# Hatchet Jobs and Hardball

## The Oxford Dictionary of American Political Slang

# Hatchet Jobs and Hardball

## The Oxford Dictionary of American Political Slang

Edited by Grant Barrett

OXFORD

UNIVERSITY PRESS

2004

# OXFORD
UNIVERSITY PRESS

Oxford  New York
Auckland  Bangkok  Buenos Aires  Cape Town  Chennai
Dar es Salaam  Delhi  Hong Kong  Istanbul  Karachi  Kolkata
Kuala Lumpur  Madrid  Melbourne  Mexico City  Mumbai
Nairobi  São Paulo  Shanghai  Taipei  Tokyo  Toronto

Copyright © 2004 by Oxford University Press

Published by Oxford University Press
198 Madison Avenue
New York, New York 10016

Oxford is a registered trademark of Oxford University Press

www.oup.com
www.askoxford.com
www.oxfordreference.com
www.oxfordscholarship.com

Library of Congress Cataloging-in-Publication Data

Hatchet Jobs and Hardball : The Oxford Dictionary of American
Political Slang / Edited by Grant Barrett / Introduction by James
Carville & Mary Matalin.
    p. cm.
  ISBN 0-19-517685-5
  1. English language—United States—Slang—Dictionaries. 2. English
language—Political aspects—United States—Dictionaries. 3. United
States—Politics and government—Dictionaries. 4. Politicians—United
States—Language—Dictionaries. 5. Political science—United
States—Dictionaries.
  PE3727.P6H38 2004
  427'.09—dc22

                                                2004009676

# Contents

# Introduction

*by James Carville and Mary Matalin*

---

Washington, D.C., is encircled by six lanes of asphalt, technically known as Route 495, but more commonly called the Beltway. Once you get inside that loop, you've not only crossed a highway, but also a border into a country where the locals speak another language.

Washingtonians divide the world into insiders and outsiders. Beltway insiders are acutely aware that something about them changed when they settled in Washington. Some transformed politicians seem to enjoy Washington so much that they've forgotten their home states: they've caught *Potomac Fever,* so named for the river, once known for its malarial swamps, that flanks the city.

Beltway insiders have a term to describe those living outside it: *real people.* In meetings of both political parties, someone will inevitably say, "Can we get a *real person* to introduce the President/Vice President/Senator, and maybe some *real people* to stand behind him/her?" A *real person* is not just an outsider to Washington, but an outsider to the political processes in which *Jane Q. Public* and *John Q. Public* themselves rarely appear.

The characteristic language of politics arises because few politicians in Washington admit to being *from* Washington, no matter how many terms they serve there. Home-state allegiances are strongly maintained inside the Beltway, where you can witness the odd spectacle of a Washington sporting event where as many fans cheer the visiting team as the home one.

Once you combine those two elements—diverse geography and an altered perception of reality—you end up with a hodgepodge that borrows elements from every region of the country, creating a supposedly universal language which, in reality, nobody understands. It's a sort of political Esperanto.

Take that slapdash Esperanto, mix it with polling data, salt it with policy jargon, send it out to be vetted by a phalanx of lawyers, spice it up with some historical references, filter it through speechwriters and communications advisers—the *spinners*—throw in equal parts of self-importance and actual importance, and propagate it to an army of reporters who then quote, transcribe, and disseminate every word, and you've found what is inside this volume: American political slang.

That unique combination of cultures, influence, inputs, and ingredients gives us *gate*-suffixed scandals and *soccer moms, angry white males* and the *anxious class*, and it allows the insider to refer offhandedly to the President of the United States as *POTUS*, the first lady as *FLOTUS*, and maybe even the wife of the Vice President as *SLOTUS*, the second lady of the United States. Such language can be hard to take if you're not an insider.

While the language of politics can be humorous or confusing or just plain inscrutable, we both feel that the practice of politics is deeply important and that every American should make his or her voice heard. The following pages will help you speak the language.

# Guide to the Dictionary

## Form and Order of Headwords

An entry begins with the headword in boldface type. The headword is given in standard form, and any exceptions are usually shown after the definition as variant forms.

Entries are listed in strict alphabetical order. Headwords with the same spelling but different parts of speech are ordered as follows:

> *n.*
> *adj.*
> *adv.*
> *v.*

## Part of Speech

Words are classified in this dictionary into the parts of speech listed above. The part of speech is given immediately after the headword or after a pronunciation. The only other label used in this position is *n.pl.* to indicate plural nouns. Phrases are not usually labeled with part-of-speech designations.

Words that occasionally function as other parts of speech without any significant changes in meaning have this noted after the definition.

*Noun* is used to classify all words with nominal function, including single words, compound or phrasal nouns, proper nouns, verbal nouns (when not treated under the verb), and nominalizations of verbs or verb phrases. When attributive use of a noun seems frequent, this is noted; if it is especially prevalent or if the meaning is notably different, this usage may be presented separately as an adjectival entry.

*Verbs* are not labeled for transitivity; in most cases, the definition and the illustrative citations make clear whether or not the verb takes an object. When a distinction is necessary but the structure of a definition makes this impossible, it is noted in a comment placed before a definition or in an internal comment.

## Etymology

The etymology appears in square brackets. It is placed immediately before the sections of an entry to which it applies, so that an etymology referring to an entire word will follow the part of speech, but an etymology referring to a single sense will follow the definition number for that sense. The etymology should not be confused with the discursive note (see *Discursive Notes,* below), which is also in square brackets but which follows the definition and does not normally cover etymological ground; longer etymological comments have in some cases been moved to or extended into the discursive note.

The majority of slang words are formed by semantic shifts from Standard English words. Etymologies are not supplied for the standard words, since these may be found in general dictionaries. Etymologies of the slang senses are discussed only when the semantic connection to the standard word might be obscure.

## Field Label

The field label (*Mil., N.Y.C.*) appears in italics immediately before the definition. Note that the field label refers to the group, subculture, etc., of people who notably *use* the word, not necessarily to those to whom the word applies. Since all headwords in this book are chosen for their political nature, most entries do not have a field label.

The decision to include field labels was made on the basis of citational evidence. While in most cases this evidence is an accurate reflection of a word's range of use, the presence of a label does not imply that the word is used exclusively by the designated group, or that persons using such words have ties to the designated group.

## Definition

Definition numbers (or letters) are given in boldface type. Individual senses of a word are usually labeled with Arabic numerals.

The degree of precision possible in the discrimination of senses depends greatly on the amount of available evidence. If the evidence for one sense is slight, this definition may be run into an existing one, preceded by a word such as "(*hence*)" or "(*also*)," even if the senses are not very close. In other cases, abundant evidence has allowed the division and definition of more closely related senses.

The reader should note that the extended context, in addition to that provided in a citation, has often facilitated the accurate placement of a citation, even though the motivation for such placement may not be obvious from the citation text. Users of this dictionary seeking full contexts of the citations are referred to the original works cited.

Certain comments can appear before or within a definition, in parentheses. The most common of these, which show the relationship between two parts of a definition, are (*hence*), which indicates that the second meaning follows logically and usually chronologically from the first; (*also*), which merely indicates that the second meaning is related to the first; and (*specif.*) and (*broadly*), which indicate respectively that the second meaning is narrower or broader than the first. Certain other comments appear internally when they affect only one part of the definition; their meanings are discussed elsewhere in this Guide.

In most cases, definitions are ordered by the date of the earliest citation. For dating purposes, bracketed citations (see *Citations,* below) are generally treated as relevant when they clearly point to the use under discussion. When a bracketed citation is simply an interesting parallel, it is discounted in the ordering of senses.

## Comments and Labels about Usage and Status

Certain definitions in this dictionary bear additional comments. These may consist of information about grammar, style, frequency, currency, and other aspects of usage. Most comments about usage are preceded by a dash, although others (such as "Now *S.E.*" or "*Joc.*") may be freestanding.

The abbreviation "usu.," meaning "almost always, though not inevitably," is used before a label to indicate that "mainstream standards" are flexible and are primarily based on situation and speaker-to-speaker relationships.

The label "derisively" implies an element of ridicule or banter that makes such terms less directly provocative than those entries marked as "contemptuous." Although many slang terms applied to human beings convey at least mild disrespect, only those senses conveying strong derision or contempt are so labeled. Labels are used only when the nature of the definition does not make its status clear; definitions of the sort "an idiot; fool" do not require labels such as "derisive" or "contemptuous."

The label "offensive" means that a term is likely to be considered offensive by the person, group, etc., to whom it refers. Used alone, it does not imply that any offense is intended by the person using the word. *Although the "offensive" label is not normally used for a word labeled as "derisive" or "contemptuous," such a word should nonetheless be considered "offensive".* As with other labels, the "usu." has been applied to terms labeled "offensive" to account for the varying reception given to words by different people. Any offensiveness lies in the context of the word's use, rather than inhering in the word itself.

Certain labels reflect the status of terms. A label of "Now *hist.*" indicates that as far as can be determined, a word is used only in historical contexts. This can mean that the referent of the word no longer exists or that the word itself, while still remembered, is no longer in active use. The "Now *hist.*" label does not necessarily mean that a word is rare or that it is no longer slang, although frequently used terms of this sort often become Standard English. This dictionary does not necessarily include recent citations for words labeled "Now *hist.*," but the label itself indicates that the word may still be encountered, especially in historical writing.

The label "*Joc.*" indicates that a word is likely considered humorous by the person using the word, but should not be regarded as inherently amusing. Some terms may be used jocularly, but can nonetheless be offensive.

The labels "Now *colloq.*" and "Now *S.E.*" are used for words that have shaken off their slang status. No attempt has been made systematically to provide recent citations for these terms. Such words should be considered in reasonably frequent use unless otherwise indicated.

## Variant Forms

Variant forms, except for those given directly after the headword, are found immediately after the definition in several formats. In this dictionary, a "variant form" is any form other than that given at the headword: different spellings or combinations, use as a different part of speech, and derived forms are all considered variants.

For variant parts of speech, see the discussion at *Parts of Speech*, above. The form is "Also as adj." or the like.

A derived form is given after a definition (as opposed to as a new entry) when it has no great independent currency and when the derivation is clear. Such derived forms are shown in boldface immediately after the definition and are preceded by the word "Hence." Cross references to derived forms are not normally given.

## Discursive Note

The discursive note, in square brackets, is usually the last element preceding the body of citations. It may cover a variety of subjects, including etymological material.

## Cross Reference

Words that are treated elsewhere in this dictionary are given in small capital type, followed by the part of speech when necessary.

## Citations

Citations are ordered strictly chronologically. For a citation with a range of dates, the last date is used for ordering. Citations from the same year are ordered by exact date if this is available.

An asterisk (*) before the date indicates that a citation is from a non–North American source. However, an English book referring to an American usage or quoting an American author will not have an asterisk, and an American book quoting British usage will have an asterisk. The reader should also note that before *ca*1820, differences between British and American slang, as between British and American English in general, are far less marked.

In this dictionary, American and Canadian English are not differentiated—neither variety has an asterisk. There are very few terms of Canadian English origin in this dictionary; see **ROC** and **neverendum**.

A citation is placed in square brackets if it does not exemplify the slang use under discussion but can contribute directly to the understanding of the history or meaning of a term; or if the allusion is clearly to the term but does not explicitly use it. See an example at the first cite under **yellow-dog Democrat**.

### *Dating and Bibliographic Style*

The overriding concern has been to supply a date that most accurately reflects the time the word was used. The citations in the dictionary will only give the specific date of the citation and enough information to allow the reader to locate the work. Various conventions have been adopted for dating a citation.

When a citation is known to be earlier than the work in which it is found, the date of the citation is followed by *in*, followed by the bibliographical reference to the work itself.

The author of a citation is usually not given if the source is a magazine or a historical dictionary. However, when an author being quoted is well-known in his or her own right, the name is given before *in*.

If the source itself cites a date earlier than the publication date, but does not give the actual citation, the style is **1947** (cited in *W10*). If the source does give the actual citation but this dictionary does not quote it, the style is **1927** in Partridge *DSUE* 21.

The abbreviation *a*, for Latin *ante* "before," is used immediately before a date to indicate that the citation was written (or the event occurred) shortly before the date given, but it is not possible to be more accurate. In all cases, citations are dated no earlier than is defensible on the basis of evidence. In no case should *a* be assumed to refer to an indefinitely long period.

The abbreviation *ca,* for Latin *circa* "about," is used similarly but more broadly. It immediately precedes a date or age, and signifies only that the date or age falls within a general range.

If a citation refers explicitly to another era, a bracketed note such as "[ref. to 1891]" is often added immediately before the citation. This practice is followed when a word appears to be characteristic of its historical reference rather than the actual date of the cited material, or when the source appears to be particularly trustworthy in depicting an earlier era from firsthand experience. For an earliest citation, it indicates that a word was probably in use earlier than is directly attested.

Oral citations have not been so labeled, but it will be clear from the lack of other bibliographical evidence that a citation is oral rather than from television, radio, print, or other sources.

Page references indicate the page on which the word under discussion appears, not where the extract begins. When quoting from alphabetical dictionaries or glossaries, volume and page numbers have usually been omitted. Occasionally, chapter references rather than page references are given, especially for books that are easily accessible in differently paginated editions.

When quoting from documents found in unpaginated digital resources, even for items that originally appeared in printed form, no page numbers have been given; however, in all cases there should be sufficient information to find the term in the digital resource, if not in the original printed form.

An author's name has been placed in brackets when a work was published anonymously or pseudonymously but the true name of the author is known. Authors known primarily by their pseudonyms have these names in double quotation marks: "M. Twain." Authors known exclusively by their pseudonyms or changed names have these names given without comment.

Citations are recorded exactly as they appear in the source with several minor exceptions. Each citation begins with a capital letter and ends with closing punctuation. Citations have been conformed trivially to the modern American standards of punctuation. For example, single quotation marks are used inside double quotation marks, and commas and periods are placed inside a closing quotation mark. Lines of verse are separated with a virgule (/), and the first word of a new line is capitalized. Spellings, use of italics (except as noted below), capitalization, etc., have not been changed.

When quoting from a dictionary, glossary, or other word list, the word or phrase being glossed has been placed in italics.

Since the main concern has been to represent the meaning of the slang word, a source has often been quoted selectively, as by starting or finishing a quote in the middle of a sentence or by use of ellipsis (...), in order to save space and emphasize the slang use. Although the citation itself has never been altered (except as noted above), some of these abridgements may change the style of an author's words. In no case should a citation be taken to represent the viewpoint of the quoted author.

*Selection*

Though the number of citations does not necessarily reflect an entry's frequency of usage, unusually common expressions are often accompanied by multiple citations. The additional citations are included for several reasons: first, to suggest the commonness of the sense; second, to indicate continuity through its history or an unusual frequency of the word in one particular period; and third, to illustrate nuances that cannot succinctly be placed in the definition. The editor has tried to supply new citations from primary sources wherever possible, rather than quoting from secondary sources; the interested reader may thus be able to find additional evidence in such sources as the *Oxford English Dictionary,* the *Historical Dictionary of American Slang,* the *Dictionary of American Regional English,* the *Dictionary of Americanisms,* and the journal *American Speech.*

In every case, the earliest citation sense is the earliest that can be documented from the available corpus. With language in general, and especially with slang, due to its oral nature, words and senses may be used regularly for some time before they are recorded in print. Many terms in this dictionary were probably in use earlier than the earliest evidence herein, for such is the nature of the historical dictionary. It has not been possible to provide up-to-the-minute examples of every sense, but many senses lacking recent citational evidence are still in use.

## Phrases

This dictionary organizes phrases under the main word of the phrase, usually the word least subject to variation. Phrases are marked with a paragraph symbol, ¶. Slang phrases often have so many variants that the main word may be the only stable one of the phrase. Where there is potential for confusion, cross references have been added.

## List of Abbreviations

*This list does not include all standard abbreviations.*

| | |
|---|---|
| * | (before the date of a citation, used to indicate a non–North American source) |
| < | is derived from |
| > | from which is derived |
| a | ante (before) |
| abbr. | abbreviation, abbreviated |
| adj. | adjective(s), adjectival(ly) |
| AmE | American English |
| Amer. | America(n) |
| AP | Associated Press |
| AS | American Speech |
| ATS | Berrey & van den Bark, *American Thesaurus of Slang* |
| attrib. | attributive(ly) |
| BDNE | *Barnhart Dictionary of New English* |
| Black E | Black English |
| BrE | British English |
| ca | circa (about) |
| Canad. | Canadian, Canadianism |
| cf. | confer (compare) |
| ch. | chapter |
| coll. | collect(or), collected (by) |
| collec. | collection |
| colloq. | colloquial(ism) |
| comb. form | combining form |
| constr. | |
| DA | Mathews, *Dictionary of Americanisms* |
| DAE | Craigie & Hulbert, *Dictionary of American English* |
| DARE | Cassidy, *Dictionary of American Regional English* |
| DAS | Wentworth & Flexner, *Dictionary of American Slang* |
| DAUL | Goldin et al., *Dictionary of American Underworld Lingo* |
| def. | define(d), definition(s) |
| dict. | dictionary |
| DN | *Dialect Notes* |
| DOST | Craigie & Aitken, *Dictionary of the Older Scottish Tongue* |
| DSUE | Partridge, *Dictionary of Slang and Unconventional English* |
| E | English (language) |
| ed. | edition, editor, edited (by) |
| EDD | Wright, *English Dialect Dictionary* |

| | |
|---|---|
| Eng. | English (in titles) |
| esp. | especially |
| et al. | et alii, et alia (and others) |
| ety. | etymology, etymological(ly) |
| euphem. | euphemism, euphemistic(ally) |
| F | French (language) |
| F & H | Farmer and Henley, *Slang and Its Analogues* |
| fig. | figurative(ly) |
| fr. | from |
| freq. | frequently; (also) frequentative(ly) |
| hist. | history, historical |
| ibid. | ibidem |
| *JAF* | *Journal of American Folklore* |
| joc. | jocular(ly) |
| Jour. | Journal (used in titles) |
| journ. | journalism |
| L | Latin |
| lang. | language |
| mag. | magazine |
| *MED* | *Middle English Dictionary* |
| mil. | military |
| N | North(ern) |
| n. | noun |
| *NADS* | *Newsletter of the American Dialect Society* |
| *NDAS* | Chapman, *New Dictionary of American Slang* |
| N.O. | New Orleans |
| No. | North(ern) |
| N.Y.(C.) | New York (City) |
| occ. | occasion, occasional(ly) |
| *OED* | Murray, Simpson, et al., *Oxford English Dictionary* |
| opp. | opposite |
| orig. | origin, original(ly) |
| p., pp. | page(s) |
| *PADS* | *Publication of the American Dialect Society* |
| perh. | perhaps |
| phr. | phrase(s) |
| pl. | plural |
| prob. | probable, probably |
| pron. | pronounce, pronunciation |
| pros. | prostitution |
| Qly. | Quarterly (used in titles) |
| quot., quots. | quotation(s) |
| ref. | refer(s), referring |
| rev. | revise(d), revision; (also) review |

| | |
|---|---|
| S | South(ern) |
| sc. | scilicet (namely) |
| S.E. | Standard English |
| *SND* | Grant, *Scottish National Dictionary* |
| So. | South(ern) (used in labels) |
| specif. | specific(ally) |
| stu. | student |
| suff. | suffix |
| sugg. | suggest(ed) |
| syn. | synonym, synonymous |
| s.v. | sub voce (under the word) |
| trans. | transitive(ly) |
| univ. | university |
| usu. | usually |
| v. | verb |
| var(s). | variant(s) |
| *WNID, WNID2, WNID3* | *Webster's New International Dictionary* [2nd, 3rd editions] |
| *W9* | *Webster's Ninth New Collegiate Dictionary* |
| *W10, W11* | *Merriam-Webster's Collegiate Dictionary*, 10th and 11th editions |
| WWI | World War I |
| WWII | World War II |

# What Does This Button Do?

Since the voting fiasco of 2000, when old-fashioned paper ballots proved controversial, the rollout of electronic voting machines (EVMs) has accelerated. The foremost goal of the direct-recording electronic (DRE) voting systems—the collective name for EVMs—is to increase trust in election outcomes.

Most e-voting machines work on the same principles as an automated teller machine (ATM). You prove to the EVM you are authorized, you do what you need to do, and then you get a receipt, everything recorded and (supposedly) secure.

Some studies have shown, however, that EVMs are easy to break into, both physically and digitally. Skeptics are looking for new assurances of reliability and verifiability. It's one thing to conduct a "paper vote hack"—an old-fashioned ballot-stuffing or get-out-the-cemetery vote—but it's quite another, they say, when one ill-intentioned ward-heeler with a computer can manipulate results, perhaps without a trace.

To prevent vote-hacking, critics of many current DRE's want the software which runs them to be "open source", meaning that its programming code would be publicly available. This, they say, would permit anyone to find flaws. If more people can find flaws, then more flaws can be fixed. Keeping the source code private, on the other hand, means only the vendor and highly motivated bad guys will know the flaws. As the geeks say, "security by obscurity" simply doesn't work.

Two kinds of tests would be run on the voting software. A *black box* check makes sure it operates as it's supposed to. A *white box* test examines the programming code itself, looking for bugs, *back doors* (secret ways in known only to the coder who put them there), or *Easter eggs* (goofy tricks or features that can only be enabled with special knowledge). These all pose security risks.

Another layer of security called *bracketing* encrypts all votes going in and going out. Votes cannot be manipulated after they have been cast (but can be while they are still on the EVM), and new votes cannot be cast without using the same encryption code. The votes are not countable until they are collected and decoded. Even two votes for the same candidate do not look alike until they are decoded.

Still other security procedures verify that an EVM has not been tampered with. An *audit trail* records everything that happens to the machine, including power-ups, tests, data changes, errors, and votes. In most cases, this information is recorded to an electronic file (called an *audit log*), and to a paper record so that it cannot be wiped out in the event of a total power failure or a malicious hacking.

Before voting begins, a *zero tape* is made. This shows that no votes are currently saved on the machine and that it is in working order. The zero tape is validated by the polling station officials and submitted with the day's results.

Some systems require a Voter Access Card (VAC)—a type of "smart card"—to be enabled by polling-station personnel after they have checked voter registration records and before a voter can choose candidates. The voter inserts the card into the EVM, then returns it. The main functions of a VAC are to permit each voter to vote only once, to make sure that a VAC from another precinct or another machine is not used, and to permit the polling station personnel to check and track each person at a polling station.

Many DREs use ATM-like touchscreens. Others use a scroll wheel, which changes the candidate that is chosen on screen, and prevents the kind of errors that might occur with a miscalibrated touchscreen. Still others work with old-fashioned pencil and paper, but without large mechanical lever systems. Voters use a number 2 pencil to fill in their choices on an optical scan ballot, which is then fed into a computer that can recognize which ovals are filled and register votes accordingly.

In a *voter-verified* system (sometimes called the *Mercuri Method* after Rebecca Mercuri, a research fellow at Harvard University's John F. Kennedy School of Government and an e-voting expert) each voter sees a paper receipt, so they can check before leaving the polling station that their choices were properly registered. Ideally, this voter-verified audit trail (VVAT) maintains voters' anonymity.

At the end of the voting day, votes from each electronic unit are loaded into a single machine to determine the total precinct vote. The result is a *totals report,* and all the paper rolls together make up the *results tape.*

Will e-voting provide more trustworthy votes? Perhaps not. Old-fashioned methods of cheating can still work. In one test of voting machines in Maryland, the lock securing the computer hardware was picked in ten seconds, and the same two keys opened all 16,000 EVMs in use there, making the hardware easily accessible.

As the computer geeks say: The only really safe computer is turned off, unplugged, put back in the box, and stored in a safe.

# Inside
# "Inside Baseball"

It's no accident that baseball, given its preeminence as the very American sport, has introduced a great many terms to standard American English. One such term is the *inside baseball* of politics.

For some, *inside baseball* means the day-to-day partisan grind, the procedures and traditions, the rhetorical splitting and re-splitting of hairs. It has a lot do with being *inside the Beltway* and the parochial interests of a one-industry town like the District of Columbia. It's about having the *inside track* or knowing the *inside*, the low-down, the scoop. It's about knowing the details so constituents and Congresspeople don't have to. It's the shoptalk among politicians and the journalists who cover them.

For others, *inside baseball* is negative: the horse-trading, the logrolling, the underhanded and under-the-table deal-making and double-dealing which make up real politics, the sausage-making part you'd rather not see or know about, but which makes the system work. It's about intentional leaks, planted news stories, and the codependent relationship of the press and the politicos they cover.

Both the positive and negative nature of *inside baseball* require an intimate knowledge of the system, the players, and the capabilities of both, just as the original diamond-shaped *inside baseball* does. Now sometimes used in any industry to describe the minutiae and inner workings of interest only to its wonks and geeks, *inside baseball*, above all, is about what happens behind the facade.

## Roots of Inside Baseball

Sometimes known as percentage baseball, small ball, little ball, base-to-base, station-to-station, the inner game, inside game, inside work, the running game, and even dirty baseball, *inside baseball* became the favored term for a new way of playing the game, even over the original and once more common term "scientific baseball."

Beginning in the late 1800s, this thinking-man's baseball focused on more strategy, probability, and teamwork. Everything that could be measured, was. Odds and statistics balanced strength and power. Proponents of inside baseball believed whipping runners around the bases on a series of singles could win more games than every slugger trying to knock one out of the park, so bunting, stealing, running, place-hitting, and the sacrifice became more important, while home runs became less important.

"What is inside baseball? Why, it's the faculty of catching an enemy off guard, taking advantage of a change, pulling off a trick, and, above all, obeying a manager's directions according to signals. That's what constitutes the supposed secrets of baseball. It's team work, hard, earnest endeavor, and that 'all-for-one' spirit." So a sportswriter for the *Washington Post* defined the theory in 1907.

Practitioners of this modern baseball included Charlie Comiskey (1859–1931), Joe Cantillon (1861–1930), Cap Anson (1852–1922), Branch Rickey (1881–1965), "Foxy" Ned Hanlon (1857–1937), and John Joseph McGraw (1873–1934). McGraw was so devoted that, as John Thorn writes in *Treasures of the Baseball Hall of Fame*, "He once fined one of his players, Sammy Strang [1876–1932], for hitting a game-winning home run—because he had missed a bunt sign."

The Baltimore Orioles built a short dynasty on inside baseball tactics, winning pennants in 1894, 1895, and 1896. In his book *Where They Ain't*, Burt Solomon writes that Hanlon, of the Orioles, eventually saw it as part of the advancement of science. "The game, like all things, has progressed, and it is today more scientific," Hanlon said. "It is in some respects like checkers and chess, and must be played upon systematic plans. Modern baseball, as played by the Baltimores, is based upon the idea to keep opposing teams guessing. It is a case of dealing out uncertainties at all times."

Not everyone agreed an inside game was a better game—they thought it was sissified or that it took a good idea too far. Pitcher Christy "Matty" Mathewson (1878–1925) was one who approached the new mode of play carefully, and in 1911 said, "Those who are too scientific stick to the rules when the rules are no good—that is worse than no rules."

## Into Politics and Beyond

*Inside baseball* came to mean more than just a "scientific" approach. There was also an element of showmanship which relied on planning and practice, practice and planning, rather than chance and raw skill. It also meant behind-the-scenes strategizing, signals between players, efforts to create psychological advantages beyond lucky charms and favorite mascots. To some, it eventually meant outright deception, trickery, and questionable ethics.

Baseball scandals added to the cynical view of inside baseball. There was the Black Sox betting scandal involving eight of the 1919 White Sox. Even after acquittal in front of a grand jury, they were still thrown out of the sport in 1921 by tough-guy baseball commissioner and former Federal judge Kenesaw Mountain Landis (1866–1944). He had been appointed to assuage the anger of fans, some who had sworn to never see another baseball game again.

Then there was the end of the "dead ball" era, when game scores were low and home runs were uncommon. Somehow, someway, batting averages skyrocketed in the 1921 season, and not everyone was happy. The ball shot around like corked rubber. Leagues, teams, and players were accused by each other and fans of using a "juiced up" ball on the sly to improve play. Pitchers worried about getting hit with the faster ball, and managers felt it changed field dynamics too much.

"The lively ball, which some players say was responsible for some of the sensational batting last summer, has been attributed by a portion of the fans to some sort of inside baseball intrigue," says an article in the December 30, 1921 *Reno (Nev.) Evening Gazette.*

Then in 1927, charges were made against Ty Cobb (1886–1961), Tris Speaker (1888–1958) and Joe Wood (1889–1985), alleging that they had tried to fix a game series for betting purposes. Commissioner Landis declared them not guilty, which, on top of the clearing of thirty-five other players in a separate betting scandal, led to repeated cries of "whitewash!"

The accused players were given dinners, parades, and public adoration, but Landis was treated as if he was somehow the guilty party. But as noted in 1926 in the *New York Times*, anyone who criticized Landis was "ignorant of one fact known to inside baseball men, namely, that a news association which was in possession of the facts went to Mr. Landis and threatened to print the story unless he gave it out officially."

The cynicism was directed at baseball, the establishment, rather than at baseball, the entertainment. Addressing that attitude, an editorial in the Jan. 13, 1927, *Decatur (Ill.) Evening Herald*, seems to make it clear there were already two kinds of inside baseball in play: "Inside baseball to fandom means strategy, the matching of wits, the employment of deception, legitimate under the rules. Inside baseball that buys favors, and calls for letting down on some-body's part is not the kind to keep the game in good standing."

In politics, too, *inside baseball* means the social and political tricks and favor-trading which rarely appear in the papers, or to the voting public. But where did the jump from sport to govern-ment took place?

Perhaps 1927 *was* the year. Speaking at a dinner for the Cartoon-ists of America in March 1927, after the ball scandal of the previous few months, New York City Mayor J. J. Walker (1881–1946) seems to be using *inside baseball* as more than wordplay. Starting the cere-monies, he said, "Looking at those on the dais, you may expect to hear some inside baseball, for a Speaker, a Cobb and a Landis are to address you."

His forced joke recognized the otherwise unnoteworthy event's status as a nexus of politics, journalists, and baseball. One featured speaker at the event was writer and humorist Irvin S. Cobb (1876–1944), who shared his name with the baseball legend Ty Cobb. Also present was Judge Landis, then holding "absolute power" over the game as baseball commissioner. He had already handled two baseball scandals, one of which ballplayer Cobb was involved. Elsewhere on the dais was U.S. Speaker of the House Nicholas Longworth (1869–1931), who was married into New York's politi-cally powerful Roosevelt clan, and shared his job title with the fam-ily name of legend Tris Speaker.

However, there's no way of knowing how, exactly, Walker meant by "inside baseball," though no doubt he was a practitioner by the modern definition. In 1932 he resigned from office under a cloud of corruption charges, and fled to Europe.

The earliest and most clear-cut use of political *inside baseball* so far found appears in a syndicated column by David Lawrence (1888–1973), published in early December 1952. "There is a right way to play ball on a team, and the evidence thus far indicates that members of the Eisenhower staff are going to have to learn their 'inside baseball' the hard way."

The negative value attached to *inside baseball* is also clear in the 1954 Congressional proceedings which ended in the censure of Senator Joseph McCarthy (R-WI) (1908–1957). Senator Herman Welker (R-ID) (1906–1957), addressing missing photostats of tele-phone records, said, "Why these calls were not brought to the at-tention of the Select Committee, when that committee was ordered by the Senate to seek out all evidence, is what I should like the two distinguished Senators [...] to find out and to report on to the Senate at the earliest possible convenience. Some inside base-ball has been played here."

In the first years of twenty-first century, some of the taint is off of *inside baseball*, but now it has become something else. Hardball wonk and statistician Bill James has pioneered substantial innovations in the statistical side of the sport—calling it *sabermetrics*—and his methods, and others like them, are used with enthusiasm by management, players, and fans alike. As Terry Golway, writing for the *New York Observer* in 2001, put it, "Inside baseball is fun when the subject is baseball; inside baseball can bore you to tears when the subject is politics."

# Tongue in Groove:
# The Blogistan Lexicon

In January of 1907, Republican Governor-elect Coe Crawford (1858–1944) of South Dakota announced at a banquet that he would not assist in attempts to defeat Republican Senator Robert Gamble (1851–1924)

> I want no bouquets from the character assassins swarming about the State like toads about a foul cellar. The gang now insisting that another man be cast aside with his character poisoned by the insinuations and innuendo is the same cabal which last Spring tried to send me to the penitentiary and now professes to want to send me to the Senate. I have higher ambitions, but they are honorable ones, and if the Senatorial toga were to be offered to me through the instrumentality of this coterie of vampires I would spurn it, I would spit upon it. With God's help, I am going to serve my time as Governor in honor. (Jan. 6, 1907, *New York Times*).

(Crawford was elected to the Senate in 1909, but failed to be renominated in 1914, after which he went back to his law practice.)

Today's politicians could take a cue from Crawford, as they seem to have equated oratorical blandness with electability. Their speeches are usually interchangeable, simplistic, lowest-denominator utilitarian obligations. The job—which is inevitably filled, no matter the era—of spewing outlandish and colorful rhetoric has therefore been gleefully taken on by the "bloggerati of Blogistan."

Blogs—online journals filled with opinion, diarylike entries, and links to recommended sites—are the source of some of our most spirited political commentary. The word *blog* (an abbreviation of *weblog*, itself a combination of *web* and *log*) appeared *ca*1999 with no known relationship to the uncommon drinking punch also known as *blog*. *Blogistan* is a newer coinage, appearing after the U.S. invasion of Afghanistan in 2001. By attaching to *blog* the suffix *-stan*, which means "land" or "place of" in Farsi and related languages, the word successfully conveys the idea that blogs in Blogistan are concerned with matters in the Stans, among them

Afghanistan and Pakistan. By extension, the suffix -*stan* also includes the Middle East, or any foreign-land-i-stan, even where Farsi is unheard. It was famously used on the December 10, 2001, in the cartoon on the cover of the *New Yorker,* in which New York City was remapped as "New Yorkistan."

To some, Blogistan is inhabited only by *warblogs,* those nonprofessional web sites primarily interested in the terrorist attacks of September 11, 2001, the subsequent American invasions of Afghanistan and Iraq, and their related implications. More generally, however, Blogistan is the entire universe of blogs—also known as the *blogosphere* and *blogdom*—regardless of whether they comment on war, remote lands, or cheese sandwiches. (*Blogosphere* is spelled less commonly as *blogasphere* or *blogisphere,* the coinage of which is usually credited to Bill Quick www.iw3p.com/DailyPundit/.)

Unhindered by looming deadlines, the editorial whims of an employer, short column inches, or scant air time, the output of the Blogistan pundits (a word of Sanskrit origin, common in English since the British controlled the Indian subcontinent) is endless. These pundits make up the *bloggerati*—a collective term for the literate, educated, and influential online commentators who resemble the *chatterati,* those people paid to bloviate offline on television or in newspapers. Both words, *bloggerati* and *chatterati* (which is also known as the *chattering class* or *chattering classes*), are inspired by *digerati*—experts in information technology—itself from *literati,* which covers the learned class as a whole.

Except for having a lot more of what political slang-dictionary writer Uno Philipson called, in his description of colloquial speech, "daring and self-assertion," online political discourse is identical to that offline: the back-and-forth of debate, the critique and criticism of opponents' ideas and behavior, the jockeying to demonstrate membership and prove allegiance, and the endless persuasive attempts to win over undecideds and the mythical open-minded opponent.

## Defining the Argument Pool

One feature of this blog-world political discussion (or "discussion") is the attempt to define the *argument pool,* to set the terms of debate so everyone knows what everyone else is going on about. Also known as *framing,* as in "framing the debate," this sometimes occurs as a storm of criticism intended to kneecap adversaries rhetorically, to force them into inflexible political stances, or to goad them into reputation-damaging statements. At other times, defining the argument pool is done with political panty-raids into enemy discussion forums, in which an opponent will *troll*, "make absurd or untrue statements out of boredom or malice in order to create outrage or to sucker the innocent," or *trawl*, "dig up opponents' statements which can be willfully misunderstood and taken out of context." A more subtle way to define the argument pool, however, is to jargonize the debate.

## Where the Words Are

New words act as advance scouts for the politics whence they spring. Online glossaries such as the "Wingnut Debate Dictionary" (stommel.tamu.edu/~baum/ethel/atrios-dictionary.html), the *Samizdata* "Blogging Glossary" (www.samizdata.net/blog/glossary.html), the "Lexicon of FreeRepublic" (www.freerepublic.com/focus/news/673536/posts), and even the venerable "Jargon File" (catb.org/~esr/jargon/), which is more concerned with the subcultures of technology than with politics, are rich sources of such new words. These lexicons, and others like them, also help give the impression that the ideas contained in the definitions are "real." They play on the widespread respect for "the dictionary" as an authoritative source: to include a word in a dictionarylike page is, for some readers, as good as canonizing it.

Like the words defined in Ambrose Bierce's *The Devil's Dictionary*, other neologisms exist only to ridicule, demean, or derogate. New words are attractive, and bloggers coin them by the shelfload. They can seem like the cutting edge of thought, even when they are really old wolves in new sheepskin. Within groups—like those served by the web sites *Little Green Footballs* (www.littlegreenfootballs.com/weblog/) or the *Independent Media Center* (www.indymedia.org)—some words enjoy the same pervasive utility that medical jargon does in emergency rooms but exist nowhere else but blogs.

Two words which are mired in Blogistan and may or may not break free are *idiotarian* and *anti-idiotarian*. Noted blogger Glenn Reynolds (instapundit.blogspot.com) is usually credited with inventing *anti-idiot* in 2002 to describe what he saw as the true nature of bloggers—they are opposed to idiots and idiocy, no matter what the bloggers' politics. From anti-idiot, Charles Johnson of *Little Green Footballs* spun off *anti-idiotarian*. The back-formation *idiotarian* was created for one's opponent—someone who supposedly espouses stupidity.

As *anti-idiotarian* was embraced by conservative, libertarian, and prowar bloggers to describe themselves, they used *idiotarian* to describe anyone opposed to their views. Now, however, *idiotarian* is often used to mean an advocate of surreal, unreal, or unrealistic political perspectives, no matter which politics they espouse.

Like so many of the Blogistan words, the spread of *idiotarian* and *anti-idiotarian* elsewhere is somewhat inhibited. Some people avoid them because they seem faddish, because they do not express enough nuance of opinion, or because they are innaccurate, or because *idiotarian* is offensive. As long-time blogger Anil Dash (dashes.com) commented in October 2002 about words such as anti-idiotarian, "Even if one lonesome loyalist ink-stained wretch felt it necessary to pander to a tiny but loud constituency by repeating our made-up words in print, we'd still not stoop to inaccuracy, childishness, or unquestioning loyalty to a doctrine in the course of our discussion of geopolitics."

If a word does catch on, one risks having it appropriated by the very people who were supposed to be maligned by it. *Yankee* and *queer* are modern American examples, and online *idiotarian* may well become another. There are places on the Internet where a conscious effort is being made to embrace that insult and wear it like a war medal. Once the word is set free, its meaning is out of the hands of its coiner, and the thesaurus defense—"that doesn't mean what you think it means"—rarely convinces anyone but the convincer.

# Election 2000:
# Maybe We Should Go
# Back to a Show of Hands

Every major event brings words, names, and meanings, into the national language. But since the Watergate era, no political drama has so galvanized the American public, or added so much to its lexicon, as the 2000 presidential election.

The thirty-six days of back-and-forth began late on election night when Vice President Albert Gore, Jr. (1948–), conceded the election to Texas Governor George W. Bush (1946–). Then, when it became clear the margin of victory was under a thousand votes, Gore called back to unconcede.

Bush was surprised. The word *unconceded* has long existed, though it is rarely used—rights, debate points, and territory can all be unconceded—but *to unconcede* is even rarer. However, the act of unconceding was not unprecedented.

As Susan Yoachum wrote in 1996 in the *San Francisco Chronicle,* "In a final mishap of a campaign marred by strategic error, [Bob] Dole conceded the race more than an hour before the polls closed in the West—only to turn around and 'unconcede' later, after vice presidential nominee Jack Kemp and other GOP leaders in California protested the effect the early concession might have on highly contested congressional races."

In 2000, after Gore's unconcession, he demanded a recount of several Florida counties, although other states still had outstanding final tallies that could have affected the election. Weeks of haggling ensued. Lawyers and the media eventually concentrated their attention on Palm Beach County, Florida, where the *butterfly ballot* was at the center of contention.

On a butterfly ballot, candidates are staggered in "wings" on either side of a vertical column. Voters use a stylus to punch holes in that center column, marking their votes on the ballot. It wasn't immediately clear to some voters that the second hole down did not belong to the second candidate on the left, but to the first candidate on the right. This led to *overvoting,* when a voter apparently chooses more than one candidate for a position, and *undervoting,* when a voter does not cast a vote for a position, or even casts an empty ballot.

In Florida, both the overvoting and undervoting numbers were high. The Gore campaign claimed the vote-counting machines were the problem. More recounts would have to be done. Hand counts were demanded, stopped, restarted by courts, and stopped by other courts. Counts and recounts returned nonmatching results. Candidates gained and lost votes depending upon when, where, and how the counting was done.

Why all the recounting? Chads: bits of paper punched out of round, square, or U-shaped holes in paper, paper tape, or cards, where each hole represents machine-readable information.

Such bits of paper—but not the name *chad* —go back as far as the pattern-making cards used in looms invented by Frenchman Jacques de Vaucanson (1709–82). (He gained greater fame from his mechanical excreting duck) Vaucanson's designs inspired those of his compatriot Joseph-Marie Jacquard (1752–1834), whose punch cards, in turn, motivated British mathematician Charles Babbage (1791–1871) to design his "analytical engine," an early mechanical computer. Such punch cards were the forerunners to the cards, reels, and strips of paper used in radiotelegraphy, and in computing, right up to the modern era.

The word *chad* appears relatively late, given the history of holey cards. The earliest print mention found so far appears in U.S. patent number 2,273,909 for a "Printing Telegraph Apparatus," filed by the Carl W. Swan Teletype Corporation in 1939 and granted in 1942. In that patent, chads are mentioned as waste material.

Given the lead time on such a patent, and the unselfconscious way in which the word is used, chad was most likely part of industry jargon before then. Chads are also mentioned in 1947 in relation to a *chadless paper* used by a radiotelegraph, meaning it does not produce chads that could foul sensitive machinery.

This was part of the problem with the Florida votes: chads from previous ballots sometimes prevented holes from being made in new ballots. Sometimes the chads weren't entirely perforated, or didn't break completely free, leading to discussions of *hanging chads, dimpled chads, pregnant chads,* and *tri-chads* (which hung by three corners). Such malformed chads made it difficult for vote-tallying machines to read the ballots accurately.

There was at least one precedent for that, too. In 1981, the *Los Angeles Times* reported, "What the city is trying to avoid is a repeat of April's Great Chad Chore, when more than 40,000 ballots had to be recounted because their chads—the punched-out portions—failed to break loose."

While the history of the *thing* chad is clear, the history of the *word* chad is less so. A complication is that the word *chad* has so many different meanings. Chad also has many synonyms: chips, selvage, perf, chaff, slugs, pieces, clippings, wads, dots, discs, computer confetti, and keypunch droppings, all of which have their own histories and their own other meanings.

The best etymological guess is that our paper chad is related to an identical Scots word referring to gravel or small stones in a riverbed, or to "subsoil; earthy matter taken from stone quarries," as defined by the *Dictionary of the Scots Language*. However, there's not quite enough in common between the two chads: they have the same name and they generally refer to a large quantity of small items, but paper chads do not have, even historically, much to do with geology.

There is one other connection. The geological chad is sometimes rendered as *chat*. Another definition of *chat*, provided by the *English Dialect Dictionary*, is a "chip of wood," which in respect to size-, shape-, and material, is similar to paper chads. *Chat* is also a synonym for *selvage*, "a thin layer of clayey or earthy matter surrounding a metalliferous vein," which is vaguely similar to the Scots meaning of chad. *Selvage*, in turn, has a second definition: "the edge (particularly when unwanted) of a strip of paper," including that used in computing and radiotelegraphy. Many chads are made not in the center of a paper ribbon or card, but on the edges. So there is a phonetic similarity between *chad* and *chat*, chat shares two similar meanings with selvage, and *selvage* itself is a synonym of the paper chad. It's all complicated and inconclusive.

Another unverifiable link is to *chaff*, a word describing small paperlike leavings after the threshing of grain. Chaff can also be refuse or worthless matter. Since World War II, *chaff* has also been the name for clouds of metal foil released to interfere with radar: lots of small, thin objects—like chads.

At the intersection of most of these forms of *chad* and *chat* is the idea of an edge, of small pieces, and of waste. As is so often the case with etymologies, there is no hard proof that any of these suggestions is more than pleasing coincidence. These one-syllable words—*chad, chat,* and *chaff*—are so simple as to make it possible that they were independently derived for their various meanings, and are in no way historically connected.

An even less reliable theory is that *chad* is a back-formation from Mr. Chadless, the supposed inventor of the Chadless Keypunch.

However, it appears there never was a man named Chadless who invented a Chadless Keypunch: *chadless* simply means "without chad." In a chadless keypunch, little pieces of paper are not, by plan, completely severed from the larger card or strip, and so cannot gum up the works.

Nor does chad seem to be an acronym for "card hole aggregate debris," which first appears in print long after the word *chad* itself. The phrase was more likely derived from the word, rather than the word from the phrase.

Unlike the election of 2000, the outcome of the debate over the origin of chad cannot be decided by a Supreme Court of word judges. Until all the votes are in (and new evidence comes to light) we only have a handful of more or less plausible candidates, with no clear winner.

# The -*Gate* to Scandal

On June 17th in the election year of 1972, five men were arrested while burglarizing the offices of the Democratic National Committee, in the Watergate complex in Washington, D.C. This botched burglary set off a turbulent period of American politics, led to the impeachment and resignation of a president, and introduced a small but persistently productive suffix to the American political lexicon.

The Watergate was then, as now, an upscale hotel, office, and apartment complex. Constructed in 1966 for $70 million, the Watergate was a favorite with Republican administration staffers who could afford its steep prices. Its name came from its position on the bank of the Potomac River, near the outlet of Rock Creek and the Watergate Steps, a ceremonial entrance to Rock Creek Park. The steps are a kind of watergate, "an access point from the land to a body of water."

*Watergate* also became a moniker for the burglary and the ensuing scandals. The press tried out the *Watergate affair,* the *Watergate extravaganza,* the *Watergate caper,* the *Watergate escapades,* the *Watergate scandal(s).* But before 1972 was out, plain *Watergate* was being used to label it all—the initial arrests, Nixon's impeachment and resignation, and the prosecution and imprisonment of administration staffers. The new usage was an easy fit: a compound noun made of two simple English words, without historical baggage. It appeared in that form on August 20, 1972, in *Time* magazine: "By coming down hard on Mitchell, the Democrats hope they can make Watergate a devastating—and durable—campaign issue."

As is often the case with new political words, journalists were the primary disseminators of the catch-all *Watergate,* and began to use it as a synonym for any scandal. One could have one's own Watergate, as one could have one's own Waterloo—or, as lefty journal *The Nation* said of Nixon in 1973, "Further revelations may yet make Watergate his Waterloo."

Various coinages using *water-* as a prefix were tried, usually in reference to the original affair—*Waterbugger, Watergaffe, Water-goof, Watergaters*. The noun was also verbed, as in the April 28, 1973, Birmingham, Alabama, *Post-Herald,* "They will be asking the voters to remember 'Watergate,' for the GOP's might be Watergating again." Journalists wrote, too, of "watergating [hiding] evidence."

But none of the other Watergate spin-offs endures like that last syllable, *-gate,* affixable as it is to almost anything. Completely disconnected from its etymological roots, it now indicates a scandal, particularly one involving a cover-up or covert activities. *Gateniks* churn out variations of this *-gate* to apply to different scandals, such as Slaughtergate and Iraqgate. The suffix has also spread to Ireland, England, South Africa, Germany, Greece, and Hungary.

As noted in the *Second Barnhart Dictionary of New English,* 1980, *-gate* as a "combining form persists in spite of the short life of most of the creations that make use of it." Most of the *-gate* coinages are one-offs, nonce usages, jokes, or journalistic shortcuts used when column inches are precious. In order for the *-gate* coinages to have legs, the scandals they are connected to must have legs as well.

The controversies of the two Clinton presidential terms turned out endless *-gates* but *Monicagate* and *Whitewatergate,* among others, proved to be ephemeral once the president's impeachment resulted in acquittal and when other charges made against Friends of Bill resulted in few convictions and even less compelling press coverage.

It's the same for most *-gates.* Although decades later *Irangate* still evokes the Nicaraguan Contras, the covert trading of arms to Iran, and the soap opera–preempting testimony of Col. Oliver North, it is still more often known as "the Iran-Contra affair." Irangate is disappearing from use, and other names for the scandal—*Iragua, Iranscam, Payatollah*—lasted only as long as the newsprint on which they were printed.

Contributing to the mayfly lifespan of some *-gate* coinages is the fact that sometimes a simple *-gate* nickname is not enough to remind one of the details. Other *-gate* coinages disappear because the coiner's hoped-for hullabaloo fails to materialize. Maybe it wasn't really a scandal. Maybe the new *-gate* word was merely the product of proximity politics, in which its "scandal" connotation was used to malign an opponent, no details or true scandal required. Who (besides the wonks) can now tell us what *Meesegate* was?

Why is *-gate* so popular? Because it continues to fill a need. Attaching *-gate* to a root word says a scandal is perceived, and that the matter is of such complexity that a shorthand will be required to avoid having to review the details every time it is discussed.

There are signs that the form is becoming standard American English at the same time it is being trivialized. *Hoagie-gate* in Philadelphia, in which fans were forbidden to bring outside food into the stadium, was hardly an earth-shattering political event, yet the suffix works. We know that some scandal involving sandwiches was aggravating Eagles ticket-buyers. The outrage in February 2004 at Janet Jackson's half-time nipple-slip (no cover-up involved there) which quickly turned out *nipplegate, boobygate,* and *tittygate,* was completely apolitical, at least until the FCC began to investigate, but again, -*gate* was able to add meaning.

Thirty years on, -*gate* coinages are still going strong, and will as long as controversy, scandals, and accusations—and the investigative journalists who live for them—are with us. What else would we call such events, but *something*-gate?

A short list of some of the forms: Abdulgate, Altergate, Angolagate, Armsgate, Batgate, Beerandbroadsgate, Begelgate, Billygate, boobygate, Briefingate, Cartergate, Cattlegate, Cellargate, Chadgate, Chelseagate, clamgate, coalgate, Contragate, Dallasgate, Debategate, diamondgate, Druggate, Enrongate, Fajitagate, Ferrarogate, Filegate, Floodgate, foodgate, Forni-gate, gategate, Goldingate, goobergate, Greekgate, H20gate, Hairgate, Halliburton-gate, Harborgate, Headachegate, Hearingsgate, Hoagie-gate, Hollywoodgate, Ice Cream Gate, Info-gate, Intimigate, Irangate, Iraqgate, Jordangate, Kachinagate, Koreagate, Laborgate, Lancegate, lettergate, Lewinskygate, Libyagate, Lobogate, lobstergate, mediagate, Meesegate, Monicagate, Motorgate, Mounty-gate, Muldergate, Nannygate, NASAgate, Nigergate, nipplegate, O'Neill Gate, Oilgate, pajamagate, Panagate, paperclip-gate, Parking-gate, Paulagate, Peanutgate, Plame-gate, Pornogate, Prisongate, Pulitzergate, Quakergate, Rashogate, rategate, Reagangate, Rebelgate, Rowland-Gate, Scrantongate, sewergate, Sexgate, Slaughtergate, Stalkergate, Stockmangate, tailgate, Teapot Domegate, Timbergate, tittygate, Travelgate, Troopergate, troutgate, Vietgate, Volgagate, Walkergate, War-gate, waste-watergate, Whitehallgate, Whitewatergate, wienergate, Windsorgate, Winegate, Yellowgate, Zippergate.

# Big Cheese Wheel Keeps on Turning

Of all the nonobscene terms we use for our elected leaders—
*bigwig, sachem, mugwump, big gun, big shot, big show, big bug, big
wheel, big boy, big enchilada, big banana, big kahuna, big toad,*
and *fat cat,* to name a few—*big cheese* has come the longest dis-
tance.

The slang word *cheese* has itself long been a positive in British
English, in which it could mean "the right thing, the correct thing,
anything genuine, pleasant, or first-rate," or more specifically,
"wealth and fame." It is recorded as early as 1835 in American English and was still going strong at the start of the twentieth century. A bit of fanciful writing passed around by American newspapers in 1900, describing a gathering of big wigs, said, "Grosvenor
VanDusen...rang the bell in a shocking manner. As it was an electric bell, the high cheese of society overlooked the manner of its
being rung."

*The cheese* could be anyone or anything important, splendid, or
influential—although *a cheese* might just be a fool. In the U.S.
today, the slang *cheese* is usually used only for something that is
*cheesy,* meaning "cheap or inauthentic," a sense that dates to at
least 1863. The only positive slang cheese left is in *big cheese,*
meaning "the most important or influential person."

In the States, actual big cheeses were a common creation for
county fairs and celebrations. When Thomas Jefferson was elected
to the presidency, the town of Cheshire, Massachusetts, took an
entire day's milk curd from every cow, and using a huge modified
cider press, made a wheel of cheese which was said to have
weighed from nearly 1,600 pounds. The big cheese was shipped to
Washington in winter, by sledge, because they trusted no wheeled
vehicle to carry it. It was said to have been the best cheese ever
tasted in Washington.

There is also the story of Mrs. Longley's big cheese, given as a gift
to the state legislature in Augusta, Maine, in 1840. The legislators
cut up the massive wheel on the spot, ate it with brown bread, and

washed it down with hard cider. This led to pandemonium, as one of the Whigs had spiked the cider with brandy. When the Speaker of the House tried to resume business, every man sought recognition on the floor, and none would yield. The Speaker shouted himself hoarse calling for order, then called for adjournment. To a thundering response of "Nay!" he adjourned the house anyway.

The *Oxford English Dictionary* (although marking it "doubtful") suggests that the *cheese* in *big cheese* is an Anglicization of a Middle Eastern word for "thing," found in Farsi and Hindi, and rendered phonetically in English as *chiz* or *ciz*. It sounds just like the English *cheese.*

Imported into the British Isles as the adjective *cheese,* meaning "good or first-rate," its spread was closely tied to the phrase "the real thing." Its popularity was part of the British fascination with India; books such as Philip Meadows Taylor's *Confessions of a Thug,* a bestseller of 1839, helped establish such imported words in English, a tongue never shy about borrowing.

# When a Tombstone
# Isn't Enough

In 1894, when the legislation creating a federal income tax was passed, Representative Uriel Hall (D-MO)(1852–1932) said, "Had I the naming of this bill, I would denominate it a measure to kill anarchy and keep down socialists." Members of Congress since have hardly resisted the temptation to go crazy with the naming.

Ordinarily, a bill has a simple, general title: the Civil Rights Act; the War Powers Act; the Agricultural Labor Relations Act.

Though a bill may have an official title, it is more likely known by the names of its sponsors. A good, but not memorable, example is the Smith-Mundt Act of 1948, which instituted the international exchange of teachers, students, lecturers, and other specialists, and established what would become the U.S. Information Agency, absorbed in 1999 into the State Department. Senators H. Alexander Smith (R-NJ), (1880–1966) and Karl Mundt (R-SD) (1900–1974) were able to resist the temptation to call it the *"Teach Them Foreigners to Read and God Bless America Act of 1948."*

The Sherman Antitrust Act of 1890, named after Senator John Sherman (R-OH) (1823–1900), set rules on interstate and international trade in order to prevent monopolies and price-fixing. Its name is still heard in classrooms and courtrooms more than a century later.

The Hatch Act of 1939, named after Senator Carl Hatch (D-NM) (1889–1963), restricted political acts of executive branch (and other) government employees and is still remembered, in part because it was amended in 1993. This is not to be confused with the Hatch Act of 1887, named after Representative William Henry Hatch (D-MO) (1833–96), which established agricultural experiment stations at land-grant universities.

Even some amendments take the names of their sponsors, at least while the matter is hot at the statehouse or Capitol. The Hatch Amendment of 1981, sponsored by another of the six

Hatches who have served in Congress, Senator Orrin Hatch (R-UT) (1934–), gives parents an explicit say in what their children learn at school. It is known in full as the Protection of Pupil Rights Amendment to the General Education Provisions Act, but, of course, nobody calls it that.

Legislation named out of respect is rare, like the 1993 Cesar Chavez Workplace Fairness Act, which bans the hiring of permanent scabs to replacing striking workers. Its result is a mixed bag. On one hand, it names Chavez in acknowledgment of his union activism. On the other hand, the word *fairness*, even muttered in Congress is such a loaded word as to make one want to read suspiciously the fine print of any bill whose name includes it.

A trend in the last two decades has been to name bills after specific victims of the crime a bill is trying to prevent. An early example is the Handgun Violence Prevention Act, almost universally known as the Brady Bill. It was named after Ronald Reagan's press secretary, James Brady, who was critically injured in the March 30, 1981, assassination attempt on Reagan by John Hinckley, Jr. The bill, passed in November of 1993, requires background checks of gun purchasers, and permits states to ban the selling of handguns to anyone indicted or convicted of a felony.

The first of the victim laws named after children was apparently Megan's Law, named after seven-year-old Megan Kanka, who in 1994 was kidnapped and killed by a sex offender who lived across the street. The 1996 law requires that communities be notified when a sex offender moves nearby.

After that, an explosion: Amber's Law, Stephanie's Law, Christopher's Law, Lee-Anne's Law, Lottie's Law, Taylor's Law, Elisa's Law, Sherrice's Law, Kathy's Law, Kendra's Law, Jillian's Law, Jenna's Law, Joan's Law, Judy's Law, Jeremy's Law, two Jennifer's Laws, the Jimmy Ryce Act, and dozens of others at the state and federal level. Also, Buster's Law, named after a cat that was set on fire.

Other laws are named to affect the reception of the legislation, sometimes in contradiction to the law's contents: the Economic Recovery Act of 1981, instead of demanding an improved economy through pure force of legislation, simply cut taxes. The Marriage Protection and Fairness Act lowered taxes for married couples in the lower income brackets who might put off getting married for fear of paying more taxes when filing jointly than when filing separately. Couples who might have considered divorce to save on taxes were now it seemed, protected. And the Senior Citizen's Freedom to Work Act? Senior Citizens have always been free to work; now, it's just that they don't suffer as much of a reduction in Social Security benefits if they do.

Acronyms are a Congressional favorite, because two messages can be shoehorned into one name. The RAVE Act, Reducing Americans' Vulnerability to Ecstasy, made nightclub owners more responsible for drugs used on their premises, but also made it known that it was the use of the drug at rave parties, rather than the drug itself, that was the most serious problem. The CHAIM Act, Comprehensive Holocaust Accountability in Insurance Measure, after the Hebrew word for *life*, addressed the problem of unpaid insurance claims from the Holocaust.

The Patriot Act, more accurately the USA-PATRIOT Act, Uniting and Strengthening America by Providing Appropriate Tools Required to Intercept and Obstruct Terrorism Act, was originally called the Financial Anti-Terrorist Act. The new name is almost a bill within a bill. In it is also a call to the flag: if you didn't support this bill then you weren't patriotic. Representative Ron Paul (R-TX) (1935–), who voted against it, told the press, "The insult is to call this a 'patriot bill' and suggest I'm not patriotic because I insisted upon finding out what is in it and voting no. I thought it was undermining the Constitution, so I didn't vote for it—and therefore I'm somehow not a patriot. That's insulting."

Naming bills after their sponsors or the victims whose tragedies inspired them, or giving them elaborate (and sometimes ridiculous) acronyms are all done to score political points. When these techniques no longer achieve that goal, new ones will certainly spring up to take their place.

# It's the Economics, Stupid

Herbert Hoover ripped Franklin Roosevelt's New Deal during the 1936 presidential campaign, calling it "Mother Hubbard economics": he wondered what would be left when the dog got home. He assailed Roosevelt as part of a socialist march. It didn't make much of an impact, and Roosevelt won reelection easily.

Nixonian economics (unlike the New Deal) depended in part upon voluntarism, entrepreneurism, and reductions in government services. Steep inflation and a 10 percent import tariff in 1971 really brought on the complaints, but as early as 1969 his economic policies were taking heat and were tagged as *Nixonomics*. The word wasn't a compliment: it meant Richard Nixon's policies were something other than good economics.

The chairman of the Democratic National Committee in 1970 said "Nixonomics means that all the things that should go up—the stock market, corporate profits, real spendable income, productivity—go down, and all the things that should go down—unemployment, prices, interest rates—go up."

*-Nomics* is two parts of the word "economics," which derives from three Greek roots: *eco*, "house"; *nom(ia)* or *nomy* (from the verb *nemein*), "to manage, deal, hold, or control"; and the *-ics*, a suffix used to form adjectives. Economics, then, meant something akin to "in the manner of managing a house," as in a household economy. The *-s* in economics is an English plural: Greek does not form plurals with that suffix. Like *politics*, economics and its spin-offs are plural but are often treated as singular. *Eco-*, like *-nomics*, is a combining form, tacked on to create words such as *ecoactivist* or *ecoterrorist*. It has also been reapplied to *-nomics* to get *eco-nomics*, meaning economics that take ecology and environmental impact into account.

After Nixon, *-nomics* became the suffix for any economic policies one didn't care for, or more simply, any economics pushed by the other guy. To tack *-nomics* onto a name was to deride the policy, to call it a black-market knockoff of the original, high-quality brand-name economics.

The *-nomics* flowed: *Fordonomics, Carternomics, Bushonomics, Reaganomics, Clintonomics, Dubyanomics* (after George W. Bush) (1946–), and even two formed long after their presidents were dead, *Hoovernomics* and *Jacksonomics*. There was also *Tsonga-nomics*, which Senator Paul Tsongas (D-MA) (1941–1997) laid out as part of his 1992 presidential campaign in a pamphlet titled "A Call to Economic Arms."

We've heard of *Daschlenomics*, after Senator Tom Daschle (D-SD) (1947–), and *Newt-o-nomics*, after former Speaker of the House Newt Gingrich (R-GA) (1943–). Even foreign leaders got the tag: *Stalinomics, Castronomics, Mitterandomics, DJnomics* (after South Korean President Kim Dae Jung [1924–]).

Like "Mother Hubbard economics," other swipes at an economic policy used the full word. George H. W. Bush's (1924–) famous *voodoo economics*, used to describe Reagan's policies during the 1980 Republican primary campaign, was morphed in a Los Angeles election by mayoral candidate Richard Riordan (1930–) into *Woodoo-economics*, playing off of the name of his opponent Michael Woo.

George H. W. Bush called Bill Clinton's (1946–) policies *Elvis economics*, taking a jab at Clinton's bubbaness and suggesting his policies were "all over the place," a reference to Elvis being spotted everywhere. *Twinkie economics* was another: sweet taste, but no substance.

Our *-nomics* bears no etymological relationship to the game *nomic*, in which rules are made up as play progresses, so that each game is different. But given that all politicians, whether implementor or decrier, seem to make up their economic policies as they go along, maybe the game nomics is a better connection.

# A

**actorvist** *n.* [*actor* + acti*vist*] a politically involved actor.

**1995** *Jet* (Oct. 9) 31:
Actor Malik Yoba is a self-proclaimed "actorvist."

**2001** *Los Angeles Times* (Mar. 14) F1:
The lure of Hollywood is so strong that even Mega, who briefly spurred controversy during the show because of his ties to the New Black Panther Party, has taken to billing himself as an "actorvist."

**2003** *Chattanooga Times Free Press* (Aug. 19) E4:
The self-described "actorvist" has been involved in organizations committed to goals from fighting AIDS to preserving wildlife to assisting Central American refugees.

**ad police** *n.* those who conduct an AD WATCH. Also **advertising police**.

**1990** *Washington Post* (May 14) F5:
The White House advertising police have been busy recently....The marketer of a cold medicine tried to score some publicity points by running an ad featuring Bush and Soviet President Mikhail Gorbachev and saluting the end of the "other" Cold War.

**1990** *Boston Globe* (Sept. 10) 1:
Mark Gearan, executive director of the National Democratic Governors' Association..., agreed that "the new aspect of negative advertising in 1990 is the ad-police aspect by the media."

**1999** *Toronto Star* (May 13) 1:
If we were the ad police, we'd throw them in jail. None of them are giving you a good enough reason to vote for them.

**advance** *n.* preparation for a (politician's) visit, esp. publicity or briefings.

**1968** Lady Bird Johnson *White House Diary* (Apr. 5) 651 in *OED*:
I knew that I was about to go home by car for a fifteen-minute advance before the press arrived at the Ranch on the bus.

**1971** *New Yorker* (June 12) 30 in *OED*:
"Good advance" means that the candidate is mobbed at the airport by fervent, unmanageable crowds.

**1979** H. Kissinger *White House Years* xix 742 in *OED*:
Whisked by a group of Communist Chinese to locations for which there had been no "advance" and in which they would have no way of telling who constituted a security risk.

**1996** *Los Angeles Times* (Oct. 29) E1:
The schedule had him flying out 18 hours later. Had to go back on the road. Had to keep moving. On Monday he worked rallies in San Diego and Anaheim. That's the business. That's advance.

**2000** *Time* (Mar. 2) 37:
Any of us should have recognized that we needed a presidential-level advance for that.

**advance man** *n.* a person sent ahead to prepare for the arrival of a larger group, including publicizing an event. Also **advance agent**, **advance**.

**1879** *Nevada State Journal* (Reno) (June 12) 3:
He goes as advance agent for a theatrical company.

**1918** *Indiana Evening Gazette* (Jan. 30) 3:
The Rev. Dr. James E. Walker, advance man for "Billy" is in the city laying final preparations for the eleven-week drive against John Barleycorn.

**1949** *Times Recorder* (Zanesville, Ohio) (Dec. 9) 17:
Most notable was his job as advance man for the Truman tour of the west in 1948.

**1973** M. Truman *Harry S. Truman* i. 31 in *OED*:
These days candidates send swarms of advance men into every city before they arrive. They are equipped with lavish amounts of money and every known publicity device.

**1998** Knight Ridder (June 30):
She later worked 21 months as the first lead advance for Kitty Dukakis.

**2003** *Washington Post* (Dec. 18) C1:
At one point an advance man used his body to block a correspondent from asking a question.

**advocacy advertising** *n.* marketing made in support of a (political) position rather than to promote a candidate. Hence **advocacy ad**.

**1971** *Chronicle Telegram* (Elyria, Ohio) (July 17) 23:
Ban on advocacy advertising.

**1975** *Wall Street Journal* (May 14) 1:
Mobil's Advocacy Ads Lead A Growing Trend.

*Ibid.:*
Advocacy advertising will be an essential part of the communications programs of many companies.

**1989** *Washington Post* (July 23) 5:
While it's often difficult to measure the effectiveness of any advocacy ad, several consultants say they can do as much harm as good.

**ad watch** *n.* the monitoring of advertising for its content; esp. for that which is unfair, untruthful, or illegal.

**1990** *USA Today* (May 14) 9A:
In Florida, *The Miami Herald* has begun an "Ad Watch" to separate the exaggerations from the facts.

**1992** *USA Today* (Oct. 7) 5A:
The press—TV especially—blamed itself after the 1988 campaign for superficial coverage dominated by photo-ops and 9-second sound bites. It vowed never to be so manipulated by politicians again. One 1992 reform is the "adwatch," in which reporters dissect the facts and fairness of each ad.

**2004** *Atlanta Journal-Constitution* (Feb. 20) B5:
Ad Watch: An occasional look at the credibility of political campaign ads.

**alderman** *n.* [ref. to the supposed stoutness of aldermen] a prominent paunch.

[**1867** W.M. Thackeray *Early & Late Papers* 85:
I wanted to beat two little boys what was playing at marbles on Alderman Paunch's monyment.]

**1929–33** Farrell *Manhood* 278:
Say, I'll be damned, Studs, if you ain't getting an alderman.

***1961** Partridge *DSUE* (ed. 6):
*Alderman.* a prominent belly...ca. 1890–1940.

**alphabet agency** *n.* a (governmental) organization designated by an acronym. Also **acronym agency**.

**1934** *Mountain Democrat* (Placerville, Cal.) (Jan. 19) 2:
It may be that when columnists throughout the country dubbed the NIRA, CCC, CWA and other government agencies as "alphabet agencies," they were thinking of that particular kind of soup which we call "alphabet soup."

**1968** *Wall Street Journal* (June 11) 1:
Acronym agencies like HELP, the "Humble Earn and Learn Plan" of Humble Oil & Refining Co. are blossoming.

**1995** *Atlantic* (July) 87:
Congress...had illegitimately delegated law-making authority to...the famed NRA, among the first of the New Deal "alphabet agencies."

**2004** *Plain Dealer Mag.* (Cleveland, Ohio) (Jan. 4) 14:
Senator Mark Mallory...calls Faith the spirit behind the Ohio Housing
Trust Fund, the OHTF in Columbus-speak, an obscure alphabet agency.

**alpha male syndrome** *n.* a (fanciful) condition in which (male)
leaders also have exaggerated masculine behavior. *Joc.*

**1998** *U.S. News & World Report* (Mar. 2) 18:
Sympathetic reporters have floated what might be called the "alpha
male syndrome"—strong leaders are victims of the hormones that go
with political success, or, as Eleanor Clift told us on MSNBC, "Libido
and leadership are linked."

**1998** *San Jose Mercury News* (Nov. 4):
It's time for corporations to take notice of the alpha male syndrome
and begin to train and support those in high positions.

**2000** *World Reporter* (Pa.) (May 12):
This is basically the alpha male syndrome at work....They're both
sitting there pointing guns at each other....They don't want to pull the
trigger and they don't want to get shot.

**2003** *Fair Disclosure Wire* (Feb. 11):
[The video game] will create a fun factor, making fun of the whole
alpha male syndrome that is part of the auto culture.

**also-ran** *n.* [orig. a racehorse that *also ran* in a race but failed to win,
place, or show] a loser in a race, contest, election, or competition of
any kind. Now *colloq.*

**1896** Ade *Artie* 16:
They ain't even in the "also rans."

**1899** Cullen *Tales* 17:
That insidious town always counted me among the also-rans before I
had a show to find out where I was at.

**1902** K. Harriman *Ann Arbor Tales* 248:
The "also-rans"...are just waiting for the end.

**1945** in *DA*:
Within a few hours some would be glorious in victory...some would be
colorless "also rans."

**1983** *National Lampoon* (Nov.) 4:
Past years as an also-ran.

**1992** *Dallas Morning News* (July 15) 17A:
Also-ran presidential candidate Paul Tsongas collected a consolation
prize Tuesday as the Democratic National Convention debated putting
four of his favorite economic ideas into the party's new platform.

**amen corner** *n.* [sugg. by congregants at the front of a church who call
out in response to the preacher.] any group (of politicians) which
gives unwavering support. Also **amen seat.**

**1860** *Harper's* (Jan.) 279 in *OED*:
The Rev. Judson Noth, a local Methodist preacher,...was one of the best "scotchers" that occupied the "Amen Corner."

**1884** *Congress. Rec.* (Apr. 24) 3207:
When...he was compelled to go to what is commonly known here as the amen corner, [he] frankly said that any seat in the Senate was better than none.

**1912** *Indianapolis Star* (Mar. 14) 9:
President Roosevelt was wont to choose the amen seat in the baldheaded row, and to sit delightedly through the whole performance, applauding every number until he was spotted in the face.

**2003** *National Post* (Toronto, Can.) (Mar. 29) 18:
Their resentment of the often-Jewish neos had expressed itself in the form of an ever-more strident hostility to the state of Israel and (in Buchanan's term) Israel's "amen corner" in the United States.

**American Taliban** *n.* fundamentalist or conservative Christians, esp. those said to believe religion should have a place in government; (*hence*) a (figurative) American government led by such a group.— usu. derogatory.

**1997** *St. Louis Post-Dispatch* (Dec. 19) C22:
Work outside the home is neither a temporary trend nor an individual aberration. Barring an American Taliban, it is an irreversible change rooted in economic necessity, opportunity and feminism.

**1999** *New Republic* (Jan. 4) 14:
The post-Newt GOP seems determined to reinvent itself as a kind of American Taliban.

**2002** *National Review* (Jan. 7):
Nothing could be better calculated to revive the Christian Right than a campaign to demonize conservative Christians as an American Taliban.

**2002** A.G. Lotz *My Heart's Cry* (Sept. 30) 163:
There have been those occasions when a listener has called into a talk show on which I was featured, vilifying me as an "American Taliban" because of my absolute conviction that the Bible is true.

**2003** S. Hawthorne *After Shock* (Sept.) 48:
Right-wing televangelists Jerry Falwell and Pat Robertson (our home-grown American Taliban leaders) appeared on Robertson's TV show.

**2003** *Baltimore Sun* (Dec. 6) 1B:
Surely the holder of the sign that read "GOP: American Taliban" with a swastika painted in the "O" of "GOP"—would have no snappy rejoinder.

**angel** *n.* one who gives (strategic) financial support (to a cause, campaign, or company).

**1917** A. Cahan *Rise of David Levinsky* 215:
I was incessantly cudgeling my brains for some "angel" who would come to my financial rescue.

**1926** *AS* (Dec.) II 136:
An "angel" in the argot of politics...is a man of wealth who makes—with not unquestionable motives—heavy contributions from his "bar'l" towards the expense of an election—election not theologically but politically speaking.

**2003** *Hispanic* (Sept.) 59 [in advertisement]:
Consider alternatives such as barter, or private investors known as "angels," who will put money into your company and may or may not want to help run the show.

**Anglo-American sphere** *n.* the loose political unit of English-speaking countries, said to have similar systems and goals.

**1905** A. Kuhn in *Proc. of Amer. Pol. Sci. Assoc.* II 88:
The Anglo-American sphere of jurisprudence is practically the only one not represented in that particular treaty union.

**1947** G. McClellan in *Amer. Pol. Sci. Rev.* XLI (Feb.) 141:
He admits we must decide whether Iran is to fall within the Soviet orbit, the Anglo-American sphere of influence, or be divided between the two.

**\*1999** in A. Tarock in *Brit. Journal of Middle East. Studies* XXVI (May) 46:
Other oil-rich states of the Persian Gulf region were under the Anglo-American sphere of influence in the 1960s and 1970s.

**Anglosphere** *n.* ANGLO-AMERICAN SPHERE.

**2000** *National Post* (Toronto, Can.) (Jan. 4):
We may see a widening gap between what writer Neal Stephenson has dubbed the "Anglosphere"—the world of English-speaking nations with strong open civil societies—and other market democracies

**2001** *2001 Washington Quarterly* (Mar. 22) 7:
He expressed a common suspicion in Europe (and particularly France) that Great Britain's real loyalties will always lie with the "Anglosphere" of English-speaking nations, dominated by the United States.

**2003** *Wall Street Journal* (Apr. 10) D8:
The underlying networks of cooperation that sustain this shy imperialism are likely to link the U.S. with such "Anglosphere" nations as Britain and Australia and perhaps, in due course, India and South Africa, which share the liberal world outlook.

**angry white male** *n.* a conservative, Caucasian male voter opposed to progressive laws, esp. those which are gender- and race-based.

**1992** Albrecht *Streetwork* 172:
Angry white males strutting around with shaved heads and aggressive

tattoos plastered all over their bodies, each with his own idea about racial equality and streetside justice.

**1998** *National Review* (Nov. 23):
Gore blasted the campaign of Virginia Republican Senate candidate Oliver North for relying on support "from the extreme right wing, the extra-chromosome right wing"—an apparent reference to the "angry white males" who, in Democratic lore, were the testosterone-crazed barbarians behind the 1994 GOP election sweep.

**2003** *Atlanta Journal-Constitution* (July 17) C2:
The war in Iraq is wildly popular with angry white males because it gives them a hormonal boost that makes them feel strong and dominant.

**anxious class** *n.* a social stratum primarily worried about its jobs and household economies.

*__1994__ *Guardian* (Manchester, U.K.) (June 6) 14:
Millions of American families, dubbed the "anxious class," are taking three jobs instead of two to make ends meet.

**1996** L. Scanlan *Heading Home* 75:
In the spring of 1995, *cutback* was the operative word...No place seemed safe, no job secure. The anxious class, as some call it, grew by the hour.

**2003** *Los Angeles Times* (Jan. 7) B13:
In the middle is a big, anxious class that's just a bit better off than a decade ago but still having trouble making ends meet.

**2004** *Nation* (Jan. 22):
Optimism and egalitarianism are being eroded. Taking their place is the cynicism of an Anxious Class that believes, rightly, that the rules aren't fair; and the hubris of a Winning Class that lives by its own rules.

**anxious generation** *n.* ANXIOUS CLASS; an age group whose members are worried they will be less well-off than their parents.

[**1987** *Barron's* (June 29):
This has become the "money society" pictured on the current cover of Fortune: an anxious generation on its way up, overwhelmed by an obsessive need to acquire before the elevator plunges.]

**1995** *Chicago Tribune* (Apr. 26) C5:
Being part of what Secretary of Labor Robert Reich calls the "anxious" generation of workers—those who never know when their jobs might simply disappear—takes its toll.

**2004** *Times-Picayune* (New Orleans, La.) (Jan. 14) 1:
Maybe we'll be the "The Anxious Generation" because of all the uncertainty in the world.

**anxious seat** *n.* the (metaphorical) location of one whose career is uncertain.

**1873** M. Ames *Ten Years in Washington* 345:
In the centre of this room, at a cloth-covered table, sits the Secretary of the Treasury and his assistants, besides, usually, a third dejected mortal, on the "anxious seat" of expectancy for office.

**1926** *AS* II (Dec.) 136:
This expression we owe to the lingo of revival meetings. At such meetings persons convicted of sin occupy the "anxious seat" or "mourner's bench." In the political usage of the term—we ought to add—there appears to be no striking implication of spiritual disquiet or conviction of sin.

**2004** *Forbes Global* (Jan. 12) 152:
Robert Sherwood: Tenterhooks are the upholstery of the anxious seat.

**apostle of hate** *n.* a bigoted or racist leader.

**1861** A. Thomson *Queens of Society*:
Robespierre, the king of blood, the apostle of hate, came among these men with a dominant resolution.

**1932** *Charleston Daily Mail* (S.C.) (Nov. 13) 7:
From Reicher he gravitates to Dr. Scollard, the apostle of hate and selfish animal brutality.

**1997** *Sun-Sentinel* (Ft. Lauderdale, Fla.) 3B:
As the regional director of the Hammerskin Nation racist movement and a veteran neo-Nazi, Leyden was an apostle of hate.

**AstroTurf** *n.* [fr. an artificial grass used to cover sports fields] an orchestrated grass-roots movement intended to appear spontaneous.

**1985** *Washington Post* (Aug. 7):
"A fellow from Texas can tell the difference between grass roots and Astro Turf," Sen. Lloyd Bentsen (D-Tex.) said of his mountain of cards and letters from opponents of the insurance provisions. "This is generated mail."

**1990** *Washington Post* (May 12) A19:
The AFL-CIO has been "flooded" with letters, phone calls and telegrams, overwhelmingly against the federation taking any position on abortion....Rather than concede the sincerity of those who want the AFL-CIO to remain neutral on abortion, he snidely remarked, "I've been around a while, and I think I can tell grass roots from Astroturf."

**1993** *Mother Jones* (Sept.–Oct.):
A massive letter-writing campaign...generated over 50,000 form letters and messages, sent to dozens of congresspersons. Not everyone was impressed. "Is it grassroots or Astroturf?."

**2001** *Electronic Engineering Times* (July 16) 51:
These spin campaigns illustrate the public relations tactic known as "AstroTurfing."

**attack ad** *n.* a campaign advertisement criticizing an opponent.

**1976** *Wall Street Journal* (Oct. 15) 12:
TV "attack ads" will deride Mr. Carter's presidential credentials, depicting him as just a one-term, big-spending governor of Georgia.

**1985** *Washington Post* (Sept. 22):
The most notorious attack ad of 1982 featured an actor dressed up as Fidel Castro lighting his cigar with a dollar bill and saying "Muchas gracias, Senor Sasser," to imply some of Tennessee Sen. James Sasser's votes had aided the communist dictator.

**2003** *New York Rev. Bks.* (July 3) 57:
Blumenthal's letter follows the basic technique of an attack ad: take an obscure detail, ascribe large significance to it, then draw a sweeping conclusion.

**2004** *Inside Politics* (CNN-TV) (Feb. 18):
The very first attack ad the Republicans have run against Kerry accused him of being too close to special interests.

**attack advertising** *n.* the use of ATTACK ADS; mudslinging.

**1982** *New York Times* (Nov. 9) A26:
As one Washington television consultant explained when asked about the new vogue for attack advertising, "Everybody in competitive races these days has enough money to buy all the name ID he needs. You just want to make sure it's negative name ID."

**1994** *Richmond Times-Dispatch* (Oct. 16) B4:
Attack advertising heats up in Senate race.

**2004** *Omaha World-Herald* (Mar. 14) 11B:
With the volume of presidential campaign speeches and attack advertising already approaching a level of frenzy, I wonder if by Election Day some eight months from now, some Americans might be inclined to look favorably on trading democracy for monarchy.

**attack dog** *n.* one who attacks on behalf of others.

**1981** *Washington Post* (Apr. 17) A13:
Any candidate who is unaware that his opponent is being trashed in half a million dollars' worth of television spots by NCPAC and its allied attack dogs isn't a good bet to have in public office.

**1994** *Times-Picayune* (New Orleans, La.) (Mar. 27) B6:
Mr. Leach, who earlier in the day had read the House a detailed list of alleged Clinton misdeeds, got a respectful hearing because he is not a political attack dog but a lawmaker known for a sharp sense of personal ethics.

**2001** *Newsweek* (June 4):
Instead of solving California's energy problems, Gray Davis is playing politics, pointing fingers and hiring political attack dogs.

**attack fax** *n.* a message, sent by facsimile machine, which criticizes an opponent or rival.

**1990** *Richmond Times-Dispatch* (Va.) (Apr. 22) D6:
In addition to "junk fax," there is now the unsavory "attack fax" that the legal bullies at the American Civil Liberties Union evidently intend to use in their typical efforts to intimidate those who do not share their nihilistic perspective.

**1992** *Washington Post* (Feb. 18) D1:
Poll-taker Harrison Hickman...has been rusticated from the campaign since being caught dissembling to the press—about his dissemination of an attack fax assailing Clinton's draft record.

**2001** *Newsweek* (June 4):
"It's everybody's fault but mine" read a recent RNC attack fax sent to Republican operatives and media outlets around the country.

**attack line** *n.* a (calculated) theme of criticism of an opponent.

**1986** *San Francisco Chronicle* (Jan. 29) E6:
In addition, Gorton was among the GOP senators who last year voted to delay Social Security cost-of-living adjustments—always a surefire Democratic attack line.

**1988** *Washington Post* (Oct. 16) C6:
This he should have started doing months ago, just as soon as the nature of the demagogic Republican attack-line became clear.

**2000** *Orlando Sentinel* (Feb. 25) A1:
McCain Attack Line—"Hey, Big Spender."

**attack politics** *n.* campaigning or day-to-day governing (said to be) primarily concerned with making accusations against opponents.

**1984** *New York Times* (Mar. 25) 22:
It is important to remember that the former Vice President's previous flirtation with attack politics helped bring disaster to him and his party. That was in 1980 when President Carter and Mr. Mondale tried to "demonize" Ronald Reagan as a threat to the nation's safety and wound up losing the White House.

**1988** *Dallas Morning News* (Nov. 19) 30A:
Mr. Atwater is responsible for a campaign that has been criticized for its superficiality and slick marketing. His specialty is "attack politics."

**2004** *Miami Herald* (Feb. 23) 7:
There's a fatigue among voters about attack politics, and there are major things at stake now. This is not a frivolous time.

**attack video** *n.* a video recording circulated to embarrass an opponent; a televised ATTACK AD.

**1987** *Washington Post* (Sept. 13) A6:
The tape, which yesterday's *Des Moines Register* described as the first example of an "attack video" launched by a political rival, showed...an excerpt from an Aug. 23 debate in Iowa in which Biden borrowed the British leader's words.

**1999** *Orange County Register* (Ca.) (Oct. 22) B8:
Naturally when campaigners took to the television screen, their products were called "attack videos."

**2004** *Nightly News* (NBC-TV) (Feb. 16):
He launched an attack video last week on his re-election Web site accusing Kerry of being an unprincipled recipient of special interest cash.

**Axis of Evil** *n.* [first used publicly, and popularized by, President George W. Bush in his 2002 State of the Union Address. It was coined by administration speechwriters David Frum and Michael Gargen as a play on the Axis Powers who opposed the Allies in World War II.] the nations of Iran, Iraq, and Korea, accused of sponsoring terrorism and developing weapons of mass destruction; (*hence*) two or more entities one finds unlikeable.

**2002** G.W. Bush *State of the Union Address* (Jan. 29):
States like these, and their terrorist allies, constitute an axis of evil, arming to threaten the peace of the world. By seeking weapons of mass destruction, these regimes pose a grave and growing danger.

**2003** *Baltimore Sun* (Aug. 10) 5C:
He did not even mention Charles Taylor of Liberia. But this one-time warlord and escapee from an American prison is part of the real axis of evil— the larger group of 44 dictators.

**2003** *New Pittsburgh Courier* (Aug. 30) A7:
We affirm the absolute necessity of standing with you against racist oppression, exploitation and repression—the real axis of evil—and of supporting your demand for reparations.

**2003** *San Francisco Chronicle* (Sept. 28) B2:
The Raiders were lured into the Super Bowl by the NFL Axis of Evil (league commissioner, other team owners and Saddam Hussein), in what was the cherry on top of the conspiracy sundae.

**Axis of Weasel** *n.* [sugg. by AXIS OF EVIL] those nations opposed to American foreign policy, esp. concerning the 2003 invasion of Iraq; (*hence*) France and Germany, or any entities one finds unlikeable. *Joc.* [The first quot. is satire and not reportage.]

**2003** S. Ott on *ScrappleFace* scrappleface.com (Jan. 22):
U.S. Secretary [of] Defense Donald Rumsfeld apologized today for referring to France and Germany as an "Axis of Weasels."

**2003** *New York Post* (Jan. 24) 1:
Axis of Weasel—Germany and France wimp out on Iraq.

**2003** *New York Observer* (Oct. 27) 4:
Can't we appeal to opposition in the Axis of Weasel? Not every German and Frenchman is a dolt or an immoralist.

*__*2004__ *Daily Post* (Liverpool, U.K.) (Feb. 19) 4:
I think my failings as a husband and father are exaggerated, especially so when mother and daughter conspire to form an axis of evil against me.

# B

**back channel** *n*. a behind-the-scenes or unusual route or method. —also *attrib.*

**1985** *Washington Times* (June 15) 1:
The paper "could become an important back channel of opposition," and a permanent fixture on the conservative side in official Washington.

**1992** *Atlanta Journal-Constitution* (June 10) A10:
An outsider with no identifiable constituency, using "back channel" media, has arisen with stunning quickness....Those so-called "back channels"—entertainment television and tabloids—have reduced serious political reporters to incoherence.

**1992** *New Republic* (Dec. 7) 12:
In an effort to smooth the negotiating process, the Arab and Israeli delegations have begun to use the press as a diplomatic back channel to sound each other out.

**2004** *Nation* (Feb. 16):
Simultaneously, many of them are engaging in a back-channel conversation on an Internet relay chat that allows hundreds of people—both those in the room and others watching the event on a live webcast—to share wisecracks, ponder dinner options and zap the speaker for everything from his clothing to his conceptualizing.

**background** *n*. information not for attribution or direct quoting. Hence **backgrounder**, n.

**1928** *Decatur Review* (Ill.) (Feb. 25) 8:
It was soon afterward ordered that in the future no references whatever should be made to the White House press conferences; that the gatherings were to be held only so that newspapermen might obtain "background" on public affairs. Already the distinguished person who speaks at these background bouts is being referred to as the "White House Backgrounder."

**1956** *Nevada State Journal* (Reno) (Dec. 14) 4:
Before Vice President Nixon made his recent speech pledging aid to Western Europe, newsmen were called in for a so-called "backgrounder." They were told for "background" that the Nixon speech was to be a great speech, another way of advising that it be given headlines.

**backstairs influence** *n.* any behind-the-scenes machinations or manipulation.

**1770** in Burke *Pres. Discontent* in *Works.* (1842) I 131 in *OED*:
A backstairs influence and clandestine government.

**1894** *Herald and Torch Light* (Hagerstown, Md.) (May 17):
When a committee of finance refuses hearings, because it knows intuitively all things, but finds by some kind of backstairs influence that it has made 400 mistakes, it is evident that that committee will bear watching.

**1934** *Sheboygan Press* (Wisc.) (June 11) 15:
Q. What is the origin of the expression, backstairs influence? N.R.A. The expression refers to private or unknown influence. It was customary to build royal palaces with a staircase for state visitors and another for those who visited the sovereign upon private matters.

**1954** *Lethbridge Herald* (Alberta, Can.) (June 8) 1:
Backstairs influence is powerless against the old man. He is the first man in Japan's history to rule out in the open with nothing but votes supporting him.

**2003** *Portland Oregonian* (Feb.10) B6:
Do Portland police officers think it's OK to use backstairs influence to help themselves when they get into trouble?

**bafflegab** *n.* [see second quot.] confusing or unintelligible speech; doublespeak.

**1952** *Berkshire Evening Eagle* (Pittsfield, Mass.) (Jan. 19) 3:
Bafflegab...Defined, tongue-in-cheek, by its coiner as "Multiloquence, characterized by consummate interfusion or circumlocution or periphrases, inscrutability, incognizability, or other familiar manifestation of obstruse expatiation commonly utilized for promulgations implementing procrustean determinations by governmental bodies."

**1952** in *AS* XXVIII 208:
Milton Smith, the assistant general counsel of the U.S. Chamber of Commerce, has coined a new word "bafflegab" designed solely for Washington bureaucrats.

**1953** in *AS* XXVIII 208:
Even I—and I've been exposed for an awfully long time to financial bafflegab—squirmed uncomfortably.

**1962** *New York Times* (Mar. 18) 35:
Rebels against the big words of "bafflegab" like to drive home their point with parodies.

**1967** *Wall Street Journal* (Mar. 14):
For collectors of bafflegab, the art of impressing an audience with verbal bushwa, the meeting of personnel officials was a gold mine....As the parade to the rostrum continued, the bafflegab glossary expanded: Narrowing parameters, functions of situational variables, diagnostic-planning activity, [etc.].

**1973** *Columbia Missourian* (May 24) 4:
Ellsberg repeatedly balked, refused and ran around the gates. Some of us had come to the studio expecting to encounter a philosopher of noble purpose, a licensed and certified martyr. We left with the impress of a bafflegab artist, recently shingled by a second-rate school of law.

**1980** J. Ciardi in *Atlantic* (Aug.) 36:
Double-talk, a form of rapid, smoothly articulated, and well-modulated baffle gab with a normal syntax but with meaningless key words, has long been a popular specialty of comedians.

**1985** *Los Angeles Times* (Sept. 5) 16:
Paper work, alas, is its own excuse for being, and the Internal Revenue Service's current fly report is, indeed, Form 5500-C and Schedule P, two pieces of bureaucratic "bafflegab" without which we all, somehow, managed to survive before 1985.

**1999** *San Francisco Chronicle* (June 29) A20:
Pure bafflegab from a president who has exhausted his friends and foes with an avalanche of lies.

**bagman** *n.* one who collects money obtained by racketeering and other dishonest means; formerly a term of mild contempt.

**1904** *Sandusky Evening Star* (Ohio) (Aug. 1) 6:
He became interested in so many different things that he almost deserved to be regarded as the bagman of high finance...He was still a Boston broker, finding his main vocation in the stock market.

**1913** *Nevada State Journal* (Nov. 4) 1:
The democratic leader...described...[him] as being the bagman of Boss Murphy, the man who gets the coin when the contractors are sandbagged on canal and highway jobs.

**1917** G. Myers *Hist. of Tammany Hall* 368:
Don't you know that Gaffney is Murphy's chief bagman? Don't you know he is the man Murphy sends out to hold up the contractors? Don't you know he is the man that held up my client...for over a hundred dollars?

**1928** *Funk's Stand. Dict.*:
Bagman (slang, U.S.), one to whom graft is paid.

**1980** *Globe and Mail* (Toronto, Can.) (Jan. 12) P6:
The total of 6½ hours would have a value of $25-million—the kind of figure that can frighten even a political bagman.

**1992** *Boston Globe* (Oct. 20) 37:
Federal prosecutors have alleged that Michael Sposito received monthly payments of $2,000 and that Sposito is a "political bagman."

**banana** *n.* [*b*uild *a*bsolutely *n*othing *a*nywhere *n*ear *a*nyone] a person opposed to all land development, esp. near residential areas.

*1991 *Advertiser* (UK) (July 31):
SPOTTED in a bulletin from WARMER, a United Kingdom organisation promoting recycling and energy production from waste, is the new acronym BANANA: Build Absolutely Nothing Anywhere Near Anyone.

**1991** *New York Times* (Dec. 15):
"The "banana" syndrome is notorious these days," Ms. Gulbinsky said, referring to an acronym for "build absolutely nothing anywhere near anyone."

**2001** *Star Tribune* (Minneapoolis, Minn.) (Jan. 28) 1A:
Industry officials have replaced the old NIMBY (not in my back yard) tag for their opponents with BANANA (Build Absolutely Nothing Anywhere Near Anyone) and, more recently, NOPE (Not on Planet Earth).

**banana superpower** *n.* a dominant nation which behaves like a weaker country with a fraction of its resources.

*1986 *Australian Financial Review* (Dec. 4) 17:
"Banana Superpower" was the headline over the lead editorial in the Baltimore Sun, which questioned how Rambophile Lieutenant-Colonel Ollie "National Hero" North, the 43-year-old former marine sacked by the President for his role in the affair, could be charged with running sensitive (and perhaps illegal) foreign operations.

**1997** *Atlanta Journal-Constitution* (Jan. 26) 2B:
A mighty democracy should adhere to prudent limits of the kind that are conspicuously lacking in the world's remaining dictatorships and tinhorn banana republics. Instead, we've become a banana superpower.

**1997** *Washington Times* (Sept. 5) A3:
Mr. Reagan criticized President Clinton for turning America into a "banana superpower" and nailed Republicans for doing nothing.

**barking head** *n.* an aggressive or loud broadcast commentator.

**1988** *Toronto Star* (Apr. 16) H1:
The barking heads have been nurturing personal styles whose only shared quality is a kind of evangelical furor.

**1998** *New York Times* (Mar. 11) A23:
Blink, and you can confuse the late-night comedy panels of "Politically Incorrect" with the barking heads of Sunday morning.

**1999** *O'Reilly Factor* (Fox-TV) (Oct. 15):
Bill, at first, you were kind of nice to watch. Now you're just another barking head. Let your guest finish a sentence, please.

**2002** *Hamilton Spectator* (Ontario, Can.) (May 25) M2:
The barking head phenomenon is better suited to a sort of hypermasculine aggressiveness.

**barnburner** *n.* [see first quot.] a radical member of the Democratic party of New York State. [Now *rare.*]

**1841, 1845** in *DA.*

**1877** Bartlett *Amer.* (ed. 4) [ref. to *ca*1810]:
This school of Democrats was termed *Barnburners,* in allusion to the story of an old Dutchman, who relieved himself of rats by burning down the barns which they infested,—just like exterminating all banks and corporations, to root out the abuses connected therewith.

**1926** *AS* II (Dec.) 138:
*Barnburners* formed the radical wing of the Democrat party.

**1977** Coover *Public Burning* 60:
I had to cool the barnburners, soften up the hardshells, keep the hunkers and the cowboys in line.

**barnstorm** *v.* [back formation from BARNSTORMER.] to travel as a BARNSTORMER.

**1884** *Daily Gazette* (Fort Wayne, Ind.) (Sept. 15) 5:
Carter Harrison is barnstorming in Illinois. He is doing the witch scene from "Macbeth," with two stock-yard henchmen as supernumeraries. They circle around the political pot and Carter says in basso profound accents, "Round the cauldron go and in your Democratic mess pork throw."

**1888** Pierson *Slave of Circumstances* 43:
Don't you go and get the barn-storming fever on you....They do say that when a girl gets the stage fever on her it's more deadly than the Yellow Jack.

**1892** *New York Times* (Mar. 16) 1:
The great political burlesque company gave one of the principal performances on its barnstorming route here to-day.

**1948** *Record-Eagle* (Mich.) (June 15) 2:
President Truman barnstormed the southwest today, sniping at the Republicans at every "whistle stop" along the way.

**2004** *Washington Post* (Mar. 1) A3:
"We are campaigning together," he told a crowd...before leaving to barnstorm the state on a red bus.

**barnstormer** *n.* Orig. *Theat.* one who tours small rural towns to give peformances; (*hence*) a politican making a rapid tour delivering campaign speeches, typically in rural areas. Now *S.E.*

**\*1859** Hotten *Slang Dict.* 3:
Barn stormers, theatrical performers who travel the country and act in barns, selecting short and frantic pieces to suit the rustic taste.

**1896** *Overland* XXVIII (Oct.) 484:
Still the West is sealed to the East by lasting ties of kinship and trade relationship, and only the "barnstormer" and "spellbinder" will talk of "bloody bridles."

**1926** *AS* (Apr.) 269:
[Baseball players] are "yannigans" on the spring training trip and "barnstormers" when they play outside their own leagues.

**1990** *Star Tribune* (Minneapolis, Minn.) (June 1) 1B:
[Khrushchev] proved to be a very good politician, the barnstormer type. Many people said then that if he had run for governor of Iowa, he could have been elected easily. He had that common touch.

**2003** *Seattle Times* (Dec. 19) C1:
[Alex] Rodriguez became nothing more than a glorified barnstormer. Like softball's old-time King and His Court. Like Meadowlark Lemon without the Harlem Globetrotters. Like Babe Ruth in the offseason, playing games against the local all-stars.

**barrel** *n.* a slush fund provided by or for a political candidate. Cf. PORK BARREL.

**1876** in *DA*:
The "barrel" is empty, the canvass ahead, And still they are crying for more.

**1884** in *F & H* I (rev.) 147:
We are accustomed to barrel-campaigns here....The Democrats depend upon carrying it with the money.

**1909** *WNID* 186:
Barrel campaign. A political campain in which money is freely used. Slang, U.S.

**1913** in *DA*:
The nominations of the party will not be the result of "compromise" or impulse, or evil design—"the barrel"—and the machine.

**beast** *n.* ¶In phrase:

¶**starve the beast** to reduce government size by cutting taxes, which in turn reduces government spending and services.

**1985** *Wall Street Journal* (Oct. 21) 16:
We didn't starve the beast. It's still eating quite well—by feeding off future generations.

**1992** *U.S. News & World Report* (May 25) 44:
Reagan tax cuts "starved the beast" so there is no money left for George Bush or Congress to spend on social programs.

**1992** Senator Daniel Patrick Moynihan (D-NY) *Federal News Service* (June 5):
The first thing to know about the budget deficit is that it was designed to paralyze domestic policy. I can testify that this is difficult to comprehend. The policy—it was known in the inside as "starve the beast"—was put in place in the first months of the Reagan administration, having been formulated the previous autumn.

**2003** *Business Week* (Feb. 17) 44:
The big fear of liberals is that if Bush's tax cuts don't act as an economic elixir, Democratic domestic spending priorities will bear the brunt of the ensuing crunch. Ultimately, Bush's strategists "want to starve the beast."

**beauty contest** *n.* CATTLE SHOW.

**1952** *New York Times* (May 8) 30:
It is the beginning of one-party government—eventually totalitarianism, of which enough has been seen by this generation. The race for the nomination should not be turned into a beauty contest.

**1959** *Stevens Point Daily Journal* (Wisc.) (Dec. 8) 11:
The Democrats held a big, four-hour "beauty contest" of 1960 presidential possibilities Monday night.

**1984** *Washington Post* (Apr. 24):
Hart won 71 percent of the vote in the March 6 "beauty contest" election.

**2004** *America Votes 2004* (CNN-TV Intl.) (Feb. 17):
The closest Sharpton came—not counting the non-binding D.C. beauty contest—was 9.6 percent in South Carolina.

**beef** *n.* [sugg. by catch phrase of a TV advertising campaign for Wendy's, Inc., in 1984] ¶In phrase:

¶**Where's the beef?** "Where is the real content or substance?"

**1984** *Los Angeles Times* (Mar. 25) IV 1:
Hart's critics say that he claims to offer "new ideas" but has so far failed to campaign on the issues. "Where's the beef?" Mondale taunts.

**1984** *Newsweek* (July 23) 40:
Mondale seized on that hamburger homily, "where's the beef?"

**1985** *New York Times Higher Ed. Supp.* (Mar. 3):
*Where's the beef?* A question asked when something is believed to be missing, as in a sandwich or a conversation seriously lacking content.

**1990** Cmiel *Demo. Eloquence* 11:
If "the dreaded 'L' word" ["liberal"] was central to the [presidential]

campaign of 1988, "Where's the beef?" served in its place four years before.

**1992** *CBS This Morning* (CBS-TV) (Apr. 6):
Charges like this have been bombarding us for weeks now. Where is the beef? Or is there any?

**2004** *Denver Post* (Feb. 19) B1:
So where's the beef? What's the point of the meeting?

**Beep** *n. N.Y.C. Pol.* a borough president.

**1952** *KEN* (Oct. 21) 5:
Borough President John Cashmore..."Beep" Cashmore.

**1980** *New York Daily News* (Tonight)(Manhattan) (Aug. 23) 5:
Still, the Queens Beep...concedes he's heard the Cabinet rumors, too.

**1985** *Our Town* (N.Y.C.) (Aug. 23) 1:
David Dinkins' Third Bid for Beep.

**1992.** *Midtown Resident* (N.Y.C.) (Oct. 5) 5:
Borough President Ruth Messenger's mayoral aspirations are well known....Several house parties have been held already for the Beep.

**belligerati** *n.* [*belliger*ent + liter*ati*] any belligerent person or group; (*hence*) as a group, pro-war commentators. Also **belligeratti**.

**2000** "Gordon" on Usenet (rec.aviation.military) (Mar. 16):
The other advisors tried to rush to the aid of their fallen belligeratti comrade, but came up short when several of the other present Africans began to point weapons in their general direction

**2001** A. Marr on Usenet (soc.culture.indian) (Apr. 10):
You are correct in observing Bush playing up to the right-wing belligerati in the recent past and moderating his tone now when the chips are down.

**2001** *Village Voice* (N.Y.C.) (Oct. 26) 59:
The Belligerati.

**2002** *Chicago Tribune* (May 16) 1:
How the war fevers raged in those days after Sept. 11. The nation's syndicated belligerati were beside themselves. Columnist Michael Kelly flayed the unconscionable pacifists as pro-terrorist and evil. Charles Krauthammer argued for bombing an enemy city, anywhere.

**Beltway** *n.* orig. the highway circling the Washington, D.C., metropolitan area, now a ref. to the city's political industry. Hence **inside the beltway,** *adj.* and **beltway insider,** *n.*

**1956** *New York Times* (Dec. 25) 23:
Hanson Highway will also run directly into the Beltway, which will go around most of Washington. The first section of the Beltway...will probably be completed within two years...The Washington Beltway will

be a 31.2-mile stretch of highway that is scheduled for completion by 1960.

**1975** *New York Times* (Oct. 12) 230:
In the White House of Richard M. Nixon, it was said that Watergate would become serious only if it "got outside the Washington Beltway"...It can be said that the myriad doubts about the Warren Commission's findings in the death of President Kennedy represent the reverse situation. The doubts would never be taken seriously until they were inside the Beltway.

**1986** R. Reagan *Let.* (Nov. 21) R.E. Weber & R.A. Weber *Dear Americans* 285:
You gave me a better press than I've been getting the last several days here inside the "beltway."

**1992** *Time* (Sept. 28) 18:
Patty Murray...cast herself as "just a mom in tennis shoes" and beat former seven-term Congressman Don Bonker for the opportunity to run against another Beltway insider, five-term Republican Congressman Rod Chandler, for the Senate seat vacated by retiring Democrat Brock Adams.

**2000** *U.S. News & World Report* (Jan 3–10) 8:
Kristol is poised to join *Fox News Sunday*, where an edgy brand of Capitol skinny is luring more and more beltway cognoscenti.

**Beltway bandit** *n.* an avaricious government contractor or consultant.

**1978** *Washington Post* (Jan. 25) quoted in Safire, 1984:
Some "Beltway bandit" ought to be hired to put one team of computer experts to work designing crime-proof defenses.

**1978** *Harper's* (June) 48:
There are also the consultants—the "beltway bandits," as they are sometimes called. These are the people who do government work for a fee.

**1989** Kanter & Mirvis *Cynical Amer.* 4:
Duplicity...by politicians...and larceny and greed by brokers and "Beltway bandits."

**1991** Dunnigan & Bay *From Shield to Storm* 463:
Most were defense consultants or scholars ("beltway bandits" is the Washington terminology).

**2004** *Fortune* (Jan. 26) 28:
Over the past few months Halliburton has been called a war profiteer, a beneficiary of crony capitalism, and a no-good Beltway Bandit.

**big bench** *n. Journ.* the United States Supreme Court.—constr. with *the.*

1929 Hostetter & Beesley *It's a Racket* 219:
*Big Bench*—The Supreme Court.

**big cheese** *n.* the most important or influential person; boss; big shot.—often used derisively. See also cheese, *n.* [See article on page 20.]

1914 in R. Lardner *Haircut* 144:
They was one big innin' every day and Parker was the big cheese in it.

1921 S.V. Benet *Wisdom* 233:
The other guy's the big cheese.

1924 DN V289:
*The big cheese, n.phr.* An important person.

1928 Treadwell *Machinal* 500:
You and the big chief. . . .You and the big cheese.

1929 "E. Queen" *Roman Hat* ch. viii:
Are you the big cheese around here?

1929–30 J.T. Farrell *Young Lonigan* 102:
He had licked Weary Reilley and become...a big cheese around Indiana.

1931 Dos Passos *1919* 257:
He started to say something sarcastic about the big cheese, as he called him.

1934 H. Miller *Tropic of Cancer* 20:
Elsa is the maid and I am the guest. And Boris is the big cheese.

1952 Bissell *Monongahela* 209:
You're the big cheese, it's all up to you.

1953 A. Kahn *Brownstone* 121:
What's the sixty-four dollar word for today from the big cheese?

1956 G. Green *Last Angry Man* 239:
You're not such a big cheese.

1970 Zindel *Your Mind* 2:
Mr. Donaldson...was the big cheese in the inhalation-therapy department.

1975 Keel *Mothman* 136:
Ashtar is a big cheese in the Intergalactic Federation.

1975 Hynek & Vallee *Edge of Reality* 197:
The guy who was in charge there at that time, the big cheese in charge of the whole area there, had been a real big shot in Japan.

**big fix** *n.* systemic corruption or graft.—usu. constr. with *the*. [Orig. associated with Chicago.]

1929 *Bookman* LXIX 12:
He discusses the "Big Fix"—an invisible part of the government which in its heyday could do anything for its favorites; he describes the cross-current influences of fraternal, political, racial and social organizations in the City.

**1930** *Appleton Post-Crescent* (Wisc.) (Feb. 15) 15:
Ask the average Chicagoan what, if anything, is wrong with his city and usually he will tell you—the "Big Fix"…"There is not a business, not an industry, In Chicago that is not paying tribute directly or indirectly to racketeers and gangsters,"…They represent but two branches of the "Big Fix."

**1959** T. Anderson *West. Pol. Quarterly* XII (Mar.) 283:
Democratic leaders had a semantic field day, charging that Knowland and Nixon had arranged a "cynical deal," a "big switch," the "big fix."

**1991** *Barron's* (July 15) 45:
Is it possible that the ongoing securities industry scandal in Japan is just another big fix that seeks to avoid a financial collapse there? Several clues that surfaced last week suggest that a conspiracy scenario isn't an unreasonable interpretation.

**bigfoot** *n.* [see 1985 quot. alluding to legendary humanoid of the Pacific Northwest] *Journ.* a prominent political journalist or news analyst; (*hence*) anyone or anything which exercises dominance.

**1980** Safire in *Good Word* 25:
Among the boys on the bus, "Big Foot" is a jocular term for a columnist, editor, or journalism celebrity who deigns to mingle with the working stiffs.

**1982** *New York Times* (Oct. 19) A18:
Mr. Bush says, as if with relief, that he has received "very little attention from the 'Big Feet,'" a colloquial reference to national political news commentators.

**1985** Safire in *Look It Up* 4:
The origin of *Big Foot*; when Hedrick Smith of the N.Y. Times with his foot in a cast, joined the press plane in the 1980 campaign, his Times colleague…Drummon Ayres, good-humoredly dubbed him that.

**1990** *New Republic* (Apr. 16) 43:
He's used his Big Foot status to get himself invited to sessions that a mere sportswriter wouldn't have been allowed near.

**1990** *New York* (Sept. 3) 10:
News stars who play Bigfoot, descending from the skies in times of crisis and crowding out lesser correspondents.

**1999** *Bangor Daily News* (Maine) (Mar. 27):
In many states, the attorney general is a political bigfoot.

**2000** *Nation* (Nov. 27) 10:
Bush was given a free pass by media that continued to hound Gore about whether he was really the model for Oliver in *Love Story*—which, by the way, he was. I guess being a Bigfoot journalist means never having to say you're sorry.

**bigfoot** *v. Journ.* to preempt or otherwise excercise one's privilege over as a BIGFOOT.

[**1982** J. Breslin in *Los Angeles Times* (Aug. 25) II 7:
In the city now we have Mayor Koch, voice braying, big-footing about the state in search of coronation.]

**1986** *New York* (Dec. 15) 15:
[Dan Rather] arrived just before the president went on the air, but Bob Schieffer was in place and [Rather] decided not to bigfoot him.

**1992** *New York Observer* (Oct. 26) 19:
Dworkin Bigfoots Abortion Book....Andrea Dworkin stopped the presses on a new book about women's reproductive health recently.

**2003** *Crossfire* (CNN-TV) (Nov. 14):
We'll look at how the senator from New York is bigfooting, overshadowing, her fellow Democrats.

**big league** *n. usu. pl.* [alluding to the major professional baseball leagues] the sphere of the most intense competition and professional activity in business, politics, research, etc.

**1924** *Washington Post* (May 2) 1:
A political lieutenant of that astute smoother and settler, Murray Crane, breaks into the big league with the announcement that Mr. Coolidge has picked his primary manager to manage his campaign.

**1956** *Christian Science Monitor* (Oct. 5) 3:
Four other Democratic women, out to break into big league politics, are rated high in ability and experience but are up against rugged political opposition.

**1974** A. Bergman *Big Kiss-Off* 47:
This guy plays in the big leagues and...you and me are pretty small potatoes to him.

**1983** *Green Arrow* (July) 13:
I know when I'm beaten, honey! I can't play in the big leagues.

**1990** *U.S. News & World Report* (Apr. 2) 39:
Stars and directors in such films...catapult into the big leagues before the smaller companies have a chance to capitalize on their fame.

**2003** *Los Angeles Times* (Dec. 11) B8:
Dean is a former governor of pint-size Vermont....Dean is playing in the big leagues.

**Big Mo** *n.* beneficial momentum, as in a political campaign. —opp. LITTLE MO.

**1980** *Washington Post* (Jan. 27) A1:
An exultant Bush, charged with Iowa's precinct caucuses victory, flew to New Hampshire to celebrate what he called "big Mo," his new momentum.

**1985** Tate *Bravo Burning* 149:
Big Mo was on our side.

**1988** *Morning Edition* (National Pub. Radio) (Feb. 19):
We've been hearing a lot in politics recently about *big mo*...momentum.

**1989** *Life Goes On* (ABC-TV):
We'll get a jump on him and start building the big mo.

**1992** *Today Show* (NBC-TV) (Feb. 18):
Tsongas...has the big mo.

**2004** *U.S. News & World Report* (Feb.16) 26:
Uh-Oh: Big Mo No Mo.

**big shot** *n.* an important person; a leader. Also **great shot, high shot**.

**1861** G. Meredith *Let.* (July 9) (1970) 91 in *OED*:
The great "shots" of Stanz parade the town with their prizes in their hats.

**1927** Ironwood Daily Globe (Mich.) (Apr. 16) 91:
That one punch made Roberts a national figure, a pugilistic big shot.

*ca*1929 D.H. Clarke *Reign of Rothstein* 40:
This year of 1917 was a hard luck year for the "Big Shot." He was robbed of $28,000 in another floating crap game in Harlem before it was over.

**1983** Globe and Mail (Can.) (Mar. 26) P10:
I tend to be too much of a populist. I should play the big shot more.

**2000** (AP) (Nov. 30):
What big-shot politician hasn't had face time in recent weeks in Florida, where the ground war over improperly marked ballots, voter intent and contested results still rages?

**big stick** *n.* [see 1900 quot.] (a display of) force or power, esp. military; (*hence*) extreme measures. Hence **big-sticker, big-stickism**.

**1900** T. Roosevelt *Let.* (Jan. 26) (1951) 1141 in *OED*:
I have always been fond of the West African proverb: "Speak softly and carry a big stick; you will go far."

**1915** *Reno Evening Gazette* (Nev.) (July 26) 1:
There is a phrase about speaking softly but carrying a big stick...The trouble is, you can't find a soft voice with a big stick. If a man has a soft voice, he doesn't want a big stick. If he gets a big stick he loses his soft voice.

**1938** *Lowell Sun* (Mass.) (Mar. 4) 16:
The United States once more has a big stick to swing. The navy must be built up to strength where it can demand respect everywhere.

**1968** *New York Times* (Aug. 5) 20:
From Teddy Roosevelt he has inherited the jingoist strain, which may

take a demented outlet such as the McCarthyism of the early 1950's or emerge in the big-stick talk of John Foster Dulles through the Eisenhower years.

**1978** *Globe and Mail* (Toronto, Can.) (Jan. 16) P8:
Indeed, for several months Ottawa has been walking softly and leaving the big stick at home in federal-provincial relations.

**1994** *Los Angeles Times* (May 22) 2:
Juries Demand Big Sticks, but Carry Soft Hearts.

**big tent** *n.* the broad policies of an organization which encompass the specific views of its factions; (*hence*) the core membership of an organization, or its center of action. Occas. **large tent**.

**1955** *New York Times* (Mar. 19) 8:
Unions that were read out off the bona fide labor movement as pawns of crooks or Communists began dickering to tie up with federation affiliates and thus worm their way into the big tent when the merger is completed this fall.

**1992** *Daily Times* (Salisbury, Md.) (Aug. 21) 12:
The Folded Tenters...have beaten Carl Lewis running from the "big tent" they used to brag about.

**2000** J. Pfeffer in R.L. Daft *Talking About Organization Science* (Feb. 10) 55:
The contents of the July 1992...issue..., although perhaps an extreme example of the proliferation of theoretical perspectives,...make the point that the field not only has, to use the current political parlance, a very large "tent," but a tent in which fundamentally any theoretical perspective or methodological approach is as valid as any other offer.

**2003** *New York Times* (June 1) A9:
Two main tenets of Bush's brand of Republicanism—the "big tent" philosophy and the "family values" agenda—seem to be on a collision course.

**bigwig** *n.* an important person or official.

*****1703** in *F & H* I (rev.) 217:
Dun or don—nob or big wig—so may you never want a bumper or a bishop.

**1792** in *OED*:
Though those big-wigs have really nothing in them, they look very formidable.

*****1815** in *OED*:
As poet-translator, no big wig ranks stouter.

**1855** Brougham *Chips* 327:
We've been spendin' a werry fashionable hour among the ar' big wigs.

**1884** Hartranft *Sidesplitter* 147:
Every blessed drop of licker he swallows there is a taxed to pay the salary of some of them ere great bigwigs.

**1935** Sayre & Twist *Annie Oakley* (film):
What will the President and the rest of the bigwigs say?

**1971** LeGuin *Lathe of Heaven* 16:
No wonder the Med School bigwigs had sent this one here.

**1973** Overgard *Hero* 89:
Now and then we get a Cuban big-wig Perez wants to show off for.

**1986** M. Skinner *USN* 21:
But even the bigwigs envy the ship's captain.

**1999** *Boston Globe* (Sept. 17) E1:
Dwyer the "master fixer" whom Beacon Hill bigwigs turned to when the district attorney was closing in.

**bimbo eruption** *n.* a sex-related scandal caused by a woman's allegations, esp. when associated with President Bill Clinton; (*hence*) any event or thing, dominated by women, that is stereotyped as overtly sexy or sexual. *Joc.*

**1992** *Washington Post* (July 26) A18:
She said that is vastly different from "opposition research" operations designed to uncover embarrassing information about a political opponent. "I don't think I've used him on anything except bimbo eruptions."

**1997** *Boston Herald* (June 4) 29:
Gennifer Flowers, Paula Jones, troopers used as procurers, bimbo eruptions and Astroturf in the back of pickup trucks—such is not the stuff of which Valentine verses are made.

**2003** *Chicago Sun-Times* (June 27) 33 [ref. to film *Charlie's Angels: Full Throttle*]:
But what, really, was so reprehensible about that high-tech bimbo eruption? Imagine a swimsuit issue crossed with an explosion at the special-effects lab, and you've got it.

**2003** *New York Times* (Oct. 19) 10:
Betsey Wright, who as Clinton's gubernatorial chief of staff learned to fight off what she called "bimbo eruptions," declares that Clinton's compulsive womanizing had "nothing to do with sex" but instead "has to do with this inferiority complex that he's carried his entire life."

**2003** *Newsday* (Dec. 28) A26:
Meanwhile, a last look at the rogues and vogues of 2003...Bimbo Eruptions.

**bimbo factor** *n.* the effect of a feminine presence, esp. when involving a sex-related scandal and a male politician. Also **bimbo syndrome**.

**1986** (AP) (July 12):
It might be what I call the "bimbo factor" in the alligator...This female has figured out the one individual who had got too close to her nest.

*__1987__ *Times* (London) May 10:
What is it that makes prominent men risk their careers? Paul Bailey says it's the bimbo factor...The bimbo syndrome does not acknowledge an all-consuming love.

**1999** *Boston Globe* (Aug. 19) A24:
Although Mrs. Blute blamed the young woman for brazenly baring her breasts, she claimed not to be upset with her husband..."It's the bimbo factor....I have never seen him sober."

**black** *adj.* Esp. *Mil.* secret, clandestine, covert; (*specif.*) not financially accountable to the government *or* accountable to Congress or the public.

**1965** *New York Times* (July 25) 30:
Black money is that not reported to the government for income tax purposes.

**1967** *Time* (Feb. 24) 17:
The group...examines in great detail every single "black" (covert) operation proposed.

**1973** *New York Times* (July 9) 22:
Both Mr. Strachan, then the Haldeman liaison to the reelection committee, and Mr. Chapin, who considered Mr. Segretti "an imaginative person" capable of dreaming up ideas of his own, thought him perfect to head the "black advance" program of spying and sabotage they had conceived.

**1974** *Harper's* (Dec.) 56:
Caulfield was convinced that Intertel was engaged in "black" operations.

**1983** *U.S. News & World Report* (Apr. 18) 33:
There are also the "black," or "illegal," operatives who have blended into American communities as immigrants or even assumed the identity of U.S. citizens.

**1983** *Los Angeles Times* (Aug. 7) I 14:
There is no significant movement in Congress to lift the "black" designation from the Stealth cruise missle.

**1984** *Atlantic* (Jan. 1985) 27:
This was "black" labor: no taxes are paid, no social regulations or minimum wages are honored.

**1985** Boyne & Thompson *Wild Blue* 229:
A black assignment is beyond Top Secret; it's done in complete secrecy with a budget that is not revealed to the public. The chief briefs the heads of the Armed Services committees, and they are sworn to secrecy.

**1988** *Newsweek* (May 16) 21:
The Pentagon begins a secret, "black" program to develop new armor, using extremely dense depleted-uranium.

**black cat** *n.* (see quots.).

[**1961** *Christian Science Monitor* (Nov. 16) 6:
With United States Secretary of Commerce Luther H. Hodges directing, Gen. Park Chung-hee of South Korea pats a black cat memento in the Secretary's office. Mr. Hodges said the cat, given to him by the San Francisco Press and Union League Club, has extraordinary powers. "You pat it three times, and everything you say is off the record," he told the Korean leader. General Park then patted the little black cat.]

**1979** Tuchman *Stilwell* 213 [ref. to 1941]:
In a "black cat" or off-the-record talk to the San Francisco Press Club...Stilwell said that war with the Japanese was certain.

**black helicopter** *n.* an aircraft believed by conspiracy theorists to be used in governmental misdeeds. —also *attrib.*

**1991** D. Allen on Usenet (alt.alien.visitors) (Aug. 9):
Twenty-two confirmed cattle mutilations had occurred...and they were accompanied by reports throughout the county of silent, unmarked, jet-black helicopters, flashing or steady anomalous lights in the air and near the ground, unmarked fixed-wing aircraft and white vans in remote and previously inaccessible areas.

**1994** *Denver Post* (Sept. 23) B1:
Black helicopters really do flutter over Colorado all the time. Those right-wing conspiracy theorists aren't crazy after all.

\***1994** *Guardian* (Manchester, U.K.) (Dec.15) T6:
Trochmann & Co. hold up dozens of pictures showing military hardware being shipped across the United States bearing UN—and even old Soviet—markings. They dig up obscure documents which purport to show how America is to be carved into 10 manageable regions. There are reports of mysterious black helicopters, spying on the innocent. Others whisper of unexplained numbers on the back of road signs, to be used to herd the masses into 43 concentration camps for dissidents, already under construction.

**2004** *Portland Press Herald* (Jan 28) 11A:
Just when I thought I couldn't imagine what else the government might be doing behind our backs, this happens...It's enough to throw the "black helicopter" crowd into a frenzy.

**blackneck** *n.* [*black* + red*neck*] a rural black Southerner who is opposed to various politically liberal programs. [All quots. ref. to Miss.]

**1978** *Los Angeles Times* (Sept. 23) I 1:
There are a weak Democratic candidate, an independent black

candidacy and a fragmenting of the "blackneck-redneck" coalition that has seen blacks and rural whites join to preserve Democratic control.

**1979** *Hattiesburg American* (Miss.) (July 19) 7:
"Redneck-blackneck" coalition.

**1980** *AS* (Winter) 294:
A term that has been a significant part of the last three gubernatorial races in Mississippi is *blackneck*...a rural black Southerner whose desires and political views may be essentially the same as those of his white (redneck) counterpart.

**1986** *Washington Post* (May 21):
Only when economics becomes the overriding issue can you put together the redneck-blackneck coalition.

**2000** (AP) (Aug. 15):
Ronnie's got to do what he has to do to get re-elected short of disowning his base, the blacknecks and rednecks.

**black Republican** *n.* a Republican supporting black emancipation. — usu. used derisively. Now *hist.*

**1856** W. Seward in *Political Speeches* (1855–57) 3:
There are three parties here: 1st, the Democracy; 2d, a branch of the opposition once known as Whigs...and, 3d, the Republicans, Black Republicans, or Abolitionists, as the other two parties happily agree in calling us.

**1876** J. Hodgson *Cradle of Confederacy* 382:
He was not willing to assert the rights of the South...to kidnap cannibals from Africa, or buy slaves of the King of Duhomey. But should a Black Republican President be installed in the Executive chair in Washington...he could pledge Virginia not to be behind Alabama.

**1929** D. Lynch *Boss Tweed* 252:
Considerable apprehension was felt for the safety of the Mayor—A Republican, a Black Republican, and an Abolitionist.

**bleeding heart** *n.* one who is sympathetic to the disadvantaged; (*hence*) any liberal. Also **bleeding heart liberal**.

**1938** *Appleton Post-Crescent* (Wisc.) (Jan. 8) 3:
I question the humanitarianism of any professional or semi-pro bleeding heart who clamors that not a single person must be allowed to hunger but would stall the entire legislative program in a fight to ham through a law intended, at the most optimistic figure, to save fourteen lives a year.

**1949** *Joplin Globe* (Mo.) (Oct. 23) 8B:
The American labor party used to include a minority of "bleeding heart" Roosevelt new dealers who now compose the American liberal party...Since the departure of the "bleeding hearts," the ALP has become completely communist.

**1988** J. Ellroy *Big Nowhere* (1994) xxvii 323:
A nice guy, if a bit of a bleeding heart.

**1993** *Albuquerque Journal* (N. Mex.) (Feb. 8) A7:
He is clearly not a bleeding heart liberal or the Alan Alda brand of feminist.

**2000** *Nation* (Aug. 7) 26:
Lindsey is...poaching on territory that used to belong to liberal Democrats...When I asked him to justify the regressive nature of Bush's tax proposal, Lindsey sounded like a regular bleeding heart.

**blink** *v.* to back down in the face of opposition; to acquiesce.

[**1962** *New York Times* (Dec. 7) 38:
Boss, we're eyeball to eyeball with you-know-who, and I think the other fellow just blinked.]

**1992** H.N. Schwarzkopf *It Doesn't Take Hero* xvii 318:
Though my intelligence experts warned...that the Republican Guard could return to an attack formation with as little as twenty-four hours' notice, it seemed that the Iraqis had blinked and that, for the first time, the likelihood of an immediate invasion had decreased.

**2003** *Wall Street Journal* (Nov. 5) A2:
Sen. Max Baucus of Montana, the leading Senate Democrat in the talks, said it would be "almost impossible" to get a bill passed if Republicans insist on using private plans to force potential reductions in the level of government support for the traditional Medicare fee-for-service program. "It's the moment of truth," Mr. Baucus said. "It's blink time."

**blinkmanship** *n.* the art of diplomatic negotiations which cedes no ground until the other side backs down from a position.

**1962** *Daily Northwestern* (Oshkosh, Wisc.) (Dec. 13) 6:
Blinkmanship is an even chancier game than Brinksmanship. Blinksmanship...is attributed to Dean Rusk, Secretary of State. During the crux of the Cuban crisis Rusk is reported as saying, vis-a-vis the U.S.-Russian position, "We're eyeball to eyeball and I think the other fellow just blinked."

**1986** *Chicago Sun-Times* (Oct. 7) 38:
The White House Blinkmanship expert told me, "Daniloff was not swapped for Zakharov. There is no link between the two men. The Soviets gave up Daniloff because they knew they were wrong, and we gave up Zakharov because he was getting to be a pain in the ear."

**1998** *Boston Globe* (Oct. 9):
Give some credit...to U.S. special envoy to the Balkans, Richard Holbrooke, the master of blinkmanship.

**blitz** *n.* a quick series of campaign events; an extensive advertising or publicity campaign.

**1948** *Time* (July 5) in Berg *New Words* 43:
The Dewey Blitz has been stopped.

**1968** Safire *New Lang. Politics* 120:
A follow-up to...a doorbell-ringing campaign is a telephone blitz.

**1984** *Washington Post* (May 6):
Jackson's state coordinator, Sherman Copelin, jubilantly credited the black preacher's campaign "blitz" through key sections of the state last weekend.

**2002** *New York Daily News* (Oct. 15) 19:
 This week's blitz, however, is merely a tuneup for a President who has politicked in 43 states.

**blitz** *v.* to hold a quick series of campaign events; to inundate with publicity or advertising.

**1966** H.S. Thompson *Hell's Angels* 78:
The group...managed to blitz the national press in 1965.

**1976** *U.S. News & World Report* (July 26) 75:
In 1968, COPE could "blitz" the country with tens of millions of pamphlets favorable to Humphrey.

**1983** *Atlanta Constitution* (Mar. 9) 1:
Democrat Candidates Blitz Ga.

**2001** *New York Times* (Aug. 12) 1:
As of Aug. 4, the nation's television viewers had been blitzed by 131,373 paid political advertisements.

**2002** *Washington Post* (Nov. 6) B4:
She blitzed through 16 stops in the same exhaustive style that characterized her campaign.

**bloviate** *v.* to blather and speechify.

**1845** *Huron Reflector* (Norwalk, Ohio) (Oct. 14) 3:
Peter P. Low, Esq., will with open throat reiterate the slang of the resolution passed by the County Convention, and bloviate about the farmers being taxed upon the full value of their farms.

**1872** W. Bausman in *Overland* VIII 62:
It was a pleasure for him to hear the Doctor talk, or, as it was inelegantly expressed in the phrase of the period, "bloviate".

**1990** *Raritan* (Winter) 110:
He would certainly have blocked the presidential nomination of...pliable Warren Gamaliel Harding, the "bloviating" senator from Ohio.

**bloviation** *n.* a lot of noise or verbose talk.

**1877** *Decatur Republican* (Ill.) (Jan. 4) 4:
The result of the conference really amounted to nothing but a large amount of commonplace bloviation.

**1901** *Iowa State Press* (Iowa City) (July 3) 2:
Right in the metropolitan section of the metropolis, with all its shouting
and bloviation over acres of new building in ten years.

**1958** *Times Recorder* (Zanesville, Ohio) (July 2) 4:
Billions of units of gaseous bloviation will be discharged on the air of
California by election day.

**1999** *Wired* (Dec.) 396:
Undoubtedly, the life of a self-employed policy mandarin is a grand
one: living large with besotted CEOs who suck on the helium of your
big-picture bloviation.

**2002** *Time* (Mar. 4) 84:
Some "journalists" take fat fees from companies like Enron in
exchange for a few hogsheads of bloviation.

**bloviator** *n.* one who BLOVIATES.

**1878** *Mountain Democrat* (Placerville, Cal.) (Aug. 24) 4:
The temperance fanatic and the anti-sumptuary bloviator, the Sunday
law Puritan and the Sunday dance Schutzenfester, the rantingest anti-
railroader and the craziest subsidist.

**1927** *Indiana Wkly. Messenger* (Pa.) (Dec. 1) 2:
How about having old Bloviator for one of our campaign speakers?

**2001** *Boston Globe* (Oct. 21) E4:
Or, for that matter,...the rest of that celebrated troupe of pundits,
mavens, ventriloquists, and solo bloviators.

**2002** *Chicago Tribune* (Jan. 13) I18:
This president seems to draw his strength not from whether the public
or the Beltway bloviators like him, but from whether he thinks he's
doing his job right.

**blue dog Democrat** *n.* [cf. YELLOW-DOG DEMOCRAT, based on paintings
by Louisiana artist George Rodrigue, which show a blue dog in
political situations] a coalition of (fiscally) moderate-to-
conservative Democratic House members; (*hence*) a Conservative
Democrat, usu. Southern.

**1995** *Washington Times* (Apr. 21) A1:
They call themselves the blue-dog Democrats—yellow-dog Democrats
turned blue by the choke hold put on them by their own liberal
leadership.

**2000** *New Republic* (Dec. 25) 42:
While some white conservatives—the so-called Blue Dog Democrats—
kept their party registration out of habit, most eventually switched to
the GOP, bringing with them control over state government.

**2001** *Newsweek* (July 15):
He is one of about 30 conservative "blue dog" Democrats who cannot
be counted on to vote the party line.

**2003** *Oil & Gas Investor* (Jan.) 8:
Blue Dogs have been active in supporting fiscal restraint...many times they craft their own position and oppose both Republican and Democratic leadership positions.

**blue flu** *n.* an organized protest action by police officers (occ. other municipal employees) in which individuals claim that influenza or some other illness prevents them from reporting to work.

**1967** Hersey *Algiers Motel* 152:
I had one day out on blue flu.

**1971** *New York Post* (Nov. 20) 3:
Acting Fire Commissioner Vincent Canty has pledged that the city will receive full fire protection despite a new epidemic of "blue flu" among uniformed firemen.

**1992** Hosansky & Sparling *Working Vice* 114:
A "Blue Flu" sick-out lasted two days.

**blue goose** *n.* a bulletproof lectern hist. used by Pres. Bill Clinton and V. Pres. Al Gore.

**1996** *New York Times* (Oct. 5) 10:
He stands behind the bulletproof lectern that the Secret Service calls the blue goose, for the color of its top and its goose-neck microphone.

**1998** *New York Times* (June 21) 4-5:
Mr. Clinton is bringing his bulletproof lectern, known as the blue goose.

**2000** *Washington Post* (Nov. 9) A34:
They unloaded a bulletproof lectern, dubbed the "Blue Goose," and positioned it in front of 17 American flags.

**2000** *New York Times* (Dec. 15) A1:
Aides brought in the "blue goose," as the vice-presidential lectern is known, and planted a forest of American flags behind it.

**2001** *U.S. News & World Report* (Feb. 19) 7:
Closeted is the hulking "Blue Goose" armored podium. In its place at most events: a simple toast lectern with a clay presidential seal dangling off the front.

**blue-light** *n.* a New England Federalist opposed to the War of 1812. Now *hist.* [According to *DA*, after "the lights reported to have been shown at New London, Conn., as a signal to the British fleet during the war of 1812–5."]

**1814, 1815** in *DA*.

**1823** *Adams Centennial* (Gettysburg, Pa.) 2:
Shall *we* who regardless of the name of *Rebel*, and in defiance of *British bayonets*, once stepped forward in defence of our country, now shrink from our duty to that country at the cry of *Federalist* or *tory*, *blue light* or *Hartford conventionist*?

**1833** J. Neal *Down-Easters* I 47:
Calling one another blue-lights, jacobins, tories, democrats and enemies to the country.

**1850** *Southern Lit. Messenger* (Dec.) 705:
When war arose and the "blue lights" were burned, and the Hartford Convention met with its doors close to plot what the southern men of that day called treason;—then it is said you were a blue light federalist.

**blue slip** *n.* a paper representing a senator's decision on a judicial nomination.

**1950** *Los Angeles Times* (Sept. 13) 28:
"Blue slips" are forms supplied by the Judiciary Committee to permit Senators to note their endorsement or objection to nominees.

**1979** *News* (Frederick, Md.) (June 2) A7:
The senators from the majority party virtually dictated the nominations of federal judges in their states by the so-called blue slip method of action...The senator had the option of returning the blue slip to the committee with a...rating, or simply pocketing the slip.

**2003** *Houston Chronicle* (Jan. 24) 14:
I'll give great weight to negative blue slips, but you can't have one senator holding up, for instance, circuit nominees.

**blue states** *n.pl.* the states whose electoral votes went to the Democrats in the 2000 presidential election; (*hence*) any liberal or Democratic state. [See also RED STATES.]

**1992** *USA Today* (Nov. 5) 6A:
I think it shows the lack of historical memory pundits have....They're a lot more excited because they see a lot more blue states than red states.

**2000** *Early Show* (CBS-TV) (May 8):
And then the tossup states—you see Bush in red and you see the blue states are for Gore.

**2004** MSNBC (Apr. 1):
A...poll taken earlier this year found that 64 percent of people living in the so-called red states—those that traditionally vote Republican—are married. That figure contrasts with the 56 percent who are married in the so-called blue states—which typically go Democratic.

**body man** *n.* a personal aide.

**1988** *Boston Globe* (April 17) 18:
Every candidate has a body man, someone who fulfills a kind of mothering role on the trail. The body man makes sure the candidate's tie is straight for the TV debate, keeps his mood up, and makes sure he gets his favorite cereal for breakfast.

**1993** *St. Louis Post-Dispatch* (Mar. 14) 6A:
As Gephardt's floor director, Stephanopoulos helped coordinate the

daily action in the House chamber and served as the "body man"—the key aide who accompanied the House majority leader everywhere in the Capitol.

**1996** *Denver Post* (June) 10 B7:
Lindsey is Clinton's body man. As the handyman, adviser and enforcer, he sticks to Clinton like a tattoo.

**2001** *Houston Chronicle* (Feb. 25) 6:
Cheney's body man, Schmitt reports, is Brian McCormack, an earnest young guy from New Jersey who considers himself a jack of all trades. He carries Cheney's coat, passes him messages, "keeps him up to date and on time" and generally sticks close by to do whatever Cheney needs.

**BOGSAT** *n.* [bunch of guys sitting around a table] policy or decision making by a small group of associates. *Joc.* Also BOGSATT.

**1961** *New York Times* (Sept. 24) E8:
Waldemar A. Nielsen...coined the word "bogsat" to have some fun with his friends on the White House staff.

**1984** *New York Times* (Feb. 9) 29:
Dan Fenn, special assistant to President John F. Kennedy, [asserted] that each President was reduced to choosing his team by a process he calls "BOGSAT"—"a bunch of guys sitting around a table."

**1986** *New York Times* (June 11) 14:
He concluded that it really was no more than BOGSATT..."Bunch of guys sitting around the table," said [Congressman Les] Aspin, an old Pentagon hand with a penchant for acronyms.

**boiler room** *n.* a political (campaign) headquarters.

**1957** *Times Recorder* (Zanesville, Ohio) 4:
After Ike was elected in '52, his brothers...hived up in the Waldorf...right across the hall from the political boiler-room operated by Arthur J. Goldsmith.

**1968** Safire *New Lang. Politics* 120:
A telephone blitz—calls made from a "boiler room" to remind favorably inclined voters to turn out on election day.

**1972** in Bernstein & Woodward *President's Men* 171:
McGovern headquarters in California was used as a boiler room to rally hard-core anti-war militants to confront the President.

**boll weevil** *n.* a conservative Southern Democrat.

**1981** *New York Times* (June 14) IV 4:
The 47 or so Southern conservatives in the House, known informally as the boll weevils, have moved to center stage....The boll weevils have been lumped togetherr in the public mind, but in fact they are quite distinctive individuals.

**1981** in *Newsweek* (Jan. 4, 1982) 32:
The "boll weevil" Democrats in the House illustrate the point:
Democrat Phil Gramm of Texas was working for the [Republican]
Administration's budget cuts almost from the beginning.

**1987** *Newsday* (CNN-TV) (Oct. 6):
A crucial vote among the so-called "boll weevils" of the judiciary
committe.

**1991** *CBS This Morning* (CBS-TV) (Mar. 15):
You've already told us about your boll-weevil Democrat credentials.

**bolt** *n.* a refusal to support a candidate, platform, or policy of one's
political party. *Now* S.E.

**1852** Eliason in *Tarheel Talk* 261:
The worst feature...is the *bolt*...from the regular nomination!

**1858** Thornton in *Amer. Gloss.* I:
It is known that there would have been some such bolt from the
nominations, had the nominations been made.

**1903** A.H. Lewis *Boss* 116:
We...are goin' to make a bolt for better government.

**bolt** *v.* to refuse to support one's political party; to refuse to support (a
candidate, policy, etc.); to leave (a political convention) in protest.
*Now* S.E.

**1814** in *DA*:
When a member wishes to "bolt," he "totes" himself out of the house
before the ayes and noes are called.

**1833** in *DA*:
Does the Doctor apprehend that the editor is about to "bolt"?

**1852** Eliason in *Tarheel Talk* 261:
This lawyer has been a "free-soiler," having "bolted" our party.

**1871** Schele de Vere *Amer.* 585:
Carl Schurz has *bolted* from the Republican party.

**1892** Garland *Spoil of Office* 88:
They're going to bolt the convention and there'll be fun in the air.

**bomfog** *n.* [*b*rotherhood *of m*an under the *f*atherhood *of* God, closing
line of a radio speech by John D. Rockefeller, Jr., on July 8, 1941; later
used as a slogan by Nelson Rockefeller; see 1978 quot.] platitudinous
political rhetoric or obfuscation. Also as **v.**

**1964** *New York Times* (May 25) 26:
Bomfog stands for "the Brotherhood of Man under the Fatherhood of
God," a phrase used regularly by the New York Governor.

**1965** *Lompoc Record* (Cal.) (May 19) 10B:
A good recent candidate, however, is BOMFOG....It describes
platitudinous political piety.

**1978** Safire *Pol. Dict.* 67:
Bomfog was originated by Hy Sheffer who was at one time [Gov. Nelson Rockefeller]'s stenotypist. Hy...started using it in the late 1959–60 national effort. Since the Governor used the phrase "the brotherhood of man under the fatherhood of God," so often, Hy began to simplify it on the stenotype machine.

**1978** *Newsweek* (Feb. 6) 30:
How to master the glut of data and improve the bomfogging reports that make up the "product" of the U.S. intelligence community.

**1979** Homer *Jargon* 35:
*Bomfog.* Any speech heavy on bombastic rhetoric and light on true substance.

**1987** Safire in *New York Times* (Feb. 2) 21:
Admiral Poindexter...pumped out some bomfog about having to check his files, never admitting...authorship.

**2004** *New York Press* (Mar. 25):
Jahncke characterized the primary result as "a significant defeat for the administration's radical new foreign policy doctrine." Of course, this statement may be just so much bomfog: The results would be significant if the mass media had paid attention to them.

**boodler** *n.* a person, esp. a politician, who seeks or accepts bribes; grafter.

**1885** *Coshocton Age* (Ohio) (Nov. 11) 4:
The coal oil corruptionists and boodlers, and by this is meant the villains who bought and sold the Senatorship last winter a year.

**1886** *Daily Republican* (May 18) 2:
The conviction of Alderman Jaehne, of New York, for bribery, has caused a cold chill to meander along the spine of many a city father in every large city...They contemplate the ease with which this boss boodler was run down.

**1888** *Catholic World* (Jan.) 563:
Where he huddles with other Irish immigrants....the cheap saloon, the pot-house politician, and the boodler boss come into being.

**1890** *Overland* (Feb.) 136:
The New York "boodler" who spoke of retiring from the "aldermanic business"used language with precision. Governor Hill's ideal in politics is on a larger scale the same as that of the "boodle" alderman.

**1957** O'Connor *Co. Q* 92:
Boodlers, thieves, cowards, troublemakers, or whatever.

**1984** P.J. Buchanan in *New York Post* (Aug. 31) 33:
But whether or not these boodlers are given "input" into spending $30 billion in social programs is our business.

**1999** *Barron's* (Oct. 18) 58:
If you had asked us a decade ago, we would have been likely to say

that anyone who would stay in the job of SEC chairman for more than six years would be a fool. Or a political boodler.

**boom** *v.* to promote (a candidate, product, local, etc.) enthusiastically. *Now* S.E.

**1883** *Moose Jaw News* Avis in Dict. Canad. 67:
Their town is all the better for not having been "boomed" to any considerable extent.

*__1888__ in *F & H* (rev.) 329:
The city of Paris is said to be diminishing instead of increasing in population. They don't know how to *boom* a town over there.

*__1891__ *OED*:
Messrs. J.S. Fry...are booming their manufacturers in a novel way.

**1904** Bierce in *Letters* 98:
Your decision to "boom" me almost frightens me.

**1906** *National Police Gaz.* (Feb. 3) 3:
What you want is a manager—someone to boom you.

**1966** in *OED*:
One minor political figure in Alabama, a certain Shorty Price, decided to boom his own wife for governor.

**boondoggle** *n.* [claimed to have been coined as a name for an ornamental leather cord] an extravagant and useless project. *Now* colloq. [The specificity and uniqueness of the first 1935 quot., in which the term means "gadget," suggest that this sense was never very common and perhaps not very old. The remainder of the quots. illustrate the usual meaning, which came to prominence in 1935 and which the first quot. attempts to explain.]

[**1935** *New York Times* (Apr. 4) 2:
"Boon doggles" is simply a term applied back in the pioneer days to what we call gadgets today.]

**1935** *Wisconsin Rapids Daily Tribune* (Apr. 11) 4:
That New York relief investigation has cleared up one thing that has always bothered us. It seems that thingumabob that fits into the hootnanny is called a boon doggle.

**1935** S. Lewis *Can't Happen* 198:
The Universal Electric Corporation....They don't mind Jews there as long as they sing at their work and find boondoggles worth a million a year to the company.

**1947** in *OED*:
The cost of this boondoggle has been estimated at perhaps 50 million dollars.

**1978** J. Webb *Fields of Fire* 106:
Tim Forbes will confess his boondoggle, and we will admire his honesty.

**1982** *New York Post* (Aug. 13) 24:
And The Boondoggles Go On.

**1983** *Morning Contact* (WKGN radio) (May 27):
That little boondoggle agency has just go itself in deeper and deeper.

**1985** *Our Town* (N.Y.C.) (Aug. 11) 2:
Now let his savvy explain that 63rd Street subway boondoggle.

**1985** Wells *444 Days* 198:
They had my passport, so they knew that I had been to all of those countries, and they wanted to know why I said, "I was on a boondoggle." Then it took me nearly an hour to explain what "boondoggle" meant.

**1992** *Los Angeles Times Mag.* (May 31) 12:
*Boondoggle* n. Business trip whose location is chosen for travel/vacation motives.

**2001** J. Franzen *Corrections* (Sept.) 360:
It is a boondoggle that I should have known better than to get involved with. However, your mother wore me down.

**boondoggle** *v.* to engage in a BOONDOGGLE. Hence **boondoggler**, *n.*

**1935** *Indiana Evening Gazette* (Pa.) (July 6) 2:
A more abundant life where the true hobo may boondoggle and follow his ancient philosophy without being forced to rub elbows with vulgar persons who would work if they got the chance, is just around the corner....Incidentally, boondoggling, disclosed as a new art during the recent New York investigations, is nothing new at all...We were the first boondogglers...In the midwest I know many old dogglers who have been doggling for years. We used to call them mushrakers. They specialized in making household utensils out of wire.

**1935** Gelman in *Photoplay* 181:
I told her I thought it was a government "boon doggler" in Milwaukee who unearthed the marriage registration of Mae West and a Frank Wallace.

**1936** Butterfield in *Post Treasury* 358:
The word "boondoggling" alarmed some New Dealers.

**1937** *AS* (Feb.) 6:
*Boondoggling* became the current term [during the 1936 elections] for describing the waste assertedly evident in...government agencies and bureaus. Administratiors of relief became *boondogglers* to the Republican press and orators.

**1939** Appel *People Talk* 12:
It's a nice park they're building....And they're not boondoggling.

**1942** in *DA*:
Boondogglers or social experimenters.

**1950** *Sat. Eve. Post* (Mar. 25) 12:
The product of these projects...is likely to be just more boondoggling.

**1963** Hecht *Gaily* 59:
I lay claim to similar ownership of years passed, and the right to boondoggle while recounting them.

**1965** Hardman *Chaplains Raid* 184:
Goodnight, you lousy boon-doggling creep.

**1970** Terkel *Hard Times* 8:
A WPA boondoggler leaning on his shovel.

**1979** Ennes *Liberty* 179:
Cumshaw experts and boondogglers.

**1985** Boyne & Thomson *Wild Blue* 468:
He accused Brown of wanting to boondoggle to Bangkok while a war was going on.

**1990** P. Theroux *Iron Rooster* 355:
It wasn't the centuries-old accretion of monuments, pagodas, ruins, factories, apartment blocks, political boondoggling and bad ideas that made up the average Chinese city.

**bork** *v.* [after Judge Robert H. *Bork,* whose appointment to the Supreme Court was blocked in 1987 after an extensive media campaign by his opponents] to attack (a candidate or the like) systematically, esp. in the media. Also as *n.*

**1987** *Chicago Tribune* (Oct. 5) 16:
As it becomes more apparent that the nomination of Bork will bite the dust, a new meaning is emerging as in "He got Borked."

**1988** *Chicago Tribune* (Nov. 30) 20:
Honest disagreement is one thing, "borking" is something else.

**1989** Sen. M. Wallop (R. Wyo.) *CBS This Morning* on (CBS-TV) (Feb. 9):
I feel strongly...that...he [sc. John Tower] is being borked....The charges that have been leveled against him...have all proved groundless, baseless.

**1991** *CBS This Morning* (CBS-TV) July 9:
An opponent of Judge Clarence Thomas said yesterday, "We're all going to bork him."

**1992** *Los Angeles Times* (Aug. 23) M6:
Perhaps...Hillary Clinton is being "borked"—attacked in the same orchestrated, systematic manner which ultimately undermined the U.S. Supreme Court nomination of Judge Robert H. Bork.

**1993** *New Republic* (May 17) 20:
More than sixty right-leaning national and state organizations will close ranks to coordinate a huge preemptive bork.

*Ibid.:*
The strategies used to bork Zoe Baird and gays in the military.

**2003** Sen. John Cornyn (R-TX) *Fed. Doc. Clearing House* (Oct. 30) transcript:
I'm particularly disturbed by this filibuster today because it represents the second judge nominated to the Fifth Circuit Court of Appeals that covers my state of Texas that has been Borked by the Democrats.

**bounce** *n.* a surge in support for a candidate or politician after a major occurrence such as a primary win or a unifying national event. Also **v** See also BUMP.

**1980** *New York Times* (Apr. 6) CN1:
This campaign, Mr. Ferree said, was marked by "an incredible amount of bounce, of volatility in people's preferences for Presidential candidates."

**1984** *Wall Street Journal* (Aug. 16) 24:
The big bounce raised anew questions about the accuracy and reliability of the election picture drawn by polls.

**1988** *Chicago Tribune* (July 27) 2:
It was evident he does not want to squander the "bounce" polls have been showing in his popularity since the Democratic National Convention in Atlanta last week.

**1992** *Seattle Times* (July 16) A3:
Get ready for a spate of "bounce" polls—surveys likely to appear within hours of Clinton's address that seek to gauge how much voter support he picks up in the wake of the convention.

**2003** *Milwaukee Journal Sentinel* (Sept. 14) 1A:
Two years after Sept. 11 and five months after the fall of Baghdad, President Bush has lost the huge political "bounce" from both rallying events.

**boy scout** *n.* a person who is idealistic and naive; (*hence*) one who is scandal-free or uncorruptible.

**1987** *Wall Street Journal* (Oct. 2) 1:
"But the bottom line is that [Sen. Paul] Simon is running for president as the boy scout who adheres to traditional liberal policies and solutions."

**1997** *Washington Post* (Mar. 4) A1:
"Gore long has been called the Boy Scout of the Clinton administration, a politician of such integrity and personal probity that even Clinton has jokingly complained about the vice president's glowing press."

**1998** *Atlanta Journal-Constitution* (Dec. 19) B5:
It came as no surprise here in suburban New Orleans when Livingston, the fabled "boy scout" of the Republican Party, admitted Thursday to extramarital affairs.

**bracket** *v.* to campaign before and after (an official or business visit or another candidate's visit).

**1996** *Washington Post* (Sept. 19) A12:
The former senator has also launched a strategy called "bracketing," or orchestrating interviews in markets being visited by the opposition.

**2003** *Boston Globe* (Oct. 19) A26:
Bush has been bracketing official events with campaign stops for months now, swooping into town on Air Force One, wowing the locals, and leaving with a pile of money.

**brain trust** *n.* a group or staff of planners or advisers; (*Mil.*) a general staff or headquarters staff.—also applied jocularly to an individual. [Popularized as S.E. in 1933 as a designation for advisers of Pres. F.D. Roosevelt.]

**1899** *Marion Daily Star* (Marion, Ohio) (Apr. 8) 16:
Since everything else is tending to trusts why not a brain trust?...Our various and sundry supplies of gray matter may as well be controlled by a central syndicate.

**1902** *Fort Wayne News* (Indiana) (May 3) 4:
Cornelius Vanderbilt and John Jacob Astor have been making inventions and taking out patents, but that is no sign that the millionaires are going to form a brain trust.

**1910** (cited by M.M. Matthews in *AS* XXXII (Feb. 1957) 57 in sense "college faculty").

**1918** Palmer *Amer. in France* 88:
Through the Chief of Staff and through the Commander-in-Chief, this "brain trust," as the line called it, had its policies executed when they were approved.

**1920** Coburn *26th M.P.'s* 55:
Is an important member of the outfit, as his suggestions are valued very highly by the "brain trust."

**1928** McCartney *Additions* 281 [ref. to WWI]:
*Brain Trust* (Am.), the General Staff.

**1937** Odets *Golden Boy* 254:
He writes he's a regular "brain trust."

**1940** *AS* (Feb.) 29:
"Brain Trust" was originally used by the line of the Army as a sort of sour grapes crack at the first American general staff established by Elihu Root in 1901....that's where the phrase came from...[Signed, General] Hugh S. Johnson.

**1942** Stilwell in *Papers* (Dec. 8):
Just had such a billet-doux from the Brain Trust.

**1972** Jenkins *Semi-Tough* 110:
Regardless of...what Big Ed the Brain Trust thinks.

**1980** S. Fuller *Big Red* 288:
The braintrust boys in London...had accumulated a mountain of OSS information.

**1983** *New York Post* (Aug. 17) 6:
Brain Trust...Francis Coppola...has enlisted the aid of author William Kennedy as a "period consultant"...on the 1930's.

**1991** *Newsweek* (Dec. 23) 24:
Even after the putsch, he has not created a brain trust for himself.

**brain truster** *n.* a member of a BRAIN TRUST.

**1933** *Lima News* (Ohio) (July 7) 6:
Brain Truster Reeves came down to Washington.

**1959** Fuller *Marines* 64:
"That's the Board of Directors," Maxwellington said sourly. "The battalion brain-trusters."

**1964** McKenna *Sons of Martha* 119:
Them braintrusters down in the ice plant.

**1980** W.C. Anderson *BAT-21* 121:
Maybe some of the brain trusts...[in the Pentagon] can come up with some ideas.

**brass** *n.* officials or executives

**1945** *Yank* (Dec. 7) 14:
My company "brass" insist that all employees wear a coat and tie to the office.

**1953** Roman *Vice Squad* film:
I know all about your influence with the political brass in this town.

**1987** *Baton Rouge State Times* 6B:
The heavy influx of Washington brass in Moscow this week may put a strain on Soviet hosts in providing enough properly bugged accommodations for the new arrivals.

**1990** C.P. McDonald *Blue Truth* 7:
Cool it, the brass!

**brass collar** *n.* extreme party loyalty, either through force or choice. *often* attrib.

**1932** *New York Times* (Mar. 27) E6:
The wets and many drys who were regular in 1928 have no objection to this pledge. The bolters of four years ago chafe under it. They call it a brass collar and a sell-out to Tammany.

**1961** *Wall Street Journal* (May 31) 12:
"I think we've proved we finally have got rid of the brass collar the Democratic party had around our necks," comments a Texas labor leader.

**1964** *New York Times* (Jan. 5) 51:
Mr. Clark...argues that Republican voters now "wear the brass collar," Texas slang for blindly voting a straight party ticket.

**brass collar Democrat** *n.* a loyal Democrat, esp. in the South.

**1952** *Daily Northwestern* (Oshkosh, Wisc.) (Oct. 14) 18:
John Garner is a brass-collar Democrat.

**1986** *Dallas Morning News* (Oct. 18) 31A:
But Democrats have misread the district; it's no longer brass-collar Democrat as it was when Tiger Teague represented it.

**2002** *Journal and Courier* (Lafayette, Ind.) (Nov. 17) 11:
I occasionally need to remind myself why I am a brass-collar Democrat and proud of it.

**bridefare** *n.* a welfare program which increases benefits if recipients are married. Cf. WEDFARE.

**1991** *Milwaukee Journal* (Wisc.) (Feb. 12) A12:
The committee's chairwoman, Rep. Rebecca Young (D-Madison), derided the proposed changes as "bridefare" a reference to two other of Thompson's controversial welfare programs, Learnfare and Jobfare.

**1994** *Phila. Tribune* (Sept. 23) 5B:
To reduce welfare dependency and to foster responsibility and strengthen family values and morals, policies designed to teach the inner city disadvantaged the importance of....not having children until marriage (WedFare and BrideFare)....have been implemented.

**2002** AP (Aug. 31):
"Bridefare" tried to get teen parents to marry, paying them extra if they did.

**bubba factor** *n.* the impact of the stereotyped unsophisticated, blue-collar, white, Southern, male.

**1987** *Dallas Morning News* (June 7) 39A:
The push will come to the shove at a moment when we are thinking with our meat rather than our minds. But the Bubba factor is only part of the problem with high-technology smart weapons.

**1988** *Chicago-Sun Times* (Mar. 6) 11:
The tacit target of Super Tuesday was the white working-class Southern male, known generically in political parlance as "Bubba."

**1990** *USA Today* (Apr. 12):
He expects a macho "Bubba factor" could work against [Ann] Richards.

**1995** *Buffalo News* (Apr. 5) 11:
The angry white male has been described as misogynistic, homophobic and racist by the high-brow media and as "the Bubba factor" by political pollsters.

**buffalo** *n.* Esp. *N.C.* a Southern abolitionist; (*hence*) a Southerner disloyal to the Confederacy. *Now hist.*

**1856** Barret in *Civil War in N.C.* 174:
Buffalo know nothings.

**1863** in *Confed. Vet.* XXIV (1916) 93:
The commanding general directs that you cause the buffalo Winslow and all other undoubted buffaloes or their aids and abettors to be arrested and sent back for further disposal.

**1864** in *DA*:
The rebels were very bitter against these "buffaloes," as they called them, for many had been on their side, and left it for the service of the union.

**bullet vote** *n.* a ballot cast to support or defeat a single candidate or issue, often ignoring all other candidates, races, or initiatives; (*hence*) casting all possible votes for a single candidate when more than one candidate can be chosen for the same position, as in a JUNGLE PRIMARY. Also **v.**

**1972** *Ironwood Daily Globe* (Mich.) (Apr. 19) 4:
The various governorship aspirants may be telling people to cast a "bullet vote"...That could mean casting all 20 votes for one man instead of spreading votes across the whole list.

**1984** *Washington Post* (Feb. 20):
One faction that has a strong bullet vote, often credited with defeating such liberals, is the right-to-life movement, and in 1980, it turned out for the sole purpose of defeating Kennedy.

**1990** *Newsday* (Mar. 16) 27:
To boost his chances in the at-large trustee race, Perlin is asking residents to "bullet vote" by casting ballots only for him, rather than for two candidates.

**2003** *Boston Globe* (Nov. 5) B6:
When he tried to bullet vote...he was told the machine would not accept his ballot unless he chose four candidates.

**bully pulpit** *n.* [orig. used by Pres. Theodore Roosevelt to explain his personal view of the presidency] a public office or position of authority that provides its occupant with an outstanding opportunity to speak out on any issue.

**1909** *Outlook* (N.Y.) (Feb. 27) 430 in *OED*:
He [sc. President Roosevelt]...swung round in his swivel chair, and said: "I suppose my critics will call that preaching, but I have got such a bully pulpit!."

**1974** *Newport Daily News* (R.I.) (July 11) 4:
[Nixon] can still reach the public from his "bully pulpit" but he can no longer be certain that his words will be taken in good faith.

**1988** B. & E. Dole *Doles* 227:
I have used the bully pulpit to wage my own war on drunk driving.

**2001** *New York* (Oct. 22) 24:
While there have been rumors that Clinton and Giuliani might co-chair a commission to rebuild downtown, his aides say he seems more likely to use his bully pulpit and play national hand-holder.

**bump** *n.* BOUNCE.

**1983** *Globe and Mail* (Toronto, Can.) (June 8) P13:
On Monday night, Labor leader Michael Foot said the polling firms were headed for the "biggest bump they have ever had."

**1988** *Sunday Oklahoman* (Oklahoma City) (Mar. 13) 1:
In polling terms, it's called a "spike" or a "bump," an event that noticeably alters the public opinion numbers.

**1999** *Houston Chronicle* (Jan. 21) 3:
An ABC News survey showed a 3 percent bump for Clinton to a 66 percent approval rating.

**bundle** *v.* to combine individual political contributions (from organization members or employees) to circumvent caps on corporate or institutional donations.

**1984** *Wall Street Journal* (July 5):
The method used by the Council for a Livable World is called "bundling." Rather than gather individuals' voluntary donations into its bank account and then write PAC checks, the pro-freeze group urges its supporters...to make out personal checks directly to the candidate's campaign. Legally, the donations are counted as coming from the individual donors, so the $5,000 limit doesn't apply...The checks are then gathered together—bundled—for delivery, so the group gets credit with the candidate.

**2004** *Washington Times* (Feb. 18):
It's called bundling...You get bundles of $2,000 maximum contributions from individuals.

**buzzard** *n.* a representation of the American eagle, as on the U.S. coat of arms, coins, etc.; (*hence*) a gold or silver dollars.

**1834** *Military & Naval Mag. of U.S.* (Oct.) 116:
He launches out a *golden buzzard* to a coachee for a ride to see the ways of the town.

**1902** Clapin *Americanisms* 89:
*Buzzard*....The silver dollar, so called derisively from the buzzard-like eagle on the coin.

**1943** Meyer in *Stars and Stripes Story of WWII* 81:
Somebody called "Jo-Jo" a sad sack the other day and he came right back with a nifty counterblow, "well, you're a disgrace to the buzzard," he told the ribber, with the gravity of a Supreme Court Justice.

# C

**campaign mode** *n.* (an artificial or aggressive) behavior adopted for campaigning.

**1984** *Washington Post* (June 26):
The political adrenaline is still flowing. I'm still in the campaign mode.

**1992** *USA Today* (Feb. 19) 2A:
Bush is going to have to start attacking back. He'll now have to govern in a campaign mode, and abandon his Rose Garden strategy.

**2003** *Boston Globe* (May 5) A14:
Marzilli said he believes Finneran is "dead right" in accusing Romney of "governing by press release" and staying in campaign mode rather than dealing with serious issues.

**2004** *New York Times* (Feb. 9) A1:
Some Republicans said Mr. Bush had been too much on the defensive in the past few weeks, and they had urged the White House to accelerate its schedule for going into full-scale campaign mode.

**card** *n.* ¶In phrase:

¶**play the —— card.** to use a (diverting or devious) tactic.

*1886 R. Churchill *Let.* (Feb. 16) in *OED*:
I decided some time ago that if the G.O.M. went for Home Rule, the Orange card would be the one to play.

[**1904** J. Commons in *Quarterly Journal Econ.* (May) XVIII 430:
These sensations undoubtedly made owners timid and retarded new enterprises; and this timidity of capital was the card, and the only card, that this union had to play.]

*1942 Lady Galway in *Journal Royal African Soc.* (Oct.) XLI 240:
Already during the last war Germany did her utmost to play the Flemish separatists' card, and exasperate Walloon feelings.

*1978 *Globe and Mail* (Toronto, Can.) (June 10):
He has been talking tough to Moscow, and sending his national

security adviser, Zbigniew Brzezinski, to Peking to remind the Russians that he can play the China card if necessary.

**\*1986** *Guardian* (Manchester, U.K.) (Sept. 3):
The introduction of visas gives the Government a beautifully deft device to play the "race card" in the run up to an election.

**1990** *Boston Globe* (Nov. 25) 29P:
To attempt something constructive...would require a lot of hard work by news reporters that might offend those who just love to play the race card.

**2000** J. Dreyer in *Amer. Pol. Sci. Rev.* XCIV (Mar.) 207:
Deng showed impressive manipulative abilities, playing the "citizen card" (i.e., the legislature as the "highest organ of state power") and the "party [committee] leadership card" through a strategy of alignment, dealignment, and realignment.

**2004** P.J. Buchanan *World Net Daily* on (Jan. 26):
He is going to play the patriot card and the nationalism card, and they trump the U.N. card every time.

**card-carrying** *adj.* having a membership card of a specified organization, esp. of the Communist Party; (*hence*) to be dedicated and committed (to a cause, group, or behavior).

**1947** *Reno Evening News* (Nev.) (Feb. 10) 1:
Do you know that one of the present and past officers of the local is a card-carrying member of the Communist party?

**1988** *Patriot News* (Harrisburg, Pa.) (Nov. 7) B1:
Vice President George Bush...essentially has labeled anyone associated with the ACLU as a "card-carrying" liberal.

**2003** *Des Moines Register* (Dec. 4) 17:
Card-carrying AARP member? Count me out.

**carpetbagger** *n.* a political interloper. Now *colloq.*

**1868** *Defiance Democrat* (Ohio) (May 9) 1:
He holds a meeting, nominates himself for office, goes about making speeches, stirs up the negro against the white...Such is the carpet-bagger. A man who has no stake in the country beyond his satchel, and yet, by the grace of reconstruction, the ruler of a black crook convention.

**1868** J. Trowbridge *A Picture of the Desolated States* 659:
If you are a Northern man, acquire citizenship by the legal period of residence, and get nominated to office, you will be ridiculed as a Yankee adventurer—a "carpet-bagger."

**1870** *St. Louis Christian Advocate* (Mo.) (Aug. 3) 7:
Now the carpet-baggers come here and tell us they are our friends and the Southern people our enemies. They tell us they set us free. Oh,

yes, they've done it all, no doubt. They set us free about like they set the mules free.

**2004** *Fort Worth Star-Telegram* (Feb. 23) 10:
Hillary Clinton—an Arkansas carpetbagger in Yankee country?

**Carterize** *v.* [ref. to Pres. Jimmy Carter.] to cause (someone, esp. a president) to appear irresolute or manipulated.

**1976** *Business Week* (June 28) 25:
Without mentioning the bill by name, the "Carterized" version in the platform commits the Democrats "to the right of all adult Americans willing, able, and seeking work to have opportunities for useful jobs at living wages"...Labor's influence.

**1982** *New York Times* (July 10) 1:
The worst thing we could do is send an uncertain signal between now and the election. It would tend to Carterize the President.

**1985** *Washington Post* (July 1) A19:
A White House official who only a few days ago expressed concern that the Mideast hijacking would "Carterize" the Reagan presidency said yesterday that Reagan "now has control of the agenda again."

**1993** *San Francisco Chronicle* (Jan. 19) A1:
Democrats are acutely aware of the pitfalls they face. "Cooperation" has become a mantra among congressional leaders, who vow that this time, they will not "Carterize" their new president.

**cattle show** *n.* an event featuring multiple, competing candidates.
Also see BEAUTY CONTEST.

**1979** *Washington Post* (Nov. 5) A2:
Reagan's low vote perhaps can be attributed to the fact that he was the only GOP presidential hopeful who did not appear before the forum...Reagan disdains all such early political cattle shows.

**1987** *Chicago Tribune* (Aug. 28) 28:
Many credit Bush's loss to Reagan in the 1980 New Hampshire primary to his stubborn refusal to join the other candidates in a highly publicized local debate sponsored by the Reagan campaign. As one seer put it, to have stiffed the others in this year's TV cattle show would have been like stepping into the same unpleasant barnyard substance twice.

**2003** *Beltway Boys* (Fox-TV) (Aug. 9):
These Democrats have gotten themselves committed to one special interest cattle show after another, and every time they go there, they pander to, to, to the audience.

**CAVE** *n.pl.* [*c*itizens *a*gainst *v*irtually *e*verything] persons who seem to oppose all (real estate or commercial) development or change.
Hence **CAVE people, CAVE dweller, CAVIE.**

**1992** *San Francisco Examiner* (Jan. 26) A11:
It bore the legend, "Remember the Grinch Who Stole Christmas?" It concluded: "Say 'No' to the Grinch and the CAVE (Citizens Against Virtually Everything) people. Don't sign the petition."

**2001** *Atlanta Journal-Constitution* (Feb. 15) JK7:
There are still some CAVE people out there, that's Citizens Against Virtually Everything.

**2002** Knight Ridder (May 28):
Chappell said some critics were Presidio neighbors who prefer that the park not become a destination point for tourists, and he described others as "CAVE dwellers"—citizens against virtually everything.

**2002** Rothman *Neon Metropolis* 365:
Retirees fit the model of the CAVIE—citizens against virtually everything—and in a city where they've come to retire and don't have deep ties, their desire to take their rewards far exceeds any feelings they have about the future of the community.

**celebrity advocate** *n.* a famous person who publicly endorses a cause. Hence **celebrity advocacy**.

**1988** (AP) (May 19):
She will be the main celebrity advocate for the foundation in dealings with government agencies.

**1990** *Denver Post* (Apr. 30) 6B:
The message came in many forms...panel discussions with celebrity advocates for environmental protection.

**1998** *Billboard* (Nov. 28) 1:
There's a tremendous opportunity for celebrity advocacy. Doctors, lawyers, teachers, politicians, and artists all used to be held in equal high regard 50 years ago, and now that's not the case.

**cemetery vote** *n.* the sum of ballots fraudulently cast in the name of dead persons.

**1891** *Newark Daily Advocate* (Ohio) (Mar. 6) 1:
It contains many names of dead men and absentees, so that the "cemetery vote" will be an important factor in deciding whether Canada wants unrestricted reciprocity or not.

**1938** *New York Times* (Feb. 17) 20:
Tom Pendergast may have lost the cemetery vote, but he can't lose Harry Truman.

**2000** *Washington Times* (Nov. 14) 2:
The Democrats don't seem to be relying on such cloak-and-daggerish devices as the "cemetery vote" or old-time ballot stuffing, exemplified by the Chicago voting machine that Nixon once noted as having recorded 121 votes for 43 voters.

**chad** *n.* a small piece of paper punched out of a paper card or tape, as from a ballot used in a mechanical polling machine. [See article on page 13.]

**1939** Teletype Corporation *US Patent 2,273,909* (Chicago, Ill.) (May 20) 1 [patent granted Feb. 24, 1942]:
The present invention provides a perforating arrangement whereby the perforations are not completely cut out, but the chads are permitted to remain attached to the perforated material.

**1988** *New Yorker* (Nov. 7) 54:
The punched-out scraps, which have come to be called "chad," are supposed to be forced between two vertical rubber strips underneath the ballot and into a chad box.

**1992** P. Shocket et al *Western Pol. Quarterly* (June) XLV 524:
The voter can "feel" the stylus break through the "chad," but cannot with ease visually verify the vote.

**2000** *New York Times* (Nov. 13) A20:
They decided, one by one, whether a ballot was a valid vote based on whether they could see a "hanging chad," which is a hole punched partly through a ballot, or a "pregnant chad," which is only an indentation created when the voter failed to pierce the ballot.

**character assassin** *n.* a person who attacks the reputation of another. Hence **character assassination**.

**1874** *Burlington Weekly Hawkeye* (Iowa) (July 30) 4:
If Tilton is a libeller and character assassin, we would like to see suit commenced against him.

**1898** *New York Times* (Oct. 4) 1:
Attempted assassination of character has been almost the sole weapon of attack employed by Senator Quay's opponents for several years.

**1901** *New York Times* (Mar. 9) 3:
Such a statute is a bad one as it enables the unscrupulous and designing to prostitute it to unworthy and ignoble purposes, and singles out the District Judges as the special marks for the character assassin.

**1907** *New York Times* (Jan. 6) 11:
I want no bouquets from the character assassins swarming about the State like toads about a foul cellar.

**1951** in *AS* XXVI 293:
A period of "the big lie," of the furtive informer, of the character assassin.

**2004** *New York Press* (Feb. 18):
Does this mean the story is true? No. It is "developing," as our

favorite cybergossip character assassin likes to say, and it may go nowhere.

**character issue** *n.* the perceived shortcomings of a person's words or deeds which become a target of an opponent's ATTACK LINE.

1920 *Washington Post* (Aug. 27) 5:
The greatest ovation of the evening came when Gov. Cox shot his reply to Chairman Hays' insinuation as to a personal character issue in the campaign.

1979 *New York Times* (Sept. 28) A27:
I have been impressed the way you have handled the character issue in the cases of Bert Lance, Hamilton Jordan, Dr. Peter Bourne, and others.

1992 *New Republic* (Aug. 10) 42:
You can't really blame Clinton and Gore for foisting all this on the public. The "character issue" is there, the "family values issue" is there, and they must be dealt with.

**checkbook diplomacy** *n.* DOLLAR DIPLOMACY; international relations in which money is used as a cure-all.

1967 *New York Times* (Aug. 12) 10:
A rigid limitation on the number of countries receiving aid was essential "as a means of discouraging foreign policy reliance on 'checkbook' diplomacy."

1990 *Dallas Morning News* (Sept. 9) 1M:
In its role as the foremost practitioner of checkbook diplomacy, the United States has built schools, hospitals, roads and power plants. Billions in federal aid and tax incentives function as a life-support system for the islands' sick economies.

**chicken hawk** *n.* a person who advocates military aggression but avoided service (or did not serve) in the military.

1986 *New Republic* (June 16):
The one group currently being handed white feathers who may deserve them are the so-called "war wimps" or "chicken hawks"—prominent Americans helping to spread war fever today who avoided service during Vietnam.

2001 *National Review* (May 7):
In the first ten days of the Quayle "draft dodging" story, the networks logged 51 evening news reports...Unlike Kerrey, Quayle was portrayed as either a liar or a dolt, and definitely a chicken hawk.

2002 *Seattle Post-Intelligencer* (Sept. 6):
It was Anthony Zinni, President Bush's special envoy to the Middle East, who first posed the politically incorrect question of whether the administration's zeal to go to war against Iraq is being driven by

civilians who have never been to war—otherwise known in some mischievous quarters as "chicken hawks."

**chicken pie** *n.* (see quot.).

> 1871 Schele de Vere *Amer.* 264:
> A curious term has, of late, sprung up in the South, to designate the necessary expenses for purchasing legislative votes and newspaper influence....These are called Chicken-pie.

**Christmas tree** *n.* a bill or piece of legislation which includes many (unrelated or excessive) special provisions. *often* attrib. Also **Christmas tree bill**.

> 1982 *Globe and Mail* (Toronto, Can.) (Apr. 2) B3:
> "As much as I would like to see this legislation, it's not going to happen in a Christmas tree fashion," Senator Lugar said, adding he would prefer to have his bill die than be loaded with amendments.

> 1987 *San Francisco Chronicle* (June 25) 8:
> "This is a Christmas tree bill...Over and over again...it takes a good issue but provides a solution that goes beyond a reasonable solution."

> 2004 *St. Paul Pioneer Press* (Feb. 1) 1A:
> They are more likely to turn appropriations measures into "Christmas tree bills" by adding unrelated projects into giant spending bills.

**chubbing** *n.* *Texas.* a form of filibuster involving a variety of delaying tactics.

> 1987 *Houston Chronicle* (May 23) 20:
> The singing and the "chubbing"—House parlance for time-killing delay—were accompanied by the formal threat of a tag-team Senate filibuster next week on the AT&T deregulation.

> 2001 *Austin Chronicle* (June 1):
> Nuke opponents smelled a rat and quickly mounted a series of parliamentary challenges, concluding with several reps "chubbing" Wilson's amendment into oblivion. Chubbing is a sort of discount, House-style filibuster.

> 2003 *National Review* (May 27):
> The art of slow-talking bills ("chubbing") was raised to include the introduction of dozens—in some cases, hundreds—of similar amendments which had no chance of passage.

**cinch** *n.* an easy or enviable office or position; sinecure.

> 1896 Ade *Artie* 82:
> Says I to myself: "This is a cinch."

> 1908 H. Green *Maison de Shine* 242:
> I think you got a cinch.

> *ca*1910 Upson *With Sherman to the Sea* 170:
> While we were eating dinner the orderly told me I had a cinch with the

old Man, as he called the [Provost] Marshall, that he never saw him take to anyone like that before.

**1956** N.Y.C. man, age *ca*70:
I tell you, you've got a cinch.

**civil serpent** *n.* a civil servant. *Joc.*

**1961** *Wall Street Journal* (Oct. 13) 12:
"My daddy," boasted one, "is a dentist." "Hmph," the other retorted, "that's nothing. Mine's a civil serpent."

**1980** Cragg (letter to J.E. Lighter, Aug. 10) 3:
When I retire from the Army I'll become a civil serpent.

**1986** Former SP5, U.S. Army:
I heard *civil serpent* at *least* fifty times in the army [during 1970's].

**1995** *Washington Times* (Jan. 2) 2:
How much would you have to pay the average civil serpent in Washington to trudge into these wild Creole slots and crannies?

**clean sweep** *n.* the winning of all available offices by a party; filling civil positions (of a board, office, or division) with cronies or other members of one's party.

**1839** *U.S. Democratic Rev.* (Nov.) 511:
There is now a decided Whig majority in the Senate....That body will doubtless immediately make a very clean sweep of all the offices within their reach.

**1875** *St. Louis Globe Democrat* (Oct. 16) 1:
A Clean Sweep. Gratifying Advices from the Buckeye State. Both Branches of the Legislature Undoubtedly Republican.

**1929** D. Lynch *Boss Tweed* 75:
This attempt by the Whigs to steal the election attracted many votes to the Democrats, who made a clean sweep of the city on Election Day, when both parties resorted to the grossest of frauds.

**1995** *Baltimore Sun* (July 9) 2F:
Republican complaints about the clean sweep of the old board and the new nominees are without merit.

**clothespin vote** *n.* [sugg. by the cartoon-inspired idea that voters must use a clothespin to protect their noses from the supposed stench of such candidates] a vote or votes made unenthusiastically for a choice which is regarded as the least objectionable.

**1980:**
(quot. at KANGAROO TICKET).

**1995** *Times Union* (Albany, N.Y.) (Nov. 9) A15:
Are they now to look askance at a field of their second choices cynical about Clinton, dissatisfied with Dole, gagging on Gingrich, bored with all the rest, in the end forced to cast a "clothespin vote"?

**clout** *n.* **1.** political influence; (*hence*) power. [The provenance of the remarkably early 1868 quot. sugg. that the term arose in New York; though it is now of national distribution, journalists often associate it with Chicago politics.]

**1868** T. Whitman in *Dear Walt* 127:
I suppose the political boiling is really more heard than felt in regard to office holding— I know lost [*sic*] of fellows in Brook[lyn] (and it is the same with Engineers) that always think they are going to be deprived of office and "*clout.*"

**1937** in *DARE*:
No one...gets anywhere in politics or business on his merits. He has to have the "clout" from behind.

**1948** Kingsley *Detective Story* 338:
What plays between you guys? What's he got on you? What's the clout?

**1970** Cannon in *Nobody Asked* 286:
He knows how to win. It is not a common trait and only guys such as Vince Lombardi, Casey Stengel and Red Auerbach had the same kind of clout.

**1981** Centi *Positive/Negative* 17:
I used to hang around with the nonatheletes and we had no clout in school.

**1981** Rucker *57th Kafka* 12:
He had the clout to get the necessary components and materials.

**2.** a politically influential friend or ally.

**1955** Deutsch *Cops* 50:
The "rabbi" in New York police parlance is the "clout" in Chicago.

*Ibid.* 51:
The man with the clout...is ruined for police work. He owes his sponsor a loyalty higher than that to his department or to the public. And there are too many clout-owned men on this force.

**1976** "N. Ross" *Policeman* 124:
First thing he had to do was see his political clout...We can't hang the clout because all they really did was help a little guy with a headache.

**1980** in *DARE*:
Who's her clout? City Hall contracts for $25,000 don't just come down the chimney with Santa.

**clout** *v.* to exercise political influence.

**1958** *AS* XXXIV 230:
He clouted himself a job.

**1980** in *DARE*:
I did not clout for her.

**1982** *Chicago Sun-Times* (Aug. 11) 51:
Investigated by the FBI (for clouting for a nursing home operator who later gave business to [his] pharmacy.)

**coalition of the willing** *n.* any alliance formed to undertake international actions, esp. when breaking with the usual post-WWII allegiances.

**1990** *Washington Times* (Oct. 5) 2:
While we have not hesitated to act alone when circumstances required, we prefer to lead coalitions of the willing whenever possible.

**1991** *Futurist* (May 1) 20:
A "club" of democracies is now becoming the gyroscope for world security, the world economy, and world development...It is a center of initiative with a habit of consultation and an activist caucus within the United Nations and other international organizations—what Massachusetts Institute of Technology political science professor Lincoln Bloomfield calls a "coalition of the willing."

**1994** *Times-Picayune* (New Orleans, La.) (Jan. 5) A3:
U.S. officials speak of a "coalition of the willing" among NATO members who would take up peacekeeping chores as part of NATO's new identity.

**2001** *Los Angeles Times* (Dec. 4) A8:
Powell and other U.S. officials have said that the United States will not have troops in the multinational force, often referred to as a "coalition of the willing."

**coat-holder** *n.* a political follower.

**1941** *Salisbury Times* (Md.) (Nov. 11) 6:
When and if the house of representatives concurs in the senate action, we have dropped the last vestige of our attitude as a coat-holder and will be in the battle without pretense.

**1955** *Bridgeport Post* (Conn.) (Jan. 20) 40:
Jonathan Daniels...confidential coat-holder to both Roosevelt and Truman.

**1972** in Bernstein & Woodward *President's Men* 206:
Mr. Bradlee [is] an old Kennedy coat-holder.

**comer** *n.* a person who shows great progress or potential. Now *colloq.*

[**1879** in *OED*:
A crab...is always very poor to begin with; but he eats everything he gets hold of, which...fattens him up some. Then he is called a "comer."]

**1913** *DN* IV 10:
He's a comer in politics.

**1934** Weseen *Dict. Slang* 138:
*Comer*—A show or actor that has good prospects; a prospective success.

**1947** Schulberg *Harder They Fall* 272:
He's a comer, Mr. Lewis...a comin' champ if I ever seen one.

**1949** in *DAS*:
He said the [baseball] club is a comer.

**1993** *New York Times* (July 7) A 3:
He was obviously picked by his superiors as a comer.

**Commie** *n.* Communist. —often *attrib.*

**1939** M. Levin *Citizens* 352:
The Commies can be just as perverse.

**1940** G. Marx in *Letters* 21:
I see...Commies under my bed.

**1954** Arnow *Dollmaker* 253:
"They'd be called a commie." "What's that?"..."A red, I reckon."

**1982** Woodruff & Maxa *At White House* 163:
"That just goes to show you that you can't trust the Commies," declared [Pres. Reagan].

**1992** *New Yorker* (Dec. 28) 150:
I am just trying to protect the President from Commie advisers like you.

**commo** *n.* COMMIE.

*****1942** in *OED*

*****1945** S.J. Baker *Australian Lang.* 265:
Communist becomes *commo*.

**1972** *National Lampoon* (Feb.) 84:
Bite the dust, Commo creeps!

**1976** *National Lampoon* (July) 72:
Show me a Commo and I'll drive a wedge in his crack.

**compassionate conservative** *n.* a centrist espousing a combination of varied left-wing policies and traditional right-wing politics. Hence **compassionate conservativism**, *n.*

**1962** *New York Times* (Aug. 19) 211:
[Speaker Sam] Rayburn was in action a compassionate Conservative.

**1981** *New York Times* (Mar. 13):
"I'm a conservative, and proud of it, but I'm a compassionate conservative," Mr. Hatch said.

**1983** *Globe and Mail* (Toronto, Can.) (June 18) E17:
A thoughtful and compassionate conservatism can acknowledge the

problem, and seek some reasonable middle ground between individual rights and the traditional moral values of the whole community.

**2000** *U.S. News & World Report* (Mar. 27) 23:
Bush was a compassionate conservative until he had trouble. Then he moved to the right and became born-again.

**Comrade** *n.* a Soviet Communist.

**1937** Goodstone in *Pulp* 9:
If I never see a Comrade again, that will be far too soon for Pat Morgan.

**1939** M. Levin *Citizens* 215:
"He's not a comrade, is he?"..."If he is, it'll be a surprise to me."

*Ibid.* 220:
The comrades have the joint packed.

**1948** I. Shaw *Young Lions* 21:
It is the one thing the Comrades have taught Europe—the end justifies the means.

**conchie** *n.* a conscientious objector to military service. Also **conshie**, **conchy**.

[**1917** *Daily Mail* (Oct. 9) 2 in *OED*:
The assembly of eleven hundred "conscientious" objectors at one spot, Princetown, on Dartmoor, where they are known as "conchies."]

**1918** *Stars & Stripes* (Aug. 30) 7:
We're "conchys" too—but we don't work at it.

**1945** in *DAS* 118:
Denies That His Son Was a Conchie.

**1985** *Civil War Times Illus.* (June) 12:
Perhaps the most fascinating is the diary of the "conshie," a drafted Vermont Quaker's account of his efforts...to get a discharge.

**concho** *n.* CONCHIE.

**1969** Maitland *Only War* 95:
But how can you hate me if you're a pacifist—a concho.

**cookie pusher** *n.* an effete man who frequents tea parties or the like; (*hence*) used as a derisive term for State Department officials or other diplomats.

**1934** Weseen *Dict. Slang* 178:
*Cookie pusher*—A male student who seeks female companions; a tea hound.

**1943** *Sat. Rev. Lit.* (July 24) 18:
"Cookie pushers" is a newspaper men's term for thwarted "career" men in the State Department...who wear striped trousers and know the proper gambits for unattractive wives of foreign secretaries.

**1989** *Capital Gang* (CNN-TV) (Feb. 18):
The striped-pants cookie-pushers in the State Department.

**coon** *n.* [alludes to the racoon emblem of the Whigs] a member or supporter of the Whig Party. Now *hist.*

**1842** in *DA.*

**1848** Lowell in *Poetical Works* 213:
Agetherin' public sentiment, 'mongst Demercrats and Coons.

**1931** Harlow *Old Bowery* 299:
Down with the coons and up with the Young Hickories!

**cop** *n.* COPPERHEAD.

**1864** Jackson in *Letters* 218:
I expect the "Cops" will begin to think they had no man in the field.

**1864** O.J. Hopkins in *Under the Flag* 169:
'Twould be worse than an old Cop.

*****1864** in *PADS* (No 70) 28:
A Captain from our regiment...could not control himself on hearing the traitors spout...I do not know how much harm he did to the cops.

**1865, 1875** in *DA.*

**copperhead** *n.* a Northerner who sympathized with the Confederacy. Now *S.E.* and *hist.*

**1862** E.H. Rhodes *All for the Union* (Feb. 6) 54:
All Copperheads should be punished, for they are too cowardly to fight us in front so they stop us in the rear.

**1864** W. Whitman in *F & H* II 182:
Exciting times in Congress. The Copperheads are getting furious, and want to recognise the Southern Confederacy.

**1965** Catton *Never Call Retreat* 104:
Vallandigham in short was speaking for those numerous war-weary Northerners who were already becoming known as Copperheads.

**cornshucking** *n.* LOG-ROLLING.

**1813** Eliason in *Tarheel Talk* 266:
Log rolling or corn shucking on Capitol Hill.

**corporate welfare** *n.* the government subsidy of industries and businesses.

**1971** *Chronicle-Telegram* (Elyria, Ohio) (Aug. 22) A3:
The current looting of the public treasury by land interests through tax subsidies and enormous "corporate welfare" without any claim must end.

**1978** *Globe and Mail* (Toronto, Can.) (Feb. 21) P1:
The corporate welfare bums have now become the corporate welfare chums.

**2003** *Orlando Sentinel* (Nov. 26) A1:
Congress has put a provision in the Medicare bill that prevents Medicare from negotiating with drug makers for better prices... This is nothing more than corporate welfare for the drug companies.

**Corwin's Law** *n.* [after Senator Thomas Corwin (Ohio).] the precept that a candidate should maintain a serious demeanor.

[**1867** L.J. Bigelow *Bench & Bar: Digest of Wit* (April 22) 175 [ref. to comment by Corwin in 1860]:
Do you know, my young friend, that the world has contempt for the man who entertains it? One must be solemn—solemn as an ass— never say any thing that is not uttered with the greatest gravity, to win respect. The world looks up to the teacher and down upon the clown. Yet, in nine cases out of ten, the clown is the better fellow of the two.]

**1956** *New York Times* (April 22) 221:
Now it appears that once more Corwin's Law is being tested.

**1996** P.F. Boller *Presidential Campaigns* ix:
The other is Corwin's law: "if you would succeed in life, you must be as solemn as an ass. All the great monuments on earth have been built to solemn asses."

**cowboy** *n.* a rash undisciplined politician.

**1882** *Daily Indep.* (Helena, Mont.) (Aug. 29) 4:
The Republicans of Pennsylvania have become tired of having this upstart and political cowboy for a master.

**1968** Safire *New Language* 95:
*Cowboy.* a political rebel, usually one opposed to party discipline.

**1977** Coover *Public Burning* 60:
I had to cool the barnburners, soften up the hardshells, keep the hunkers and the cowboys in line.

**cracking** *n.* the splitting of a block of like-minded voters when redistricting, a form of GERRYMANDER.

**1983** AP (July 30):
The rejected districts were faulty because they had the effect of "packing" almost all of Boston's black voters into two districts and "cracking" the Hispanic vote among six districts. The result...would be that blacks could never elect more than two candidates, while Hispanic voters would likely be shut out altogether.

**1991** *Boston Globe* (May 19) A29:
Cracking, stacking and packing: the methods of gerrymandering...With gerrymandering, undesirable voting blocs are packed or stacked tightly

together to have as narrow an influence as possible or cracked apart into several separate districts to dilute their power.

**1999** *New Statesman* (Oct.11):
A popular tactic, known in psephology-jargon as "cracking," split concentrations of black voters into several constituencies to prevent a black majority.

**2003** *New Yorker* (Dec. 12):
Cracking divides a group's voters into other districts, where they will be ineffective minorities.

**cutor** *n.* a prosecutor or district attorney.

**1925–26** Black *You Can't Win* 227:
"He'll appear when you go an trial...," said the "cutor."

**1927** *DNV* 443:
*Cutor*, n., A prosecuting attorney.

**1928** Hammett *Red Harvest* 66:
You'll have the 'cuter get a stiff out of here?

**1933–35** D. Lamson *About to Die* 194:
An' the 'cutors put on these three witnesses.

**1938** Chandler *Big Sleep* 31:
Then next day she comes down to the D.A. and gets him to beg the kid off with the U.S. 'cutor.

# D

**dark horse** *n.* [fr. horse-racing slang] a candidate who unexpectedly receives the nomination when the convention has failed to agree upon any of the other, leading candidates.

**1844** M. Egan in *Catholic World* XXXIX 755:
The Young Men's Reform Club...have at length announced their "dark horse" who will enter the race for nomination our legislature.

**1896** J. Bishop in *Century* LII (June) 307 [ref. to 1844]:
It was the first convention to develop a "dark horse," the first to bring about a nomination by means of a "stamped," and the first to have its proceeding reported by telegraph.

**1929** D. Lynch *Boss Tweed* 291:
For four days the delegates were deadlocked. On the twenty-second ballot the dark horse of the convention, the presiding officer, was nominated for President.

**2000** D. Lynch *U.S. News & World Report* (May 22) 24:
Now there is also Theodore J. Forstmann, a dark horse Wall Street billionaire whose greatest asset is his ability to foot the bill for his own campaign.

**dead president** *n.* [U.S. law prohibits the likeness of a living person from appearing on its currency] U.S. banknote.

**1944** Burley *Harlem Jive* 136:
*Dead President*: A dollar bill, paper money of any denomination.

**1946** Boulware *Jive & Slang* 3:
*Dead President*...Dollar bill.

**1989** *Newsweek* (Aug. 14) 6:
We found a briefcase full of dead presidents in the trunk of the Caddie.

**deal** *n.* a secret or underhand agreement for mutual advantage; scheme.

**1881** in *OED*:
[The party boss's] power of making "deals."

**1882** in *Century Dict.*:
The President had definitively abandoned the maxims and practices of...machine politics in New York, with the shifts and expedients and *deals* which had illustrated his political prominence.

**1988** *21 Jump St.* (Fox-TV):
Now is this one of your deals—or is it serious?

**declinism** *n.* the belief that (something) is decreasing or is not what it once was, esp. a nation's power.

**1984** M.J. Nye in *Isis* LXXV (Dec.) 697:
A recent example of contemporary declinism.

**1988** *Boston Globe* (Dec. 25) A27:
There is the phenomenon of what Samuel P. Huntington...calls "declinism," the proposition that the United States or the industrialized world or both are decadent and doomed to go down the tubes, if not tomorrow, pretty soon.

*****1992** M. Smith *Intl. Affairs* LXXVIII (Jan.) 114:
It led to the phenomenon of "declinism" and agonized debates about the United State's future role.

**2003** *Los Angeles Times* (Feb. 2) R6:
Triumphalism (in contrast to declinism) has negative connotations, but there was ground for satisfaction that a continent which had been at the end of its tether in 1945 had purged itself of the heritage of totalitarianism, had developed firmer democratic institutions than ever before, had resurrected itself from the ruins, had buried the hatchet.

**Dem** *n.* a Democrat. Now *colloq.*

**1875** Hayes *Diary* 6:
Dems oppose discussion, agitation of this topic.

**1897** Schaaf in *Dooley* 146:
Dooley on the County "Dems."

**Demmy** *n.* a Democrat.

**1840** in *DAE*:
We had dubbed our parties Feds and Demies—that is, Federalists and Democrats.

**1849** in *DAE*:
Malicious "demmys" did say he preached for hire.

**1884** in Lummis *Letters* 75:
There is a general impressions [*sic*] that the Demmies "got thar."

**1892** F. Remington in *Sel. Letters* 156:
We will have to lick the Demmies.

**demo** *n.* (usu. *cap.*) a Democrat.

**1795** Whiting in *EAP* 105:
The devil is to pay among the demo's.

**1796** Tyler in *Verse* 48:
Southern Demos...represent our brother negroes.

**1798** in *DAE*:
In vain each Demo spouts and bellows.

**1948** in *OED*:
The program chairman kept peace between GOP and Demos.

**1987** *Daily Beacon* (Univ. Tenn.) (Jan. 7) 1:
Demos rule reconvening Congress.

**Democrat gloves** *n.pl.* men's white gloves. *Joc.* Now *hist.*

**1977** Monaghan *Schoolboy, Cowboy* opp. 116 [ref. to *ca*1910]:
The man wearing glasses and "Democrat gloves" is the Mexican spy in this book.

**democrazy** *n.* a democracy in which unusual or unequitable situations arise even when the system works as intended. [The first quot. is a dialect representation, though context shows that the joc. idea of an unruly democracy was likely intended.]

[**1919** *Sheboygan Press* (Wisc.) (Sept. 6) 8:
Dey call idt der land of libert, Schmaltz and democrazy, und freedamn. Bull! You schpeak, but you done said somdings, Schmaltz.]

**1989** *Los Angeles Times* (Apr. 30) 2:
My favorite, however, is "Democrazy."...It was used in 1946 at the Japanese War Trials by Shumei Okawa, a former propaganda minister of Japan.

**1992** *National Review* (Aug. 31) 80:
The traditional lesbian is no more. In the name of "democrazy," feminists rolled her up in her tweeds, weighted her with her scholarly tomes, and threw her overboard. The last thing she heard was, "Everybody's gotta right to be a lesbian."

**2001** *BusinessWorld* (June 13):
We have a democrazy not a democracy. Democracy is a numbers game and if your electorate can be fooled because they are ignorant, then the game goes to the cheaters and the rabblerousers.

**Demopublican** *n.* REPUBOCRAT.

**1984** *Daily Oklahoman* (Oklahoma City) July 31:
It looks like Oklahomans will have two choices in November—Libertarian and Demopublican.

**1995** *News & Observer* (Raleigh, N.C.) A12:
What it really is, is part of this tax-cutting mania afflicting Demopublican Governor Hunt as he tries to outdo the legislature.

**demosclerosis** *n.* [*demo*cracy + arterio*sclerosis*] the resistance of government to change.

**1992** *Washington Post* (Sept. 8) B7:
It's called…"Demosclerosis," and it's no more optimistic than the one before…Rauch uses the term to describe the current paralysis of the federal government; by his reading, Washington is the prisoner of its past policies, impervious to change.

**1994** J. Rauch *Demosclerosis: Silent Killer of Amer. Govt.*:
(work title)

**dinosaur** *n.* a person who clings tenaciously to conservative or outmoded beliefs.— used derisively.

**1970** *Playboy* (Sept.) 56:
Hidebound conservatives…"Give us an insight into the needs of these men," says one of the local dinosaurs.

**1987** Taubman *Lady Cop* 74:
Some of the dinosaurs in the precinct teased them.

*Ibid.* 268:
*Dinosaur:* Derogatory term used to describe an old-fashioned cop.

**1987** C. Joyner *Prison* film:
Joel, the man is a dinosaur.

**dip** *n.* a diplomatic passport; a diplomat.

**1977** *New York Times* (Jan. 9) IV 3:
Starting last Jan. 1 all "dips," as the documents are called in the trade, must carry a five-year expiration date.

**1991** *Newsweek* (Sept. 2) 8:
J. Matlock…ex-dip rakes in TV bucks.

**dipper** *n.* a government employee who enjoys more than one source of governmental income.

**1979** Homer *Jargon* 28.

**dirty tricks** *n.pl.* undercover or clandestine operations; (*hence*) deceitful stratagems intended to subvert an opponent's campaign for office.

[**1867** J. Parton *Famous Americans* 204:
Mr. Speaker…I have but one word to say….The measure to which the gentleman has just alluded originated in a dirty trick!]

**1870** W. Gray *History of Oregon* 378:
As a politician, he considered all little dirty tricks and slanders against an opponent justifiable.

**1973** *New York Times* (July 9) 22:
One of Colson's responsibilities [at the White House] was that he was the dirty-trick expert, the counter-demonstration guy.

**1983** *Business Week* (May 9) 50:
The Newfoundlander has injected this plain talk into a...campaign otherwise dominated by dirty tricks on the part of the front-runners.

**1999** *New York Times Mag.* (Oct. 24) 77:
Perot won the nomination, using what the Lamm people regard as dirty tricks.

**Dittohead** *n.* a fan of conservative talk show host Rush Limbaugh.

**1989** *Los Angeles Times* (Nov. 25) 1:
Many Limbaugh fans—or "dittoheads," as he calls them—are willing to dish out fistfuls of cash for Limbaugh T-shirts, satin jackets, "dittohead" mugs and "Rush to Excellence" videocassettes.

**2003** *Chicago Sun-Times* (Nov.19) 11:
Would the reaction from Limbaugh and his dittoheads be compassionate understanding, or howls of derision?

**DJ** *n.* an agent of the U.S. Department of Justice.

**1935** *Lit. Digest* (June 22) 38:
"G Men" have also been called "Feds," "Dee Jays," and "Whiskers" (*Uncle Sam's* Agents).

**dog-and-pony show** *n.* an elaborate formal occasion or undertaking; (*specif.*) an official briefing or visual presentation, usu. for public relations purposes. *often* attrib. Hence **dog-and-pony.**

**1957** Hecht *Charlie* 14 [ref. to 1916]:
Black Jack Pershing, in charge of the hostilities, dubbed it "Colonel Foreman's Dog and Pony Show."

**1974** Terkel *Working* 71:
I go into my act: we call it dog and pony time, show time, tap dance....[The client] says..."How much will it cost us?."

**1981** *Harper's* (Dec.) 38:
The September 1980 decision [was] almost ignored by the press because it occurred during the quadrennial dog-and-pony show held to select the leader of the Free World.

**1989** J. Weber *Defcon One* 114:
The president didn't care for officious functions. He referred to the rituals as dog-and-pony shows.

**dollar diplomacy** *n.* a foreign policy that seeks to further the country's financial and commercial interests. See also CHECKBOOK DIPLOMACY.

**1910** *Newark Advocate* (Ohio) (Feb. 5) 4:
So bitter has the opposition grown to this particular kind of state department procedure that it has come to be known as "dollar diplomacy."

**1913** Heaton *Story of a Page* 290:
As "Dollar Diplomacy" it made the attempt to force a loan upon China

that China neither needed nor asked for, and various menaces of Central American states, odious to the people.

**1999** Pendergrast *Uncommon Grounds* 176:
The region's stability, important to North American businessmen, was guaranteed by the "dollar diplomacy" that sent U.S. Marines into Haiti and Nicaragua to protect American business interests.

**doo-doo** *n.* [euphem. for *deep shit*] trouble.—usu. constr. with *deep*. [Popularized in a speech by President-elect George H. W. Bush in January, 1989.]

**1989** *CBS This Morning* CBS-TV (Jan. 17):
*Real* Texans do not describe trouble as "deep doodoo."

**1994** N. McCall *Wanna Holler* 301:
I got myself into deeper doo-doo while trying to clean up my act.

**2004** *Your World With Neil Cavuto* (Fox-TV) (Mar. 25):
Social Security, something has to be done to fix that before it gets in deep doo-doo.

**dopester** *n.* a (political) forecaster or analyst.

**1907** in *OED*:
As we talked on a corner not long ago, a Dopester...stepped up to us.

**1910** T.A. Dorgan, in *New York Eve. Journal* (Feb. 16) 14:
Figuring up the Jeffries-Johnson fight, the way the dopesters get at the ponies, is a very interesting thing.

**1965** *World Bk. Dict.*:
Dopester...an analyst.

**dope story** *n.* (speculative or false) information planted or leaked (as part of an agenda).

**1929** *New York Times* (Jan. 3) 3 [said by former N.Y. Gov. Alfred E. Smith]:
When you get these reports that I'm going to take all kinds of jobs; that I'm going to be a baseball player on the Giants; why, I wish you wouldn't come running up here to ask me about them because you'll know there's nothing to all these dope stories.

**1947** *Zanesville Signal* (Ohio) (Feb. 26) 4:
All this adds up to make a plausible political dope story. Only trouble with it is that isn't an accurate picture of what's going on.

**1988** *Record* (N.J.) (July 1) B9:
The reporter...opted to pacify the demanding editor with what is called a political-dope story. The newsman put together a speculative piece about a scramble for leadership jobs among Assembly Republicans. Although Kean wasn't seeking any spot—or even thinking about it—the writer just popped Kean's name into the article.

**doubledome** *n.* a scholar or intellectual, esp. a highly educated person who holds impractical or unrealistic views.

**1943** H.A. Smith *Putty Knife Factory* 207:
Arthur Birsbane [ 1936]...was known among fellow newspapermen as Old Double Dome.

**1953** Michener *Sayonara* 11:
Then the doubledomes in Washington set a deadline.

**1966** Longstreet & Godoff *Wm. Kite* 173:
She got next to this double-dome from Columbia, a molecular physicist.

**doughface** *n.* a northern congressman who did not oppose slavery or its extension; (*hence*) a northerner who favored the Confederacy. Now *hist.*

**1830** in *DA*:
The protecting duty will be repealed, if the anti-tariff party can get enough dough faces to join them.

**1859** J. Brown, in *Mo. Hist. Rev.* XVII (1923) 278:
All pro-slavery, conservative, Free-state and dough-face men and Administration tools are filled with holy horror.

**1956** P. Murray *Proud Shoes* 116:
You must be a damned doughface or a secesh!

**dove** *n.* a person, esp. in public office, who advocates peace or a conciliatory national attitude. Now *S.E.* [Given wide currency in journalistic accounts of the Cuban missile crisis of Oct. 1962; 1930 quot. is atypical of its period. Cf. HAWK.]

**1930** Nason *Corporal* 189:
If this is war,...then give me peace at any price. Man, I'm a dove from now on!

**1962** *Sat. Eve. Post.* (Dec. 8) 20:
The hawks favored an air strike to eliminate the Cuban missile bases...The doves opposed the air strikes and favored a blockade.

**1964** J. Lucas *Dateline* 43:
The 15,500 U.S. military personnel in Viet Nam are divided into two camps—the "Hawks" and the "Doves." The Hawks believe...[the] solution...is to kill the Viet Cong. The Doves...believe in something called "civic action."

**1967** "M.T. Knight" *Terrible Ten* 52:
A reporter...had facetiously inquired if she was a hawk or a dove.

**drag** *n.* influence. Cf. PULL.

**1896** Ade *Artie* 60:
He knows I've got a drag in the precinct.

**1898** Dunne *Peace & War* 203:
I have a dhrag at th' station.

**1912–14** E. O'Neill in *Lost Plays* 44:
Oh, he's got a drag somewhere. He squares it with the cops so they don't hold me for walkin' the streets.

**1914** Ellis *Billy Sunday* 29:
Well, he had some drag with me and influenced me.

**1924** in Nason *Three Lights* 23:
You go ask him, Simmons. You got a drag with him.

**1928** *AS* II (Feb.) 219:
*Drag.* Influence, pull. "She must have a drag with Agnes, to get away with that stuff."

**1932** Lorimer *Streetcars* 26:
You'll have an eternal drag with me if you'll dance with her.

**1951** Bowers *Mob* film:
What's your angle, Flynn? Where do you get your drag?

**1957** E. Brown *Locust Fire* 19 [ref. to 1944]:
They can't ground Pappy. He has a big drag with Colonel Rogers.

**DRE** *n.* [*d*irect *r*ecording *e*lectronic] a polling booth which is completely computerized, usually offering voting choices on a video screen. Also *attrib.*

**1988** *New York Times* (Nov. 2) D8:
Computerized voting machines fall into three categories—key punch devices, optical scanners and direct recording electronic machines.

**1992** P. Shocket et al *Western Pol. Quarterly* (June) XLV 524:
The possibility of overvoting is shared by any manual system that uses paper-and-pencil and is not shared by either mechanical or direct recording electronic systems (D.R.E) which can be programmed to prevent overvoting.

**2004** *Boulder News* (Col.) (Feb. 3):
The county Clerk and Recorder's Office...was poised to fork out millions of dollars for a hi-tech, "direct recording electronic" voting system...The problem with DREs is that the average citizen can never be fully assured that his or her vote is recorded accurately or that the software is tallying the vote correctly.

**drink the Kool-Aid** Cf. KOOL-AID

**dry** *adj.* opposed to, prohibiting, or free from the sale of alcoholic beverages. Now *S.E.*

**1853** W.W. Brown *Clotel* 196:
I suppose you have told 'em we are a dry set up here?

**1870** in *DA.*

**1887** in *OED*:
Athens...is a dry town.

**1888** Farmer in *Amer.*:
If a county has voted...and gone dry.

**1910** W. Archer *Afro-Amer.* 157:
Between "wet" counties and "dry."

**1948** *Time* (Apr. 26) 14:
The natives voted...to keep the town dry.

**1984** Cunningham & Ethell *Fox Two* 48:
Navy ships are dry, so we tipped our soda pops and commenced to celebrating.

**1987** *Time* (July 13) 33:
Kansas [was] the first state to go dry (in 1881).

**dry** *n.* a supporter of alcohol prohibition. Now *S.E.*

**1889** *Century Dict.*:
*Dry*...a member of the Prohibition party.

**1910** *New York Eve. Journal* (Feb. 5) 3:
Chicago "Drys" March to File Grant Petition.

**1920** in *Dict. Canad.* 225:
The drys cannot pretend much longer that Alberta is "prohibition."

**1948** in *DA*

**1977** P. Wood *Salt Bk.* 161:
You'd get calls from people that were on the side of the dries.

**dynamiter** *n.* a violent anarchist or communist. Now *hist.*

**1877** in *Mo. Hist. Rev.* XVIII (1924) 205:
In the United States they are "dynamiters;" in Canada they are "dynamiteurs;" in England they are "dynamitards." They are cowardly scoundrels everywhere.

**1884** Lummis in *Letters* 10:
A friendly confab of politics. Thank heaven, there are no dynamiters this far West.

**1890** Howells *Hazard* 158:
"By-the-bye, March, I saw that old dynamiter of yours round at Beaton's room yesterday." "What old dynamiter of mine?" "That old one-handed Dutchman."

**1915** *Report on Colo. Strike* 26:
A bunch of Democrats—a bunch of dynamiters, Jeff called them.

**1947** W.M. Camp *S.F.* 304:
Haskell...was among the first of the "dynamiters" and...did not hesitate to advocate the most violent methods for achieving a worker's revolution.

# E

**earned media** *n.* cost-free publicity. Also **free media**.

**1986** *Daily Oklahoman* (Oklahoma City) (Apr. 7):
Calling it "earned media," she said she can gain publicity on county projects and other official activities.

**1990** AP (Aug. 28):
The dozen or so events have drawn favorable—and free—media coverage...."It's a good way to generate some free earned media, because I don't have a big campaign war chest."

**1999** *New York Times Mag.* (Oct. 24) 77:
Rather than merely shaking hands, he has always campaigned more by snatching "free media"—showing up at dawn at local television stations, for example, to offer himself to content-starved morning shows.

**2004** *Newsweek* (Feb. 20):
All Edwards can count on for sure is "earned media, earned media, earned media"—the plentiful press coverage Edwards will garner now that he's locked in a two-man race.

**echo chamber** *n.* an environment or group of people in which ideas or beliefs are repeated, esp. when they are circularly reinforced, confirmed, or validated. Cf. MEDIA ECHO CHAMBER.

**1955** *New York Times* (Aug. 5) 2:
Geneva became an echo chamber for rumors, one often contradicting the other.

**1979** *Washington Post* (May 15) A12:
[French Health Minister Simone] Veil is heading the campaign of President Valery Giscard d'Estating's own party in the first direct elections for the European Parliament, which amounts to the legislature of the European Common Market. That body has largely been a powerless echo chamber.

**1980** *Globe and Mail* (Toronto, Can.) (Jan. 29) P6:
Commie-bashing is an indoor sport normally associated with election

year in the United States. It's a bit unsettling to find the Prime Minister of Canada playing the game, sounding like a pocket Ronald Reagan and smiting the dreaded Reds with the full sonority of his echo-chamber rhetoric.

**\*1990** R. Critchfield *Among British* 231:
It has been a society whose almost miraculous political tolerance, even under great strain, has been based on a shared—I would like to call it as in physics—a shared echo chamber of verbal articulacy, fluency, elegance, and reference.

**2004** *U.S.A. Today* (Mar. 4):
House Democratic leader Nancy Pelosi...said Democrats will create "an echo chamber" on the issues of jobs, health care, education, the environment and national security.

**2004** *New York Times* (Mar. 13) 9:
Mr. Krebs, who got similar results when he conducted the same experiment last year, calls this pattern the "echo chamber" effect: for the most part, he found, buyers of liberal books buy only other liberal books, while buyers of conservative books buy only other conservative books.

**ecofreak** *n.* an environmental activist.—used derisively.

**1970:**
(cited in *W9*).

**1972** *U.S. News & World Report* (Apr. 10) 92:
Convince inner-city residents that conservationists "are not 'eco-freaks'—middle-class whites interested only in stopping things like power plants which will provide heat and jobs for the ghetto."

**1977** *Time* (June 6) 63:
Ecofreaks.

**1982** *Time* (May 24) 86:
People with only limited commitments to environmental preservation will tend similarly to allude not to environmentalists but to eco-freaks.

**1992** *Richmond Times-Dispatch* (Va.) A3:
The Bush campaign plans to lambaste Clinton as an environmental weakling and Gore as an eco-freak.

**eelskin** *n.* (see quot.) Cf. PASTER.

**1877** Bartlett *Amer.* (ed. 4) 199:
*Eel-Skin.* A thin, narrow slip of paper, with the name of a candidate on one side, and coated with mucilage on the other, so as to be quickly and secretly placed over the name of an opponent, on a printed ballot.

**embed** *n.* [see first quot.] a journalist assigned to a candidate for the duration of a campaign. Also, **embedded journalist, campaign embed.**

**2003** *Los Angeles Times* (July 17) E5:
The Iraq war's "embeds"—journalists who lived and traveled with U.S. and British troops to produce up-close reports on their activities—have spawned a "campaign embed" program at MSNBC. The cable news channel said it will send one-person video-journalists, who will function as reporters, producers and camerapersons, into the field, one to a presidential candidate.

**2003** *Wall Street Journal* (Dec. 29) A4:
He had quit NBC, however, and moved to Oregon...when MSNBC asked him to audition for Campaign Embed.

**enemies list** *n.* [fr. Richard Nixon's counsel John Dean's list of opponents] a (real or imagined) blacklist.

**1973** *New York Times* (June 27) 49:
The Nixon White House kept and continually updated an "enemy list," John W. Dean 3d testified today, and often used Government investigators to harass the people on it.

**1982** *Daily Oklahoman* (Oklahoma City) (Apr. 14):
The word is getting around, he said, that the administration will take the attitude that it should "reward your friends and ignore those who have not quite made it to the enemies list, yet."

**2004** *New York Post* (Feb. 2) 2:
If you're on an enemies list—for whatever reason—you're turned down. Yet another guy can walk in with the exact same evidence, or less, and get the pension.

**express advocacy** *n.* a call to vote for or against a specific candidate.—opp. ISSUE ADVOCACY.

**1987** *Orange County Register* (Ca.) B6:
He also prescribed standards—the first by any federal appeals court—for deciding whether a given statement was "express advocacy" of a candidate's election or defeat.

**2000** *Chronicle-Telegram* (Elyria, Ohio) (Nov. 5) A8:
The ads run by the chambers of commerce, though highly critical of Resnick, do not call for her defeat or O'Donnell's election. That makes them "issue advocacy" rather than "express advocacy" ads and hence immune from campaign laws requiring groups to disclose their contributors.

# F

**fair-fight district** *n.* a voting area which is redistricted to favor no political party, usu. the result of a GERRYMANDER.

**1982** *New York Times* (Apr. 11) 32:
There remains the matter of what the "fair fight" district will look like.

**1989** *Congress. Quarterly* (Nov. 4) XLVII:
Should the state lose three seats, a "fair fight" district might be created, perhaps in metropolitan New York City or in the Albany/central New York regions.

**1999** *Washingtonian* (Dec.) 43:
The 11th district was designed as a "fair-fight" district that could go either Republican or Democratic.

**2003** *New Yorker* Dec. 8:
Representative Benjamin Gilman, an upstate Republican, said that during the 1982 redistricting he was promised by the majority leader of the state senate that "if I accepted that challenge of a fair-fight district, I would never again be asked or forced by the state to face that prospect of a fair fight once again."

**faithless elector** *n.* a member of the electoral college who votes for a candidate other than that pledged.

**1967** *New York Times* (Jan. 3) 13:
They were acting to preserve the integrity of the Electoral College system against the "faithless elector."

**1980** *Globe and Mail* (Toronto, Can.) (Oct. 21) P13:
The last person to fetch the vote of a "Faithless Elector" was Ronald Reagan, in 1976. One man from Washington state ran on Gerald Ford's Republican slate, but insisted on casting his Electoral College ballot for Mr. Reagan, who had been defeated by Mr. Ford for the Republican nomination that year.

**1984** *Capital* (Annapolis, Md.) (Dec. 27) 6:
The first faithless elector was a Pennsylvania Federalist who voted in 1796 for Jefferson rather than for Adams.

**1988** *Chicago Sun-Times* (Nov. 1) 23:
"Faithless" electors could swing a close election. In the 1976 election, one elector for a state won by Gerald Ford actually voted for Ronald Reagan.

**family values** *n.pl.* a code term for a set of religious, moral, and social beliefs said to be created and strengthened by families. [Popularized during the 1992 presidential election.]

**1978** *Globe and Mail* (Toronto, Can.) (Sept. 27) P10:
Bishops plan family-values campaign.

**1993** *Boston Herald* (Apr. 27) 25:
How long have we been listening to our politicians pontificate about "family values?" The phrase has been on everyone's lips for the past year, but the concept has existed forever.

**1996** *Spectrum* (Winter) LXIX 26:
Christian Right candidates are less likely now to say that God told me to be a Democrat or "it's your Christian duty to vote for me." Instead they say, "cut taxes, reduce government spending, promote family values."

**Farley's Law** *n.* [see quot.] a dictum which postulates that voters have made their presidential choice before Labor Day (the first Monday in September) and are unlikely to later change their minds.

**1948** *New York Times* (Nov. 28) 63:
The Ohio results and voter reaction also cast aside "Farley's Law," the theory of James A. Farley, former Democratic National Chairman, that voters do not change their minds after early September, and that formal campaigning by Presidential candidates, therefore, has little effect on election results.

**1959** *Reno Evening Gazette* (Nev.) (Oct. 30)(Nev.) 4:
F—For Farley's Law: The idea that elections are decided by Labor Day is forever repealed.

**1996** P.F. Boller *Presidential Campaigns* ix:
One of them is Farley's Law: that nothing happens between nominating conventions and election day to change the minds of voters.

**2000** Z. Karabell *Last Campaign* (Apr. 4) 199:
Roper was operating on a widely held assumption of voter behavior called "Farley's Law." According to New York State Democratic Chairman James A. Farley, voters made up their minds by early September at the latest.

**2000** *Jewish World Review* (Sept. 6):
James A. Farley was one of Franklin Roosevelt's chief political

operatives, and he stated that there was no use campaigning after Labor Day because voters had already made up their minds by then. In other words, whoever was ahead on Labor Day won. Farley's Law is not followed today—polls show a large number of voters make up their minds after Labor Day.

**2000** *Gazette* (Oct. 31)(Montreal):
Over half a century ago, before Harry Truman upset Thomas E. Dewey in 1948, many politicos accepted Farley's Law.

**fat cat** *n.* a wealthy and privileged individual, esp. a financial backer of a political campaign.

**1925** *Denton Journal* (Md.) (Nov. 7) 2:
A primary in which there is a collection of Fat Cats is almost too good to be true.

**1928** F.R. Kent *Pol. Behavior* 59:
These capitalists have...money to finance the campaign. Such men are known in political circles as "Fat Cats"....Any "Fat Cat" able and willing to spend as much as is necessary can get whatever he wants in state politics.

**1950** Truman in *Dear Bess* 561:
I had the pleasure of telling off a lot of "fat cats" last night.

**1992** Sen. Albert Gore, Jr. (D-Tenn.) , in *New York Times* (July 27) A11:
They couldn't care less about the people who live downwind of pollution. They only care about the fat cat who owns the smokestack.

**fat-frying** *n.* coercive fund-raising from groups, corporations, or individuals which have benefitted or will benefit from an officeholder's efforts. Now *hist.* [Fr. the presidential campaign of 1888.]

**1889** *Gettysburg Compiler* (Pa.) (Jan. 8):
If, upon the other hand, they adopt the Democratic policy of adjusting the tariff to the requirements of the times, and if they cease robbing the people, they will then break faith with the manufacturers, who, finding that they are not to participate in this expected plunder, will never again submit to the process of "fat frying."

**1893** *Atlantic* (Mar.) LXXI 425:
Such terms as..."fat-frying"...belong to the more recent unsavory imbecilities of politics.

**1913** J. Heaton *Story of a Page* 75:
The...corruption of the "fat-frying" agents of protected interests had much to do with the result.

**1921** *Indianapolis Star* (Sept. 22) 1:
The "fat fryers" worked overtime during that campaign and yet if you will look back over the files of that evening newspaper you will see,

judging from their silence on the subject, that political fat frying was a good thing in 1917.

**1928** *Daily Northwestern* (Oshkosh, Wisc.) (Mar. 6) 10:
If a democracy cannot exercise its electoral function and govern itself without expenditures on such a huge scale as to necessitate fat-fyring from individuals or interests, selfishly concerned and self-seeking, then that democracy fails.

**favorite son** *n.* a poltician popular with delegations or voters from his hometown, region, or state, esp. when nominated as a candidate at the national level.

**1852** Democratic Natl. Conv. (June) 64:
We are now united and most heartily and cheerfully join in the nomination of New England's favorite son, Franklin Pierce, of New Hampshire.

**1888** Bryce *Amer. Commw.* II III lxx 552 in *OED*:
A Favourite Son is a politician respected or admired in his own State, but little regarded beyond it.

**1919** *Fort Wayne Journal* (Ind.) (June 11) 4:
It begs them for once to forbear making themselves foolish by going to the next national convention with a favorite son.

**1967** *News* (Frederick, Md.) (Jan. 30) 17:
[Ohio Gov. James Rhodes] is expected to control Ohio's 58 votes and there have been reports that some other Western states might string along with him as a favorite son to see how the nomination race shakes down.

**2004** *Toledo Blade* (Ohio) (Feb. 22):
It remains unclear how much support Mr. Kucinich, a favorite son, will win in Ohio.

**Fed** *n.* **1.** a Federalist. Now *hist.*

**1788** in *DAE*:
Antis, and Feds, usurp the glory,/So long enjoy'd by Whig and Tory.

*ca*1818 in *Harlow Old Bowery* 178:
I'm ashamed to be seen, sir, among such a set of Clintonians, Tammanies, Coodies and Feds!

**1830** [S. Smith] in *Letters of Downing* 4:
Calling Adams a tory and a fed.

**1834** Foner in *Labor Songs* 26:
None but such as Hartford Feds/Oppose the poor and—Jackson.

**2.** a federal official, esp. a member of the FBI.

**1916** A. Stringer *Door of Dread* 53:
Seein' Kestner and yuh'd told me the Feds had ev'rything fixt, I gave him the glassy eye.

**1930** Irwin *Tramp & Und. Sl.*:
Feds...Federal law enforcement officers, especially those charged with suppressing the liquor or drug traffic.

**1935** Mackenzie *Been Places* 44:
They had the goods on him for bumping off the three Feds.

**1955** *PADS* (No 24) 47:
The Feds got the letter where I sent him $400.

**1984** Kagan & Summers *Mute Evidence* 89:
Many...would have found it easy to believe that the Army, Air Force, CIA, or the feds were behind it.

**1991** "R. Brown" & R. Angus *A.K.A. Narc* 205:
The Fed strode in, three-piece suit, sunglasses and all.

**3.** the federal government.

**1965** Tavel *Godiva* 183:
Chuck the fanfare, baby, I'm here on Fed business.

**feminazi** *n.* a committed feminist or a strong-willed woman. —usu. derogatory.

**1992** R.H. Limbaugh *Way Things Ought to Be* 55:
Here then is the definition and real agenda of the feminazi: radical feminists whose objective is to see that there are as many abortions as possible.

**1995** *Denver Post* (June 11) C8:
I may be a left-wing, radical, ACLU card-carrying liberal feminazi who wants to save the whales.

**2004** *New York Times* (Feb. 15):
Just as Hillary Rodham Clinton was more complicated than her feminazi image, surely Laura Bush has a few currents, a little tension, in her inner life.

**fire-eater** *n.* an uncompromising partisan of Southern interests before and during the Civil War. Now *hist.*

**1846** in *DA*.

**1855** in *DAE*:
I would say...to all true Georgians, whether Whigs or Democrats, Union men or Fire-Eaters, whither are you drifting?

**1879** [Tourgée] *Fool's Errand* 30:
An original Secesh, a regular fire-eater.

**527 organization** *n.* a political group covered by section 527 of the Internal Revenue Code, which specifies how such groups are taxed. Also **527 committee**, **527**.—usu. spoken as *five twenty-seven.*

**1999** *Roll Call* (Sept. 20):
The IRS, the tax-code watchdog, does not even require 527 organizations to publicly disclose their existence.

**2000** *Houston Chronicle* (May 26) 3:
The Doggett proposal...is designed to crack down on so-called "stealth PACs" or "527 organizations" that get special tax breaks by claiming to be political fund-raising groups but avoid federal campaign disclosure laws by denying any political affiliation.

**2003** *American Prospect* (Dec. 1):
Much of the good news for Democrats these days is coming from a variety of organizations (dubbed "527s" in the argot of election law) that have been set up to do the kind of campaign work that, in theory, the DNC used to perform but which the funding restrictions of the McCain-Feingold campaign-finance law now make impossible.

**2004** *New York Times* (Feb. 18):
The commission's ruling on so-called 527 committees could have profound effects on the 2004 election by helping Democrats.

**fix** *v.* **1.** to secure the cooperation of (someone) through the payment of a bribe.

**1790** in *DA*:
It is expected of us that we should fix the Governor of Pennsylvania.

**1872** Burnham *Secret Service* 72:
When Biebusch saw *this* man in Court, whom he fancied he had fixed for certain, the criminal wilted.

**1921** Conklin & Root *Circus* 167 [ref. to *ca*1880]:
The town was said to be "fixed" or "safe." If it was not possible to "fix" a town the gamblers and fakers usually "took a chance," perhaps being a little more cautious and careful and on the alert for trouble.

**1951** Pryor *The Big Play* 351:
Sterling stated unequivocally that Transworld had succeeded in "fixing" him.

**1979** Terkel in *Amer. Dreams* 250:
They set up a store, fixed a guy in Western Union.

**2.** to arrange the outcome of an election by secret, dishonest, or unlawful means; rig. Now *colloq.*

**1880** *New York Clipper Alamanac* 44:
*Fixed.*—A race which is decided, before coming off, to go a certain way, is said to have been "fixed."

**1889** in *DA*:
Where the "boss" and the fixer of elections are unknown.

**flag-waver** *n.* an enthusiastic, demonstrative patriot.

**1925** *AS* I (Oct.) 37:
The "flag-waver" who flourishes the flag for applause is despised by everyone.

**1942** Huie in *Can Do!* 103:
All those flag wavers who just sit pretty and look cute.

**\*1944** in *OED*:
The Pretoria flag-wavers.

**1982** *New York Times* (Oct. 26) D26:
Herb Brooks, an old-fashioned sort who calls himself a "flag-waver," was the coach of the American [men's ice hockey] team.

**flak-catcher** *n.* a public-relations specialist or spokesperson hired to reply to criticism of his or her employer. Hence **flak-catching**, *n.*

**1970** T. Wolfe *Radical Chic* 110:
This man is the flak catcher. His job is to catch the flak for the No. 1 man.

**1975** *Harper's* (July) 73:
There was a *frisson* of relish, a tendency to regard flak-catching as a Learning Experience.

**1987** *Wkly. World News* (July 14) 12:
A public relations flak-catcher...said, "Dr. Ruth doesn't give reactions to these kinds of things."

**flap** *n.* ¶In phrase:

¶**keep (one's) flaps down** [of aviation orig.] to keep from attracting unnecessary media attention.

**1979** Homer *Jargon* 40:
Ever since he was criticized on the ERA vote, the Senator's kept his door locked, his mouth shut, and his flaps well down.

**flatfoot** *n.* (see quot.).

**1887** in *DA*:
An American "flatfoot" is a man who stands firmly for his party.

**floater** *n.* a person who has not committed to any political party, orig. one whose vote may be purchased.

**1847** *Knickerbocker* XXIX 329 in *OED*:
Early the next morning the "floaters" were marched in single file with votes in hand, to the ballot box.

**1883** H. George in *N. Amer. Rev.* (Mar.) 203 in *OED*:
"How many of them floaters?" i.e. merchantable voters—continued the candidate. "Four hundred" was again the answer.

**1913** *Fort Wayne Daily News* (Ind.) (Nov. 7) 8:
One dollar was the prevailing price paid the floaters for each vote...The

floaters would be taken around a corner and money handed to them as if such transactions were perfectly legitimate.

**1926** *AS* II (Dec.) 136:
A "floater" is a person who shifts from one party to another, and whose vote is purchasable.

**1983** *New York Times* (Mar. 2) B8:
Some say it doesn't matter whether an individual is a "floater," one who gives advice to several candidates,...or one of the "faithful," provided he is pleasant enough and very talented.

**2000** *Star Tribune* (Minneapolis, Minn.) (Aug. 31) 22A:
A lot of voters won't firm up their decision until the last minute. So the campaigns will be chasing those fickle floaters.

**flop** *n.* a turnaround or sudden change of policy or the like; flip-flop.

**1880** in *OED*:
Mr. Skinner's apparent flop on the railroad question is injuring his chances in the Speakership struggle.

**1904** in *DA*:
That a flop by the most militant of the unionists is under contemplation has been denied.

**1911** H. Harrison *Queed* 230:
The editor, instead of seeing in West's letter a spontaneous act of magnanimity,...maliciously twisted it into a grudging confession of error...So ran the editorial, which was offensively headed "West's Fatal Flop."

**flopper** *n.* a person who deserts one political party for another.

**1884** in *DA*:
The kept organ refers to the great masses of the people...who conscientiously oppose Mr. Steven's election...as a "little band of floppers and kickers."

**1905** in *DA*:
Assemblyman Rogers is a flopper because he withdrew from the speakership race and re-entered it.

**FLOTUS** *n.* [first lady of the United States]

**1983** *Washington Post* (Sept. 20) C1:
To their Secret Service shadows they may be "POTUS" and "FLOTUS," but to each other out on their 688-acre California ranch he's still her "Ronnie" and she's still his "Nancy."

**1990** *Electronic Buyers' News* (Apr. 9) 42:
The Secret Service has begun referring to President Bush as "Potus" and Mrs. Bush as "Flotus"—for President and First Lady of the United States.

**2004** *Boston Globe* (Jan. 9) D5:
POTUS is miffed, and FLOTUS is—well, only Goodall's indecisive Southern accent registers.

**flush-bottom** *n.* a wealthy contributor.

**1983** R. Thomas *Missionary* 34:
Over the years Replogle had come to specialize in political fund-raising, which he always called "shaking down the flush-buttoms back East."

**FOB** *n.* [*friend of Bill*] a supporter or acquaintance of Pres. Bill Clinton.

**1992** *Wall Street Journal* (Mar. 12) 1A:
Nobody collects friends like Bill Clinton—And nobody puts them to better use. Inside the Clinton campaign, they are known as the FOBs—Friends of Bill's—and they make up a remarkable network.

**1997** *Business NH Mag.* (Jan. 1) 12:
A lobbyist and "FOB," friend of Bill (as in Clinton).

**2003** *St. Louis Post-Dispatch* (May 30) 2:
Dolan doesn't know Clinton and certainly is not an FOB (friend of Bill's).

**Foggy Bottom** *n.* the U.S. Department of State. *Joc.* [Located in Foggy Bottom, a district in Washington, D.C.; as applied to the State Department, the name is employed for its connotations of befuddlement and obscurity.]

[**1883** *Washington Post* (Apr. 26) 4:
He would take Anderson's heart to Foggy Bottom that night.]

[**1947** J. Reston, in *New York Times* (May 25) VI 7:
The State Department has moved its principal offices...from Pennsylvania Avenue to Foggy Bottom, which, for the benefit of any cynics, is not an intellectual condition but a geographical area down by the Potomac.]

**1950** *Sat. Eve. Post* (July 29) 60:
Another reporter asked a taxi driver to take him to Foggy Bottom, as the new State Department Building is known.

**1951** *Time* (June 25) 18:
Johnson had noted in Foggy Bottom a seeming hostility to Chiang's government.

**1982** in *New York Times Mag.* (Jan. 2, 1983) 15:
This philosophy is making for certain changes at Foggy Bottom.

**football** *n.* (see 1968 quot.). [In the 1959 film comedy *The Mouse That Roared*, an actual football, equipped with wire coils, was used to represent a doomsday weapon.]

**1968** Safire *New Lang. of Politics* 151:
A new, more ominous use of "football" refers to the small, thirty-pound

metal suitcase containing codes that can launch a nuclear attack. It is carried by a military aide to the President and follows the Chief Executive wherever he goes.

**1971** *New Yorker* (Jan. 9) 56:
Wherever the President travels, he is shadowed by "the man with the football," an individual whose single function is to carry a bag holding a variety of codes that pertain to the release—or recall—of one or more nuclear bombs.

**1982** Woodruff & Maza *At White House* 10:
The ever-present military aide with the "football,"...a black bag that contains top secret military and communication codes that follows the President wherever he goes, to be used in the event of a national security crisis.

**1982** *Time* (Mar. 29) 18:
Their other responsibility: not to drop the briefcase. Hence its irreverent nickname—"the football."

**1991** *Newsweek* (Sept. 2) 57:
The briefcase containing launch codes for Soviet missiles—"the football," as Americans say.

**foot-in-mouth-disease** *n.* [pun on hoof-and-mouth disease] an instance or habit of putting (one's) foot in (one's) mouth (see 1968 quot.). *Colloq.*

**1952** *Lethbridge Herald* (Alberta, Can.) (Apr. 16) 4:
President Truman has a bad case of foot-in-mouth disease, an ailment which commonly affects politicians.

**1968** Safire *New Lang. of Politics.* 151:
*Foot-in-mouth disease*: tendency to blunder when ad-libbing; error prone.

**1978** *Business Week* (Jan. 30) 41:
A period when foot-in-mouth disease is endemic in the Carter Administration.

**1983** L. Wachtel, on WINS Radio News (Dec. 12):
A leaning on the part of the administration team on foot-in-mouth disease.

**1990–93** M. Moore *Woman at War* 168:
I learned a long time ago I have foot-and-mouth disease, so I plan on keeping my mouth shut.

**2004** *St. Petersburg Times* (Jan. 27) 2:
Is this all so simple as "foot in mouth" disease?

**14th Amendment citizen** *n.* a member of a minority group granted citizenship and other rights by the 14th Amendment to the U.S. Constitution. [Favored by the Freemen and Constitutionalists who recognize only the first ten amendments to the Constitution.]

**1988** *Colorado Springs Gazette Telegraph* (July 17) A1:
Hellman calls the second class "14th Amendment citizens," who, because they were granted their rights by governmental action, "are liable to regulation and taxation upon their limited statutory citizenship."

**1993** *Chicago Tribune* (Sept. 23) C2:
That health care card. That smacks of a national identity card... That obligates you to be a 14th-Amendment citizen.

**1994** *Denver Post* (Nov. 29) B8:
The citizens learned from that report that illegal immigrants and their 14th Amendment-citizen children represented a net annual taxpayer burden of almost $600 million.

**1996** *Kansas City Star* (Mar. 23) A1:
Under common law, a citizen must declare himself "sovereign" to exercise those God-given rights. Otherwise, according to their interpretation, one is a 14th Amendment citizen, a creature of an illegitimate government.

**Freeper** *n.* a member of the conservative web site "Free Republic." Also **FReeper**.

**1998** L. Goldberg on Usenet (alt.current-events.clinton.whitewater) (June 20):
Trixie—one angry Freeper.

**1998** *Newsday* (Oct. 11) A8:
The e-mailed responses came pouring in, signed with special "Freeper" names.

**2002** *Tennessean* (Nashville) (Nov. 24) 19:
The term "Freepers" comes from Free Republic, at freerepublic.com, "an online gathering place for independent, grassroots conservatism"...It was a Freeper, Pierce said, who designed the parody of the Gore-Lieberman 2000 logo calling it "Sore Loserman."

**friendly** *n.* a political supporter (of a particular candidate).

**1984** *WINS Radio News* (Sept. 3):
President Reagan will begin his campaign in Orange County [Cal.] because, in the words of an adviser, "He wants to kick off his reelection bid with an audience of known friendlies."

**Friend of Bill** *n.* see FOB.

**front porcher** *n.* [Cf. *S.E. front-porch campaign,* in Safire *New Lang. Pol.,* p. 156] a political candidate who is reluctant to campaign widely.

**1977** Coover *Public Burning* 432:
I like campaign trains, I'm no front porcher, but this was too goddamn much!

**frontrunneritis** *n.* the condition of being a leading candidate, esp. a tendency to coast or to be under increased scrutiny by the press.

**1995** *Charleston Daily Mail* (S.C.) (Aug. 21) P1A:
But "frontrunneritis," as the Ames results vividly showed, also can foster complacency among a candidate's managers.

**1997** *Globe and Mail* (Toronto, Can.) (Nov. 8) A7:
Mr. Martin is suffering from a serious case of frontrunneritis...Wherever he goes and whatever he does these days, the Finance Minister is scrutinized with the presumption that he lusts after Mr. Chretien's job.

**2004** *Morning Edition* (National Pub. Radio) (Jan. 23):
I think frontrunneritis tends to take over in Massachusetts.

**Fudge Factory** *n.* the U.S. Department of State. *Joc.*

**1983** R. Thomas *Missionary* 270:
I'm retiring from the fudge factory in exactly two months and nine days.

**1986** Former U.S. Asst. Secy. of State B. Kalb, (public lecture, Knoxville, Tenn.) (Nov. 18):
The building that is known everywhere affectionately as the Fudge Factory.

# G

**gag rule** *n.* a rule, ruling, or law forbidding discussion of certain issues or specifics. [First adopted by the House of Representatives in May 1836, renewed in subsequent years, and made part of the standing orders of the House from 1840–4, stating that petitions relating to slavery should be laid aside without being read aloud, debated, printed or referred to committee.] Now *hist.*

**1810** *Centinel* (Gettysburg, Pa.) (Feb. 7) 2:
The gag rule was before the house this afternoon, but the majority, tho' they called up the question, had not courage to go through with the discussion.

**1840** J.Q. Adams *Journal* (Feb. 11) in Mem. (1876) X 216 in *OED*:
I enquired...if the slavery resolutions of Rhett, and Anderson, of Kentucky were within the recent gag-rule.

**1845** *Amer. Whig. Rev.* I (Mar.) 227:
A very different spirit now required conciliating, and the famous "Gag Rule" was the sacrifice.

**1992** *Village Voice* (N.Y.C.) (Apr. 7) 33:
The "gag rule," preventing family planning clinics...from even informing women of abortion as an option, must be repealed.

**2001** *Vanity Fair* (Aug.) 177:
She then launched into her list of "pullbacks" by the Bush administration., admonishing the secretary for the "continuing misunderstanding of the global gag rule".

**gate** *suffix.* [fr. Water*gate*] (used as the final element in journalistic coinages, usu. nonce words, that name scandals resulting from corruption and cover-ups or other improprieties in government or business). [This continues to be an enormously productive combining form; additional examples of its use in a wide range of contexts may be found in the "Among the New Words" column in

*American Speech* LIII (Fall 1978) 3 and LVI (Winter 1981) 4, *OED*, and elsewhere. See article on page 17.]

**1973** in *AS* LIII (Fall):
There have been perisistent rumors in Russia of a vast scandal....Implicated in the "Volgatgate" are a group of liberal officials.

**1974** *AS* LIII (Fall):
"Watergate" became an international symbol of corruption. (A French vintage scandal became "Winegate"; crooked Southeast Asian unions produced a "Laborgate.")

**1977** *U.S. News & World Report* (Aug. 29) 18:
Reactions to "Koreagate." Michel, who is Republican whip in the House, often was asked about the Korean payoff scandal.

**1980** *Los Angeles Times* (July 28) II5:
Jimmy Carter's proven ability to cut his own throat—most recently by the "Billygate" episode involving his brother's role as a lobbyist for Libya.

**1983** *Mother Jones* (June) 6:
The squalid Environmental Protection Agency affair some dubbed "Sewergate" has now joined a dozen other larger and lesser "gates" in the nation's scandal archives.

**1984** *Time* (Sept. 10) 76:
It may now be time to close the -gate. Ten years is a long time for any political fashion....In that decade we have had Watergate, Koreagate, Lancegate, Billygate and now Ferrarogate, with Meesegate and Debategate temporarily on hold.

**1992** *New York Daily News* (Mar. 18) 18:
Rep. Joe Early (D-Mass.), one of the leading House check bouncers, yesterday angrily attacked House Speaker Tom Foley for his handling of "Rubbergate."

**1993** *Nation* (Mar. 1) 256:
Sessionsgate: Why did F.B.I. Director William Sessions get caught in such a tangled web?

**gerrymander** *n.* [f. surname of Massachusetts Governor Elbridge Gerry (1744–1814), under whose guidance that state's districts were redrawn in 1812. Credit for the coinage is usually given to artist Gilbert Stuart who claimed a redrawn district looked like a salamander, and Benjamin Russell, editor of the *Boston Sentinel*, who suggested "gerrymander" was more appropriate.] a method of redistricting which unfairly or disproportionately favors one party over others; (*hence*) one elected by such methods; any sort of dubious manipulation or negotiation. Also as *v.* and *attrib.* Cf. PACKING, CRACKING, FAIR-FIGHT DISTRICT, KIDNAPPING.

**1812** *Columbian Centinel* (May 23) 2 in *OED*:
The sensibility of the good people of Massachusetts is...awakened to this "Gerrymander."

**1839** *Southern Lit. Messenger* (Virg.) (Dec.) 797:
The fine old height, from which it once proudly surveyed the country round, is the abode of a brick-and-mortar monster, compared with which the gerrymander was grace and proportion itself.

**1892** *Daily Northwestern* (Oshkosh, Wisc.) (Mar. 25):
Their organs have been calling for an extra session of the legislature not knowing whether it was or not to have, through the their bosses, been threatening the Republicans with an apportionment so much worse than their first that the Republican leaders will be sorry they ever questioned the validity of the last gerrymander.

**1938** *Pop. Sci.* (Nov.) 152:
Both man and monkeys, evolutionists hold, are descendants of an animal known as the *a* lemur *b* wombat *c* ocelot *d* gerrymander.

**1955** *Waukesha Daily Freeman* (Wisc.) (Oct. 29) 152:
Waukesha county came into being through gerrymander tactics between 1845–56, dividing what was then Milwaukee county into two parts.

*****2002** *New Internationalist* (Aug.) 2:
Look at the US where half the electorate do not vote, the gerrymander is firmly in place and the President is appointed by the court.

**gerrymander** *v.* to engage in a GERRYMANDER; to manipulate or skew.

**1813** *Salem Gazette* (Dec. 22) 2 in *OED*:
So much...for *War* and *Gerrymandering*.

**1869** C. Buckalew *Proportional Representation* (1872) 218:
There is hardly a State of our Union in which the congressional districts are not gerrymandered in the interest of party.

**1873** *Appleton's Journal* (N.Y.) (Sept. 20) 362:
Bill Gurney himself was arrested, for the fifth or sixth time, in New York; but soon found himself at liberty once more, through some gerrymandering process known only to himself and those who then held him in custody.

**1959** *Sheboygan Press* (Wisc.) (July 16) 44:
To gerrymander is to fix the bounds of electoral districts in such a manner as to give built-in advantage to the party in control of a legislative body.

**1993** *Harper's* (Dec. 24) 26:
One could argue, for instance, that the introduction of the concept of "brain death" in the 1960s was nothing more than a well-intentioned effort to gerrymander the line between life and death in order to increase the [organ] donor pool without inflaming public opinion.

**G-guy** *n.* G-MAN.

**1932** D. Runyon in *Collier's* (June 11) 7:
It seems that these G-guys are members of a squad that comes from Washington, and...do not know that Good Time Charley's joint is not supposed to be busted up.

**1935** S. Miller *"G" Men* (film):
I don't want to get tangled up with you G guys.

**G-heat** *n.* pressure or trouble from federal law enforcement agencies; (*also*) federal law enforcement agents.

**1937** Hoover *Persons in Hiding* 114:
You're hot. It's G heat! We don't want to lay eyes on you!

**1940** Longstreet *Decade* 357:
He chalked out a momser, and the coppers...and G-heat are on him.

**1949** in *Harper's* (Feb. 1950) 74:
The G-heat may assume it has been stolen and enter the case on that basis.

**1955** E. Hunter *Jungle Kids* 102:
Also he was getting G-heat because...he transported some broads into Connecticut for the purpose of prostitution.

**1966** Longstreet & Godoff *Wm. Kite* 277:
No G-heat on you?

**glad-hander** *n.* a person, often a politician, who greets others effusively and often insincerely; one who seeks self-aggrandizement through flattery and feigned cordiality.

**1918** Clover in *Stop at Suzanne's* 134:
Well, this...[fellow] is a glad-hander, besides being a mighty clever man.

**1929** Merriam *Chicago* 275:
One type [politician] is the good fellow, the mixer, the "joiner," the glad hander, whose chief reliance is the cultivation of the personal friendship of invididuals and the acquaintance with all sorts of groups and societies of a non-political nature.

**1934** Weseen *Dict. Slang* 342:
*Glad hander*—A person who is always very friendly and cheerful. He is often suspected of ulterior motives.

**1963** Gant *Queen St.* 156:
He was a glad-hander,...a tinhorn politician.

**1972** Hannah *Geronimo Rex* 108:
In their ranks were the hard-lipped scowlers for Jesus and the radiant happy gladhanders for Jesus.

**1986** *New York* (Dec. 15) 36:
Reagan...is the glad-hander most at home at the ceremonial functions other politicians abhor.

**globaloney** *n.* [*glo*bal + b*aloney*] (an unrealistic) foreign policy or global outlook.

**1943** *New York Times* (Feb. 10) 27:
Characterizing much of Vice President Wallace's "global thinking" as "globaloney," Mrs. Luce said that "usually the higher the plane Mr. Wallace puts his economic arguments upon, the lower, it turns out, American living standards will fall."

**1985** *Seattle Times* (May 31) A11:
While such aberrations in a society are fatal, there is another threat to the globaloney concept. This is the "Technological Revolution."

**1989** *Washington Post* (Apr. 30) X4:
If we all now lived in a global village, Marshall McLuhan—witty, audacious, energetic—was the man with just the right "Globaloney" for the moment.

**2002** *Newsweek* (Dec. 16) 43:
Congresswoman Clare Boothe Luce apparently coined the term "globaloney" in 1943 to trash what Vice President Henry Wallace liked to call his "global thinking," particularly a plan to promote peace by building airports all over the planet.

**G-man** *n.* [government *man,* first applied (*a*1917) to political detectives in Ireland; see *OED*] a special agent of the Federal Bureau of Investigation.

**1930** Pasley *Al Capone* 33:
He offered a G man (government agent) ten gran' to forget it.

**1935** Pollock *Und. Speaks*:
G. man, federal officer.

**1935** R. Graves *Speed Limited* (film):
I think they're G-men.

**1935** *G-Men* (NBC radio) (July 20):
(title)

**1942** Boucherk *Werewolf* 20:
Anybody can marry an actor or a G-man; but a werewolf—.

**1949** *New York Times* (May 1) IV 2:
G-Men Act.

**1952** Himes *Stone* 116:
It took the G-men to get Sid in here.

**1957** H. Danforth & J. Horan *D.A.'s Man* 41 [ref. to *ca*1935]:
Do you want the G-men raiding the joint!

# go

**1974** Bernstein & Woodward *President's Men* 184:
The G-man paused for another 30 seconds or so.

**1977** *New York Post* (Aug. 5) 1:
Godfather picked up by FBI...The move by G-men cast him back into his usual image as a racketeer.

**1981** *Time* (Nov. 9) 39:
The pilot was a hit with G-men, at least. At a screening at the bureau...the show won knowing nods and murmurs.

**1993** *Newsweek* (July 26) 29:
J. Edgar Hoover hung on for decades as the nation's G-man by collecting damaging information on his employers.

**go** *adj.* [orig. aerospace] ready or favorable, esp. for action.

**1962** in *DAS (Supp.)* 704:
As the astronauts say...all signs are go in the National League.

**1965** Hardman *Chaplains* 14:
Men...First Battalion, 16th marines, is a go outfit. We go.

*Ibid.* 14:
In this outfit,...everything that's right is [called] go.

**1972–79** T. Wolfe *Right Stuff* 210:
His system was "go."

**1985** Ferraro & Francke *Ferraro* 109:
As far as the Zacaros are concerned, it's all go.

**go** *v.* ¶In phrase:

¶**go dark** to cease television advertising.

**1988** *Washington Post* (Nov. 13):
Each Friday, Bush campaign operative Janet Mullins got a report on where Dukakis was buying commercials...Three weeks before the election, a red flag came in: Dukakis had suddenly "gone dark" in Ohio, suggesting he was giving up in the state.

**2002** *Deseret News* (Oct. 15):
With three weeks to go to election day, GOP 1st District hopeful Rob Bishop has canceled immediate plans for a television ad campaign, a strategic move referred to in political slang as "going dark" and something that usually signals a candidate is out of money with no hope of raising more, or he is so far ahead in the race there is just no need to continue the media blitz.

**2003** AP (Dec. 13):
We will begin our national advertising on that day. The DNC will never go dark for a single day.

**goat** *n.* (see quot.).

**1855** in *Kans. Hist. Quarterly* vii (1938) 413:
Goats...Free Soilers in Kansas are so designated.

**God squad** *n.* the Endangered Species Committee, a cabinet-level committee formed in 1978 and authorized to reduce the protection of species under the Endangered Species Act to benefit business.

**1991** *Time* (Dec. 9) 72:
Interior Secretary Manuel Lujan Jr. announced he would convene the so-called God Squad, a Cabinet-level committee that can override the Endangered Species Act in the regional or national interest.

**1992** *Nation* (Mar. 30) 417:
This allows the President to convene a panel, dubbed the "god squad," to exempt protected species from coverage of the act.

**1992** *New Republic* (Aug. 10) 4:
Examples include the Endangered Species Act God Squad reducing the protection of the Olympic Forest and Spotted Owl.

**goldbug** *n.* a plutocrat (*obs.*); (*also*) a person in favor of the free circulation of gold; a gold speculator.

**1878** *Harper's Wkly.* (Feb. 23) 156:
Bloated Bondholder. Gold Bug.

**1878** in *DA*:
[Our forefathers] carried on business in gold...In short, they were "goldites," "gold-bugs," and "gold-sharps."

**1878** Sperber & Trittschuh *Amer. Pol. Terms.* 172:
The "gold bugs"—in the elegant language of Western statesmen— have the power to squeeze the debtor by making gold scarce at the time of payment.

**1896** F.P. Dunne, in Schaaf *Dooley* 129:
Misther Hinnissy here...was jus' tellin' me th' advantages iv th' free coinage iv silver. Misther McKenna is a gould bug.

**1903** T.W. Jackson *Slow Train* 87:
You take President Roosevelt. He is a big gold bug.

**1973** *Business Week* (May 19) 70:
Dr. Franz Pick, outspoken currency expert, devout chrysophile (gold bug), [etc.]

**1976** Hayden *Voygage* 366:
Them bloomin' gold bugs'll spend th rest of their lousy lives trying to undo the scramble.

**1976** *Business Week* (Aug. 23) 42:
A $70 price for gold is a far cry from the $300 that the goldbugs widely predicted.

**1980** *ABC Network News* (ABC-TV) (Sept. 17):
A handful of so-called "gold-bugs" claim that gold is the only real money and advocate a return to the gold standard.

**1981** Wambaugh *Glitter Dome* 96:
The two old geezers were goldbugs from Spring Street...[who] had been buying and hoarding gold in their store.

**golden rolodex** *n.* a vast network of contacts.

**1987** *FW* (Apr. 21) 94:
The Man With the Golden Rolodex.

**2002** *Chicago Daily Herald* (Aug. 27) 1:
Austin recommends networking with a "Golden Rolodex" of people who know and care about you.

**2004** *Chicago Tribune* (Jan. 18) 1:
Leading America's efforts on behalf of Iraq is James Baker, the man with the golden Rolodex.

**goo goo** *n.* [sugg. by phr. *good* government, infl. by *goody-goody*] an idealistic supporter of political reform.—used derisively.

**1895** T. Roosevelt in *Letters* I 466:
The Goo-Goos, and all the German leaders...have attacked me.

*Ibid.* 483:
And those prize idiots, the Goo-Goos, have just played into their hands by...nominating an independent ticket of their own.

**1909** O. Johnson in *Lawrenceville* 150:
Down with the Goo-Goos...Rally to the Federalists and Down the Dickinson Goo-Goos.

**1931** Steffens *Autobiog.* 255 [ref. to 1890's]:
The reformers called goo-goos after their Good Government clubs.

**1938** Adamic *My American* 24 [ref. to 1912]:
Mayor Alexander...ran on the Good Government League ("Goo-Goo") ticket.

*Ibid.* 26:
The "Goo-Goos"...had only one more card to play.

**1958** in S.H. Adams *Tenderloin* 364:
The goo-goos haven't got a look-in.

**1984** Formisano & Burns *Boston* 147 [ref. to 1903]:
Their electoral attempt did produce a reputation for arrogant self-righteousness and their nickname of Goo-Goo.

**1988** *Newsweek* (May 16) 27:
The Chicago electorate [is] so inured to influence-peddling and other shenanigans that good-government types are derided as "goo-goos."

**1988** *McLaughlin Group* (synd. TV series) (Sept. 4):
It's going to hurt him with the googoos—the good government crowd.

**1992** *New Republic* (Dec. 14) 23:
The goo-goos should know better, because the budget deal didn't even work on its own political terms.

**2003** *Christian Science Monitor* (Oct. 31) 2:
Even the good-government groups, known affectionately around Gotham as the "Goo Goos," have gotten into the fray.

**goose** *n.* ¶In phrase:

¶**sound [or right] on the goose** (among proponents of slavery in Kansas) strongly supporting the issue of slavery; (*hence*) sound in one's adherence to any specific orthodox belief.

**1862** M.V. Victor *Unionist's Dtr.* 40:
What do you suppose brought him 'way down to Nashville to volunteer, if he wasn't sound on the goos?

**1871** Schele de Vere *Americanisms* 267:
Now, *sound on the goose* means simply to be staunch on the party question, whatever that may be for the moment.

**1872** *Galaxy* (Mar.) 430:
Our theologians are sound on the goose.

**1889** Cox *Frontier Humor* 332:
He was sound on the goose, he was.

**1893** Hampton *Maj. in Washington* 138:
He's sound on the Southern goose and know's where he's "at."

**gotcha** *n.* a surprise or error; (*hence*) an attempt to trick, trap, or expose (a candidate or opponent). —also *attrib.*

**1984** *Washington Post* (Aug. 29):
In a tactical "gotcha," Cuomo made the four-years-in-Albany promise.

**1984** *Wall Street Journal* (Aug. 30):
For one thing, they could stop playing follow the leader in games of "catch-up" and "gotcha."

**1987** *Dallas Morning News* (Oct. 12) 5C:
I think quite frankly that you're making much ado about nothing...You are playing the game of "I gotcha." I didn't set my resume up to be analyzed under a microscope...I don't need to add any embellishments to my life.

**1998** *Chicago Sun-Times* (Sept. 27) 40:
As politics increasingly becomes a game of "gotcha"—almost the only reason anyone watches political debates anymore is to see if one of the candidates will say something spectacularly stupid.

**2000** *Los Angeles Times* (Nov. 4) A20:
Hughes asserted "gotcha politics" was the reason that the 24-year-old drunken driving incident surfaced in the closing days of the presidential race.

**2002** *Houston Chronicle* (Mar. 2) 33:
Instead of playing a game of "political gotcha" over the Enron debacle,

Congress should prevent companies from creating dummy corporations to hide debt, as Enron did.

**gov** *n.* state governor.

**1846** J.H. Ingraham *P. Fenning* 81:
I live at the Gov's.

**1867** S. Clemens in *Twain's Letters* II 115:
Remember me to the Gov.

**1928** W. Rogers *Chews to Run* 33:
They nominated Gov, or Senator Jasbo.

**1942** *ATS* 787:
*Gov, guv*...governor.

**1984** *New York Daily News* (Aug. 10) 10:
Top lottery winner checks in with the gov.

**graft** *n.* personal advantage, gain, or profit obtained through corrupt political or commercial practices, esp. money paid for bribes or protection; commercial and political corruption in general. Now *S.E.*

**1901** "J. Flynt" *World of Graft* 4:
The Under World has had occasion to approach him for purposes of graft and found him corrupt.

*Ibid.* 23:
The City Hall people want their graft just as much as I do.

**1905** Riordan *Plunkitt* 3:
Everybody is talkin' these days about Tammany men growin' rich on graft, but nobody thinks of drawing the distinction between honest graft and dishonest graft.

**1907** "O. Henry" *Works* 1449:
You know, Mac...they're trying Inspector Pickering on graft charges.

**1911** H.B. Wright *Barbara Worth* 213:
I mean...the way these four-flushers...attempt to work their graft right under our eyes. Did you hear about this man Worth getting that franchise out of the council?

**1914** *Century Dict.* (Supp.):
The word graft...came suddenly into extensive use in the political and journalist language of the United States about 1901, as a new term more convenient in some respects than the equivalent terms bribery, corruption, dishonesty, blackmail, "boodling," all of which it connotes and of which it is a succinct synonym.

**1917** W.A. White in *Letters* 180:
I wasn't jawing at Jose for exposing graft.

**1929** T. Gordon *Born to Be* 36:
His wife put the sheriff on Louie and he was run out of town; that necessarily cut our graft again.

**1929–30** Farrell *Young Lonigan* 12:
His old man kicked about pay for [a certificate] because he thought it was graft.

**1931** J.T. Flynn *Graft in Business* 37:
The characteristic vice of business today is graft.

*Ibid.* 39:
Graft is, I believe, comparatively recent as a term for describing a certain form of parasitic profit.

**1937** Reitman *Box-Car Bertha* 78:
They say that she pays a big graft...for protection.

**1952** Bradbury in *Golden Apples* 91:
We have to pay big graft to keep our franchise.

**1955** Q. Reynolds *HQ* 329:
No one blamed the citizens who did not hesitate to pay out graft to avoid traffic tickets.

**graft** *v.* to acquire money, gain, or advantage through the practice of political corruption, esp. bribery or extortion.

**1901** "J. Flynt" *World of Graft* 4:
A "grafter" is one who makes his living, and sometimes his political fortune, by "grafting." He may be a political "boss," a mayor, a chief of police, a warden of penitentiary, a municipal contract, a member of the town council, [etc.].

**1901** "J. Flynt," in *McClure's* (Apr.) 572:
I'd like to see this town run by thieves once more. Course they'd graft...but not any more'n the police do.

**1905** D.G. Phillips *Plum Tree* 61:
Politics is on a money basis now...I don't see how those in politics that don't graft, as they call it, are any better than those that do.

**1909** O. Johnson in *Lawrenceville* 155:
Turn the Robbers Out. No More Grafting.

**1910** Asburgy in *Gem of Prairie* 267:
Hell, they all graft. There is not a policeman around here that doesn't hold us girls [prostitutes] up.

**grafter** *n.* a person, esp. a politician or official, who takes advantage of his position to gain money or property unethically or illegally, as by taking bribes, levying extortion, diverting funds, etc. Now *S.E.*

**1901:**
(quot. at GRAFT, *v.*)

**1903** in *DAE*:
Every member of the union knew the exact character of Parks, that he was a "grafter."

**1904** F. Lynde *Grafters* 298:
You were to crush the grafters in this railroad struggle...and climb to distinction yourself on the ladder from which you had shaken them.

**1914** Atherton *Perch* 58:
Butte...has her pestilential politicians, her grafters and crooks.

**1953** Pohl *Star of Stars* 48:
It was an informal club for goldbricks and staff grafters who carouse within.

**granfalloon** *n.* [coined by Kurt Vonnegut, Jr.] any large, amorphous organization without real identity; see 1960 quot.

**1960** K. Vonnegut Jr. *Cat's Cradle* 91:
A seeming team that was meaningless in terms of the ways God gets things done, a textbook example of what Bokonon calls a *granfalloon*. Other examples of *granfalloons* are the Communist party, the Daughters of the American Revolution, the General Electric Company, the International Order of Odd Fellows—and any nation, anytime, anywhere.

**1985** *Washington Post* (Sept. 22):
Galapagos is a book that makes me glad to declare my membership in that granfalloon ("a proud and meaningless association of human beings").

**2002** U-Wire (Jan. 7):
The bogus, pseudo-religious patriotism currently sweeping the nation is nothing more than propaganda, encompassing both the granfalloon technique (people bound by meaningless symbols, which in this case would be the American flag) and the bandwagon trap.

**graymail** *n.* [sugg. by *blackmail*] a method of preventing prosecution, as for espionage, by threatening to reveal or subpoena classified government information in court.

[**1964** *Newsweek* (Aug. 24) 32:
Political blackmail is becoming...a commonplace...Perhaps there should be gradations of the term..."whitemail" and "graymail," for starters.]

**1973**:
(cited in *BDNE3*).

**1979** *New York Times*, in *BDNE3*:
Secret proceedings would not eliminate graymail.

**1984** *Time* (Nov. 19) 115:
The CIA's worries were rekindled when Boyce threatened "graymail": the introduction of sensitive information in his testimony.

**1987** Levinson & Link *Terrorist* (film):
*Graymail*—the threat to reveal classified information in court.

**1990** *Newsweek* (Jan.) 19:
Noriega's lawyers are already saying they will require reams of classified material for their defense. U.S. officials say the graymail problem isn't insurmountable.

**grease** *n.* political influence; PULL.

**1941** *Guide to Naval Acad.* 151:
Grease. Pull or influence.

**1980** Gould *Ft. Apache* 155:
Hey, Murphy, your brothers have a little grease downtown, don't they?...Do you think they could pull me a transfer?

**gridlock** *n.* a situation in which it is impossible to make progress; an impasse, stalemate, or deadlock.

**\*1983** *Financial Times* (London, U.K.) (May 16) 2:
The political "gridlock" in Congress might mean that no budget resolution could be passed for fiscal year of 1984.

**1992** *Village Voice* (N.Y.C.) (Apr. 7) 23:
The stranglehold of plutocrats, pundits, pollsters, and power brokers also effectively chokes every vital issue before the American public... This gridlock has nothing to do with democracy.

**1994** *Critical Intelligence* (Oct.) 1:
Is it possible he might still...break through Washington gridlock and reinvent the fundamental ways government works?

**Gucci Gulch** *n.* the corridors outside the Senate Finance Committee or the House Ways and Means Committee offices; (*hence*) the K Street district in Washington D.C., or all lobbyists in the city.

**1986** *Atlanta Journal-Constitution* (May 25) E2:
It must withstand "Gucci Gulch," the gauntlet of lobbyists for industries.

**1994** *Vanity Fair* (May) 53:
Along Gucci Gulch, the corridor outside the Finance Committee offices, plied by expensively shod lobbyists, Moynihan has been heard lecturing other senators on, say, the reasons Romania was a model of Stalinist government.

**2000** *U.S. News & World Report* (Nov. 27) 10:
"Gucci Gulch," slang for the capital's legal, lobbying, and PR industry, is uncorking the champagne.

**2001** *New York Times Mag.* (Oct. 14) 42:
This is useful information for Washington pundits: when I see a lobbyist on K Street's "Gucci Gulch," I'll look down at his shoes and say, "Nice *snaffle-bit* buckle."

**2003** *Wall Street Journal* (Oct. 20) B1:
One of the most lucrative squealing operations in America is run out of

a comfortable suite of offices near Gucci Gulch, the K Street lobbying district in Washington, D.C.

**2003** *Roll Call* (Sept. 29):
Capitol Hill's Godfather of campaign finance reform initiatives fought efforts to ban contributions from Gucci Gulch during the Senate's last debate over campaign reform issues in March 2001.

**gut** *adj.* (of a political issue or the like) of fundamental importance; of extraordinary concern tto voters, often evoking a visceral reaction. Hence **guttier, guttiest**.

**1964** *Newsweek* (Sept. 21) 29:
The one issue that the President feels is the "guttiest" of the campaign, and on which he also feels Goldwater is the most vulnerable: peace.

**\*1964** in *OED*:
Combined with a concentration on gut issues.

**1968** Safire *New Lang. Pol.* 179:
A peripheral issue in one campaign can be a gut issue in another.

**1969** *Newsweek* (May 26) 48:
The gut issues in the forthcoming election are not dramatic ones.

**1988** Univ. Tenn. instructor:
There aren't any gut issues in this campaign. You call the Pledge of Allegiance a gut issue?

**gut-fighter** *n.* a candidate or political operative who wages an unusually aggressive, uncompromising campaign, especially against a politically stronger opponent.

**1962** *Time* (Feb. 23) 62:
Brusque, sly and opportunistic, Standton...was the special blend of gut-fighter and idealist that Lincoln wanted and needed.

**1968** in Safire in *New Lang. Pol.* 179:
The people voted for the homely, rumpled, irrational gutfighter, Harry Truman.

**1968** *Ibid.*:
Gutfighters are at their best dealing with "gut issues."

**1984** Univ. Tenn. instructor:
I guess the classic example of a poltical gutfighter would be Richard Nixon.

**1992** *Capitol Gang* (CNN-TV) (July 19):
Bill Clinton is very much of a gut-fighter.

**G-woman** *n.* [sugg. by G-MAN] a woman who is an FBI agent.

**1984** *New York Post* (Aug. 30) 24:
G-Women Mugged. Two female FBI agents having lunch at Central Park's lake were mugged yesterday by two men who stole their guns and handcuffed them together.

# H

**hard** *n.* an advocate of hard money as a national standard. Now *hist.*

**1843** Sperber & Trittschuh *Amer. Pol. Terms* 187:
The hards and the softs have at last resorted to the keen weapons of wits!

**1844** in *DAE*:
The locofocos are divided in that State [Missouri], and are known [as] "Hards" and "Softs," in consequence of their views upon the currency question.

**1847** in *DAE*:
He has occupied the position of what is termed a "hard."

**1848** Robb *Squatter Life* 91:
Hards, softs, whigs and Tylerites were represented.

**1855** in Meserve & Reardon *Satiric Comedies* 125:
Being a hard himself, [he] does not intend an insult.

**hardball** *n.* aggressive or ruthless competition, esp. in politics or business; in phr. **play hardball** or [as *v.*] **hardball it** to engage in such competition; to do whatever is necessary to prevail or succeed. Often attrib. Now *colloq.*

**1972** in Bernstein & Woodward *President's Men* 173:
This is the hardest hardball that's ever been played in this town. We all have to be very careful, in the office and out.

**1973** in *Submission of Pres. Convers.* 223:
He is playing hard ball. He wouldn't play hard ball unless he were pretty confident that he could cause an awful lot of grief.

**1975** *New York Times* (Aug. 24) IV 19:
Nixon was a mean, tough, hardball politician.

**1979** Eble *Campus Slang* (Mar.) 4:
*Hard ball*—tough, given to ruthless tactics: He's a real hard ball businessman.

**1982** *Los Angeles Times* (Nov. 21) IA 6:
Paul's really hard-balling it now. They're locked in a relatively high level for competition.

**1983** *Los Angeles Times* (Oct. 26) I 6:
[Sen. J. Biden] accused White House counselor Edwin Meese III of deciding "to hardball it."

**1983** W. Walker *Dime to Dance By* 68:
The opposing counsel was serving notice that he intended to play hardball.

**1987** *RHD2*:
He wasn't ready for the hardball politics of Washington....Reporters asked the president some hardball questions.

**1988** Kienzle *Marked for Murder* 114:
He plays hard ball.

**2003** *Cincinatti Post* (Apr. 26) A1:
Scholars and historians say the Bush administration has set a new presidential standard when it comes to playing hardball politics with Congress.

**hardballer** *n.* one who excels in an atmosphere of hardball; one who plays hardball.

**1976** *Time* (Dec. 27) 52:
Grodin plays the honcho as a hardballer.

**1981** *Maclean's* (Jan. 12) 20:
The political hardballers always seem to win in Ottawa.

**1983** Wambaugh *Delta Star* 205:
"Internal Affairs is gonna nail him one a these days." "Naw, he's a hardballer....A hardballer."

**hard hat** *n.* a person who clings stubbornly to a nationalistic political position.

**1970** *Time* (May 25) 20:
[On May 8], a gang of 200 hardhats, equipped with U.S. flags and lengths of lead pipe, had waded into a crowd of antiwar students in Wall Street. Police...stood by as some 70 peace demonstrators were beaten....Almost overnight, "hardhats" became synonymous with white working-class conservatives.

**1971** *Time* (June 14) 41:
Gradually, [Mr. Nehru] became a hardhat on the Tibetan border question.

**hard money** *n.* funds which, according to law, may be used to support a specific (federal) election campaign; (*hence*) donations to candidates rather than to political organizations. Cf. SOFT MONEY.

**1984** *Washington Post* (June 6):
Contributions to a candidate...were not tax deductible—they were "hard" money the giver would never see again. Contributions to the nonprofit organizations...were all tax deductible, "soft" money.

**2004** *Chicago Sun-Times* (Oct. 13) 3:
The distinction between candidates' spending and political parties' spending is important because federal candidates can only receive "hard money"—contributions that are highly regulated.

**hard-shell** *n.* an obstinate, uncompromising, tough, or extremely conservative person; (*specif.,* in 1850's) a conservative member of the New York State Democratic party.

**1853** in Bartlett *Amer.* (ed. 2):
The difference between a Hardshell and a Softshell is this: one favors the execution of the Fugitive Slave Law and goes for a distribution of the offices among the Nationals, while the other is a stickler for Union and Harmony.

**1854–55** in Sperber & Trittschuh *Amer. Pol. Terms* 188:
A Whig said "I am a whole hog—I am a Hard-shell."

**1858** in *DA*:
We have, however, one or two specimens in our eye of the genus, hard shell, who still do as their daddies did.

**1860** in Sperber & Trittschuh *Amer. Pol. Terms* 188:
The Soft Shells and the Hard Shells of New York are terribly distressed just now.

**1900** in *DAE*:
The elder observed that certain of the "hardshells" were looking askance at the fiddle.

**1916** H.L. Wilson *In Red Gap* 135:
A grouchy old hardshell with white hair and whiskers whirling about his head.

**1919** in *OED*:
I've ridden up here from Tall Timber Junction to get acquainted with you hardshells.

**1922–26** Scoggins *Red Gods* 26:
And when work's done, you can get drunk, or play poker with a gang of homesick hardshells.

*a*1956 Almirall *College to Cow Country* 227:
His welcome to newcomers wasn't a universal one. There were some "hardshells" around that cow country that envied the fact that others did what they couldn't.

**1971** Keith *Long Line Rider* 144:
They're bringin' a bunch in from Tucker. All hard shells.

**1977** Coover *Public Burning* 60:
I had to cool the barnburners, soften up the hardshells, keep the hunkers and cowboys in line.

**hatchet** *v.* to perform a HATCHET JOB on; to be a HATCHET MAN.

**1962** *Time* (Dec. 21) 18:
He and/or his aides were out to hatchet Adlai.

**1968**:
(quot. at HATCHET JOB).

**1970** in *Atlantic* (Jan. 1971) 35:
The description and fabrication of cold fact was all Time's not unusual procedure for hatcheting.

**2003** *Capital Gang* (CNN-TV) (Aug. 9):
[Margaret] Carlson: But he's going to have to have more to say than he's had yet, and 60 days is not that long to learn everything, if the press is doing its job and manages to question him... [Robert] Novak: Hatcheting him, you mean.

**hatchet job** *n.* an instance of character assassination, malicious distortion, or excessively harsh criticism.

**1940** *Daily Northwestern* (Oshkosh, Wisc.) (Aug. 26) 7:
It was one of "Donald Duck" Ickes' hatchet jobs, consisting of subtle intimations, innuendoes and outright falsehoods.

**1943** *Berkshire Eagle* (Pittsfield, Mass.) (Jan. 12) 8:
We have seen the political hatchet job that was done on the President's seven-point program for war sacrifice equality.

**1944** *Time* (Oct. 23) 20:
Exuberant hatchet jobs were done on Foster Dulles because of his Wall Street connections.

**1947** J.P. Cannon in *Notebook* 149:
I noticed the hatchet job most of the critics of the big press were doing on the picture.

**1965** Horan *Seat of Power* 45:
The bum is good for any hatchet job [City] Hall wants.

**1968** Safire *New Lang. of Politics* 185:
The work performed is called a "hatchet job" as well as "hatcheting." Harry Truman's assessment of the Republican party in the 1948 campaign "Gluttons of privilege...all set to do a hatchet job on the New Deal."

**1974** Strasburger *Rounding Third* 134:
At least we'll leave one person pure at the end of this hatchet job.

**1980** Berlitz & Moore *Roswell* 47:
A "most unscrupulous journalist from San Francisco" who may have been paid off to do "the hatchet job" on Scully.

**1980** Key *Clam-Plate* 108:
Even a hatchet-job review would invite heat from the ad agencies.

**1986** N. George in *Buppies, B-Boys* 310:
As if he suspected I was out to do a hatchet job.

**1999** *New York Times Mag.* (Oct. 24) 77:
After a long silence, he angrily declared it was a "hatchet job" on his book.

**2003** E. Alterman *What Liberal Media?* (Feb. 4) 88:
The transformation of the public discourse is categorically a different undertaking than merely publishing a best-selling right-wing hatchet job—particularly one that is purchased in bulk by conservative organizations.

**hatchet man** *n.* a loyal supporter who engages in HATCHET JOBS or similar activities on behalf of a particular candidate or cause.

**1898** *Fresno Weekly Republican* (Cal.) (Jan. 28) 4:
As Chief Hatchetman of the Literary Highbinders he has some of the prominence of disrepute that distinguishes the Chief of Tammany, but none of the enforced virtue of the latter. He is a lower, meaner and more disreputable scoundrel than Dick Croker, the man who has become a millionaire by "doing" politics.

**1938** *Daily Independent* (Monessen, Pa.) (Apr. 19) 2:
His attack is evidence of the fact that he is trying to make good in the role of the hatchet man, but the decent people of Pennsylvania will not be taken in by this jack of all parties.

**1941** B.O. Davis, Jr. in *Davis* 79:
One other officer, the Hatchet Man, I am told.

**1949** in *DA*:
Truman's hatchetman...announces that he is sending organizing teams into the South to work for the defeat of Congressmen and Senators who oppose the Truman-CIO legislative program.

**1951** *Sat. Eve. Post* (June 16) 130:
Stalin might send his hatchet men to do away with a tool that could compromise him.

**1957** Blumgarten *Mr. Rock & Roll* (film):
Your hatchet man boss already told the truth—coast to coast!

**1964** *Newsweek* (July 27) 27:
He'll be the hatchet man, just like Nixon was in '52.

**1966** F. Harvey *Raiders* 100:
Executive assistant ("hatchet man" was the term used in Washington).

**1974** Bernstein & Woodward *President's Men* 24:
Charles W. Colson, special counsel to the President of the United States, was the White House "hatchet man," he said.

**1984** J. McNamara *First Directive* 210:
They were administrative captains, hatchet men.

**haul up** *v.* to call or hale to account before a legal or administrative authority.

**1851** B. Hall *College Wds.*:
In many colleges, one brought up before the Faculty is said to be *hauled up*.

**\*1882** in *OED*:
They were all young officers and probably at times require to be hauled up sharply.

**1890** *Overland Mo.* (Feb.) 123:
I want him hauled up. Can't ye make out the papers?

**1925** Z. Grey *Vanishing Amer.* 131:
I'll put you in jail....I'll haul you up for this.

**1938** Inman in *Diary* 879:
The bull wouldn't haul me up in Petersburg because he said the courts dere didn't have nothin' against hobos.

**hawk** *n.* a person, esp. in public office, who advocates a warlike, aggressive, or deliberately confrontational national military policy. Now *S.E.* Cf. DOVE.

**1962** *Sat. Eve. Post* (Dec. 8) 20:
The hawks favored an air strike to eliminate the Cuban missile bases....The doves opposed the air strikes and favored a blockade.

**1964**:
(quot. at DOVE)

**1967** J. Flaherty in *Chez Joey* 7:
The Hawks in May: A Day to Remember.

**1973** *U.S. News & World Report* (Aug. 27) 32:
The "hawks" in the Soviet leadership are believed to be arguing that a quick military operation could solve all of these problems at a single stroke.

**1981** *Time* (July 27) 11:
If the Administration persists..., warn some of the most fervent hawks in Congress, the present consensus for heavy defense spending could evaporate.

**1987** M. Hastings *Korean War* 186:
In the eyes of the "hawks" the change of mood in Washington represented a weakening of the American position.

**1990** *Daily Beacon* (Univ. Tenn.) (Aug. 27) 4:
The hawks are certain that American air power can virtually eliminate Iraq's air force.

**1994** *New Republic* (July 4) 10:
Celebrated by David Halberstam as the dove among the Vietnam hawks.

**heads-up** *n.* a warning. Also *attrib.* Now *colloq.*

**1989** T. Clancy *Clear & Pres. Danger* 319:
The shooters got a heads-up for an important job several days ago.

**1990** Stoll *Cuckoo's Egg* 125:
My boss wanted me to call our funding agency, the Department of Energy—"Give them a heads-up."

**1991** in Kross *Splash One* 254:
Got a heads-up from the public information officer about a negative story running in the States.

**1994** *Time* (Aug. 1) 21:
He gave White House officials a "heads up" briefing on the RTC probe.

**1994** *New York Times* (Nov. 6) IV 2:
He took care, too, to send an early heads-up to his Pentagon and Congressional overseers.

**1995** *New Yorker* (Apr. 17) 64:
Commissioners were left to decide whether a document or a media contact or a political request required a heads-up to City Hall.

**heeler** *n.* a hanger-on or adherent of a politician or political party who usu. carries out the orders of political bosses in the hope of personal aggrandizement. —used contemptuously. Now *rare* except as WARD-HEELER.

**1876** in AS XXVII (1952) 165:
As the crowd dispersed a gentleman happened to say that the gang in the room was composed of Tammany "heelers," when a Tammany retainer taking umbrage at the epithet knocked the gentleman down.

**1877** in Bartlett *Amer.* (ed. 4):
Wirt Sykes as a journalist would make as good a consul as Wirt Sykes the politician, who has been a heeler about the capital, or Wirt Sykes the army bummer.

**1884** T. Fortune *Black & White* 131:
Demagogues, tricksters, and corruptionists who figure in the newspapers as "bosses," "heelers," and "sluggers."

**1886** T. Roosevelt, in *Century Mag.* (Nov.) 78:
The "heelers" stand at the polls.

**1900** J.R. Spears *Amer. Slave Trade* 4:
He was what ward politicians would call a "heeler" of the Earl of Warwick.

**1903** in *DA*:
The local man, often called a "heeler," has his body of adherents.

**1904** in "O. Henry" *Works* 513:
We get the heelers out with the crackly two-spots.

**1904** *Life in Sing Sing* 249:
Heeler—A politician in a small way.

**1909** *WNID*:
*Heeler* One who follows at the heels; specif., a subservient hanger-on of a political patron. Polit. Cant, U.S.

**1915** *DN* IV 201:
*Heeler*, a political fellow ready to do dirty work.

**1917** U. Sinclair *K. Coal* 210:
The foreman of the jury [was] a saloon-keeper, one of Raymond's heelers.

**1944** E.C. Smith & A.J. Zurcher *Dict. Amer. Pol.* 151:
*Heeler.* A party worker who runs errands for a district or precinct leader, distributes literature, canvasses for votes, arranges for open or disguised bribery of individual voters, and gets out the vote on election day.

**1942–49** Goldin et al. *DAUL*:
*Heeler* Any ward politician whose tactics are those of a ruffian.

**1950** P. Green *Peer Gynt* 101:
A thief and a heeler come in at the right front.

**highbinder** *n.* an unscrupulous politician or political intriguer. [The 1835 quot. either anticipates or plays upon this sense.]

[**1835** *Knickerbocker* (July) 65:
Benjamin Smith...was a...loafer....I was surprised...that he never was sent to the Legislature; for he was one of our distinguished "high-binders," and deserved...office.]

**1890** in *OED*:
Highbinders applied to political conspirators and the like.

**1903** A.H. Lewis *Boss* 136:
Them high-binders at the top o' Tammany.

**1920** Ade *Hand-Made Fables* 72:
Tax Dodgers and amateur High Binders.

**1920** Safire in *New Lang. Politics* 415:
A lot of old high-binder standpatters who haven't had an idea since the fall of Babylon.

**1942** *ATS* 787:
Political intriguer. *Highbinder.*

**1952** in *DAS*:
The AFL-News Reporter covered the winter meeting of the grand inner circle of high-binders at Miami Beach.

**Hindu** *n. Cal.* a member of the Know-Nothing Party.

**1855** in *Cal. Hist. Soc. Quarterly* IX (1930) 41:
The anti-Catholic test, which here in California the Hindoos (Know Nothings) profess to repudiate.

**hippie** *n.* a usu. young, longhaired person who dresses unconventionally, holds various antiestablishment attitudes and beliefs, and typically advocates pacifist or radical politics. *orig.* used disparagingly. Now *S.E.* Also as **hippy** and as *adj.*

**1966** Young & Hixson *LSD* 8:
The poundage of LSD swallowed by college "hippies" is a minuscule amount.

*Ibid.* 63:
Harvard "druggies"—that label being preferred in Cambridge to the Western term "hippies."

**1966** Goldstein *1 in 7* 73:
Ah, the Harvard hippie. I knew him well. Ready to prove that Kennedy and Dostoevsky and Holden Caulfield have not lived in vain. He defies his parents by sleeping with his girl friend, his neighbors by letting his hair grow, and his university by smoking pot.

*Ibid.* 121:
The real hippies—I mean the ones that matter under the purple sunglasses—go in for stronger stuff.

**1967** Tamony *Americanisms* (Mar.) (No. 17) 15:
After late December, 1966, news stories and column comment on the San Francisco hippies appear daily in the *San Francisco Chronicle* and almost daily in the *San Francisco Examiner*.

**1967** J. Flaherty, in *Village Voice* (N.Y.C.) (May 18):
Hippies are not un-American.

**1967** J. Flaherty in *Chez Joey* 7:
If your hair was slightly too long, your chin foliated, your dress too hippy,...you were best off south of...Sixty-second Street.

**1967** Brelis *Face of S. Vietnam* 100:
"The music is good. Real American. Hippy." "What's hippy?" "The latest. Modern."

**1983** Leeson *Survivors* (film):
Take that little hippie girl with you.

**1986** Stinson & Carabatsos *Heartbreak* 31:
Man, there ain't been any hippies around for centuries.

**1989** *Murphy Brown* (CBS-TV):
You talkin' about the wimpy guy in the hippie outfit?

**1993** *News-Sentinel* (Knoxville, Tenn.) (July 20) B1:
You have to wonder how many hippies travel with nail polish.

**hog** *n.* (esp. among radical political groups) a police officer; pig.—used contemptuously.

**1970** *New York Post* (July 10) [ref. to 1968]:
Sure, I've been to Nam (Vietnam), and I'd rip off (attack) a hog (policeman) in a minute.

**1972** Smith & Gay *Don't Try It* 203:
*Honda Hogs.* Division of San Francisco Tactical Squad that rides little Honda motorcycles.

**1978** *UTSQ* [terms for police]:
Watch out for the pigs, hogs, heat.

**1967–80** Folb *Runnin' Lines* 242:
*Hog(s), the.* Police.

**1980** *AS* (Fall) 197.

**hook** *n.* Esp. *N.Y.C.* an influential patron or associate; political influence. Cf. RABBI.

**1931** Wilstach *Under Cover Man* 160:
You're a good hook, Jones.

**1968** Radano *Walking Beat* 134:
If your hook is big enough you can get any job.

**1971** N.Y.U. student:
They say, "you gotta have a hook. That guy's got a long hook around here." It means influence, pull, somebody you know.

**1972** J. Mills *Report* 99:
Oh, she got in on a hook.

**1973** Schiano & Burton *Solo* 23:
You gotta have a hook. You gotta know the mayor or some senior officer to get in something like that.

**1973** Droge *Patrolman* 57:
Near the end of March all the probies called their "hook." A hook is a person who claims he can get you the exact assignment you want, and sometimes he can. In the telephone company we called him a "rabbi."

**1978** Strieber *Wolfen* 107:
That's their whole career, that and figuring out who has the biggest hook, who is the biggest hook for that matter.

**1983** Flaherty *Tin Wife* 286:
I used a hook to get my kid off a felony.

**1987** Taubman *Lady Cop* 268:
*Hook:* Someone of higher rank who can bring someone up, provide references for better assignments or even order transfers on their own authority.

**1991** McCarthy & Mallowe *Vice Cop* 52:
Gussman became McCarthy's "hook," his "rabbi."

**hook-up** *n.* a joining of forces; (*hence*) a political or other connection. Now *colloq.*

**1903** A.H. Lewis *Boss* 116:
It'll put us in line for a hook-up with th' reform bunch in th' fight for th' town next year.

**1928–30** Fiaschetti *Gotta Be Rough* 139:
That was interesting, provocative....Wasn't there a hook-up somewhere?

**1930** Lait *On the Spot* 30:
You know what hook-ups he's got. You know the precin't captains...are in with him.

**1957** Ness & Fraley *Untouchables* 13:
They could be brought in from other cities...to insure that they had no hookup with the Chicago mobsters.

**horse** *n.* (see quot.).

**1989** *Newsweek* (Oct. 2) 8:
A horse is a congressman who introduces or supports a lobbyist's bill.

**horse-race journalism** *n.* the media coverage of election season which emphasizes popularity polls and inter-campaign battles, esp. that little concerned with issues.

**1986** *Dallas Morning News* (Oct. 29) 19A:
Horse race journalism—who's in front in today's polls—is much easier to provide than is an analysis of complex issues.

**1994** *Buffalo News* (July 5) B3:
One reason the substance of policy is not communicated is that reporters carry over to their coverage of government the campaign mind set of horse-race journalism. Process stories predominate, and the emphasis is on who is gaining or losing, not on what is being done.

**2004** *Ottawa Citizen* (Feb. 17) A13:
Horserace journalism is spreading, which is a disaster. More horserace chatter means fewer newspaper pages and broadcast minutes for everything else: Policy issues not raised by politicians are ignored, important studies are not read, myths are not corrected and lies go unchallenged.

**horse-shed** *v.* to attempt to influence individual voters, witnesses, or jurors, esp. while feigning impartiality.

**1846** J.F. Cooper *Redskins* 240:
This "horse-shedding" process...is well-known...and extends not only to politics, but to the administration of justice. Your regular "horse-shedder" is employed to frequent taverns where jurors stay, and drop

hints...touching the merits of causes known to be on the calendar....It is true there is a law against doing anything of this sort.

**1856** B. Hall *College Wds.* (ed. 2) 258:
*Horse-Shedding.* At the University of Vermont, among secret and literary societies, this term is used to express the idea conveyed by the word electioneering.

**1901** in *DN* VI (1933) 369:
There was no opportunity, as Mr. Lincoln used to say, to "horse-shed" [the witnesses] before they were brought in.

**1914** *DN* IV 108:
We don't expect to horseshed any witnesses.

**hot button** *n.* a strongly emotive, popular, or controversial concern or issue. Also *attrib.*

**1966** *New York Times* (Jan. 9) 7:
Dr. Martin E. Marty, Lutheran theologian..., acknowledges that the "God Is Dead" theologians have their finger on the "hot button."

**1990** P. Taylor *See How They Run* 6:
They were the ones who had reduced media-age politics to a dismal science: take a poll, find a "hot button" issue, feed it back to the voters in the form of a picture, a symbol and a pre-masticated attack line.

**hunker** *n.* a member of the conservative element of the New York State Democratic party; (*hence*) a politically conservative person. Now *hist.*

**1843** in *DAE:*
Let the "Hunkers" and "Barn-burners" contend.

**1849** Bartlett in *Amer.* (ed. 2) 208:
He is now the leader of the hunkers of Missouri.

**1853** P.H. Myers *Emigrant Squire* 10:
There are the Hunkers and the Barnburners.

**1863** R.G. Carter in *4 Bros.* 345:
Too many hunkers present, who voted what they believed rather than what the merits of the debate established.

**1864** J.R. Browne *Crusoe's Island* 52 [ref. to 1849]:
I'm a [manifest-]destiny-man myself. I'm none of your old Hunkers.

**1926** *AS* II (Dec.) 136:
The "Hunkers" were regular or conservative Democrats—in antebellum days—who were accused by the "Barnburners" of "hunkering" or "hankering" for power.

**1977** Coover *Public Burning* 60:
I had to cool the barnburners, soften up the hardshells, keep the hunkers and the cowboys in line.

**hunting license** *n.* exceptional license to take unauthorized action against individuals, proposals, programs, or the like.

**1979** Homer *Jargon* 41:
But don't mess with the Sanitation Commissioner—he has a hunting license.

**hyper-power** *n.* a nation without an economic, martial, or political superior or equal.

*1988 *Economist* (Feb. 28):
There is one hyper-power, and seven powers with world influence—Russia, China, Japan, India, France, Germany and Britain.

**1998** *Rocky Mountain News* (Denver, Colo.) (May 24) 45A:
These trends pose a particular challenge to the U.S. as the "hyper-power" to which the world turns to solve many of its problems.

**1998** *Washington Times* (Dec. 23) A14:
Some observers believe that plan is being crafted mainly to reduce what French officials describe as the "hegemony of a hyperpower"—the United States—and to "rehabilitate" the authority of the U.N. Security Council.

**2004** *Citizen-Times* (Asheville, N.C.) (Mar. 25):
Even though we are the "hyperpower" in the world, we're probably the least educated on global issues.

# I

**immunity bath** *n.* a condition of being free from threat of all prosecution.

**1987** *Atlanta Constitution* (Jan. 6) A13:
Occasionally, a witness will be successfully prosecuted for a crime after he has given immunized testimony. The federal statute is not an immunity bath. On the other hand, one federal judge has correctly observed that criminal prosecution of defendants is uncommon after they have been granted immunity.

**1994** *All Things Considered* (National Pub. Radio) (May 14):
The question raises whether or not the fortuity that he subsequently was elected president is sufficient automatically then to give him a constitutional immunity bath from having to answer in court at all to contest that claim in any way or just to turn it aside.

**2000** *Wall Street Journal* (Aug. 25) 9:
Once Mr. Cheney has availed himself of the same immunity bath, the Democrats would be on treacherous ice.

**inside baseball** *n.* [see article on page 4] the intricate knowledge and actions (of a process, a system, a sport, an organization, etc.) not usually known to the public; (*hence*) technical and uninteresting details.

[**1927** *Decatur Herald* (Ill.) (Jan. 13) 4 [ref. to baseball scandals]:
Inside baseball to fandom means strategy, the matching of wits, the employment of deception, legitimate under the rules. Inside baseball that buys favors, and calls for letting down on somebody's part is not the kind to keep the game in good standing.]

**1927** *New York Times* (Mar. 19) 20 [ref. to political and baseball figures]:
Looking at those on the dais, you may expect to hear some inside baseball, for a Speaker, a Cobb and a Landis are to address you.

**1952** *East Liverpool Rev.* (Ohio) (Dec. 8) 4:
There is a right way to play ball on a team, and the evidence thus far indicates that members of the Eisenhower staff are going to have to learn their "inside baseball" the hard way.

**1954** *New York Times* (Dec. 2) 12:
Why these calls were not brought to the attention of the Select Committee, when that committee was ordered by the Senate to seek out all evidence, is what I should like...to find out....Some inside baseball has been played here.

**1999** *New York Times* (Oct. 4) A22:
The Vice President dismissed the matter as "inside baseball" and said voters were not interested in it.

**2002** Po Bronson *What Should I Do With My Life?* (Dec. 24) 269:
This was the sort of inside baseball D.C. goes nuts over.

**instant policy** *n.* strategies or opinions stated (by an official) with minimal deliberation, consultation, or detail, esp. when done off-the-cuff in a public setting, or in quick response to current events.

**1962** *Wall Street Journal* (May 9) 1:
People want "instant policy." But one of the main ideas of the briefings is to eradicate the idea that foreign policy is easy and simple.

**1978** *Globe and Mail* (Toronto, Can.) (Jan. 16) 1:
He added that he was not sure that the four-dollar minimum should apply equally to someone who has the benefit of tips as for someone who relies solely on his wages. After Mr. Cassidy had spoken, Ian Deans (Wentworth) told the audience of about 60 in a Timmins union hall: There you have it—instant policy.

**1989** J. Sununu in Federal News Service (Dec. 13):
I think that what we are watching happen has been complicated by...the immediacy of television....The images that come forward evoke emotions and a desire for instant response, instant gratification, instant policy.

**1998** *Weekend Edition Sunday* (National Pub. Radio) (Nov. 22):
Officials will tell you they often learn of important developments on CNN before they hear from embassies or from the CIA. Often officials, aware that citizens are seeing what they are seeing, must improvise instant policies.

**invisible primaries** *n.* the campaigning, fund-raising, polling, and negotiating which take place before the party primaries. See UGLY SEASON.

**1988** *Boston Globe* (Mar. 23) 8:
They could be effective in the invisible primaries, conventions, straw polls and caucuses.

**1995** *Boston Herald* (Feb. 20) 1:
There are these invisible primaries, these events that mean nothing but get played up by the candidates to their own advantage. This year it's, "You've got to have $20 million in the tank or you're not a serious presidential candidate." Where is it written that you need that kind of money to run?

*1995 *Australia Fin. Rev.* (Nov. 20) 16:
The Florida poll is the last of the "invisible primaries" before the formal process of nominating the Republican presidential nominee begins in February with the Iowa caucus and the New Hampshire primary.

**2003** *Virginia-Pilot & Ledger Star* (Norfolk) (Nov. 24) E1:
Dean has won what I call the "invisible" primaries, which is to say he's ahead in the polls and leads the other Democrats in raising money.

**Iraqification** *n.* the process of removing American presence and control in Iraq and returning them to Iraqis.

*2003 *Observer* (Apr. 6) 7:
How long will the "Iraqification" of a post-Saddam government take?

**2003** *New York Times* (Oct. 31) 5:
Bush, staring at the campaign hourglass, has ordered that the Iraqification of security be speeded up, so Iraqi cannon fodder can replace American sitting ducks. But Iraqification won't work any better than Vietnamization unless the Bush crowd stops spinning.

**iron triangle** *n.* any three-part combination of industry, media, SPECIAL INTERESTS, and government which acts as a self-reinforcing loop, esp. when involving the defense industry.

**1978** *Evening Capital* (Annapolis, Md.) (May 27) 2:
[Pres. Jimmy] Carter said in the prepared speech that an "iron triangle" of bureaucracy, congressional committees and lobbies can mobilize opposition to needed reform.

**1984** *Omaha World-Herald* (Neb.) (Mar. 2):
The "Iron Triangle," he said, consists of the Pentagon, defense contractors and congressmen whose districts depend on military contractors and subcontractors for jobs.

**1988** *Chicago Sun-Times* (Dec. 20) 27:
President Reagan was blaming the federal budget deficit on an "iron triangle" of Congress, lobbyists and the news media.

**2002** *Dollars & Sense* (Jan. 1) 16:
The "Iron Triangle" forms the U.S. military establishment's decision-making structure and includes its major interest groups. One side of the triangle includes the "civilian" agencies that shape U.S. military policy....A second side includes the military institutions....At the base of the triangle are the 85,000 private firms that profit from the military contracting system.

**issue advocacy** *n.* an attempt to persuade (voters, viewers) on a particular subject without specifically calling for the election or defeat of a candidate. —opp. EXPRESS ADVOCACY.

1987 *Chicago Sun-Times* (Dec. 20) 20:
More basic to the religious groups' cause is the right to get involved in "issue advocacy."

1998 *Gettysburg Times* (Pa.) (May 21) 7:
His win also suggests that issue-advocacy advertising, which promises to be a force in November, can backfire.

2000 *Chronicle-Telegram* (Ohio) (Nov. 5) A8:
The ads run by the chambers of commerce, though highly critical of Resnick, do not call for her defeat or O'Donnell's election. That makes them "issue advocacy" rather than "express advocacy" ads and hence immune from campaign laws requiring groups to disclose their contributors.

2004 *Boston Globe* (Feb. 16):
MoveOn.org now consists of an issue advocacy group, a political action committee, and a Voter Fund for battleground-state advertising in 2004.

**issue positioning** *n.* the act of defining policies or politics (of a campaign, candidate, party, etc.).

1975 M. Jennings & R. Niemi in *Amer. Pol. Sci. Rev.* (Dec.) LXIX 1335:
No single model adequately describes the issue positioning of the two generations over time...The youth cohort remains more liberal after an eight-year interim.

*1983 *Economist* (July 16) 41:
The "gender gap" has now passed into the American political vocabulary to take its place beside "name recognition," "issue positioning," "focus group evaluation" and the other phrases visited upon the language by pollsters, consultants and political scientists.

1988 *Washington Post* (Nov. 5) A1:
To judge by their biographies and their cautious issue positioning, the contest this year is between two candidates from the center of two parties that are both reaching toward the center.

1997 *Campaigns & Elections* XVIII 34:
Gilmore vs. Beyer: how a Republican won the Virginia governorship with a focused message and smart issue positioning.

# J

**jack** *n.* a Jacksonian Democrat. Cf. earlier Brit. pol. sense, "a Jacobite," as in bracketed quot.

[*a1720 D'Urfey in *Pills* I 28:
Ye Jacks of the Town,/And Whiggs of renown.]

1830 in *DA*:
The masons, as the antis say, are clearly unfit for office—the Jacks are just as bad.

**Jane Q. Public** *n.* [modeled on JOHN Q. PUBLIC] the general female public; a woman who is typical of the general public. Also **Jane Q. Citizen**.

1977 *Aviation Week and Space Technology* (May 9) 70:
Those of us who have watched the Apollo or Viking projects financially and technically struggle may have a different perspective on our numerous space accomplishments than does the general public, be they John Q. or Jane Q. Public.

1986 *NDAS*:
*Jane Q Citizen* (or *Public*)... Any woman, esp the average or typical woman.

1995 *New York Times* (June 14) A20:
Mr. Perot has invited all members of United We Stand and also John and Jane Q. Public to this three-day conference.

**jawbone** *adj.* persuasive or cajoling but noncompulsory. Cf. JAWBONE, *v.*

1941 *Wall Street Journal* (Feb. 8) 3:
Price Administrator Henderson admits he is fixing prices by the "jawbone method," that is by talking and bluffing. OPA...price schedules "proclaim" and "direct," but they do not order.

1959 *New York Times* (Feb. 8) IV E3:
A "jawbone" attack on the private forces, which takes the form of an appeal for restraint by business and labor.

**1961** *New York Times* (Oct. 1) 6E:
Some of the President's less reverent aides call this the "jawbone approach" to price stabilization—one that relies on conversation, rather than compulsion.

**1969** *U.S. News & World Report* (Apr. 28) 46:
Q Are you saying the "jawbone" approach is dead for this Administration? A Yes, if you mean trying to preach people into forgoing wage or price changes that market conditions encourage.

**1978:**
(quot. at JAWBONE, V.).

**jawbone** *n.* the practice of persuasion rather than compulsion as a means of accomplishing political goals.—constr. with *the.* Cf. JAWBONE, *v.*

**1969** *Business Week* (Mar. 15) 29:
The Nixon Administration is being driven toward using the jawbone to supplement monetary and fiscal restraints against inflation.

**1979** *Business Week* (Nov. 12) 32:
Volcker's use of the jawbone to keep the prime down has a precedent.

**jawbone** *v.* to admonish or persuade, esp. to urge voluntary compliance upon. Cf. corresponding and slightly earlier JAWBONE, *adj.*

**1965** *New York Times* (Oct. 24) E7:
What is perhaps irreverently known in some circles as Presidential "jawboning"—that is, the attempt on the part of any White House occupant to persuade the citizenry to do, for the good of the country, what the President thinks is right.

**1969** *Time* (Sept. 19) 36:
Since June, Feather has been jawboning his union chiefs on the virtues of labor discipline on the shop floor.

**1969** *U.S. News & World Report* (Dec. 1) 8:
The Administration's most ambitious effort yet to "jawbone" businessmen into supporting its anti-inflation campaign.

**1974** *U.S. News & World Report* (July 22) 87:
All that the Government can do is "jawbone"—attempt to get voluntary co-operation from labor and management in holding down wage settlements.

**1974** *Business Week* (Aug. 10) 8:
The "jawboning" by congressmen of the $850-million Citicorp floating rate note issue is another obvious attempt by the government to intervene and manipulate the free market to the detriment of borrowers, savers, and investors.

**1978** Safire *Pol. Dict.* 346:
*Jawboning.* The use of presidential admonition as a tool of incomes policy. "The jawbone method" was the phrase used by Walter Heller,

chairman of the Council of Economic Advisers in 1962, to describe guidelines set down to restrain prices and wages.

**1979** *New York Times* (June 24) 1:
The Department of Energy has been jawboning oil companies into increasing their production and sales of gasoline.

**1983** *Morning Line* (WKGN radio) (Mar. 23):
Now the President's jawboning the banks about interest rates.

**1983** *Newsweek on Campus* (May) 19:
Some schools have consciously stiffened standards—simply jawboning professors can help.

**1989** *CBS This Morning* (CBS-TV) (Feb. 28):
The President will weigh in with a little old-fashioned jawboning and even some arm-twisting.

**jayhawker** *n.* an ardent or violent Kansas abolitionist during the Free-Soil conflict of 1857–60. Now *hist.*

**1858** in *Coll. Kans. Hist. Soc.* V 559:
Mr. Fosset also stated that two of the "jayhawkers" [abolitionists] stayed all night with him that he was afraid to refuse the "jayhawkers" to stay.

**1858** A.D. Richardson in *Beyond Miss.* 125:
Found all the settlers justifying the "Jayhawkers," a name universally applied to Montgomery's men, from the celerity of their movements and their habit of suddenly pouncing upon an enemy.

**1860** in *DAE*:
By the term "Jayhawkers" is here [Mound City, Kans.] understood the active, fighting abolitionists.

**1861** S.Z. Starr in *Jennison's Jayhawkers* dust-jacket photo of recruiting poster:
Independent Kansas Jay-Hawkers. Volunteers are wanted for the 1st Regiment of Kansas Volunteer Cavalry to serve our country During the War....Aug. 24, 1861.

**1861** in *Ibid.* 38:
I am authorized by the "Southern Kansas Jay-Hawkers" to tender you the thanks of the company, for a beautifully wrought specimen of the American flag.

**1868** Rosa in *Gunfighter* 36:
The term "Jayhawker" was applied by the pro-slavery men to mean "thief" and after it became of general use, they ceased using any other term than "Jayhawkers" to all the Free State people of the territory.

**1915–18** *Coll. Kans. State Hist. Soc.* XIV 203:
In July, 1857 there existed in Linn county an organization known as the "Jayhawkers," brought together for mutual defense against the incursions of parties known as border ruffians of Missouri.

**1940** Gaeddart *Birth of Kansas* 9:
The leaders were active abolitionists who called themselves Vigilantes, but their enemies called them Jayhawkers. They operated in southern Kansas as early as 1857.

**1953** Breihan *Jesse James* 76:
Quantrill's only brother had been murdered by Jayhawkers.

*a***1962** Strother *Underground R.R. in Conn.* 176:
Free Soil "jayhawkers" with Sharps rifles rushed in from Northern states.

**Jim Crow** *adj.* segregationist; (*also*) racially prejudiced against blacks. Now *S.E.*

**1904** *Nation* (Mar. 17) 202:
The "Jim Crow" bills now before the Maryland Legislature.

**1919–21** Chi. Comm. Race Rel. *Negro in Chi.* 63:
They might use it to overthrow "Jim Crow" laws in certain states.

**1943** P. McGuire in *Jim Crow Army* 171:
Plenty of down dixie Boys enforce Jim Crow laws.

**1946** Halsey *Color Blind* 78:
But there are Jim Crow laws in South Carolina and no Jim Crow laws in New York.

**1962** T. Berger *Reinhart* 25:
Everybody who believed that was perforce Jim Crow.

**1975** T. Berger *Sneaky People* 89:
That Buddy's business was Jim Crow was all Clarence knew or cared to know.

**1979** Terkel in *Amer. Dreams* 355:
The army was strictly Jim Crow at the time.

**1992** in *Reader's Digest* (May 1994) 145:
Along the Mississippi in the era of lynchings and Jim Crow laws.

**1989–93** K. Grover *Make a Way* 123:
That was rich, rich people, but they was so Jim Crow.

**1994** Bak *Turkey Stearnes* 105:
Local Jim Crow customs and ordinances.

**Jim Crow** *n.* anti-black racism, esp. in the form of segregationist legislative policies. Now *S.E.*

**1919–21** Chi. Comm. Race Rel. *Negro in Chi.* 302:
There's no lynching or Jim Crow.

**1933** Heyward *Emperor Jones* (film):
There ain't no chain gangs or Jim Crow.

**1940** Zinberg *Walk Hard* 18:
There's places you can forget about jim-crow, but you need money—
real money.

**1944** *New Republic* (Mar. 13) 339:
Jim Crow in the Army.

**1946** *Amer. Sociol. Rev.* XI 713:
To the Negro any joke is particularly humorous if it shows Jim-Crow
"backfiring" on a Southerner.

**1953** Manchester *City of Anger* 109:
Get the delegation talking Jim Crow.

**1957** Rowan *Go South* 3:
The Southland braced for the decisive battle that both whites and non-
whites had termed "Jim Crow's last stand."

**1988** *Channel 2 News at Five* (WCBS-TV) (June 29):
Jim Crow is alive and well in New York.

**1992** *Sonya Live* (CNN-TV) (Sept. 1):
A friend of mine was very active in the anti-Jim Crow movement, before
the '60s.

**Jim-Crow** *v.* Esp. *Black E.* to subject to anti-black discrimination, esp.
by law. Now *hist.*

**1918** *New York Age* (Apr. 27) 1:
Pupils Strike at Musicale When Negroes Are "Jim-Crowed."

**1918** *Scribner's* (Aug.) 176:
They was looked down at an' Jim-Crowed an' teetotally put on the
wrong side of th' fence.

**1919–21** Chi. Comm. Race Rel. *Negro in Chi.* 301:
Few white people realized how uncertain the southern Negro felt about
making use of his new privilege of sitting anywhere in the car, instead
of being "Jim Crowed."

**1922** W. White *Fire in the Flint* 116:
No wonder the South lynched, disfranchised, Jim-Crowed the Negro.

**1925** Van Vechten *Nigger Heaven* 45:
Why, in one or two places, they've actually tried to do a little jim-
crowing!

**1928** Bradford *Ol' Man Adam* 68:
Can't you Jim Crow 'em?

**1929** T. Gordon *Born to Be* 182:
Would you believe it, there are places right here in beloved Harlem, run
by white men, where negroes can't go unless they are jimcrowed?

**1940** Zinberg *Walk Hard* 187:
There isn't a colored man in the country that doesn't know he's been
jim-crowed.

**1945** A.C. Powell *Marching Blacks* 4:
They could not fly in the air corps or fight in the marine corps and were Jim-Crowed in the army.

**1945** P. McGuire in *Jim Crow Army* 179:
Negroes have been jim-crowed at this theater ever since I came here in 1942.

**1956** Childress *Like One of Family* 46:
Folks hatin' and Jim Crowin'.

**1966** *New Yorker* (Sept. 3) 82:
Negroes could be described, in the words of the late Kelly Miller, as "anybody who'd be Jim-Crowed in Virginia."

**1971** N.Y.U. professor:
When I heard that, I knew I'd been Jim-Crowed again!

**1978** A. Rose *Eubie Blake* 66:
They used to Jim Crow the [phonograph] records in those days. They called 'em race records.

*a*1973–87 F.M. Davis *Livin' the Blues* 5:
Negroes [in Kansas] were not jim crowed on transportation.

**1989–93** K. Grover *Make a Way* 123:
We was Jim Crowed a lot.

**1996** *Harper's* (Apr.) 56:
We were perceived as a separate people—enslaved, Jim Crowed, and segregated.

## Joe Citizen *n.* a man who is a typical U.S. citizen.

**1932** *Appleton Post-Crescent* (Wisc.) (Mar. 26) 6:
No matter WHO gets socked on that tax, you know who pays it ultimately...Mister Joe Citizen, the kind of gent most of us are.

**1938** *Lima News* (Ohio) (Apr. 4) 4:
Mr. Smith from Middletown has become well known as the typical Joe Citizen in "Middletown," and "Middletown in Transition," published studies of the "typical midwestern city."

[**1973** *Chopper* (Jan.) 60:
You can't fight the man, City Hall, and Johnny Joe Citizen.]

**1986** *Campus Voice* (Sept.) 62:
Most police officers go through more adrenalin pumps in a shift than Joe Citizen does in a lifetime.

*a*1990 in C. Fletcher *What Cops Know* 23:
And every Joe Citizen in the world has to flash their lights at you and tell you your lights are off.

**1990** Ruggero *38 N. Yankee* 276:
Start pulling Joe Citizen out of the workplace and America would sit up and take notice.

**John-Brown** *adj.& adv. So.* damned.

> **1954** Killens *Youngblood* 160:
> He seems to be a John-Brown good teacher.

> **1987** Stage magician, Knoxville, Tenn. , age *ca*65:
> I still can't work the john-browned thing.

**John-Brown** *v.* [ref. to the hanging of John Brown, U.S. abolitionist (1800–59)] Esp. *So.* to execute by hanging (now *hist.*); in phr. **be John-Browned** to be "hanged" or damned.

> **1869** *Overland Mo.* (Aug.) 130:
> You need apprehend nothing dreadful, for boobies seldom "John Brown" each other.

> **1870** *Overland Mo.* (May) 477:
> No White Man as respects hisself is ever gwine to do it. He'll be John-Browned fust.

> **1905** *DN* III 84:
> I'll be John(ny) Browned.

> **1924** Clarke in *Amer. Negro Stories* 27:
> I'll be john-browned if there's a monkey-chaser in Harlem can gyp him if I know it.

> **1928** R. Fisher *Jericho* 230:
> Well, I'll be john-browned.

> *ca***1965** IUFA *Folk Speech* [111]:
> I'll be John Brown if I'll do it.

> **1966, 1975, 1978** in *DARE*:
> [all for John Browned "damned"].

**Johnny Congress** *n.* the U.S. Congress.

> **1816** *Ohio Repository* (Sept. 19) 1:
> What roaring cheer/Was spent by Johnny Congress O!

> **1827** in *DA*:
> In the rural, but significant speech of the swains, this body is called Johnny congress.

> **1835** *Gettysburg Republican Compiler* (Pa.) (Jan. 6) 4:
> Johnny Congress has been busily engaged for some time past in raising the pay of Naval officers.

**John Q. Public** *n.* the general public; a man who is typical of the general public. Also **John Q. Citizen, John Q.** Cf. JANE Q. PUBLIC. Now *colloq.*

> **1922** *New York Evening Mail* (Aug. 10) 12:
> John Q. Public Tells Views On The Giants.

> **1930** *Washington Post* (Jan. 2) 1:
> It was 12:30 o'clock before the President could take time out to grab a

sandwich and a cup of coffee and be back on the line to start greeting Mr. and Mrs. John Q. Public promptly at 1 o'clock.

**1937** *N & Q* (Mar. 6) 177:
John Q. Public.

**1937** in *New York Times Mag.* (Dec. 19, 1982) 19:
We are all the children of John Q. Public.

**1939** "E. Queen" *Dragon's Teeth* 22:
Look at it this way, Master-Mind, because this is the way it's going to be looked at by John Q. Public.

**1941** *Pittsburgh Courier* (Nov. 1) 7:
Presently Old John Q. gets his number.

**1947** in *DA*:
Plain John Q. Citizens.

**1960** *Twilight Zone* (CBS-TV):
You're John Q. Citizen. You're Tom, Dick and Harry.

**1970** R. Vasquez *Chicano* 290:
No one ever before brought items of culture to the front door of Mr. and Mrs. John Q.

**1973** Schiano & Burton *Solo* 120:
You protect yourself as well as John Q. Citizen.

**1973–76** J. Allen *Assault* 105:
Say John Q, Average American, played OOO every day.

**1977** Butler & Shryack *Gauntlet* 12:
The average John Q Public. What the hell could you talk to a John Q about?

**1980** Brands Mart ad (WINS radio) (Aug. 30):
And we're open to the public. That means you, John Q.

**1984** "W.T. Tyler" *Shadow Cabinet* 184:
So I'm trying to live up to the John Q. Public image.

**1994** Ft. Worth, Tex., policeman, on *Cops* (Fox-TV):
The hell with John Q. If they're gonna fight with the police I don't care if they're a man or a woman.

**1995** *New Yorker* (May 15) 33:
At the expense of Mr. and Mrs. John Q. Public.

**juice** *n.* personal or political power or influence, often of a corrupt nature.

**1935** Pollock *Und. Speaks*:
*Juice*, corrupt influence (shake-down) for protection to operate unlawfully.

**1957** Fenton & Haines *Wings of Eagles* (film):
"How'd you do it?" "Same as you. Drag. Pull. Juice."

**1961** L. Bruce in *Essential L. Bruce* 77:
Cause it's juice, man. That's it. The only rights you got are knowing the right guy.

**1963** Breen *PT 109* (film):
You got the juice in Washington...Juice, muscle, glycerine. Don't they teach you any practical talk at Harvard?

**1963** Braly *Shake Him* 144:
Dino must be out of his gourd unless he's got giant juice.

**1966** Elli *Riot* 211:
He had some juice. His uncle owns one of the biggest hotels in this state.

**1966** *New York Times* (Dec. 4) II 13:
The important thing now is I got juice as an actor.

**1972** *Banyon* (NBC-TV):
I got enough juice in this town to shock you right out of business.

**1974** *Police Story* (NBC-TV):
You got juice.

**1977** Bunker *Animal Factory* 184:
I've got long juice with this dude.

**1978** *New York Times Mag.* (July 23) 23:
Clout has been replaced by juice, and the System is now the process.

**1978** Nolan & Mann *Jericho Mile* (film):
Now I know yo' man's got the juice.

**1984** J. McNamara *First Directive* 5:
No-balls Foley, in the face of that kind of political juice, had quickly put three homocide dicks on the case.

**1984** S. Hager *Hip Hop* 13:
The toughest guy...had the juice to do what he wanted.

**juice bill** *n.* (see 1988 quot.).

**1985** *Los Angeles Times* (July 5) 1:
Let's face it; it's a real juice bill. Big bucks are at stake.

**1986** *Newsday* (Dec. 15) 1:
In California, we have a term, "juice bill." You can use it to juice political contributions out of the parties involved.

**1988** Safire, in *New York Times Mag.* (Feb. 7) 13:
A legislative bill that causes lobbyists to loosen the purse strings is known as a juice bill—"so named for the hundreds of thousands of dollars that could be squeezed from it."

**2003** *Sacramento Bee* (Calif.) (July 18):
This is the juice bill of the year, the most blatant cash-for-influence legislation.

**jump Jim Crow** *v.* [alluding to the chorus of T.D. Rice's minstrel song, which describes a dance step introduced in Rice's performance: "Ebery time I wheel about I jump Jim Crow"] to do a dexterous turnabout in one's principles.

*ca*1832 T.D.Rice *Original Jim Crow* (song) in Lhamon *Jump Jim Crow* (2003) 98:
You'd gain popularity / By jumping Jim Crow.

**1836** in *OED*:
A Mr. Collier of Virginia has "jumped Jim Crow."

**1840** in *DA*:
Fo he's the man to jump Jim Crow,/And prove that black is white.

**1842** in *DA*:
The Kentucky delegation jump Jim Crow to perfection. They found the people would not sustain them in their former course.

**1844** in *DA*:
If they were honest in going for Harrison and a Bank in 1840, then never did any set of politicians jump Jim Crow more expeditiously.

**jungle primary** *n.* a form of primary election in which any voter may vote for any candidate, regardless of either's party affiliation. Cf. BULLET VOTE.

**1986** *Congress. Quarterly Wkly Rpt.* (Sept. 20) XLIV:
Adams won virtually the same number of primary votes as Gorton—a significant achievement under Washington's unique "jungle primary" system, which is regarded as a dry run of the general election.

**1996** *Boston Globe* (Sept. 29) A18:
Under the "jungle primary" system in Washington, where voters are free to support candidates from either party and the top Democrat and leading Republican win their party's nomination.

**2002** *Arkansas Democrat-Gazette* (Little Rock) (Nov. 22) 24:
The jungle primary. Throw everybody into the mix, including Republicans. Result: two Democrats usually found themselves in the runoff.

**junkyard dog** *n.* [sugg. by cliché *meaner than a junkyard dog*] a person in a position of authority who is notably vigorous about investigating graft.

[**1981** *Washington Post* (Jan. 22) A5:
We want people that are meaner than a junkyard dog in ferreting out waste, fraud and mismanagement.]

**1983** *U.S. News & World Report* (July 25) 50:
Leading the charge are the inspectors general—or "junkyard dogs," as the White House has labelled them—that he appointed early in his term to ferret out waste.

[**1989** *New York Times* (July 30) Week in Rev. 22:
Nothing would be more in the Administration's interest than to pursue the political abuses in H.U.D. like a junkyard dog.]

**1990** *Washington Post* (May 22) A23:
A self-described "junkyard dog," Robinson as the controversial sheriff showed an uncanny talent for gaining media attention.

**1992** *Washington Post* (June 3) 7:
Kusserow is a "shake-the-boat, junkyard-dog kind of IG [Inspector General]. He knows where to look."

**1993** *Washington Post* (Jan. 2) A19:
Portions of that transcript had been read into the Congressional Record by that junkyard dog, Rep. Robert K. Dornan (R-Cal.).

# K

**kangaroo** *n.* (among itinerants) KANGAROO COURT.—also used attrib.

**1902** "J. Flynt" *Little Bro.* 124:
Both he and Blackie were summoned by one of the prisoners to appear before the "Kangaroo."...It don't pay, pris'ners, to buck against the Kang'roo.

*Ibid.* 128:
An' the Kang'roo is adjourned.

**1935** Algren *Boots* 168:
This is about all what's left o' my kangaroo money.

**kangaroo** *v.* Orig. *Pris.* to convict by means of a prisoners' KANGAROO COURT; (*hence*) to convict unjustly in an actual court.

**1907** *Reader* (Sept.) 344:
The bunch used to kangaroo me something fierce and make me boil myself and my clothes about nine times a week.

*a*\1909 Tillotson *Detective* 92:
Kangarooed—Given a false trial.

**1912** *Hampton's Mag.* (Jan.) 848:
No guy was ever kangarooed like Portsmouth Fat in that Los Angeles stir.

**1921** U. Sinclair *K. Coal* 210:
His circulars had been confiscated, his posters torn down, his supporters "kangarooed."

**1923** Kornbluh in *Rebel Voices* 91:
Kangarooed again, by God!

**1934** Kromer *Waiting* 28:
[The judge] is kangarooing them. They haven't got a chance.

**1935** Algren *Boots* 145:
I guess I must of kangarooed twelve Mexes in that jailhouse.

**1935** Pollock *Und. Speaks*:
Kangarooed, sentenced to prison when innocent.

**1983** Goldman & Fuller *Charlie Co.* 312:
"They kangarooed me"—found him guilty and sentenced him to six months' hard time in the stockade.

**kangaroo court** *n.* [the orig. allusion, presumably to Australia, is now obscure; cf. 1862 quot., perh. sugg. that the kangaroo's appearance seems to defy laws of nature] an unauthorized or irregularly conducted court; (in 1853 quot.) such a court created on the frontier before the establishment of territorial law; (*also*) *Pris.* a mock court set up by prisoners to initiate and extort money from new inmates; (now usu.) a flagrantly unfair court or similar proceeding. Now *colloq.* or *S.E.*

**1853** "P. Paxton" *In Texas* 205:
Judge G. was elected to the bench, and the "Mestang" or "Kangaroo Court" regularly organized.

[**1862** A.P. Hudson in *Humor of Old So.* 376:
As in the case of the Kangaroo, the law was altogether inoperative against this dangerous class of man.]

**1890** in *DAE*:
Organizing "kangaroo courts" for the slightest offense, were some of their daily amusements.

**1895** "J. Flynt" , in *Harper's Mag.* (Apr.) 718:
The "Kangaroo Court" is found almost entirely in county jails. The "Kangaroo Court" consists of all the prisoners.

**1902** "J. Flynt" *Little Bro.* 124:
There were thirty inmates all told, and one notified the fresh arrivals that they were in the presence of the local "Kang'roo Court," and that they were under indictment of having money in their pockets.

**1917–20** J.M. Hunter in *Trail Drivers* I 68:
We organized a kangaroo court and tried the engineer for disturbing the peace of passengers.

**1930** Irwin *Tramp & Und. Slang* 115:
*Kangaroo Court*....the prisoners waiting for trial...try each newly received prisoner on a charge of "breaking into jail."

**1951** C. Palmer *Sellout* (film):
A prisoners' court. Kangaroo court....Some new fish for you, Little Jake.

**1981** Gilliland *Rosinante* 162:
This is a kangaroo court and I will file an immediate appeal.

**1982** L'Amour *Shadow Riders* 3:
They're fixin' to hang him. Kangaroo court.

**kangaroo ticket** *n.* a political ticket, as for the offices of president and vice president, where the principal candidate is less appealing to voters than the running mate.

**1848** *Zanesville Courier* (Ohio) (June 21) 2:
We may say of this ticket, thus formed, as some one said in 1844, when the Baltimore Convention nominated Silas Wright as Vice President with James K. Polk, that it is "a kangaroo ticket, with all its strength in its hind legs."

**1856** J.P. Hambleton *Sketch of Henry Wise* 162:
Some Antecedents of the Kangaroo Ticket.

[**1862** W.G. Brownlow *Sketches of Secession* 411:
In 1860, I was for Bell and Everett, and I am for the hind-legs of this kangaroo yet. A better or a more nobly disinterested man than Everett never lived.]

**1971** *New York Times* (Oct. 23), in Safire Pol. Dict. (1978 ed.):
[John Connally would run for vice president if asked by President Nixon, but] he would insist that the Nixon-Connally partnership be advertised as a "kangaroo ticket."

**1977** Coover *Public Burning* 384:
It was virtually a kangaroo ticket after that, old war hero at the top or no.

**1980** Safire in *Good Word* 138:
A couple of kangaroo tickets will lead to a big clothespin vote.

**1984** *New York Post* (Sept. 3) 11:
"It's a kangaroo ticket," sighed one disappointed Texas politician after FDR's nomination [in 1932]. "Stronger in the hindquarters than in the front."

**kidnapping** *n.* a GERRYMANDER which places a legislator's residence outside the district to which he was elected; (hence) a reapportionment which pits two incumbents of the same party against each other. Cf. GERRYMANDER, n., CRACKING, PACKING.

**2003** *New Yorker* (Dec. 1):
Kidnapping places two incumbents from the same party in the same district.

**2004** *Atlantic Monthly* (Jan–Feb.) 50:
The oddly shaped Twelfth District in Pennsylvania...is a good example of "kidnapping"—in effect, moving an incumbent's established constituency out from under him or her.

**kingfish** *n.* a powerful political organizer or boss. [Now familiar as the nickname of Huey P. Long (1893–1935), governor of Louisiana.]

**1926** Finerty *Crim.* 33:
*Kingfish*—an organizer or backer.

**1933** H.P. Long *Every Man* 277:
We from time to time termed various of our political enemies the "Kingfish," most prominent of which was a certain corporation lawyer.

**1982** Braun *Judas Tree* 135:
He's no kingfish or power behind the throne.

**1993** Spot promo *(AMC-TV):*
There he was—the big cheese, the kingfish, the top dog.

**kite** *n.* ¶In phrase:

¶**kite to keep the henyard in order** early name for Constitution.

**1787** S. Schmucker *Life of Thomas Jefferson* (1857) 155:
Our Convention has been too much impressed by the insurrection of Massachusetts; and on the spur of the moment, they are setting up a kite to keep the henyard in order.

**1926** *AS* II (Dec.) 138:
Speaking of the Eighteenth Amendment or any other amendment brings to mind early nicknames for the Constitution,—"New Roof," "New Breeches," "Gilded Trap," "Triple-Headed Monster," and Jefferson's phrase, "A Kite to Keep the Henyard in Order."

**knife** *v.* to strike at treacherously; betray. Now *colloq.*

**1888** in *DA*:
The strongest men in the party cannot be nominated, because they are hateful to the Blaine faction, and are certain to be knifed in the Convention in case Blaine does not get the nomination.

**1889** in *Century Dict.*:
*Knife*...To endeavor to defeat in a secret or underhand way in an election, as a candidate of one's own party. (Political slang, U.S.).

**1891** Maitland *Slang Dict.* 161:
*Knife* (Am.), to knife a person is to do him harm, to stab him in character, if not in person.

**1911** Harrison *Queed* 323:
What chance'd there be of namin' to lead the party in the city the man who had knifed the party in the State?

**1918** E.E. Rose *Cappy Ricks* 70:
Why, that old rascal would knife his mother in a business deal!

**1922** Hemingway in *Sel. Letters* 64:
Its [*sic*] hell when a male knifes you—especially when you still love him.

**1927–28** R. Nelson in *Dishonorable* 157:
If I don't put this over with you, they'll knife me, next election.

**1929** McEvoy *Hollywood Girl* 79:
Test turned out swell but that Chiquita knifed me.

**1932** Farrell *Guillotine Party* 187:
This fraternity cannot afford to have members who knife their...fraternity brothers.

**1948** in *DA*

**1964** D. Berg *Looks at U.S.A.* (unp.):
I wonder how many guys he knifed in order to get that job?

**Kool-Aid** *v.* ¶In phrase:

¶**drink the Kool-Aid** [from the 1978 Jonestown, Guyana, massacre, in which 913 cult members committed suicide by taking a poisoned-laced drink] to commit to or to agree with (a person, a course of action, a party platform, etc.).

[**1985** *Washington Post* (Sept. 23):
What he didn't want, Foley was telling Joyce Aboussie, Gephardt's campaign manager, was "what I call the politics of Jim Jones, you know, that let's drink the Kool-Aid kind of downer."]

**1986** *San Francisco Chronicle* (Dec. 10) 35:
Most of them are also put off by a new program called Krone that will turn the worker bees into Krone-clones who have to be "choiceful" to create a "potentiated" organization. Don't drink the Kool-Aid.

**1993** *Columbia Journal Rev.* (May 1) XXXII 27:
If Pete Hamill said, "Drink the Kool-Aid," I'd drink the Kool-Aid. He's the only thing right now that's holding this paper together.

**2000** *New York Times Bk. Rev.* (July 30) 16:
Giuliani...fatally flawed, a man...whose effectiveness is undermined by ruthlessness and a compulsive need to hog the spotlight. You drink the Kool-Aid when Rudy tells you to.

**2004** *Oregonian* (Feb. 19):
When Dean's candidacy began to falter, she became embroiled in more than one online argument with supporters she thought were too quick "to drink the Kool-Aid" and buy the campaign's assurances that it knew how to get things back on track.

**labor faker** *n.* a political agitator among workers.

> **1915** *Puck* (Feb. 13) 18:
> I call on all those who believe in justice and brotherhood to leave this crowd of bunk labor fakers, fake revolutionists, opportunists, and cockroach capitalists, and come out into the open air.

> **1938** Steinbeck *Grapes of Wrath* 209:
> You sure you ain't one of these here troublemakers? You sure you ain't a labor faker?

> **1938–39** Dos Passos *Young Man* 257:
> No, Mr. Connolly wasn't a crook or a social-fascist labor faker any more, he was a noble progressive fellow traveller.

> **1946** *Amer. Mercury* (Apr.) 462:
> Learn the truth about the labor fakers, get into the One Big Union.

**lame duck** *n.* an elected official or legislative body whose term of office is nearing an end, esp. a legislator still in office after losing an election or a U.S. president not running for reelection. —often used *attrib.* Now *S.E.*

> **1910** in *DAE*:
> The Congress which assembled Monday for its last session is full of what they call "lame ducks," or representatives who failed of re-election and senators who will fail when the legislatures meet.

> **1922** *New York Times* (Dec. 6) 18:
> Senator Norris is all for the plan "to have the convening of Congress moved up to avoid lame-duck Congresses."

> **1924** in *DAE*:
> A "lame duck" Congress is not likely to be very competent.

> **1934** Weseen *Dict. Slang* 361:
> Lame duck—A politician in office who has been defeated for re-election.

**1948** *Amer. College Dict.*:
Lame duck...a Congressman who has failed of re-election and is serving at the last session of his term.

**1975** Boatner et al. *Dict. Amer. Idioms* 195:
In the last year of their second terms, American presidents are lame ducks.

**1982** Flexner *Listening to Amer.* 539:
In 1932 the Lame Duck Amendment, the Twentieth Amendment to the Constitution, was passed, calling for Congress and each new Presidential administration to take office in January instead of March and eliminating the lame duck session of Congress.

**1989** S. Robinson & D. Ritz *Smokey* 183:
I knew what it meant to be a lame-duck President.

**1994** Univ. Tenn. professor, age 50:
You know [a senator serving the remainder of another's term but not running for reelection] is a lame duck.

**1994** *World Today* (CNN-TV) (Nov. 29):
The first lame-duck session of Congress since 1982. The last hurrah for the lame ducks on Capitol Hill.

**lay pipe** *v.* to engage in any of various forms of political intrigue.

**1848** Bartlett in *Amer.* 251:
The result of the Pennsylvania election would be in the least doubtful, if we could be sure of fair play and no *pipe-laying.*

**1848** *Ibid.*:
To lay pipe means to bring up voters not legally qualified....The term...arose from an accusation brought against the Whig party of...New York...some years ago, of a gigantic scheme to bring on voters from Philadelphia....As if for the purpose of concealment,...the number of men hired to visit New York and vote, being spoken of as so many yards of pipe—the work of laying down pipe for the Croton water being at that time in full activity....The accused were acquitted. The term "*pipe-laying,*" however, was at once adopted as a synonym for negotiations to procure fraudulent votes.

**1856** Bartlett in *Amer.* (ed. 2) 323:
There is a magnificent scheme of pipe-laying and log-rolling going on in Pennsylvania.

**1862** in *DAE*:
To charge him, in the technical language of his party, with "pulling wires," and "laying pipes" for the Presidency.

**1877** Bartlett *Amer.* (ed. 4) 468:
Pipe-Layer A [?political] trickster.—*N.Y. Tribune.*

**1888** in *F & H* IV 212:
There are not a few who are pipe-laying and martialling forces for the fray.

**1891** Maitland *Slang Dict.* 165:
*Laying pipe*, making arrangements to ensure the passage or defeat of some measure before a legislative body.

**1893** in *DA*:
The Irish...who began by laying our water-pipes...now lay a different kind of pipe, and make our city government.

*a*1890–96 *F & H* IV 212:
*Pipe-layer*...(American).—A political intriguer.

**1942** *ATS* 794:
*Pipelaying*, political intriguing, securing illegal votes.

**leak** *n.* a disclosure of secret, esp. official, information; (*also*) the source of such a disclosure. Now *S.E.*

[**1933** Ersine *Prison Slang* 76:
The cops took him into the bullring and he turned on the leaks.]

**1939** Brookhouser in *Our Years* 456:
The presence of two New York police cruisers startled Hoover as well as Lepke. The G-man later admitted he feared "a leak."

**1949** *New York Times* (Sept. 26) 3:
So vital a bit of information should not be the subject of a "leak" but should be released with solemnity.

**1954–60** *DAS*:
*Leak*...The person who "Leaks" news or secret information.

**1960** *Time* (Feb. 15) 46:
Because of his partisanship he was fed the first official "leaks."

**1964** *Atlantic Monthly* (June) 8:
Minor leaks to the press about his plans infuriate him.

**1974** *New York Times* (June 29) 13:
"The leak is the safety valve of democracy," and without it the country would get only Government-controlled news.

*Ibid.*:
By Washington's definition, a leak is an unauthorized disclosure of confidential official information, usually by an unidentified "source."

**leak** *v.* to divulge (a secret); —also used intrans. Now *S.E.*

**1859** Matsell *Vocab.* 50:
*Leak.* To impart a secret.

**1933** Ersine *Prison Slang* 50:
*Leak*, v. To squeal, rat.

**1949** *New Yorker* (Nov. 5) 64:
Johnson, however, who likes to talk, leaked his news to the press before Calder had decided whether to take the job or not.

**1952** *Sat. Eve. Post* (Mar. 22) 37:
The congressmen had leaked news of the executive session to the press.

**1958** *Time* (July 14) 38:
Colonel John Nickerson, court-martialed for leaking Army rocket secrets to newsmen.

**1960–61** Steinbeck *Discontent* 224:
You won't leak, Ethan?

**1966** *Harper's* (Mar.) 42:
In the totalitarian countries, of course, there is no "leaking" of information at all, except on pain of death.

**1974** *New York Times* (June 29) 13:
Isn't it illegal to leak official information or accept it?

**1975** V.B. Miller *Deadly Game* 11:
I don't like to worry about how they'll be leaked off.

**1982** *U.S. News & World Report* (Dec. 20) 38:
It isn't that difficult to find out who's leaking. When you see some really sensitive stuff oozing out, fire somebody.

**lefty** *n.* a leftist. Also as **adj.**

**1935** C. Odets *Waiting for Lefty* [title of play].

*1937 Partridge in *Concise Dict. Sl.* 261:
Counterblast to Lefties.

**1948** *Sat. Eve. Post*, in DAS:
Truman's Central Error: Fear of Libero-Lefties.

**1977** Coover *Public Burning* 416:
Our decision to burn them two lefties.

**1977** Sayles *Union Dues* 75:
So it was some lefty hotshot from Rolling Stone.

**1978** Hamill *Dirty Laundry* 35:
The Communists were in the hills, the government was full of Lefties.

**1979** Terkel in *Amer. Dreams* 233:
I know Seeger's a leftie, but I like his music.

**1983** *Newsweek* (Feb. 28) 50:
They're a bunch of lefties, aren't they?

*1984 T. Jones *Heart of Oak* 160:
All the Lefties on board were in a state of high excitement.

**1992** *Crier & Co.* (CNN-TV) (Sept. 30):
That's a typical lefty response.

**1994** *New Yorker* (Sept. 5) 110:
An unreconstructed lefty.

**1996** *New Yorker* (May 13) 38:
A brilliant Strangelovian "modest proposal" hatched by a bunch of New York lefties.

**leg treasurer** *n.* one who flees with stolen government funds. Cf. SWARTWOUT.

**1839** *Ohio Repository* (Canton) (Aug. 29) 2:
Another Leg Treasurer. Owen Hamlin, entrusted by Mr. Dixon, Rail Road Commissioner, with a check for $11,600 on the State bank of Illinois, collected the money and Swartwouted.

**1840** *Huron Reflector* (Norwalk, Ohio) (Apr. 28) 2:
Another Leg-Treasurer Off! Mr. James, Van Buren Federal Treasurer, of Logan, absquatulated, leaving the county of Hocking minus six or eight thousand dollars.

**1848** *Zanesville Courier* (Ohio) (Jan. 17) 2:
More Leg-Treasurers.—It was rumored in Washington, on Saturday week, that a Clerk in the Treasury had absquatulated with $25,000 and another in the Post Office had swartwouted with $50,000. These are the beauties of the Sub-Treasury!

**1934** *Newark Advocate* (Ohio) (May 25) 4:
Then comes the announcement under the head of "Another Leg Treasurer Off," telling about a Kentucky postmaster who stole all the money in his office and then "Swartwouted."

**lib** *n.* **1.** LIBBER. [As an abbr. of *liberation (movement)*, this term has always been *colloq.*]

***1973** in *OED*:
Lillian Thomas is a member of the Suffrage Fellowship Movement and is delighted with the Libs.

**1981** Jenkins *Baja Okla.* 127:
Libs ran in clusters, like motorcycle gangs.

**2.** a political liberal.

**1981** Ehrlichman *Witness* 102 [ref. to 1969]:
President Nixon was under great political pressure to nominate a "lib."

**1987** *New York Daily News* (July 2) 5:
Libs hone their hatchets.

**libber** *n.* a supporter of the women's liberation movement; feminist. [The form *women's libber* has always been colloq.]

**1972** *Village Voice* (N.Y.C.) (June 1) 26 in *OED*:
Now the star-maker has decided to calm the libbers with another token.

**1972** Eble *Campus Slang* (Oct.) 4:
*Libber*—one who believes in women's liberation.

*a***1976** Roebuck & Frese *Rendezvous* 178:
These screwy women libbers. If they lived in my world they wouldn't want to be libbers.

**1978** S. King *Stand* 549:
She got to be an even bigger libber than the roomie.

**1978** Pici *Tennis Hustler* 83:
And that's nothing to be ashamed of—even for a libber.

**1981** Sann *Trial* 26:
The libbers are very strong for pants suits.

**1981** Thom in *Letters to Ms.* 175:
What is your wife, one of those libbers?

**1986** R. Walker *AF Wives* 434:
Don't get one of those libber types.

**1991** J. Lamar *Bourgeois Blues* 76:
Let her be a libber!

**libby** *n.* LIBBER.

**1974** Millard *Thunderbolt* 87:
You damn freak. I only wanted to make love to you like a gentleman. So what the hell are you, sister, a goddam libby?

**lily-white** *adj.* bigoted against black persons; segregated racially.

**1903** *N.Y. Times*, in *OED*:
The report that the President was seeking reconciliation with the "lilywhite" faction, which eliminated the negro from the last State Convention.

**1932** in *DA*:
The "lily white" movement in the Southern Republican party was another indication of the South's opposition to Negro suffrage.

**1943** Ottley *New World* 115 [ref. to 1933]:
A store that did not employ Negro help in any capacity was labeled "lily-white."

**1950** *New York Times* (Oct. 15) I 51:
Labor unions are doing away with "lily-white policies."

**1952** *Mt. Pleasant News* (Iowa) (June 3) 6:
Officially, the party organization, known as the "lily-whites" because it is comprised predominantly of white people, voted to send a five-man delegation to the national convention at Chicago uninstructed.

**1956–60** J.A. Williams *Angry Ones* ch. xx:
What is it you can't accept, Lois—that Negroes can think and feel and want revenge? Is that what your lily-white mind tells you?

**1964** R. Kendall *Black School* 140:
The Muslims are gonna have the lily-whites pickin' up their garbage!

**1971** *Ramparts* (Nov.) 54:
The Zephyr, a straight, lily-white restaurant.

**1982** *Los Angeles Times* (Sept. 3) I 3:
More blacks are moving into formerly lily-white arenas.

**limousine liberal** *n.* a wealthy liberal. Also **limo liberal**.

**1969** *New York Times* (Aug. 18) 37:
Lindsay seen candidate of "limousine liberals."

**1969** *Progess* (Curwensville, Pa.) (Nov. 3) 8:
Lindsay, however, has put together a polished and expensive campaign that appears to have overcome Procaccino's law-and-order strategy and his attacks on the mayor as a "Limousine Liberal" who plunged the city into its worst racial crisis.

**1970** *Burlington Times-News* (N.C) (June 2) 5B:
The candidate received applause when he referred to his Democratic opponent, L. Richardson Preyer, as a "limousine liberal" who calls the communist conspirators "misguided idealists."

**1970** *New York Times* (Oct. 26) 36:
Canada is most fortunate to have a Premier who is willing to tell the bleeding hearts and limousine liberals what he thinks of them.

**1986** *Chicago Sun-Times* (Feb. 16) 20:
Ranney squirms at "limo liberal" tag.

**2003** *Edmonton Journal* (Can.) (Aug. 22) E13:
It's the myth of the limo liberal vs. the Ford Taurus conservative. All liberals are out of touch and wealthy. That myth has been a useful tool for the right.

**Lincoln** *adj. Civil War.* of or from the federal government.—often in jocular nonce coinages. Now *hist.*

**1864** A.W. Petty in *3d Mo. Cav.* 55:
We were anxious to get some Lincoln coffee, as were getting very tired of our substitute.

**1864** Wightman in *To Ft. Fisher* 220:
We had some codfish, which the boys called "Lincoln trout," and a few rations of dried herring, which they have christened "Lincoln's sardines."

**1862–65** C. Barney *20th Ia.* 64:
The lady informed us that "Lincoln money" would not be received.

**1866** Shanks *Personal Recollections* 272:
He did, however, give Sherman his rations—of the plainest materials he could gather—"Lincoln platform" (hard bread) and rye coffee.

**1867** in *DA*:
Nectar in the likeness of Lincoln coffee—no bad substitute either to hungry and toil-worn soldiers.

**1885** Cannon *Where Men Only* 171:
"Lincoln coffee" and "Jeff. Davis coffee" [were] names for the real article or a substitute [in E. Tenn.].

**lip** *n.* ¶In phrases:

¶**read** [or **watch**] **my lips** listen closely to my words; (*hence*) I assure you I speak the truth. [Popularized as a political slogan by George H. W. Bush in the 1988 presidential campaign.]

**1984** *Night Court* (NBC-TV):
Read my lips, Dan. Does the State object to a fine and time served?

**1985** *Miami Vice* (NBC-TV):
Read my lips, Richard—nobody's buying!

**1985–87** Bogosian *Talk Radio* 34:
Am I speaking English? Read my lips.

**1987** "J. Hawkins" *Tunnel Warriors* 144:
Hey! Read my lips, dildo nose.

**1988** *Evans & Novak* (CNN-TV) (Jan. 24):
Daniel Ortega and his people promised those very same things nine years ago—watch my lips—nine years ago.

**1988** TV ad for Eggo NutriGrain waffles:
It's—read my lips—nutritious!

**1988** G.H.W. Bush (acceptance speech, Republican National Convention) (Aug. 18):
The Congress will push me to raise taxes and I'll say no, and they'll push and I'll say no, and they'll push again. And all I can say to them is, "Read my lips. No new taxes."

**1988–89** Safire in *Quoth Maven* [ref. to 1978]:
I would say to him, "We got it that time," and he would say, "Read my lips—we didn't." That phrase arrested me.

*Ibid.* 243:
In my high school days in the late 60's we would mouth [an expected] obscene answer after calling for the questioner to "read my lips."

**1989** P. Benchley *Rummies* 171:
Hey! Read my fucking lips.

¶**shoot from the lip** [sugg. by equivalent fig. usage of S.E. *shoot from the hip*] to make incautious remarks. *Joc.*

**1952** *Lethbridge Herald* (Alberta, Can.) (Feb. 11) 3:
I have a matchless draw, and I shoot from the lip, but perhaps this parable will illustrate just why I practise verbal restraint.

1961 *New York Times Mag.* (Sept. 17) 16:
The politician's quarry is not a dumb animal: it is always another politician. And his method, as Raymond Moley once explained it, is to "shoot from the lip."

1978 *Globe and Mail* (Toronto, Can.) (Nov. 9) P8:
George Ben always shoots from the lip, she said. That's why we call him the Bionic Mouth.

1995 *TV Guide* (Nov. 18) 5:
Shooting from the Lip.

1996 *Good Morning America* (ABC-TV) (June 13):
He kind of "shoots from the lip," so to speak.

**Little Mo** *n.* very little momentum (in a campaign). —opp. BIG MO.

1980 *Washington Post* (Feb. 26) B1:
All I hear is momentum. Big Mo and Little Mo. It would be refreshing if someone asked me about an issue instead of a poll.

1996 *St. Petersburg Times* (Fla.) (Mar. 4) 3A:
In 1988, George Bush dubbed it the Big Mo, for momentum—that moment in a campaign when the tide shifts and the wind is at your back. In Dole's case, it's nothing so dramatic. Call it the Little Mo.

2003 *Star Tribune* (Minneapolis, Minn.) (Nov. 2) 12A:
The question is always, "Is it Big Mo? Or is it Little Mo?."

**lobby** *v.* to influence (legislators) on behalf of a third-party; (*hence*) to persuade or petition (someone). Now *S.E.*

1837 *Cleveland Herald* (Ohio) (Oct. 6) 2 in *OED*:
Gen. Bronson...spent a considerable portion of the last winter in Columbus, lobbying to procure the establishment of a Bank at Ohio City.

1839 *Republican Compiler* (Gettysburg, Pa.) (Apr. 9) 4:
The hasty remarks thrown out a few days since on the subject of boring and lobbying.

1841 *Ohio Repository* (Canton) (Mar. 4) 1:
Two years ago, a certain person was lobbying around the Legislature, nearly a whole session, to procure the re-charter of the Manhattan Bank.

1847 *U.S. Dem. Rev.* XX (Mar.) 199:
We are at a loss to perceive, however, that the present system of "lobbying" and "log-rolling," to procure the allowance of exorbitant claims, frequently where none is justly due, is a more dignified course than for the people collectively to submit to the majesty of the laws of their own creation, and to satisfy the claims of individuals according to strict justice.

**1850** O. Turner *Pioneer History* 465:
In the winter of 1802, Mr. Ellicott spent a considerable time in Albany, "lobbying" as such visits to our state capital were afterwards termed.

**1917** G. Myers *Hist. Tammany Hall* 77:
The Sachems were lobbying at Albany for charters of banks of which they became presidents or directors.

**1929** D. Lynch *Boss Tweed* 290:
Tweed testified that he paid Hastings richly for his work, which consisted of lobbying for bills.

**Loco** *n.* [after a brand or type of sulfur matches; see 1842 quot.] a Locofoco, a member of the "Equal Rights" or radical faction of the N.Y. Democratic Party; (*hence*) a member of the faction, or any Democrat. Now *hist.*

**1837** P. Hone *Diary* (Sept. 6) in *OED*:
The President's message...is locofoco to the very core.

**1840** in Eliason *Tarheel Talk* 282:
The democrats or locos.

**1842** J. D. Hammond *Hist. of Politcal Parties New York* 491–92:
A very tumultuous and confused scene ensued, during which the gas-lights...were extinguised. The Equal Rights party...had provided themselves with loco-foco matches and candles, and the room was re-lighted. Immediately after this outbreak at Tammany Hall, the Courier and Enquirer, a whig, and the Times, a democratic (aftwards conservative)...newspaper, dubbed the anti-monopolists with the name of the Loco-Foco Party, a sort of nick-name which the whigs have since given to the whole democratic party.

**1860** R.B. Browne in *Lincoln-Lore* 337:
How the frightened Locos run/From Uncle Abe the honest.

**1929** D. Lynch *Boss Tweed* 48:
This is alarming, certainly, but nothing more than a carrying-out of the Loco-Foco [Democratic] principles of the people of the State.

**logroll** *v.* to practice favoritism or cronyism; (*specif.*) to use political influence or connections; accomplish or obtain (something) through such influence. Now *colloq.* Hence **logroller**, n.

**1812:**
(cited in *W11*)

**1827** *Sentinel* (Gettysburg, Pa.) (Apr. 4) 3:
The Canal bill—is not finally disposed of in Senate; and it is very probable, that by aid of the log-rolling system, it may be passed in all its magnitude.

**1835** D. Crockett *Tour* 120 in *OED*:
My people don't like me to log-roll in their business, and vote away pre-

emption rights to fellows in other states, that never kindle a fire on their lands.

**1845** Corcoran *Pickings* 75:
I calls that downright log-rollin'.

**1899** Thomas *Arizona* 17:
I log-rolled a transfer down here in the desert, where she can't possibly escape.

**1929** E. Haycox *Chaffee* 152:
There was something of the glorified log roller about him.

**1949** *New York Times* (Sept. 25) VI 2:
It is a subtle conspiracy to logroll appointments through the Senate without opposition.

**1950** *New York Times* (Dec. 26) 22:
The logrollers, the social-economic doctrinaires and the wasters are able to discredit the effort.

**1963** *Time* (Nov. 1) 50:
Delegates lobbied and logrolled to gather votes.

**loose cannon** *n.* an uncontrollable and usu. dangerous person or thing.

[**1900** *Internat. Journal Ethics* 11 18:
How far in general is a newspaper calculated to keep a nation reasonable or informed of the truth? About as well as loose cannon on a ship's deck are calculated to serve the ship for ballast.]

[**1918** *Washington Post* 8:
What happened to the Claymore, a British sloop-of-war, a hundred years ago, when a..."24-pounder" broke loose, has been vividly described by Victor Hugo in his popular novel, "Ninety-three"...."You can reason with a bulldog, astonish a bull, fascinate a boa, frighten a tiger, tame a lion; but you have no resource against this monster, a loose cannon."]

[**1946** W.A. White *Autobiog.* 339 [ref. to 1901]:
[Theodore Roosevelt] was worried about what he would do after he left the White House. He said: "I don't want to be the old cannon loose on the deck in the storm."]

**1973** R.M. Nixon, diary entry for Apr. 14, in *RN: The Memoirs of Richard Nixon* (1979) II 351:
I have a note here saying, "the loose cannon has finally gone off," that's probably what could be said because that's what Magruder did when he went in and talked to the U.S. Attorney.

[**1976** *Business Week* (Nov. 15):
"That money," says Arnold Packer, a senior Senate Budget Committee economist who is helping Carter draw up his shadow budget, "is like a

loose cannon rolling around the deck" because a sudden reappearance of the funds could be inflationary.]

**1977** *Washington Post* (Mar. 13):
New political sobriquets are heaped upon [Andrew] Young almost as fast as he breaks into the headlines: the Moynihan of the Left, the loose cannon, the wayward missile of the Carter administration, the "Andy Young Problem."

**1977:**
(cited in *BDNE3*)

**1981** *Washington Wk. in Review* (PBS-TV) (Feb. 6):
Is [he] a loose cannon?

**1982** *News & Observer* (Raleigh, N.C.) A5:
After all, Young had been something of a loose cannon on the deck of the Carter administration as ambassador to the United Nations, a black who seemed quick to find racism all around him.

**1983** R. Thomas *Missionary* 261:
You know, Morgan, sitting here listening to you just now, one phrase kept popping into my mind: loose cannon.

**1985** Boyne & Thompson *Wild Blue* 451:
But he was a loose cannon on the flight line.

**1986** in D. Tate *Bravo Burning* 33:
The lovable loose cannon of military megalomania.

**1986** *CBS Evening News* (CBS-TV) (Dec. 24):
It could help answer the question of whether he was a loose cannon operating on his own—or a loyal soldier following the instructions of superiors.

**1988** Headline News network (Aug. 14):
He has a reputation as a loose cannon.

**1990** *Time* (Nov. 5) 42:
Saddam is a loose cannon with terrible weapons that must be eliminated.

**1993** Namus *Shattered Dreams* (film):
You're a loose cannon, Shari. You don't know how to control yourself.

**lunch-bucket** *adj.* being or concerned with blue-collar issues. Cf. LUNCHPAIL.

**1956** Rowin in *Go South* 151:
In the audience was a liberal lunch-bucket representation.

**1983** *Los Angeles Times* (Feb. 28) I 2:
It's a lunch bucket issue. The dump would mean 100 jobs to an area where most people "are lucky to make $6,000 a year, if they have a job at all."

**1987** Kent *Phr. Book* 154:
Not exactly a lunch-bucket type of crowd.

**1991** *New Republic* (Mar. 18) 43:
Lunch-bucket liberal causes like labor and social welfare legislation.

**lunch lid** *n.* a meal-time moratorium on news from the White House.

**1986** *New York Times* (May 11) 7-9:
The announcement at the White House that "the lunch lid is on" means reporters are free to go to lunch knowing war will not be declared while they're eating a corned beef on rye and, in fact, nothing newsworthy will happen until after 3 o'clock.

**1993** *Washington Times* (June 11) C1:
Miss Myers issued a clarification during the so-called "lunch lid," when news conferences and statements are suspended so White House reporters can eat their sandwiches in peace.

**1993** *Houston Chronicle* (June 15) B9:
The White House correspondent for CNN...said there was a "lunch lid" on things: Reporters could go grab a bite, she'd been told, nothing big was going to happen right away.

**lunchpail** *n.* a blue-collar worker. Earlier **lunch-pailer**. Cf. LUNCH-BUCKET.

**1958** *Time* (Nov. 3) 35:
I don't need votes from lunch-pailers.

*Ibid.:*
For the "lunch-pailers" he plugged "free, autonomous trade unions."

**1977** Sayles *Union Dues* 187:
He was touching Inez then, softer than you'd expect from a lunchpail, more like one of those executive-suite smoothies just read the Kama Sutra.

*Ibid.* 191:
Over six hundred dollars. A lunchpail with that much.

**1984** Vice-Pres. W.F. Mondale, at Dem. National Convention (July 19):
Young and old, native and immigrant, male and female, yuppie and lunch-pail—we are all united here.

**1992** *New York Times Mag.* (Aug. 2) 50:
Traditional lunch-pail liberals and progressive Democrats are beginning to question the vitality of their own programs.

# M

**majority-minority** *n.* a national minority which constitutes the majority of a voting district.

[**1978** *Globe and Mail* (Toronto, Can.) (May 19) P12:
[The Parti Québecois is] open, in a new type of association, to a monetary union with Canada, provided it is based on equitable dispositions, not a majority-minority relationship.]

**2002** *Boston Globe* (Oct. 13) B6:
It took a federal lawsuit in 1986, which made its way to the US Supreme Court, to force states to allow the creation of "majority minority" districts. Thornberg v. Gingles paved the way for the redrawing of the first two majority black congressional districts—both of them in North Carolina.

**2003** *New Yorker* (Dec. 8):
Republicans recognized the value of concentrating black voters, who are reliable Democrats, in single districts, which are known in voting-rights parlance as "majority-minority."

**man** *n.* Orig. *So.* & *Black E.* **1.** any man or group in a position of authority; authority as an abstract entity.

**1918** G. M. Battey *70,000 Miles in Submarine Destroyer* (1919) 302 in *OED*:
Any body in authority is "the man."

**1928** R. Fisher *Jericho* 306:
*The man*: designation of abstract authority. He who trespasses where a sign forbids is asked: "Say, biggy, can't you read the man's sign?."

**1929–32** in *AS* (Dec. 1934) 288 [Lincoln U.]:
*Man*. Anyone in authority. When I rode in that exam I took the Man out! means "When I cheated in that exam I put one over on the professor!."

**1959–60** R. Reisner *Jazz Titans* 160:
*Man, The*...Also anyone in a position of authority.

**1968** *Business Week* (Nov. 23) 34:
The Negroes are keeping their cool, giving "the man" a chance. They show no vindictiveness toward the new Chief Executive.

**1977** Sen. J. Abourezk (D.-S. Dak.), in Terkel *Amer. Dream* 340:
You're not gonna get in trouble with The Man if you just let him do what he wants. The privileged can always manage to legalize whatever they want.

**1995** *New York Press* (May 17) 20:
William Wallace, a low-born Scotsman who just wants to live in peace. But as usual, the Man (in this case, the occupying English) fucks it all up by killing [his wife].

**2.** *Black E.* white people collectively regarded as oppressors of blacks; (*hence,* in radical politics) the white ruling class or U.S. government; (*rarely*) a white person.

**1931** L. Hughes & Z. N. Hurston *Mule Bone* (1991) 142 in *OED*:
Dis railroad belongs to de man—I kin walk it good as you, cain't I?

**1954** Killens *Youngblood* 22:
How about going into the man's army?

**1964** *Newsweek* (Aug. 3) 16:
It is time to let the Man know that if he does something to us, we are going to do something back.

**1965** *Time* (Aug. 27) 17:
Told by Black Nationalists and civil rights demagogues that "The Man"—the white man—is responsible for his savage hopelessness.

**1966** in *Trans-action* IV (Apr. 1967) 6:
"The man" (the man in power—the police, and by extension, the white man).

**1967** *DAS* (Supp.):
*Man, the*...A white man white people, the white race; the white establishment, society, or culture.

**1969** *U.S. News & World Report* (May 19) 37:
Avowed aim of the "Yippies" is to destroy "the Man"—their term for the present system of government.

**1970** *Harper's* (June) 55:
Now we've got the man where we need him and we can't take no promises. Black people are not gonna be pushed around anymore.

**1977** Sayles *Union Dues* 190:
Go up against the Man when he's got tanks and heelicopters and fighter jets and paratroops an all that? Forget it, sucker.

**1979** *Easyriders* (Dec.) 110 (ad):
California residents add 6% [sales tax] for The Man.

*a*1981 D. Travis *Black Chi.* 113:
How can you be happy when the man is constantly kicking your ass?

**1981** N.Y.C. man, age 25:
Numbers is better than state-run cause you don't gotta give nothin' to the Man [in taxes].

**1988** Poyer *The Med* 369:
After Tet the Man was scared.

*a*1994 in N. McCall *Wanna Holler* 292:
They talked white and thought white and even dressed goofy like the man.

**mashed-potato circuit** *n.* a round of after-dinner speaking engagements. Cf. RUBBER-CHICKEN CIRCUIT.

**1941** *Mountain Democrat* (Placerville, Cal.) (Oct. 23) 4:
Jay Allen...is on what he elegantly calls "the mashed potato circuit" speaking at lunch clubs—where mashed potatoes never fail to appear.

**1965** Reagan & Hubler *Rest of Me* 286:
And the speaking I'd done in the industry's behalf along the "mashed potato circuit."

**1988** *U.S. News & World Report* (Nov. 21) 21:
Gerald Ford, who rates $20,000 per talk, regularly performs for pay on what Reagan fondly calls "the mashed-potato circuit."

**1988** R. Reagan, on *ABC News* (ABC-TV) (Dec. 22):
I'm not going to retire. I'm going back out on the mashed-potato circuit.

**media echo chamber** *n.* the tendency of media to react to its own reporting; (*hence*) the tendency to cover the same stories as competitors. Cf. ECHO CHAMBER.

**1990** *Los Angeles Times* (Aug. 18) 18:
Within a week, however, they note that the media echo chamber—operating at hyper-speed—seemed to have run full cycle.

**1996** *Boston Globe* (Apr. 7) 12:
The image hit the media echo chamber, reverberating across the nation with devastating effect.

**2004** *Newsday* (Jan. 19) B6:
In truth, it's tough to say how much of Stewart's perceived clout is just the reverberation bouncing between the walls of the media echo chamber.

**Mediscare** *n.* a tactic (usu. targeted at the elderly) which claims Medicare will be cut or canceled.

**1995** *Washington Times* (May 22) A6:
Change the name of "Medicare" to "Mediscare."

**2003** *Fresno Bee* (Cal.) (Nov. 26) A1:
Bush alluded to that possibility in a speech Tuesday in Las Vegas, saying the vote was a triumph over "Mediscare"—a word long used by

Republicans to deride Democratic warnings of a GOP threat to Medicare.

**memcon** *n.* [*mem*orandum of *con*versation] written record of a conversation.

**1985** *Washington Post* (Feb. 20):
Ask John Hughes if he would find it convenient to write a Memcon on our luncheon with the Chief Justice to capture that historic moment for our future reference.

*****2003** *Agence France-Presse* (Oct. 7):
"You won't get violent protests from Washington if something happens during the night, while I'm flying," [Kissinger] said, according to the MemCon. "Nothing can happen in Washington until noon tomorrow."

**Mercuri method** *n.* [after Rebecca Mercuri, a research fellow at Harvard University's John F. Kennedy School of Government, who proposed such a system.] a voter-verified electronic ballot system (see quots.)

**2002** *Spectrum Online* (Oct.):
A method of voting described by this author over a decade ago, referred to as the Mercuri Method, requires that the voting system print a paper ballot containing the selections made on the computer. This ballot is then examined for correctness by the voter through a glass or screen, and deposited mechanically into a ballot box, eliminating the chance of accidental removal from the premises. If, for some reason, the paper does not match the intended choices on the computer, a poll worker can be shown the problem, the ballot can be voided, and another opportunity to vote provided.

**2002** *Toronto Star* (Nov. 4) D1:
The ballot may be presented to the voter behind a glass screen on the voting machine, then, once approved, dropped and mixed into a ballot box. A quick electronic tally can then, a few days later, be compared to a slower manual tally. This has been dubbed the Mercuri Method.

*****2004** *Politics.ie* (Ireland) (Feb. 4):
We are also calling for the Mercuri method to be applied, i.e. a paper copy of the vote, verified by the voter, to be held for the purpose of independent recount and for parallel manual counting be used for a period so that voter confidence is enhanced.

**millionaire loophole** *n.* the U.S. Supreme Court's 1976 *Buckley v. Valeo* ruling which said limiting the amount one could contribute to one's own campaign would violate the First Amendment.

**1996** *Wall Street Journal* (Apr. 4) A12:
Then Steve Forbes ran right through the millionaire loophole.

**2003** *U. of Chic. Law Rev.* (July 1) LXX:
The new law, the Bipartisan Campaign Reform Act of 2002 (BCRA), better known as McCain-Feingold, included a provision to deal with the so-called Millionaire Loophole.

**minarchist** *n.* [*min*imal + an*archist.*] an anarchist in favor of minimal government sufficient only to protect citizen rights and provide civil defense. Also *adj.*

**1984** S. Newman *Liberalism at Wits' End* 94 in *OED*:
Following Locke, minarchists simply do not trust people to act justly or to display unbiased judgement when their interests are at stake.

**1985** *Los Angeles Times* (Nov. 1) 1:
The two main divisions within the modern libertarian movement are the anarchist libertarians, who believe in no government, and the "minarchist" libertarians, who believe that a shred of government is tolerable.

**1993** *Peoria Journal Star* (Apr. 16) C12:
"The process we're protesting here is institutional, organized theft," said Miller, a self-described "minarchist" who believes the only legitimate functions of government are the court system and the military.

**Mister Whiskers** *n.* [sugg. by the image of "Uncle Sam"] the U.S. government or one of its law-enforcement agencies.

**1933** Partridge in *Dict. Und.* 767

**1953** T. Runyon *In for Life* 234:
But toward the minions of Mr. Whiskers' justice machine I still had plenty of resentment.

**1967** "M.T. Knight" *Terrible Ten* 81:
Mr. Whiskers' snoopers [couldn't make you talk].

**mo** *n.* [shortened from BIG MO] momentum, as of a political campaign. Cf. LITTLE MO.

**1980** *Maclean's* (Oct. 27):
The central figure in this quickening American presidential campaign is a character called Mo. Everyone wants Mo on his side, but Mo's loyalties are fickle.

**1988** *McLaughlin Group* (synd. TV series) (Sept. 4):
A week after Labor Day, who will have the big mo—Dukakis or Bush?...Four say that the mo will be with Bush.

**1989** *Capital Gang* (CNN-TV) (Aug. 5):
"Does the abortion lobby have the big mo now?" "Well, I think they have a little mo."

**mole** *n.* [introduced into current vocab. by "John Le Carré" in 1974 novel; see quot.] a spy who works from within an enemy's government or spy agency; (*hence*) a person who spies on an organization from within.

**\*1922** *Morning Post* (Dec. 28) 7 in *OED*:
It is...necessary...to describe this document in detail, so that those who may be directly or indirectly affected by the underground burrowings of our Bolshevist moles will be familiar with their methods and plans.

**1960** G. Bailey *Conspirators* (1961) 124 in *OED* [in 1935]:
"Ivanov"...displayed such a disconcerting knowledge of the innermost workings of the White military organizations that Fedossenko decided to join his network in order to discover the source of his information. He was recruited under the alias of "The Mole."

**1974** "J. Le Carré" *Tinker Tailor* 62:
Ivlov's task was to service a mole. A mole is a deep penetration agent so called because he burrows deep into the fabric of Western imperialism.

**1978** *New York Post* (Mar. 17) 27:
The suspicion that there was a Soviet "mole" high in the CIA who helped on this is the most disquieting part of the story.

**1978** *Los Angeles Times* (Aug. 16) I 30:
Agents who have no ostensible connections to official foreign delegations and who attempt to infiltrate quietly into positions from which they can obtain information. In the trade, they also are known as "moles."

**1980** *Time* (Jan. 28) 40:
This does not preclude the presence of a Soviet "mole," lurking within the [Yugoslav Communist] party and waiting to stir up trouble when Tito dies.

**1983** *New York Times* (June 9):
Apparently a Reagan mole in the Carter camp had filched papers.

**1984** *U.S. News & World Report* (Oct. 29) 38:
A KGB "mole" spent years working inside Britain's code-breaking center.

**1992** G. Wolff *Day at the Beach* 83:
I was a spook, a mole, a Company Man.

**1994** *Newsweek* (May 9) 24:
The KGB has always been in the market for moles, or "deep-penetration agents," as they are more properly known.

**2004** *Democratic Underground* (Feb. 13) 24:
The high-ranking GOP mole—formerly inside the White House and now in another government agency—had talked with me numerous times over the past year and a half.

**mossback** *n.* an elderly, old-fashioned, or extremely conservative person.—used derisively. Hence **mossbacked**, adj.

**1872** *Daily Republican* (Decatur, Ill.) (Dec. 26) 8:
Now and then a moss-back may pipe out unconstitutional, or centralization of power, but that is all claptrap.

**1874** *Daily Republican* (Decatur, Ill.) (Aug. 13) 2:
A letter from Springfield, to the St. Louis Democrat, says that the real old simon-pure moss-back, bat-winged democrats...insist that the...meeting...and its platform gag were all vanity and vexation of spirit.

**1885** in *DA*:
Everybody rejoices over the passage of the bill except a few intense mossbacks, who were known during the war as copperheads.

**1888** in *DA*:
Mossback seems to have originated in the swamps of North Carolina, where a particular class of the poor whites were said to have lived among the cypress until the moss had grown upon their backs.

**1889–90** Barrère & Leland *Dict. Slang*:
Moss-backs (American), old fogies, "fossils," men behind the times.

**1899** Robbins *Gam* 73:
Then they set the old moss-back afire, beginning with his boots.

**1933** Hemingway *Winner* 33:
"Goddamned mossbacks," she said.

**1935** J. Conroy *World to Win* 227:
He wasn't one of those mossbacks who claim a woman's place is in the home and all that old-fashioned hooey.

**1937** Mason & Heerman *Stella Dallas* (film):
That bunch of mossbacks.

**1938** Krims *Sisters* (film):
Who cares what he says, the old mossback!

**1947** Boyer *Dark Ship* 149:
Listen, you little mossback, I've a good mind to throw you out the window!

**1950** *Harper's* (Mar.) 33:
None of these men is very radical; on the other hand, the mossbacks are few.

**1955** O'Connor *Last Hurrah* 202:
There must be a few mossbacks in the electorate who don't bother to tape-record every political speech they hear.

**1968** Johnson & Johnson *Count Me Gone* 121:
The old mossbacks down at the court house.

*ca***1969** *Gunsmoke* (CBS-TV):
You and that old mossback you're ridin' with.

**1978** Maupin *Tales* 60:
All the old mossbacks would stop us and say how nice it was to know there were still some decent, upstanding young men left in the world.

**1979** Cassidy *Delta* 2:
They're so moss-backed up there in Saigon.

**1994** *New Republic* (Oct. 24) 39:
Arch-conservatism in investment philosophy. I should disclose that I myself figure among the mossbacks.

**mossbacker** *n.* MOSSBACK

**1884** Lummis in *Letters* 9:
No doubt about their politics—all are moss-backers and hungry for spoils.

**Mug** *n.* MUGWUMP.

**1894** Bangs *Three Weeks in Politics* 12:
Diss is what comes o' puttin' up a Mugwump. Dere ain't no life in de Mugs!

**mugwump** *n.* [fr. Massachusett *mugquomp* (also in form *mummugquomp*) war leader (1663 in Eliot's *Massachusett Bible*, freq. translating "officer," "captain," and "duke")] (often *cap.*) a person, esp. a politician, who withdraws support from his own party; a bolter; (*hence*) one who refuses to take a strong stand on an issue when expected by colleagues to do so. —also used attrib. Now *colloq.* [Applied orig. in this sense to Republicans who would not support the party's presidential candidate, James G. Blaine, in the election of 1884.]

**1884** in *DA*:
It may be that in a few years...a little group of British Mugwumps...will arise in their might.

**1885** M. Keller in *T. Nast* plate 238:
Democratic and Republican Mugwumps.

**1886** Nye *Remarks* 37:
To the President.—I write this letter on behalf of a personal friend of mine who is known as a mugwump.

**1887** in *F & H* IV 383:
Mugwump is now generally applied to those who profess to study the interests of their country before those of their party.

**1887** F. Francis *Saddle & Moccasin* 188:
I am uncertain what the burro's politics were; some of the boys asserted that he was a Mugwump.

**1894** in *DAE*:
I'd have believed anything but that you [a Democrat] would be a dashed Mugwump!

**1902** Mead *Word-Coinage* 179:
"Mugwump" will be in every dictionary in the year 1950, just as the good slang of fifty years ago is in the lexicons of to-day.

**1905** Riordan *Plunkitt* 12:
Fifty-five Republicans and mugwumps!

**1909** O. Johnson in *Lawrenceville* 151:
Crazy Opdyke had organized a Mugwump party.

**1919** Fiske *Midshipman* 86:
Mr. Cleveland was elected [in 1884] with the assistance of the so-called "mugwumps," who were Republicans who revolted against Blaine.

**1950** *New York Times* (Oct. 4) 21:
This suggestion pleases that small group of political mugwumps in Washington.

**1952** C. Sandburg *Young Strangers* 163 [ref. to 1884]:
I heard a Blaine Republican say, "A mugwump is a man who sits with his mug on one side of the fence and his wump on the other."

**1989** Rawson *Wicked Words* 260:
The classic definition of a mugwump is "a man with his mug on one side of the fence and his wump on the other" (attr. [to] Harold Willis Dodds, president of Princeton University, 1933–37).

**1992** *Capital Gang* (CNN-TV) (May 16):
The problem with George Bush is he's a mugwump.

**mugwump** *v.* to behave in the manner of a political MUGWUMP.

**1889** in *DAE*:
E. D. Graves "Mugwumped to Cleveland," in 1884 because he "could not conscientiously support James G. Blaine."

**1958** *Time* (Mar. 3) 12:
Brossard mugwumped, but the other five members all said no.

**muscle** *n.* power of intimidation; political influence.

**1931** Partridge in *Dict. Und.* 457:
He lets his "muscle" speak for him. When the police drag his name into every gang killing or big shot feud he makes no denial. This circumstance has given Madden that terrorizing thing known in the underworld as "muscle."

**1963** D. Tracy *Brass Ring* 310:
He had the muscle to back up what he said.

**1972** J. Mills *Report* 48:
He said that to get along in the world everyone has to have some kind of muscle, some kind of power.

**1981** *National Lampoon* (Mar.) 44:
They got the best legal muscle in town.

# N

**NASCAR dad** *n.* a white, working class father, seen as an ideal campaign target.

**2002** *Washington Times* (June 30) A2:
The Democrats appear to have just discovered this electoral fact and are publicly admitting they have a "NASCAR-dad gap."

**2003** *Daily Advertiser* (Lafayette, La.) 6:
NASCAR dads voted for Bush not because they especially like third-generation money, but because he was running against Al Gore. Gore comes off as wooden and pretentious, and pretension is not a quality prized among blue-collar, rural people.

**2004** *Boston Globe* (Feb. 19) A15:
NASCAR Dad is man of the political year. He's the XY chromosome heir to the Joe Six-Pack, Reagan Democrat, Angry White Man types and stereotypes of years gone by.

**nervous Nellie** *n.* a foolishly fearful or timid person. Also as quasi-*adj.* [Orig. in derisive ref. to Frank B. Kellogg, Secretary of State 1925–29.]

**1923** *Coshocton Tribune & Times-Age* (Ohio) (Dec. 8) 6:
We therefore welcome the chastening to which Ambassador Designate Kellog, known as "Nervous Nellie," will be subjected in the Senate by Messrs. La Follette, Shipsted et al. before his appointment to the court of St. James will be confirmed.

**1925** *New York Herald Tribune* (Jan. 18) 1 in *OED*:
[Kellogg] was labeled "Nervous Nellie" by those who were irritated at his maneuvering during the League of Nations fight.

**1944** *S.F. News* (May 13) 7 (Tamony Coll.):
Nervous Nellies who still fear a Japanese raid on Market Street.

**1947** Blankfort *Big Yankee* 134 [ref. to Jan. 1927]:
It was all "Nervous Nellie's" fault. That damned [Secretary of State Frank B.] Kellogg! He let the damned pacifists talk him out of [further military action in Nicaragua].

**1953** *ATS* (ed. 2):
Nervous Nellie. a jittery person.

**1962** *Time* (Nov. 2):
There were some Nervous Nelly reactions in the U.S.

**1966** Gallery *Start Engines* 21:
So he's a nervous Nellie whenever anything unusual happens.

**1966** Pres. L.B. Johnson, in *Time* (May 27) 17:
There will be some nervous Nellies and some who will become
frustrated and bothered and break ranks under the strain.

**1966** J. Daniels Time *Between Wars* 149 [ref. to 1927]:
Kellogg, known in the Senate as "Nervous Nellie," had been
unenthusiastic.

**1971** Michelson *Very Simple Game* 71:
We're a bunch of nervous Nellies. I'm very high-strung.

**1975** *Business Week* (Oct. 20) 102:
Some nervous nellies might go to their banks and turn their deposits
into currency.

*a*1986 D. Tate *Bravo Burning* 103:
If we let these Nervous Nellies run things, there's no telling who'll do
us in first.

**1987** da Cruz *Boot* 62:
The shouting scares only the Nervous Nellies.

**1988** P. Beck & P. Massman *Rich Men, Single Women* 5:
What a nervous Nellie.

**1995** *New Yorker* (Sept. 4) 63:
Tell the Nervous Nellies it'll be their time before they know it.

**neverendum** *n.* [*never* + refer*endum*] a series of referendums initiated
until the desired outcome is achieved, (*specif.*) referendums on the
status of Quebec.

**1992** *Gazette* (Montreal, Quebec) (Feb. 1) A2:
Thank you for participating in the neverendum referendum.

**2001** *Ottawa Citizen* (Jan. 27) A15:
Canada has had its own special problem in Quebec separatism, the
"neverendum."

**2003** *Toronto Star* (June 14) H1:
The new Anglo separatists are geared for a neverendum battle until
they win back their old towns.

**New Europe** *n.* the multi-state European Union, esp. those former
communist-bloc states joining the European Union in 2004; (*hence*)
those European nations which support American foreign policy
following the terrorist attacks of Sept. 11, 2001. Cf. OLD EUROPE).

\*1989 *Independent* (Nov. 1):
In his vision of Europe in the year 2000, Robert Cottrell...asks whether a date can be fixed at which the "old" Europe began subverting the "new."

2003 *Newsweek* (June 23) 36:
On the critical economic front, New Europe looks either increasingly like Old Europe, or uninspired to press change on the founders.

2003 *Wall Street Journal* (Aug. 14) A13:
Of course, the always-assertive American defense chief also neglected to tell the people of Poland, clearly part of any "New Europe," how they feel.

**niggerize** *v.* to relegate to a position of marginal power or opportunity.—usu. considered offensive. Hence **niggerization**, n.

[1890 *Star & Sentinel* (Gettysburg, Pa.) (Nov. 18) 2:
This club solemnly avers that the Democratic charge, that Republicans have endeavored to "niggerize" the offices of the State of Florida is without any foundation...There were not in the entire State...more than half a dozen colored men who were candidates for office.]

1969 *San Francisco Chronicle* (May 24) 8:
The Presidio GIs—all of them white—who took part in an alleged mutiny last October 14 were "niggerized" on that day, a black San Francisco psychiatrist testified...."On that day, they were in the stockade, and they couldn't run away or drop out, so on that day they became controlled by what I call the concept of 'niggerization.' They were 'nigerized.' That means they identified with the black people as being oppressed. They felt they were a minority."

1972 *Harper's* (Oct.) 57:
There's a whole lotta people out there who are afraid to win because they don't think of themselves as running the show. They've been niggerized, the only way they know is suckin'.

1973 F. Kennedy, in *Bartlett's Quots.* (16th ed.) 739:
Niggerization is the result of oppression—and it doesn't just apply to black people. Old people, poor people, and students can also get niggerized.

1976 *Village Voice* (N.Y.C.) (Sept. 13) 31:
Champion of black people, native Americans, women, Hispanics and artists and farm workers, prison inmates and lesbians and whores, and all the niggerized of the world.

1976 *Harper's* (Nov.) 66:
Women can afford the kind of political action they [*sc.* blacks] now shrink from. But it's easier to cringe and talk about being "niggerized."

1979 *Village Voice* (N.Y.C.) (Jan. 29) 27:
He was allied with the poor and the oppressed and had been "niggerized" by the press and government.

**1982** *Harper's* (July) 68:
Life in these here United States is a series of niggerizations. The schools, she said, "niggerize" us, the churches "niggerize" us, the police and the federal government "niggerize" us.

**NIMBY** *n.* [*not n my b*ackyard] opposition to any project or institution perceived as injurious to a residential or other local neighborhood; (*hence*) a person holding such an attitude. Also as *attrib.*

**1980** *Christian Science Monitor* (Nov. 6) B5:
A secure landfill anywhere near them is anathema to most Americans today. It's an attitude referred to in the trade as NIMBY—"not in my backyard."

**1982** in *Atlantic* (Aug. 1987) 88:
A few years ago ANS [American Nuclear Society] stalwart Walton Rodger coined the acronym NIMBY to describe the syndrome that urges the immediate rejection of almost any large construction project in any local area.

**1987** *Atlantic* (Aug.) 88:
The Nimbys—those who want no construction that might disturb the character and real estate value of their neighborhoods.

**1988** *Ch. 2 News at Five* (WCBS-TV) (June 29):
Neighbors got caught up in the NIMBY syndrome—"Not in my back yard."

**1988** *Time* (Dec. 26) 29:
Playing Atomic NIMBY; Pileup of radioactive waste may close a bomb plant.

**1989** "Capt. X" & Dodson *Unfriendly Skies* 65:
We're in the well-known "Nimby" (Not in my backyard) Syndrome.

**1991** *Nation* (June 17) 805:
Services and other institutions that no organized community wants in its backyard—prisons, sanitation works and other "NIMBYs"—have followed.

**1992** *New York Observer* (Dec. 7) 12:
Some Nimbys learned that a methadone clinic was planned for West 110th Street.

**1994** *New York Times* (July 17)(Arts & Leisure) 1:
All politics is local, and the local perspective is a recipe for disaster: ignorance, Nimby selfishness, isolationism, tribal and racial strife.

**NOTA** *n.* [*none of the a*bove] a ballot choice which rejects all candidates.

**1980** *New York Times* (June 6) A17:
We've already had Nota—"none of the above"—in the primary season.

**1992** *Journal of Commerce* (June 3) 8A:
Time will tell whether Ross Perot, the candidate of the NOTA Party (None Of The Above), can make a difference.

**2003** *San Francisco Chronicle* (July 17) A22:
If the recall ballot gives us little choice other than Gray Davis, Bill Simon, Arnold Schwarzenegger or Darrell Issa, then I'm writing in NOTA—None Of The Above.

# O

**October surprise** *n.* the release of important news in the month before election, in hopes of affecting the outcome, esp. by an incumbent.

**1980** *New York Times* (Sept. 1) A7:
Republicans worry about an "October surprise" in foreign policy.

**1980** *Globe and Mail* (Toronto, Can.) (Oct. 3) P15:
George Bush, in Eugene, Ore., warned that Mr. Carter may spring "an October surprise" in his campaign.

**2003** *Seattle Times* (Nov. 29):
The phrase "October surprise" has become a part of the political-campaign lexicon, the notion that an incumbent president can make some major announcement or take some substantial action in the monthlong run-up to Election Day.

**2004** Chris Matthews Show (NBC-TV) (Feb. 8):
I'd go with a prediction that now that you've have the WMD final results put off until next year, don't be surprised if there is an October surprise, perhaps a finding of a small vial, another piece of equipment that we didn't have before that adds more of a solid case behind Bush's claim.

**off-off election year** *n.* a year with no presidential or congressional elections.

**1989** *Wall Street Journal* (Nov. 2):
The irony is that the attack commercial, after getting a boost in last year's presidential campaign, has come of age in an off-off election year with only a few contests scattered across the country.

**2001** *Columbian* (Wash.) (Nov. 10) C2:
The lowest turnout in recent years for an off-off-election year was 1989's 48 percent.

**off the reservation** *adj.* not in line with (organization or party) policy; off-message.

---

**1909** *Atlanta Constitution* (Mar. 20) 1:
The committee will confine its punitive measure to a mild correction of the twenty-three independents and a warning not to get off the reservation again.

**1910** *Indianapolis Star* (Feb. 4) 2:
The senator from West Virginia has more than once exhibited an inclination to get off of that reservation.

**1926** *Barron's* (Mar. 22) 4:
There is an old and an honored adage that there is more joy in Washington over one senator "getting off the reservation" and kicking his heels on some trouble-making excursion than there is for all the other ninety-five who practice the regularity which is known as "going along with the party."

**1984** *Record* (N.J.) (July19) A15:
A lieutenant-general in the Marine Corps went equally off the reservation at the same symposium, so much so that President Reagan disavowed his remarks.

**1991** *Chicago Sun-Times* (June 24) 27:
The congressman views Sununu as "an instinctive conservative there to remind Bush when he gets off the reservation as no one else would or could."

**2003** *Christian Science Monitor* (Sept. 24) 1:
At times, Ashcroft has appeared to go off the reservation—such as the time he announced from Moscow the capture of a key terrorist, ahead of what the administration had planned to say.

**Old Europe** *n.* France, Germany and their traditional Western European allies, esp. those who oppose American foreign policy following the terrorist attacks of Sept. 11, 2001. Cf. NEW EUROPE.

**2003** *Boston Globe* (Jan. 23) A1:
You're thinking of Europe as France and Germany. I don't. That's old Europe. If you take a look at the entire Europe today, the center of gravity has shifted east.

**2003** *Los Angeles Times* (Aug. 19) B13:
Both the federal government and the states are requiring new high-stakes tests that put Old Europe to shame.

**on message** *adj.* adhering to (campaign) strategy or (party) policy.

**1992** *Dallas Morning News* (Nov. 12) 1A:
He has to stay on message. He cannot be diverted from his economic message by social issues.

**1996** *Chicago Sun-Times* (Oct. 4) 5:
Political experts and the campaigns themselves said the candidates were trying to stay "on message" by using speeches and arguments already researched, shaped and approved by their staffs.

**2001** *Houston Chronicle* (Dec. 1) 35:
It showed a shouting Eckels on an overpass making a case for the bond issue over noisy traffic. Nice image, but hard to stay on message when 18-wheelers are zooming around.

**oppo** *n.* OPPOSITION RESEARCH. Also attrib.

**1992** *New York Times* (May 7) A24:
Officially, their job is drearily called "opposition research"—or "oppo" for short.

**1992** *Kansas City Star* (June 29) B3:
Opposition research—"Oppo" to its practitioners —is now a computer-dominated tracking operation that collects in its database virtually every speech, public statement, vote or major financial transaction made by a candidate or potential candidate.

**1992** *Washington Post* (July 2) A1:
"I've hired outside assistance to look into whether the [Silverado] case was handled properly, whether the case was treated differently than other cases relating to S&L crooks," said Dan Carol, DNC research director and chief of the party's "oppo" unit.

**2004** *Tampa Tribune* (Feb. 16) 17:
People tout their skills at "oppo" along with fundraising, direct mail and image-building.

**opposition research** *n.* information gathered on other candidates; esp. information which is scandalous or otherwise embarrassing. Cf. OPPO.

**1984** *Washington Post* (Feb. 3):
The $52 million Republican budget includes...$850,000 for opposition research.

**1988** *Boston Globe* (Mar. 17) A29:
Two employees of the Republican National Committee were in town last week, gathering "opposition research" on Gov. Dukakis.

**1994** *St. Petersburg Times* (May 23) A1:
Opposition research is the way you compare your candidates' strengths and weaknesses with that of the opponent.

**2004** *Houston Chronicle* (Feb. 24) 34:
Opposition research—the campaign work designed to find information about one's political opponent—is in full swing across the political spectrum.

**overvote** *n.* to cast a ballot for more than one candidate for an office when only one choice is permitted.

**1970** *Edwardsville Intelligencer* (Ill.) (Oct. 21) 3:
Mechanical safeguards built into the machine prohibit spoiled ballots, blank ballots and overvoting a particular office.

**1987** *Chicago Tribune* (Nov. 20) C3:
The attorney defending the city's election board, agreed that

undervoting and overvoting occurred. But he says that such practices have not always cut against black voters.

**1988** *Omaha World-Herald* (Oct. 28) 11:
Rather's report featured an interview with a person who indicated that punch cards used by voters could be altered before being given to voters to produce an "overvote" that would not be counted in a race.

**1992** *Los Angeles Times* (June 1) B1:
Writing in Perot's name and punching out a presidential candidate on the ballot—called an overvote—will disqualify the vote for the qualified presidential candidate.

# P

**pacifico** *n.* a pacifist.

> **1942** *ATS* 13:
> *pacifico*, a pacifist.

> **1944** *Slanguage Dict.* 53:
> *pacifico*—one who is against war; a pacifist.

**pack** *v.* to select or make up (a jury or a deliberating or voting body) so as to influence the debate or outcome.

> **1587** Harisson *England* (1877) 53 in *OED*:
> Grieued, that she had...wrested out such a uerdict against him, and therein packed vp a quest at hir owne choise.

> **1871** Bagg *Yale* 46:
> *Pack*, to organize or to join with "a crowd," with a view of securing some desired honor, especially a senior-society election. The crowd thus made up is itself called a pack.

> **1891** Maitland *Slang Dict.* 197:
> *To pack a meeting*, to have it filled up by persons pledged to a particular course.

> **1921** *Variety* (Feb. 18) 10:
> But, it is said, Hynicka "packed" the meeting, with the result Long was ousted from the presidency.

¶In phrase:

**¶pack the rigging** (see 1942 quot.)

> **1942** *ATS* 504:
> *packing the rigging*, distributing propaganda literature.

> **1946** *Amer. Mercury* (Apr.) 467:
> Yet Old War Horse Boose...is still packing the rigging, as they say of active IWW organizers.

**packing** *n.* the consolidation of similar voters into distinct voting districts. Cf. GERRYMANDER, *n.*, CRACKING, KIDNAPPING.

**1983**:
quot. at CRACKING.

**1991** *Boston Globe* (May 19) A29:
With gerrymandering, undesirable voting blocs are packed or stacked tightly together to have as narrow an influence as possible.

**1999** *New Statesman* (Oct.11):
The result of packing black voters into a small number of constituencies was to bleach surrounding areas.

**2003** *New Yorker* (Dec. 12):
Packing concentrates one group's voters in the fewest possible districts, so they cannot influence the outcome of races in others.

**palm-grease** *n.* bribe money. *Obs.* [Ref. to palms itching for money go back to Shakespeare's *Julius Caesar:* "Let me tell you Cassius, you your selfe/Are much condemn'd to haue an itching Palme."]

**1888** Bidwell *Forging His Chains* 64:
$600 worth of "palm-grease."

**1900** in F & H *Slang* V 130:
I think she'll take us up, William,...but she will want a lot of palm-grease.

**1918** Ruggles *Navy Explained* 102:
The sailormen of the navy probably coin more words for money than any other body of men....Sheckles, iron men, washers, clackers, jack, cart wheels, simoleons, kopex, mazuma, palm grease, evil metal, oro, jingles, liberty bait, gilt, sou, armor plate, holy stones, joy berries, and many others.

**1938** *Nevada State Journal* (Reno) (May 28):
Thus State and local politicians frame legislation affecting these developments in accord with Federal wishes—lest the annual Washington palm grease is not forthcoming.

**1951** *Reno Evening Gazette* (Nev.) (Oct. 9):
There legitimate industries were running well, killing was reduced to a minimum, and the forces of law and politics had been so anointed with olive oil, and palm grease, the illegitimate dodges almost seemed legal.

**panda-hugger** *n.* a specialist in American-Chinese relations said to be too accommodating to Chinese perspectives.

**2000** *Political Transcripts* (June 21):
The China field...members don't like to disagree with each other in public. We like to all pretend like we all pretty much think the same way...This really cheats outsiders from a rigorous debate where people would say, "You're a panda hugger," and somebody else would say, "Well, you're a McCarthyite."

**2002** *Insight Mag.* (June 17) 16:
Congress tried to give INSS a strong China shop but refused funding when a panda hugger was to be appointed to run it.

**2003** *Washington Post* (Dec. 15) A29:
At the same time, hard-liners had long seen Moriarty as a "panda hugger," meaning too soft on the Chicoms in Beijing.

**paper-pusher** *n.* an office worker, as a clerk or an administrator.

**1943** *Reno Evening Gazette* (Nev.) (Jan. 4) 4:
After we figure up our new taxes we are going to be pretty mad whenever we see or hear of a single paper-pusher or payroller who isn't absolutely needed.

**1953** *Newport News* (R.I.) (Feb. 5) 14:
George calls himself a paper pusher and would laugh at any one who said that pushing paper was an art. He would admit it needs two skills; know what paper to push and where to push it.

**1961** Joswick & Keating *Combat Cameraman* 161:
Headquarters paper-pushers, I reflected, and paid no attention to them.

**1969** Searls *Hero Ship* 6:
Harmless paper-pusher yesterday or chief of naval operations-elect today.

**1981** Rogan *Mixed Co.* 171:
Most of these people are going to be medics and paper pushers.

**1991** Marcinko & Weisberg *Rogue Warrior* 105:
Subject to even more bean counters and paper pushers.

**1992** *Batman* (FOX-TV):
I'm just a paper-pusher. I can't change the laws.

**1993** *Lois & Clark* (ABC-TV):
You sit there with those gutless paper-pushers in Washington.

**parlor pink** *n.* [sugg. by earlier S.E. *parlor socialist*] a person, usu. of a wealthy or intellectual background, who espouses left-of-center views but is not politically active.

[**1911** *Atlanta Constitution* (Mar. 5) 3:
Our churches are full of men and women wanting a little parlor pink tea religion.]

**1926** *Sun Herald* (Lime Springs, Iowa) (Feb. 25) 8:
The demagogue, the parlor pink,/The poets using purple ink,/The naughty books, the nasty plays—/Oh, I am happy lots of ways.

**1941** Schulberg *Sammy* 150:
"Well, maybe not Reds," Paine said. "...But they're goddam palor-pinks and that's just as bad."

**1944** Inman in *Diary* 1205:
Parlor Pinks from Washington.

**1965** LeMay & Kantor *Mission* 560:
Your Parlor Pink, your Self-Appointed Crusader, grinds a column out of his typewriter—one in which he proves glibly that there is little to choose from in comparison of the two ideologies now opposing each other on this planet.

**paster** *n.* EEL-SKIN.

**1870** *Congress. Globe* (Apr. 13) 2659 in *OED*:
There were ten tickets...which were scratched and had pasters with the name of Caleb N. Taylor.

**1875** G.W. McCrary *Treatise on Amer. Law of Elections* 311:
It has accordingly been held that the placing of a "paster" containing one name over another name, on a ticket, indicates an intention to substitute one name for another.

**1877** U.S. Electoral Commission 969:
If they find a printed name pasted over another name on the ticket, they reject the name on the paster.

**1880** W.G Sumner in *Princeton Review* I 283:
The party managers have also recently invented devices for preventing scratching. The names are printed solid. No margin is left, and it would be difficult even to use a "paster."

**1895** *Rept. of Invest. of Police Dept. of New York C.* 5152:
And were these $2 given to you by Benjamin in consideration that you would vote the paster he gave you?

**1915** *Fort Wayne Daily News* (Ind.) (Mar. 12) 13:
Nothing in the act shall prevent any individual voter at any general election from using the paster ballot as now provided by law.

**1938** *Helena Daily Independent* (Mont.) (Nov. 5) 2:
Unless the county clerk does affix the pasters they would not be affixed at all on absent voters' ballots, and thus such voters would not be given an equal opportunity to express their choice.

**pax Americana** *n.* the (notional) stability and peace resulting from American dominance (in a region or the world); formerly, stability and peace in the U.S. itself.

**1894** *Forum* (Aug.) 633:
The true cause for exultation is the universal outburst of patriotism in support of the prompt and courageous action of President Cleveland in maintaining the supremacy of law throughout the length and breadth of the land, —in establishing the pax Americana.

**1898** F. Adler in *Intl. Journal Ethics* IX (Oct.) 3:
It would be the saddest possible aberration...if instead of establishing the *Pax Americana* so far as our influence avails throughout this

continent we should enter into the field of Old World strife and seek the sort of glory that is written in human blood.

**1926** F.J. Turner in *Annals Assoc. Amer. Geographers* XVI (June) 91: The Pax Americana is not without its influence upon the war-torn continent of the Old World.

**1936** E.C. Stowell in *Amer. Journal Intl. Law* XXX (Apr.) 272: Such measures of cooperation between the American Republic will undoubtedly have considerable influence in the practical establishment of a pax Americana, based, not upon the fiat of the great Republic of the North, but upon the friendly and rational solution of misunderstandings and differences between the various States of this continent.

**1954** *Barron's* (Jan. 4) 1: The misson of Britain was not...to beat down the oppressed...It was to range power on the side of order, of justice and of law...That job has irrevocably fallen on the United States...We may well witness...the beginning of the Pax Americana.

**pay** *v.* ¶In phrases:

¶**pay as you go** the funding of a project as a prerequisite for its existence; (*hence*) a budget-balancing provision stipulating that tax cuts and spending must not increase the Federal deficit. Cf. PAY-GO.

**1984** *Washington Post* (Sept. 11): [Walter Mondale] also said that he would institute "pay as you go" budgeting, which would require that a source of revenue be found before a spending increase could be proposed by his administration.

**1987** *Atlanta Constitution* (Oct. 23) A1: "I have always believed in balanced budgets," he says, calling himself a "pay-as-you-go" Democrat.

**1993** *Chicago Sun-Times* (Mar. 5) 6: Former President George Bush approved three previous extensions of the benefits, but in each case the legislation included necessary funding, in keeping with the "pay as you go" provisions of the 1990 budget agreement between Congress and the White House.

¶**pay to play** to contribute money (to a campaign, a party, a political action committee, etc.) in order to participate (in politics, in government, in contracts, etc.).

**1982** *New York Times* (Aug. 25) A12: "It was very clear that if you didn't 'pay to play,' PUSH would work very hard to make sure you did not reap any of the benefits" of trade from Anheuser-Busch.

**\*1986** *Australian Financial Review* (Aug. 15) 15: The authors of this book make no bones about who is scooping the cream off the top—and taking an undue share of the milk, too. While managers and promoters scoot about in soft-top Mercedes, the vast majority of musicians still have to "pay to play."

**1986** *Washington Post* (Sept. 1) A15:
The motto of the carnival barker is apt: "You gotta pay to play." Without chips, the Russians won't be in on the bargaining whether they are observers or not.

**1999** *Venture Capital Journal* (Feb. 1) 1:
It's very uncomfortable when there is the inference that your professional fate could be affected, usually negatively, if you don't pay to play.

**2001** *New York Observer* (Aug. 27):
This charming arrangement is known in the trade as pay-to-play. Want to make widgets for the state Department of Small-Time Scams? You would be well advised to make a hefty contribution to those elected officials who administer the department: the Governor for sure, and maybe a big-shot state legislative leader. Does your investment house want a piece of a municipality's pension-fund action? Your competence may be measured by the size of your contribution.

**2004** *Tri-Town News* (N.J.) (Mar. 4):
Pay-to-play is the practice that has come to describe a system in which professionals such as engineers, planners and attorneys make campaign contributions to candidates for government office with the expectation they will subsequently receive public contracts for which there is no competitive bidding.

**paycheck protection** *n.* the right of workers to approve their union's political donations.

**1997** Sen. Trent Lott (R-MS) *Fed. Doc. Clearing House* (Jan. 21):
The Paycheck Protection Act...forbids corporations and labor unions to take money from their stockholders, employees, or members for political purposes without their express consent.

**2001** *Washington Post* (Dec. 5) A9:
Its members charged that, as governor, he had opposed school choice measures and "paycheck protection" legislation barring unions from collecting compulsory dues.

**2001** *Wall Street Journal* (Mar. 23) A14:
The Senate also ditched paycheck protection, which would have finally enforced the 1988 Supreme Court Beck decision that held that union members can't be compelled to contribute dues for political activities they disagree with.

**pay-go** *n.* See *pay as you go* s.v. PAY.

**1984** *Globe and Mail* (Toronto, Can.) (Mar. 8) B11:
I think we accept this situation because if we keep the CPP pay/go, at least you have to account to the people and tell them where they are putting the funds.

**1990** *Baltimore Sun* (Dec. 2) 2:
Everybody misunderstood pay-go; it was never a philosophy.

**1995** *Amer. Banker* (June 7) 3:
Pay-go is Washington idiom for "pay as you go."

**2003** *Christian Science Monitor* (Dec. 8) 1:
These include caps on discretionary spending and PAYGO provisions, which require offsets for new programs.

**payola** *n.* money offered or paid as a bribe; bribery.

**1938** *Variety* (Oct. 19) 41 in *OED*:
Plug payolas perplexed.

**1940** *AS* (Apr.) 205 [show business]:
Payola. Bribery, the unethical practice of exploitation.

**1955** Graziano & Barber *Somebody Up There* 320:
As far as bribes in fighting are concerned, "payola" offers for throwing a bout come your way all the time.

**1959** *Life* (Nov. 23) 45:
The U.S. was becoming familiar with a new word, "payola," trade jargon for bribes to promote certain records over the air.

**1962** E. Stephens *Blow Negative* 248:
"Wanted to make his C.O. a hero....Loyalty." "Or payola."

**1967** Kolb *Getting Straight* 127:
Some kind of graft or payola.

**1968** W.C. Anderson *Gooney Bird* 118:
It's all very hush-hush, involving the CIA, Buddhist uprisings, king-sized defections, barrels of intrigue, all topped by a large dose of payola.

**1972** in *Dance World of Swing* 38:
I could have made an extra thousand dollars from payola.

**1972** *New Yorker* (Dec. 23) 34:
Payola...exists still.

**1974** in *Mad Super Special* (No 64) 39:
Your church stinks! Your bishops take payola!

**1976** N. Ross *Policeman* 30:
Police and Blacks alike realized that it's better for both parties to succumb to the evils of "payola" than be bothered with traffic citations and court dates.

**1968–77** F. Wallace *Poker* 76:
Quintin threatens to expose Sid's payola on city paving contracts.

**1980** in *National Lampoon* (Jan. 1981) 80:
Now that I'm back, I'm going to need some of that old payola to start my life anew, know what I mean?

**1985** "Blow dryer" *Mod. Eng.* 30:
Payola...Is what the police get when a club wants to stay open.

**1987** *Miami Vice* (NBC-TV):
Thought this was just your garden-variety payola case.

**1989** Headline News Network (Dec. 2):
Payola is not new.

**1994** N. Karlen *Babes in Toyland* 147:
Freed pleaded guilty to accepting over thirty thousand dollars in payola from six record companies.

**peace creep** *n.* a strident pacifist or war-resister.—used derisively.

**1965** *New York Times* (Nov. 22) 5:
He was followed by four young men bearing a hand-lettered sign reading "Peace Creeps Should Be Tried for Treason."

**1970** Eisen *Altamont* 128:
I'm not no peace creep by any sense of the word.

**1983** K. Miller *Lurp Dog* 79:
Enough to turn a...Special Forces veteran into a babbling peacecreep.

**1987** in Bunch & Cole *Reckoning for Kings* 194:
This ain't no time to be a peace creep.

**peacenik** *n.* [*peace* + *-nik* < Rus. & Yid. 'a person involved with sth.'] a pacifist or war-resister. Derisive.

**1963** *New York Times Mag.* (May 19) 17:
Peace groups bud (and wither) with such frequency that even the experts can't keep track of them. They come in all shapes and sizes—professional groups..., religious groups, demonstrators and nondemonstrators, sophisticated groups and peacenik amateurs.

**1965** *Time* (Apr. 23) 13 in *OED*:
(heading) War & Peaceniks.

**1967** Michaeles *Suicide Command* 103:
Well, these critics—the peaceniks and college professors—are almost all liberals.

**1967–68** von Hoffman *Parents Warned Us* 53:
Toughs out after peaceniks to beat up.

**1968** Klein *Police* 111:
Peacenik demonstrators are determined souls, and,...ever conscious of the newspaper and TV cameramen whose lenses were aimed their way, they put on quite a show.

**1968** Zerwick & Brown *Cassiopeia* 22:
She's sort of a peacenik. He likes that.

**1970** J. Flaherty in *Chez Joey* 150:
Peaceniks are fags.

**1970** *Playboy* (Sept.) 98:
All he could say was something about "those peaceniks."

**1971** Vaughan & Lynch *Brandywine's War* 153:
"I'd say you were a peacenik," B. Dowling Mudd scowled.

**1982** *Time* (May 24) 86:
To speak of a pacifist or peacemaker as a peacenik is, through a single syllable, to smear someone with the suspicion that he has alien loyalties.

**1983** N. Proffitt *Gardens of Stone* 248:
I'm no peacenik, sir. I'm just not in favor of this particular war.

**1983** E. Dodge *Dau* 111:
These peaceniks....they're marching in the streets.

**1987** Lame *Monkey Manif.* (Univ. Tenn.) (Jan. 28) 4:
Perhaps these Peaceniks have forgotten that the United States now nearly stands alone for freedom in the world?

**1988** Clodfelter *Mad Minute* 118:
Those cocksuckin' draft card burning peaceniks.

**1988** *Parade* (Feb. 21) 4:
It was easy being 18 and a peacenik.

**1990** *World Tonight* (CNN TV) (Oct. 17):
Lesser known politicians, peaceniks, and ordinary citizens [have also visited Baghdad].

**1991** *War in Gulf* (CNN TV) (Jan. 31):
An assortment of 70 peaceniks from around the world.

**Peoria** *n.* [ref. to a city in Illinois] a place other than a major U.S. city; middle America; (*hence*), a notional bellwether town populated by JOHN Q. PUBLIC and JANE Q. PUBLIC.

**1942** *ATS* 44:
Imaginary "Hick" Town....Peoria.

[**1949** *Sat. Eve. Post* (Feb. 12) 21:
More are resentful of the implication that "Peoria" is synonymous with "hick town."]

¶In phrase:

¶**play in Peoria** to be well-received by the average American.

**1969** *New York Times Mag.* (Aug. 3) 6:
When a newsman asked him why the President had made a certain move that had aroused criticism in Washington, Ehrlichman replied crisply: "Don't worry. It'll play in Peoria."

**1972** *Daily Northwestern* (Oshkosh, Wisc.) (June 10) 20:
"It'll play in Peoria" will be broadcast as part of the weekly "Comment!" series.

**1984** Wallace & Gates *Close Encounters* 205:
I felt that it would not "play in Peoria" and other less indulgent parts of the country.

**1993** J. Ehrlichman in Safire *New Pol. Dict.* 580:
"Play in Peoria" appeared in a Wall Street Journal story after I'd run the school for advance men in NYC in 1968....It personified— exemplified—a place, removed from the media centers on the coasts, where the national verdict is cast, according to Nixon doctrine.

**permanent campaign** *n.* a nonstop pursuit of funds and votes, esp. when not associated with a specific race or campaign; (*hence*) occupying oneself more with self-promotion than with executing the duties of an office. Also as *v.*

**1977** *Walla Walla Union-Bulletin* (Wash.) (Mar. 16) 27:
Carter is now running a "permanent campaign."

**1993** *Los Angeles Times* (Apr. 4) 2:
Clinton is running a permanent campaign—town halls, speaking tours, call-in shows and meetings with children. All on television.

**2003** *Boston Globe* (Mar. 14) A19:
The governor has chosen to engage in permanent campaigning, characterized by pat slogans,...photo ops,...or staged "town meetings,"...where Republican mayors handpicked the audiences and screened questions.

**photo-op foreign policy** *n.* a disconnected series of (superficial) diplomatic actions or statements, esp. related to a crisis or problem, which result in media exposure, but that have little effect.

**1993** *Atlanta Journal* (Oct. 8) A12:
Somalia is of utterly no importance to this nation. We're there because of a photo-op foreign policy, first by George Bush and then by Bill Clinton, reacting to the nation's impulse to do something to relieve the images of starvation they were seeing nightly.

**1996** *Dayton Daily News* (Ohio) (Aug. 30) 6A:
The feckless, photo-op foreign policy of this administration has put us in grave danger.

**2002** *American Morning* (CNN-TV) (Apr. 17):
Too often the administration has pursued a feckless photo-op foreign policy with little or no effort to define a coherent plan for U.S. engagement in the world or to establish a set of strategic priorities to guide us in a post-cold war era.

**P.I.** *n.* political influence; one who has political influence.

**1942** *Lowell Sun* (Nov. 5) 8:
The brass hats, who had to be a hard-of-hearing congress for peace-time pittances, will do everything in their power to reject congressionally-backed applicants for commissions. They'll make their

applications with that dreaded pencil notation, "P.I." It doesn't stand for the Philippine islands. It means "political influence" and it's a horrid curse, no matter how eligible the would-be officer is.

**1955** Shapiro *Sixth of June* 164:
Are you one of these queer American fish known as a P.I.?...P.I. stands for political influence. We have 'em in the British army too, only we call 'em DBNs. You know. Don't be nasty to this chap sort of thing.

**1971** Murphy & Gentry *Second in Command* 405:
An officer who gets his assignments and promotions through "PI"— political influence—is a marked man.

**piebiter** *n.* a greedy person or animal; one receiving political patronage.

**1863** in *Contrib. to Hist. Soc. of Mont.* I 231:
We overtook George Hillerman (alias "Pie-Biter").

**1871** *Harper's* XLIII 160:
Not so the "Great American Pie-Biter." He parted his shaggy beard, opened a mouth so vast and wide that it might have served for a mountain cavern, insert the pile of eleven pies, and bit clean through them, not only with ease, but apparently with relish and satisfaction.

**1881** Nye *Forty Liars* 130:
The...imperial pie-biters of the realm...congregate on a special date and put the kibosh on the new czar.

**1890** *Weekly Gazette* (Colorado Springs) (Nov. 15) 3:
Life here is so colorless that if a Washington restaurant keeper could hire Senator Hoar to come here and eat his usual midday luncheon of crackers and milk that restaurant keeper's fortune would be made. Or, if he couldn't get Hoar, Senator Blair, as the great senatorial pie biter, would do quite as well.

**1908** *Evening News* (Ada, Okla.) (Sept. 18) 4:
H.G House, secretary of the committee, is a pie-biter of the small fry, and was only squeezed away from the federal crib when statehood put an end to his job as deputy clerk of the federal court.

**1908** W.R. Hunt in *North of 53°* (1974) 225 in *OED*:
Persons interested in other points, and paid knockers and piebiters may pound and hammer until their auditors are deafened.

**pig** *n.* (among radical political groups) a greedy or brutish exploiter of the proletariat.—used contemptuously.

**1952** Himes *Cast Stone* 147:
Passive resistance was the order of the day....All you could hear was "down with the pig." The committee ran all activities within the walls.

**1964** Gover in *Trilogy* 369:
Them goddam...capitalist pigs.

**1967** H.S. Thompson in *Shark Hunt* 452:
Digger chieftain, Emmett Grogan, 23, called a local butcher a "Fascist pig and a coward" when he refused to donate meat scraps.

**1977** L. Jordan *Hype* 164:
We're going to invade the masculine pig stronghold!

**1985** J.M.G. Brown *Rice Paddy Grunt* 341:
These Weathermen had finally come up with the line that, "America is made up almost entirely of pigs, except the blacks."

**pink** *n.* a person whose politics are left of center, but to the right of a *red*; PINKO. Cf. PARLOR PINK.

[*1837 De Quincey in *Tait's Mag.* (Feb.) 71 in *OED*:
Amusing it is to look back on any political work of Mr. Shepherd's...and to know that the pale pink of his Radicalism was then accounted deep, deep scarlet.]

**1927** U. Sinclair *Oil!* 313 in *OED*:
He's nuts on this red-hunting business, and the pinks are worse than the reds, he says.

**1930** G. Schuyler *Black No More* 89:
In time of peace he was a Pink Socialist but when the clouds of war gathered he bivouacked at the feet of Mars.

**1936** H. L. Mencken in Riggio *Dreiser-Mencken Letters* II 602:
My belief is that pinks never tell the truth.

[**1938** *Amer. Mercury* (Nov.) 374:
Think of the thousands of Pinkies in Russia.]

**1942** Epstein & Epstein *Male Animal* (film):
If you can't find any reds, get the pinks!

*1944 "G. Orwell" in *Partisan Rev.* 408:
The pinks deprecate any criticism of the USSR on the ground that it "plays into the hands of the Tories."

**1945** G.A. Smith in *Jim Crow, John Bull* 225:
All the social "do-gooders,"...the reds and the pinks, the disciples of Eleanor [Roosevelt].

**1952** Lait & Mortimer *USA* 6:
The pinks have infiltrated the...thinking of an entire nation.

**1953** Wicker *Kingpin* 41:
All the stinking pinks...voted for that Anson.

**pinko** *n.* one who sympathizes disloyally with socialism or communism; a disloyal American socialist or communist.

**1936** J. G. Cozzens *Men & Brethren* 104 in *OED*:
She's a good girl....now only a healthy pinko. I've snatched her like a brand from the Young Communist League burning.

**1953** Wicker *Kingpin* 29:
How swell...for a real American to win over a pinko.

**1954** Voorhees *Show Me a Hero* 29:
You better get gone, pinko.

**1963** D. Tracy *Brass Ring* 204:
A goddam young pinko, an atheist, a free-love advocate.

**1968** Safire *Lang. of Politics* 336:
Pinko....epithet for anyone in a spectrum ranging from liberal to communist, but most often applied to "fellow travelers," a smear word....In 1926, when Time magazine was popularizing the Homeric adjective ("Berkshire-cradled," "Beethoven-locked," "Yankee-shrewd") its editors were fond of "pinko-liberal" and "pinko-political."

**1972** *National Lampoon* (July) 52:
Your hands are tied by domestic pinkos!

**1972–75** W. Allen *Feathers* 144:
You're all a bunch of...commie pinkos.

**1975** W. Allen *God* 24:
New York left-wing Jewish intellectual commie pinkos.

**1977** Carabatsos *Heroes* 6:
They're pinkos. I'm warning you.

**1984** Ehrhart *Marking Time* 44:
Commie hippie pinkos and bleeding hearts.

**1985** *New York Daily News* (Aug. 26):
Ron snitched on Pinkos in '40s.

**1986** C. Horrall & C. Vincent *Wimps* film:
But this university has been infiltrated by a board of Commie pinkos.

**pinko** *adj.* leftist, with communistic leanings.

**1957** O. Nash *You can't get there from Here* 84 in *OED*:
So what do you want on yours—a lot of pinko longhairs, or red-blooded athletes and drum majorettes?

**1979** Gutcheon *New Girls* 135:
Pinko professors.

**1993** *Donahue* (NBC-TV):
You pinko communistic creep!

**play the —— card** Cf. CARD

**pocketbook nerve** *n.* a sensitivity to personal financial issues, esp. concerning taxes.

**1903** *New York Times* (Apr. 19) 16 [advertisement]:
Your Pocket Book Nerve is attached to our spinal column.

**1905** *Cambridge Jeffersonian* (Ohio) (Nov. 30) 7:
The pocketbook nerve of some men is much more sensitive than their domestic nerve.

**1932** *Landmark* (Statesville, N.C.) (Jan. 26) 8:
A people does not long remain apathetic when a government starts drilling on the pocketbook nerve.

**1935** *Frederick Post* (Md.) (Sept. 3) 6:
Not only is the pocketbook nerve among the most tender, but talk about taxes always intertwines itself with the general business situation.

**1947** *Portland Press Herald* (Maine) (Dec. 30) 4:
The Forum on price control comes at a time when the rising cost of living is biting into the pocketbook nerve, and Congress and the Administration are fearful of the effect in the election.

**1961** *Great Bend Daily Tribune* (Kan.) (July 25) 4:
If they are convulsively sensitive to the pocketbook nerve at ruinous cost to personal integrity, there is little help for them.

**1996** *San Francisco Chronicle* (Mar. 21) A1:
The recession of the early 1990s was really severe, the worst in a long time, and the public is still cautious. The pocketbook nerve is the most sensitive nerve in your whole body.

**pocket veto** *n.* the automatic killing of a bill by means other than an explicit executive-branch veto or a legislative vote, usu. by the chief executive failing to sign a bill but not returning it to the representative body for reconsideration before the end of the legislative session; (*hence*) the annulment of any proposed rule, law, bill, or question by failure to act.

**1842** *Ohio Statesman* (Dec. 19) 3 in *OED*:
The pocket vetoes.

**1843** *Huron Reflector* (Norwalk, Ohio) (Apr. 25) 6:
He also wanted the avails of the public lands to swell the pool of corruption, and so the party wound up by approving the pocket veto, and of the sending of the bill to the Senate where it had no business to be—with reasons...to convince the gulls of the Nation that the pocket veto was all right.

**1851** *Political Landmarks* 221 [ref. to 1845]:
A bill making appropriations for certain harbors and rivers, passed both houses, near the close of the session, but was retained by the president, and thus failed to become law, in consequence of what was called a "pocket veto," which was that last act of Mr. Tyler's administration.

**1911** *Washington Post* (Sept. 25) 6:
Washington employed the veto only twice in his eight years in office, and Lincoln only four times, one of these being a pocket veto.

**2001** *Las Vegas Review-Journal* (Apr. 5) 9B:
Without a quorum, there can't be a vote, and without a vote, the proposal doesn't show up on the ballot. Call it a pocket veto.

**2002** *Time* (Mar. 4) 84:
Ask a roomful of fledgling journalists if they would be willing to die for the truth, and not a hand will be raised. They do not mean no, exactly. They simply give the hypothesis a pocket veto.

**pol** *n.* a politician.

**1931** Steffens *Autobiog.* 382 [ref. to 1902]:
These Minneapolis pols are bums.

**1934** Berg *Prison Nurse* 41:
I'd have thought you must have one hell of a big drag with some "pol" to rate all that attention.

**1942** Inman in *Diary* 1101:
There wasn't any bribing or fixing them. They weren't pols.

**1961** Cannon in *Nobody Asked* 141:
But the way they carry on, you'd think no pol ever gave a poor bum a deuce to vote the straight ticket.

**1970** La Motta, Carter & Savage *Raging Bull* 223:
He's a friend of the pol who knows the judge.

**1983** R. Thomas *Missionary* 22:
An old pols' hotel.

**1991** B. Adler *Rap!* xvi:
The pol with a head of wood and a heart of stone.

**policy wank** *n.* [a play on POLICY WONK, and *wank*, v., 'to masturbate'] POLICY WONK; one who participates in a pointless discussion of policy details; the event itself. Also *v.* and **policy wanker**.

[**1992** K. Karplus (Aug. 3) on Usenet (alt.usage.english):
Does anyone (besides me) think that "policy-wonk" was originally "policy-wank"?]

***1999** R. Allison *Catchword* (Victoria, Australia) (July) 11:
A six month contract was spent with Water and Catchment Policy at the Victorian EPA where I officially became a "policy wanker."

**2000** Shepherd *Express Metro* (Aug. 24):
But my goals should be sort of nonspecific 'cause I don't want to come off like some kind of policy wanker the way Big Al [Gore] does.

**\*2003** *Canberra Times* (Australia) (Nov. 3):
It is widely seen as "that policy-wanker stuff."

**policy wonk** *n.* see WONK.

**politainer** *n.* a politician who is also an entertainer.

**2000** *Star Tribune* (Minneapolis, Minn.) (May 4) 18A:
Jesse Ventura and the Brave New World of Politainer Politics.

**2002** *City Pages* (Minneapolis, Minn.) (Mar. 6):
David Schultz, a professor in the graduate school of public administration at Hamline University in St. Paul, and his students...first coined the term "politainer": "Somebody whose identity as an entertainer and a politician can't be separated."

**2003** *San Francisco Chronicle* (Sept. 17) D1:
Angelyne may be the contest's original politainer.

**political football** *n.* an issue for which blame or responsibility is passed.

**1857** *Whig & Courier* (Bangor, Maine) (Oct. 12) 2:
Smart of the Belfast Free Press is laboring with all his might to keep the temperance question as a political football.

**1890** *New York Times* (Oct. 19) 2:
Eustace...like his unscrupulous chief, regards the judiciary, like everything else, from the political football standpoint.

**1910** *Indianapolis Star* (Jan. 21) 1:
A disposition to play political football with the whole affair is glaringly manifest.

**1915** *Lancaster Daily Eagle* (Ohio) (Oct. 29) 3:
The proposed amendment to limit elections on twice defeated constitutional proposals and to prevent abuse of initiative and referendum is offered so that agitators may not make the Ohio constitution a political football.

**1977** *Globe and Mail* (Toronto, Can.) (Nov. 17) P6:
It has been a painful experience to me to observe the Opposition parties making a political football of the Force in the House of Commons.

**politician** *n.* a person who pursues success cynically or ruthlessly; a schemer, sharper, operator.

**1863** T. Whitman in *Dear Walt* 26:
He tells me that he (Webster) is a "politician" and that he will help you...provided that he thinks that it will not interfere at all with him.

**1931** Erdman *Reserve Officer's Manual* 450:
Sea Lawyer. One with a gift of gab. One who by his smartness avoids hard duties—synonymous with "politician."

**1933** Ersine *Prison Slang* 58:
Politician, n. A convict who plays up to prison officials.

**1938** Connolly *Navy Men* 81 [ref. to 1904]:
A politician in the Navy is a man with a soft job, or a job that doesn't call for being shipwise.

**polly** *n.* a politician or office holder.

**1932** Nelson *Prison Days & Nights* 37:
Where do you think I'd be right now if I didn't know a pile of pollies and big shots?

**1942** in *ATS* 787:
Politician....polly, poly.

**1961** Scarne *Complete Guide to Gambling* 84:
The pollies (politicians)...happened to be against the bookie operation.

**poly sci** *n.* political science. Now *colloq.*

**1927** *AS* II (Mar.) 277:
Poly Sci. Political science.

**1971** N.Y.U. Student:
He's majoring in poly sci right now.

**1978** Truscott *Dress Gray* 100:
Gotta poly sci paper due, man.

**pork barrel** *n.* a government appropriation, bill, policy, agency, etc., that supplies funds for local improvements designed to ingratiate legislators with their constituents; (*hence*) such funds; pork.

**1873** *Defiance Democrat* (Ohio) (Sept. 13) 1:
"Holy Abraham,...What a fuss about a little piece of pork?"....Recollecting their many previous visits to the public pork-barrel, the much bigger loads lugged away on those occasions, the utter indifference displayed by the people,...this salary grab...puzzles them quite as much as it alarms them.

**1902** *Des Moines Leader* (Iowa) (Mar. 7) 4:
This is the sum of his campaign—no argument other than the one that he can get his arm a little farther into the national pork barrel than could Judge Prouty.

**1909** *Westm. Gaz.* (June 1) in *OED*:
The Democratic Party...has periodically inveighed against the extravagance of the administration, but its representatives in the Legislature have exercised no critical surveillance over the

appropriations. They have preferred to take for their own constituencies whatever could be got out of the Congressional "pork barrel."

**1915** *Coll. Kans. State Hist. Soc.* XIV 79:
I suppose that the average reader will say that the senator's methods must have savored of the "pork barrel."...the "pork-barrel" proposition.

**1949** H.S. Truman in *Confid.* 102:
But when it comes to "pork barrel," and this is a "pork barrel" project, they are right in the front line with hats off and their hands out.

**1974** H.S. Thompson in *Shark Hunt* 343:
Any incumbent president...has a massive amount of leverage when it comes to using the political pork barrel.

**1983** *Morning Report* (WKGN radio) (Mar. 7):
Critics of the [tax] package say it's strictly pork barrel.

**1984** Caunitz *Police Plaza* 263:
A pork barrel like the Board of Ed.

**1987** *Academe* (July) 3:
The "academic pork barrel" issue continues to divide the academic community.

**post office party** *n.* a local branch of a national party with only a superficial presence.

**1991** E.J. Dionne *Why Americans Hate Politics* (May 15) 182:
Through 1952, the Southern Republican party was basically a "post office" party—a tiny organization that existed mainly to win patronage benefits (such as postmasterships) for its members.

**2001** R. Perlstein *Before the Storm* (Mar.) 46:
State Republican organizations survived as shells, "post office parties" that existed only to deliver their "black-and-tan" delegations at Republican conventions in exchange for federal patronage if the GOP won the White House.

**Potomac Fever** *n.* a passion to be involved in politics, esp. nationally.

**1944** *New York Times* (Aug. 25) 14:
It is evident that Mr. Berge because of Potomac fever, has seemingly lost his sense of direction.

**1975** *U.S. News & World Report* (May 12) 30:
Potomac fever...Reagan is dying to run for President.

**1977** *Washington Post* (Jan. 15) A4:
Potomac fever has started to replace sickle cell anemia as the black people's disease.

**1994** *Esquire* (Apr.) 87:
"I will never come back to government. I have zero Potomac fever. I don't have the patience anymore."

**2002** *Washington Post* (Aug. 1) A27:
It is supposedly something of a disease or a compulsion, a variant of the oft-debilitating Potomac Fever in which the victim seeks the nation's highest office over and over again or simply cannot stay away from government service.

**POTUS** *n.* [*p*resident of *t*he *u*nited *s*tates] (see quots. at FLOTUS and VPOTUS).

**Powerhouse** *n.* the rectory of the archdiocese of New York considered as a source of political influence.—constr. with *the.*

**1968** Radano *Walking the Beat* 135:
The biggest hook of all, the biggest rabbi, is called The Powerhouse: this refers to the pressure emanating from the rectory at 50th Street and Madison Avenue.

**1984** Caunitz *Police Plaza* 8:
He wanted the Powerhouse to know that they owed him one.

**prairie-dog court** *n.* KANGAROO COURT.

**1936** R. Adams *Cowboy Lingo* 203:
By "prairie-dog court" he meant kangaroo court.

*a*1940 in Lanning & Lanning *Texas Cowboys* 143 [ref. to 1880's]:
The hands had what they called a prairie-dog court....There were fines for breaking the rules.

**1980** *CBS Mystery Theater* (WHEZ radio) (May 14):
A woman's word don't count for much in the prairie-dog courts the men run around here.

**prebuttal** *n.* a prepared response which anticipates an opponent; an instant response.

**1996** *Washington Post* (May 26) A18:
President Clinton's White House and campaign team have been drawing favorable reviews for their rapid response operation and penchant for picking off issues before Senate Majority Leader Robert J. Dole (R-Kan.) even gets his TelePrompTer warmed up. Vice President Gore calls it "prebuttal."

**2000** *Newsweek* (Nov. 20) 78:
Fabiani actually believed in what he called "prebuttal": blunting an attack before it ever got launched.

**2003** *American Prospect* (Apr.) 15:
They did that by unveiling their economic-stimulus plan before

President Bush released his proposal, and also by giving a "prebuttal" to the State of the Union address.

**presidential fever** *n.* a form of POTOMAC FEVER, manifesting itself as a desire for the presidency.

**1857** J. Weiss *Life of Theo. Parker* (1864) 194:
But all the distinguished Northern politicians are subject to a peculiar disease, which renders them wholly unreliable for patriotic work, viz. "the Presidential fever."

**1884** *Harper's* (May) LXVIII 944:
William H. Crawford, Secretary of the Treasury, was touched with the Presidential fever.

**1985** *Chicago Sun-Times* (Aug. 1) 46:
Presidential fever, Baker said, "is like malaria—you never really get over it, although there are periods of remission."

**2003** *Live from the Headlines* (CNN-TV) (Aug. 7):
I am, though, reminded of Mo Udall, the former presidential candidate, former congressman, who once said, "The only cure for presidential fever is formaldehyde."

**presidential timber** *n.* see TIMBER.

**press the flesh** *v.* to shake hands; (*hence*) to greet by physical contact.

**1918** Grider *War Birds* 148:
Well, I have pressed the flesh of royalty now. My hand has gotten accustomed to the grasp of nobility.

**1926** Maines & Grant *Wise-Crack Dict.* 8:
*Press the flesh*—shake hands.

**1968** Safire *New Language* 355:
*Press the flesh.* Handshaking; any form of physical contact between candidate and voter. The phrase...was politically popularized by Lyndon Johnson in 1960.

**1982** WINS radio news (Aug. 14):
Politicians are expected to be pressing the flesh at LaGuardia Place today.

**1993** *CBS This Morning* (CBS-TV) (May 13):
Yesterday the President was back out pressing the flesh with the people.

**prex** *n.* a president (usu. of a student body, college, etc.). Also **prexy**.

**1828** *Yankee* (Portland, Maine) (July 16) 232 in *OED*:
Our Prex says this: You surely miss [etc.].

**1846** *Yale Banger* (Nov. 10):
That skull and bones of college mysteries, the Prex's room.

**1856** Hall *College Wds.* 375:
*Prex.* A cant term for President.

**1835** Strong *Diary* I 4:
Then comes a preachment from the Prex which I shall not take the trouble of writing down.

**1869** Carmina *Princetonia* 54:
Stamping in the chapel makes the Prex so mad.

**1871** *Yale Naught-Ical Almanac* 26:
The Prex. behind the lofty desk/Lifts up his figure slim.

**1871** Bagg *Yale* 46:
*Prex,* the president.

**1871** in *DA*:
*Prex* or *prexy,* n. President of a college or university. First form is general; the second is used at [34 colleges].

**1905** Compton in *Librarian* 183:
I'm not going to cry during the valedictory or while "Prexy" is making his speech.

**1917** in Kimball & Balcolm *Sissle & Blake* 33:
Students, alumni, professors and prexy are rooting for you to win this game.

**1949** Robbins *Dream Merchants* 242:
Edge had been elected prexy of the company.

**1966** K. Hunter *Landlord* 112:
If weather stripping is applied to the prexy's windows.

**1970** D. Long *Nia* 16:
Prof. Jones is screwing the/prexy's wife.

**1972** Barker & Lewin *Denver* 141:
A new prexy, Joseph Royall Smiley, arrived from Texas.

**1976** Lee *Ninth Man* 276:
The Oval Office. Prexy sent word about ten minutes ago.

**pseudo-event** *n.* an event staged for publicity or rehearsal.

**1962** R. Spiller in *Amer. Quarterly* XIV (Summer) 216:
Once one has accepted [Daniel Boorstin's] thesis, the journey through "pseudo-events" of news-making, of hero-faking, travel-sterilizing, dissolving art forms and advertising is a sheer and spine-tingling joy.

**1984** *Washington Post* (Aug. 20):
During the war games in San Francisco, for example, Douglas Kiker of NBC recalls that even technicians had trouble taking the pseudo-event with solemnity when Rod Prince, the Chicago bureau chief who is tall,

black and male, was forced to pose as LaBelle Lance, the diminutive wife of Georgia Democratic Party chairman Bert Lance.

**1988** *Seattle Times* (Mar. 25) C1:
Good planning, or good luck, can transform one pseudo-event into many, multiplying the benefits.

**2003** *Denver Post* (July 11) FF2:
A pseudo event comes about because someone has planned, planted or incited it. Typically, it is not a train wreck or an earthquake, but an interview.

**public diplomacy** *n.* foreign policy directed at foreign citizens rather than foreign governments; acts of non-secret foreign policy.

**1907** A. Hart in *Amer. Journal of Intl. Law* I (July) 634:
A result of this swift and eventful diplomatic experience is that Americans hold to an ideal of open and almost public diplomacy.

**1977** *Globe and Mail* (Toronto, Can.) (Dec. 26) P33:
The notion of public diplomacy among nations is not a new one. President Woodrow Wilson's call for "open covenants openly arrived at" in the peace negotiations after the First World War was an effort in that direction, based on the moral imperatives of democracy.

**2003** *New York Times* (Dec. 29):
The government's public-relations drive to build a favorable impression abroad—particularly among Muslim nations—is a shambles...That effort, known as public diplomacy, lacks direction and is starved of cash and personnel.

**pull** *n.* political influence; a source of such influence. Cf. DRAG. Now *S.E.*

**1887** in *DA*:
He's got a great pull down yonder.

**1889** *Harper's Mo.* (Mar.) 630:
If it wasn't for the pull he has, I think they'd hang him.

**1891** Maitland *Slang Dict.* 212:
*Pull* (Am.), an advantage held over another person...."to have a pull," to be possessed of influence; a word much used in the political world.

**1892** Gunter *Miss Dividends* 164:
Don't this give the church a pull upon the daddy.

**1892** Frye *From Hgs.* 167:
Youse must have pull enough fer t' get me de place on de drum.

**1893** *Life* (Feb. 2) 77:
"A Man With a Pull."

**1893** Macdonald *Prison Secrets* V:
My opponents' attorney "had a great pull." The judge admitted his falsehoods and completely forgot the law of the land.

**1893** F.P. Dunne in Schaaf *Dooley* 227:
They had a pull like a bridge horse.

**1895** J.L. Williams *Princeton* 172:
I shall have to get used to boot-licking and getting pulls.

**1900** Ade *More Fables* 130:
His Father worked a Pull and got him a Job with a Steel Company.

**1900** *DN* II 52:
*Pull* n. 1. Influence, or favor with anyone. 2. Favor, sometimes gained by deception.

**1907** London *Road* 129:
The one thing obvious is that the man has a "pull."

**1910** W. Archer *Afro-Amer.* 15:
"How are negroes placed in these positions?"..."Why, through various political 'pulls.'"

**1914** London *Jacket* 19:
You can weave the political pull of San Francisco saloonmen and ward healers into a position of graft such as this one you occupy.

**1958** S.H. Adams *Tenderloin* 17:
Evidently the attempted murderer had a pull.

**1979** T.R. Kennedy *Gotta Deal* 64:
I had a lot of pull 'round here.

**pull-aside** *n.* a private, informal meeting at an otherwise structured event.

**1994** Safire in *New York Times Mag.* (Aug. 28) 6-22:
A similar construction goes from the verb "to pull aside," to the diplomatic noun, a pull-aside, which means "a private meeting at a public event."

**1996** U.S. Newswire (transcript) (Mar. 13):
I'm going to get a fuller list from him—he's had, during the course of moving back and forth, some individual, one-on-one conversations with additional leaders in a pull-aside format.

**2001** *Washington Post* (Dec. 11) A8:
The lowest-level presidential meeting is known as the "pull aside," in which the president breaks away from a larger meeting for a few minutes of private time with a foreign leader. When the president chooses not to take his date into a private room, the meeting is called a "drive-by." Another such meeting is the presidential "drop-by," in which the foreign leader has a session with a lesser U.S. official and the president pokes his head in the room.

**pundit** *n.* [< Hindi *pandit* < Sanskrit *pandita* 'a learned man.'] one who claims or is said to be a learned expert or teacher; a commentator.

[**1816** "QUIZ" *Grand Master* III 73 in *OED*:
For English pundets condescend Th' observatory to ascend.]

**1960** *Oshkosh Northwestern* (Wisc.) (June 29) 20:
All newspapermen, I suppose, secretly think of themselves as potential pundits. We fancy that if we could get free of the fetters of facts, we could write penetrating analyses that would soon set the work straight again.

**1967** *Tri-City Herald* (Wash.) (Dec. 17) 10A:
A leading English intellectual and pundit attempted this week to debunk the debunkers with a lengthy, closely argued assertion that the Warren Commission was basically correct.

**1987** W. Percy *Thanatos Syndrome* (1988) 263:
Worst of all were the...NBC anchormen, *N.Y. Times* pundits, show-biz gurus.

**1990** *New York Woman* (Apr.) 57:
Maybe it was the very breadth of NOW's political vision that inflamed the pundits.

**1992** *Playboy* (Nov.) 67:
I enjoy the job I have, which is the best job in the world. And sure, there's power in being a pundit—and responsibility, too. You have to be very careful not to hurt somebody inadvertently or to pop somebody who is not powerful. My motto is "Kick 'em when they're up," and I always try to.

**1999** *Baltimore Mag.* (Md.) (Apr.) 55:
The archetypal pundit and crank, Mencken was a mix of Aristotle, Thomas Paine, and W.C. Fields.

**punditariat** *n.* the collective body of PUNDITs.

**1999** *American Prospect* (Mar. 1) X:
I love reading Weekly World News and the National Enquirer, because they are true to their mission. But that mission hardly fits the pretensions of the punditariat that kept the Monica story alive.

**2001** *Chicago Sun-Times* (Jan. 21) 51:
One is embarrassed that the American punditariat can do no better than repeat these cliches, both of which are patently false.

**2004** *Denver Post* (Jan. 24) C15:
From what I read of the rantings of the punditariat, that tactic didn't work well for him, either.

**punditeer** *n.* a PUNDIT, esp. a novice.

**1989** *Newsday* (Nov. 15) 69:
The words of the secretary and the punditeer naturally lead a columnist to heed the call of a third authority.

**1999** *New York Times* (Dec. 26) 6-24:
Instead of great cold war statesmen, we have Clinton, Gingrich, Hastert and Carville. Instead of Walter Lippmann, we have 20-something punditeers on MSNBC.

**2000** J. Novak on *National Review Online* (Dec. 14):
For Bush, to not only, as every punditeer will solemnly intone, remember that he "was not elected to serve one party, but to serve one nation," but also to pick people for his administration who believe in something—and have the cojones to do something, too.

**2002** *San Francisco Chronicle* (Jan. 6) D2:
That's the question many a punditeer is asking lately about 2001.

**push** *n.* a group of associates or supporters.

**1893** Dreiser in *Journal* I 125:
The 40 odd members of "The Republic's push," for such is the name they are becoming to be known by.

**1896** Ade *Artie* 7:
Well, what'd a couple o' hot knock-abouts do to this push.

**1899** Whiteing *John St.* 287:
The papers chimed in, and our push suddenly found we were monsters, when all we wanted was to have a dance.

**1904** in "O. Henry" *Works* 30:
These new guys always win out with the push.

**1904** *Life in Sing Sing* 251:
Push.—Associates; a crowd.

**1907** in "O. Henry" *Works* 1609:
My governor is one of the hottest...of the Wall Street push.

**1908** "O. Henry" *Works* 327:
Our peaceful little swindle was constructed on the old saying: "The whole push loves a lover."

**1941** *AS* (Feb.) 24 [Indiana]:
Push. Group "I met the whole push as I was going to town."

**1943** Wendt & Kogan *Bosses* 11:
This young Coughlin has got a nice little push.

**push poll** *n.* a false voter survey which gives misleading information about candidates in the form of questions.

**1994** *Rocky Mountain News* (July 29) 5A:
Bird also continues to be outraged by a "push poll" conducted by

Benson last week...that was designed to alert voters to Bird's alleged political failures.

**2004** *Orlando Sentinel* (Feb. 19) B1:
Mulvaney says the calls amount to an illegal "push poll," a campaign tactic used to sway voters for or against a candidate under the guise of a survey.

# Q

**Quadriad** *n.* the president's four leading economic advisers.

**1963** *Wall Street Journal* (June 17) 10:
The term "troika" so far has proved an apt description—adopted joshingly among themselves—for President Kennedy's three central framers of economic policy....When a fourth man joins this group for occasional meetings with the President, the label illogically switches from Russian to Latin...and the group calls itself the "quadriad."

**1989** *San Francisco Chronicle* (Feb. 1) C1:
The Fed chairman said he and Bush are friends of long standing and he expects to have periodic meetings with the president, along with the secretary of Treasury, the director of the Office of Management and Budget and the chairman of the Council of Economic Advisers—a four-person advisory group known in the past as the Quadriad.

**2003** *Fed. Reserve Bank of Minneapolis* (Sept. 1) XVII 16:
Well, by the time we get to the '50s, there are other ways in which they can influence things and one of them is congressional hearings, lean on the chairman, try to get them to do things, start regular meetings between the Fed chairman and the president and other officials, later called the quadriad.

# R

**rabbi** *n.* *N.Y.C.* someone with CLOUT or PULL. Cf. HOOK.

**1952** in *ATS* 783:
*rabbi*, one who aids in the securing of special privilege or favor.

**1955** Deutsch *Cops* 50:
The "rabbi" in New York police parlance is the "clout" in Chicago.

**1968** Radano *Walking the Beat* 135:
The biggest hook of all, the biggest rabbi, is called The Powerhouse: this refers to the pressure emanating from the rectory at 50th Street and Madison Avenue.

**rag baby** *n.* [after the cotton rag used to print money] paper currency; the movement in favor of such, or a supporter of it.

**1876** Democratic Party Natl. Comm. *Campaign Textbook* 753:
If Mr. Hayes voted honestly, which we can not doubt and with the intelligence of a man fit for President, he was then in full sympathy with the "Rag Baby" financial creed.

**1896** *N. Amer. Rev.* CLXIII 272:
The last fierce fight for the "rag baby" was made in Ohio in the fall of the same year.

**rainmaker** *n.* an influential political operative or lobbyist, typically one who can attract large donations or other funds.

**1940** *Nation's Business* (Feb.) 28:
It was shown recently in two state elections that there are more people who mistrust the economic nonsense of Browder and Townsend than there are who follow such political rainmakers.

**1977** Coover *Public Burning* 599:
Every rainmaker becomes a bore at last, so zip your lip!

**1984** NYC attorney, age ca37:
A *rainmaker* is a politician or an attorney or [*sic*] claims that he can—

or actually can—exercise influence, pull strings, get lots of things done. Someone with clout.

**1984** *Wall Street Journal* (Feb. 15) 1:
Just last month one of Washington's best-known "rainmakers," Thomas Boggs, threw a $500-a-person reception at his home for Mr. Gore.

**rapid response** *adj.* offering quick rebuttals to opponents' tactics.

**1988** *Washington Post* (Nov. 13):
The Bush "army" also had a secret team known as the Rapid Response Group. Every week, they telephoned major television stations in 20 contested states to find out what commercials Dukakis had booked.

**1992** *Boston Globe* (Aug. 13) 1:
The Clinton-Gore campaign's rapid response team, at the ready 24 hours a day, had doused the flames of two political fires by early Tuesday afternoon.

**1994** *Washington Post* (Oct. 5) A26:
He is surrounded by a large circle of associates, friends of Tony, who speak of "rapid response" campaign tactics.

**2004** *Milwaukee Journal Sentinel* (Feb. 16) 1A:
The pre-debate drawing of lots so the grown men who want to live at 1600 Pennsylvania Ave. could have first dibs on...who got the biggest holding room and "rapid-response" suites, where frenzied staffers with laptops and caffeine colas do opposition research.

**raptivist** *n.* a politically active hip-hop peformer.

**1987** *Los Angeles Times* (July 19) 58:
Chuck D., a self-proclaimed "raptivist" whose black-consciousness message is more consistently and pointedly political than those of other contemporary rappers.

**1992** *Boston Globe* (Oct. 2) 62:
If white America doesn't come to grips with the anger of "raptivist" Sister Souljah...then the country will tear itself apart economically as well as every other way.

**2001** *San Francisco Chronicle* (Nov. 18) 58:
Political activism and love of music ran in the family, and by the time he turned 20, Riley was both a Communist youth organizer and budding "raptivist."

**rat-fucking** *n.* sabotage; (*hence*) the act of disrupting (the opposition). Also **rat-copulation, rat-dinging, rat-kissing**.

**1928** Nason *Sgt. Eadie* 110 [ref. to 1918]:
This time to-morrow, Jake, I'll be with my own outfit and that's the only ray of sun in my black sky at present. All other troubles fade when I think of that. No more of this rat-kissing.

**1928–29** Nason *White Slicker* 88:
You know, I had a sergeancy clinched if we hadn't run into all this rat-kissing!

**1930** Nason *Corporal* 139:
Well, in all the rustle and tussle in this here gigantic rat-copulation they call a war....

*Ibid.* 171:
This isn't going to be the same kind of a damned disgusting blank-cartridge rat-copulation such as we've been going through on the Border...is it?

*Ibid.* 260:
This will be just the same old rat-dinging all over again.

**1944** P. Smith in *Letter from Father* 391:
*Rat fucking*...at Hanover [N.H.] means the raiding of the students rooms on one floor by the students from another floor—the boys go in groups of eight or ten—turn everything upside down...even fire buckets of water are employed to make the wreck complete.

**1972** in *Ibid.* 132:
Yes, political sabotage is associated with Segretti. I've heard a term for it, "ratfucking."

**1974** Bernstein & Woodward *President's Men* 131 [ref. to 1962]:
The Trojans called their brand of electioneering "ratfucking." Ballot boxes were stuffed, spies were planted in the opposition camp, and bogus campaign literature abounded.

*Ibid.* 134:
I don't think he's involved in the ratfucking. But he's capable of anything.

*Ibid.* 138:
Ratfucking? He had heard the term. It meant double-cross and, as used by the Nixon forces, it referred to infiltration of the Democrats.

**1996** G. Gordon Liddy *Will* (Nov. 15) 282:
By this time I knew that *rat-fucking* was a University of California fraternity term for glorified Halloween pranks.

**2002** D. Brock *Blinded by the Right* (Mar. 5) 81:
David Sullivan was...a master of bureaucratic intrigue and strategic leaking to the press—"rat fucking" the enemy, in Sullivan's words.

**2003** *Time Out* (May 8) 176:
Do you ever feel like taking revenge on the cast? HS: by rat-fucking 'em in the story? Probably now and then.

**2003** *New Yorker* (Dec. 8):
The unholy alliance—between black Democrats and white Republicans—shaped redistricting during the eighties and nineties. [...] Benjamin Ginsberg, a Republican redistricting operative who

helped to construct the unholy alliance during the 1990 cycle, referred to the initiative as "Project Ratfuck."

**reach** *v.* to influence illicitly, as by bribery or coercion.

**1906** A. H. Lewis *Confessions of Detective* 72 in *OED*:
I'd been squared; it was known that I could be reached.

**1908** H.C. Fisher in *A. Mutt* 59:
Baby Jack...disguised as a politician trying to reach one of the jurors.

**1955** Deutsch *Cops* 34:
Somewhere along the line in the law-enforcement system, somebody has been "reached."

**1976** Hoffman & Pecznick *Drop a Dime* 53:
They'd "reached" seven of the fourteen-member panel.

**read** *v.* ¶In phrase:

¶**read out of the party** to be expelled from one's party.

**1846** *Ohio Repository* (July 25) 6:
Is there anything in these sentiments which are anti-democratic, and for which my hard money friends will read me out of the party?

**1851** *Report Const. Convention* 537:
But should a democrat now express the opinion which Jackson expressed in 1832, I suppose, he must, of course, be read out of the party.

**1947** *Waukesha Daily Freeman* (Wisc.) (May 20) 2:
Wallace told the Women's National Democratic club here in March, 1946, that Democrats should be read out of the party or refused assistance in their campaigns if they bucked the administration on major issues.

**1992** *Seattle Times* (Nov. 26) E5:
A minority view says the Religious Right should be read out of the party.

**2003** *Times Union* (Albany, N.Y.) (May 28) A1:
An endorsement like that never would have happened before. Someone who tried to do that would have been read out of the party.

**Reagan Democrat** *n.* a registered Democrat who voted for Ronald Reagan in 1980 or 1984; (*hence*) any white, working class, blue-collar Democrat who votes for a Republican.

**1984** *Washington Post* (Mar. 25):
"I don't care if you are poor or if you are a millionaire," said Maria Rodriguez, a Reagan Democrat who left Cuba in 1960, just after the revolution that brought Fidel Castro to power.

**1992** AP (Mar. 16):
In Heart Of Reagan Democrat Country, A Yearning For Change.

**2004** *Baltimore Sun* (Feb. 19) 17A:
In case you don't wear designer labels, NASCAR Dad is man of the political year. He's the X-Y chromosomes heir to the Joe-Six-Pack, Reagan-Democrat, Angry-White-Man types and stereotypes of years gone by.

**red-headed Eskimo** *n.* a precisely targeted bill, law, or piece of legislation.

**1986** *Washington Post* (Apr. 5):
"It's a red-headed Eskimo," legislative parlance for a narrowly constructed bill that applies to only one person or company.

**2004** *Baltimore Sun* (Feb. 18) 4B:
The legislation is what those around Annapolis call a "red-headed Eskimo"—a bill designed to aid just one person, business or interest.

**red states** *n.pl.* the states whose electoral votes went to the Republicans in the 2000 presidential election; (*hence*) any conservative or Republican state. See BLUE STATES. [Maps used in the aftermath of the 2000 presidential election showed states whose electoral votes went to the Democrats in blue and those whose votes went to the Republicans in red. The colors were not consistent in previous elections. See also BLUE STATES.]

**1992** *Boston Globe* (Oct. 15) 19:
But when the anchormen turn to their electronic tote boards election night and the red states for Clinton start swamping the blue states for Bush, this will be a strange night for me.

**2000** D. Frankel (Nov. 6) on Usenet (alt.religion.wicca):
Now, we're all stuck to our CNN for the biggest horserace of the Millenium (so far anyway:) and we're looking at the Red States (Bush) and the Blue States (Gore) and the Swing States (Gray) and all I know is that I agree with pretty much everything Ralph Nader says and I wish all those states were GREEN:).

**2000** *Deseret News* (Dec. 30):
2000 was the year of The Map. You know the one: red states, blue states, false states, true states, me states, you states.

**2002** *American Votes 2002* (CNN-TV) (Nov. 9):
What you are beginning to see here, blue is Democratic and red is Republican. Just think red states, blue states.

**2004** *Chicago Tribune* (Feb. 15) 1:
Since the 2000 census, a few more electoral votes have migrated from blue states to red states.

**regime change** *n.* a change of leadership.

**1956** *New York Times* (Nov. 8) 18:
Regime Changes Delayed...The announcement of far-reaching changes

in Government personnel that was to have been made at the Sejm today was postponed.

**1971** J. Loewenberg *in Comparative Politics* III 182:
Recent European political history offers numerous examples of instability culminating in the form of sudden regime change, from the Weimar Republic to the Nazi dictatorship, or from the Fourth to the Fifth French Republics.

**1980** *Wall Street Journal* (Mar. 7):
There is...an 8% chance of regime change in Finland.

**2004** *Atlanta Journal-Constitution* (Feb. 19) 17A:
The Iranian people are demanding a United Nations-supervised referendum on the establishment of a democratic system and regime change.

**2004** *Newsday* (Feb. 19) B3:
Lefton's a long-haired kid with long-haired parents, a class activist and espouser of progressive politics whose refrigerator has a MoveOn.org ad urging US "regime change" below a notice about SAT scores.

**REGO** *n.* [*re*inventing *go*vernment] an initiative by former Vice President Albert Gore, Jr., to trim and reorganize government agencies.

**1993** *Newsday* (Sept. 3) 34:
The "REGO" (Reinventing Government) report is a combination of proposals for both immediate and long-range changes for how the federal government does its business.

**2000** *Tulsa World* (Okla.) (Aug. 15) 9:
Gore was pushing REGO, reinventing government.

**rep** *n.* a representative.

**1841** in Bleser *Secret & Sacred* 40:
Our Reps nevertheless took it up.

**1877** Hayes *Diary* 80:
Many senators and Reps were introduced to me.

**1978** in Lyle & Golenbock *Bronx Zoo* 124:
I held a meeting to elect the new player rep.

**1994** *New Yorker* (Dec. 26) 148:
Freshman Rep. (yep) Sonny Bono.

**repeater** *n.* (see 1891 quot.).

**1868** in *OED*:
When every town and city in the United States is voting at the same time, and "colonists" and "repeaters" are needed at home.

**1891** Maitland *Slang Dict.* 221:
*Repeater* (Am.), one who votes early and often at an election.

**1929** D. Lynch *Boss Tweed* 75:
Ballot boxes were stuffed, violence was common, and repeaters journeyed in gangs. Some repeaters votes as often as twenty times in the course of a day.

**Repubocrat** *n.* a Republican who behaves like a Democrat, or vice versa. See also DEMOPUBLICAN.

**1990** *Washington Times* (Nov. 7) A4:
Only radical surgery could have transformed the "read-my-lips" man in New Orleans into the tax-and-spend Repubocrat of the budget fiasco in Washington.

**2001** *Denver Post* (Nov. 24) E7:
In the last election, Libertarians fielded 75 candidates for the 84 seats up in the Colorado Legislature—often providing the only alternative to the Demol-ican or Repubocrat parties in the 21 districts where one or the other of the major parties didn't field a candidate.

**2004** *St. Petersburg Times* (Fla.) (Feb. 14) 1:
One voter is a registered Repubocrat.

**retail campaign** *n.* precisely targeted electioneering. Cf. WHOLESALE.

**1965** *New York Times* (June 5) 18:
His organization for the mayoral campaign will resemble a super-market chain, even to the opening of 76 store-front branches in the city's 76 Assembly Dictricts. "This is going to be a decentralized, retail campaign."

**2000** *Marketing News* (Feb. 28) XXXIV 10:
The presidential campaign is shifting from town halls to television sets as candidates trade the retail campaigning of Iowa and New Hampshire for a multistate advertising blitz.

**2002** V. O'Regan & S. Stambough, in *White House Studies* (Sum.):
This retail politics is nearly impossible in highly-populated states dominated by mass media markets and wholesale campaigning. Sparsely-populated states are more conducive to retail campaigns where the voters expect to meet and know the candidates personally.

**reverse McCarthyism** *n.* discrimination against conservatives; bias in favor of liberals. [First quot. is an unrelated nonce usage, referring to then representative, but later Sen. Eugene McCarthy (D-MN) (1916–), not Sen. Joe McCarthy (R-WI) (1908–1957).]

[**1954** *Washington Post* (June 24) 25:
Rep. W. M. (Schine Ball) Wheeler pitched a no-hitter against the Do-Nothing Republicans. And you might say that the Democrats applied some reverse McCarthyism to pull this game out.]

**1965** *Chronicle Telegram* (Elyria, Ohio) (Mar. 18) 3:
In a kind of reverse McCarthyism, moderate Negro leaders, white

liberals, and government officials have feared to point out the degree of communist infiltration.

**1975** I. Light in *Amer. Journal of Soc.* LXXX (Mar.) 1265:
A kind of reverse McCarthyism is at work. One dare not say anything that might be at all unfavorable to any "oppressed" group lest one play into the hands of the "oppressors."

**1983** *Wall Street Journal* (May 17) 1:
He is trying to make grants available to worthy projects of all stripes and won't practice "reverse McCarthyism" by ruling out conservatives.

**1985** *Los Angeles Times* (July 3) 1:
Artukovic's son, Radoslav, denied charges that his father was involved in the murder of thousands of Serbs, Gypsies and Jews during World War II and accused federal prosecutors of engaging in a "kind of reverse McCarthyism" in allegedly prodding Yugoslavia into action.

**RIF** *n.* [reduction in force] government layoffs.

**1953** *Gazette & Bulletin* (Williamsport, Pa.) 6:
Thousands of other "RIF" slips are scheduled to go out shortly. "RIF" is govermentese for "reduction in force."

**1981** *Washington Post* (Feb. 15) B2:
Federal agencies have been dusting off RIF plans, in anticipation of the substantial jobs cuts that Reagan willl propose this week.

**ripper** *n.* legislation designed to deny opponents power or positions, esp. when they are of a minority party.—often *attrib.*

**1893** *Century* XLV (Mar.) 780:
Since the majority of the legislature was changed in the last election, the ejected Vinopolitans are now before that body with a bill simply "reversing the ripper," as they call it—pitching the incumbents out of office, and reinstating their own gang.

**1895** *Columbus Dispatch* (Ohio) (Apr. 1) 4 in *OED*:
The Merryman ripper bill looks very much as if the Republicans of this city were going to the legislature for offices.

**1917** G. Myers *Hist. Tammany Hall* 354:
It was at this session that a strong effort was made to enact the Tammany-Gaynor "Ripper" Charter...[which] would have arbitrarily deprived them of many of their most important functions of office...An attempt was made to pass the Sullivan Inferior Criminal Courts "Ripper" bill which, by making city magistrates elective instead of appointive, would have restored the old pernicious, demoralizing system of local political influence.

**1937** J. R. Schultz in *AS* XII 319:
The word "ripper" is commonly used in Pennsylvania political parlance to describe a bill that abolishes an office or commission of state or city. Such an act is said usually to have as its purpose the elimination

of an officer or member of a commission who is unfriendly to the party in power.

**ROC** *n.* [rest of Canada] the Canadian provinces, excluding Quebec.

**1991** *Toronto Star* (Sept. 7) D2:
In the rest of Canada, ROC—I'm sorry for this awful acronym; can you suggest something better?—a lot of people also asked themselves if independence in the Baltic states would help Quebec, and wondered how Ottawa could deal with independence elsewhere without weakening its stand at home. This term refers to Canada outside Québec.

**1995** *Boston Globe* (Nov. 3) 3:
"ROC" is shorthand for a big place: the Rest of Canada.

**2003** *Montreal Gazette* (Sept. 14) B3:
This is living proof that when the ROC (Rest of Canada) wants to be as cheesy (*quetaine*) as Quebec, it succeeds brilliantly.

**Rockefeller gesture** *n.* [see 1996 quot.] an obscene gesture of contempt made by closing the fist and extending the middle finger, often with a jab upward; the bird; the finger; L. *digitus impudicus.*

[**1976** Safire in *New York Times* (Sept. 23) 41:
The Washington newspapers gleefully front-paged the use of the hitherto taboo word just as they published the picture of Mr. Rockefeller's breakthrough middle-fingering.]

**1986** *Chicago Tribune* (Jan. 6) C1:
He saw them give the old thumbs-up (a sign of approval except in certain place, such as Sardinia, where it is tantamount to the infamous Rockefeller Gesture).

**1996** *San Jose Mercury News* (June 20):
In 1976, then Vice-President Nelson Rockefeller flipped off hecklers at a campaign stop in Binghamton, NY. That incident gave the maneuver a new moniker, according to San Francisco folklorist Archie Green. "People who wrote about it began to call it 'the Rockefeller Gesture.'"

**rogue state** *n.* a nation acting outside the international rule of law or traditional alliances.

[**1943** *College English* V (Oct.) 47:
Mexican picaresque novels, anti-epics of individualism satirizing the rogue world and the rogue state.]

**1977** J. Lieberman in *Philos. Public Affairs* VII (Autumn) 63:
They will be substantive rules; in short, legislation, which may go well beyond the limited functions of the minimal state. And notice that these are not rules that only a rogue state will adopt.

*Ibid.* 66:
To hypothesize an autonomous state as the defining agency is simply

to maximize the chance of the minimal state's becoming a rogue state, for there will then be no check on its power to transcend its Nozickian limits.

**1985** *Chicago Tribune* (Dec. 10) 23:
Before the war, the Soviet Union had deliberately isolated itself. Its role was that of a rogue state, a revolutionary power that challenged all the others.

**2000** S.D. Cohen *Making of U.S. Intl. Econ. Policy* 40:
Disagreements among all but so-called rogue states are now dominated by such technical issues as measures utilized by governments to alter export and import flows, techniques for correcting balance of payments disequilibria, and the dangers of destablizing private capital flows.

**rope lines** *n.pl.* barriers intended to separate a politician from crowds (of supporters or media); (*hence*) the crowds themselves.

**1980** *Christian Science Monitor* (Oct. 31) 22:
Children have been warned back of a rope line.

**1988** *Chicago Tribune* (July 21) C9:
Trash any rope lines and ignore all Secret Service directives.

**1988** *U.S. News & World Report* (Sept. 12) 14–17:
Keep the media off guard by approaching them at rope lines or on airport tarmacs.

**1991** *Washington Post* (Feb. 2) A15:
Hundreds, mostly women, pressed against security rope lines waving virtually anything that would take a signature for his autograph and shouting support.

**2004** *San Francisco Chronicle* (Feb. 13):
Clinton is the gold standard for working "rope lines," political parlance for the queues of voters hemmed in by gates or ropes as they await a candidate's greeting.

**Rose Garden rubbish** *n.* minor statements made by the president; (esp.) remarks given at ceremonies held in the White House Rose Garden.

**1966** *Wall Street Journal* (June 16) 1:
Mr. Kintner...has also taken over Mr. Valenti's assignment of riding herd on what White House men call the "rose garden rubbish"—the more-or-less routine speeches ground out for the President to give to assorted groups in the White House rose garden.

**1977** *Coshocton Tribune* (Ohio) (May 18) 4:
Califano recalls that it was his duty to review the "Rose Garden rubbish"—brief remarks typed on small yellow cards—before they were passed on to the President to deliver before small visiting groups,

such as Boy Scouts or nurses. The President never looked at the remarks before he read them publicly.

**1988** *Record* (N.J.) (Apr. 17) A21:
Most of the routine paper issued in the president's name is dubbed by White House insiders as "Rose Garden Rubbish."

**1988** K.H. Jamieson *Eloquence in an Electronic Age* 213:
Eliminating inconsequential speeches, labelled "Rose Garden Rubbish" by the press, would free the president for more important thoughts and acitivites.

**1997** *Christian Science Monitor* (Feb. 4) 1:
Speech writers also produce smaller, briefer utterances for the president—toasts at state dinners, greetings to important visitors, and other seemingly innocuous remarks that Eisenhower's two speech writers called "Rose Garden rubbish."

**rubber-chicken circuit** *n.* a series of ceremonial public dinners which must be endured. Cf. MASHED-POTATO CIRCUIT.

**1953** *New York Times* (Nov. 1) 26:
Pity the poor coach. This is his twenty-first engagement on the "rubber-chicken circuit" in the past month and he has to drive 200 miles to the next town after he has finished his pleas for John and the other departing seniors.

**1978** *Globe and Mail* (Toronto, Can.) (Apr. 6) P7:
Constituents demand endless hours of work on their pension cheques and passports, as well as flawless attendance on the rubber-chicken circuit.

**1989** P. Auster *Moon Palace* 11:
No more dance tunes. No more drunken weddings. We've quit the rubber chicken circuit for a run at the big time.

**rump session** *n.* [fr. *rump* 'a remainder of a body of persons, esp. when legislative' (see 1950 quot.)] orig., a meeting held by a group lacking authority which refuses to disband; (*hence*) an ad hoc meeting; a discussion of off-agenda or out-of-policy ideas, esp. by a splinter group.

**1881** *Int. Rev.* (Aug.) 107:
The "rump session," as it was then called, became more and more dismal as it dragged its slow length into the fall months.

**1906** *Reno Evening Gazette* (Nev.) (Aug. 8) 8:
Albert Young, who aspires to succeed Shen, led a bolt movement and his followers, refusing to attend the regular convention, held a rump session in another hall.

**1950** *Independent Record* (Helena, Mont.) (Mar. 5) 2:
The term "rump session" first was used in 1648, when the Rump

parliament of some 60 members continued in session after the purge of 96 members by Cromwell's army.

**1963** *Barron's* (Mar. 11) 5:
Despite exhortations from some industry leaders for a boycott, Mr. Silbaugh's rump session drew more than 100 savings and loan executives and other interested parties.

**1997** W. Holton in *William & Mary Quarterly* (Apr.) LIV 432:
The dual purposes of nonimportation...were best expressed by the man who proposed the first association to a rump session of the burgesses in May 1769.

**rusticate** *v.* [fr. S.E. 'to go to or stay in the country' and Br.E. 'to be expelled (from university)'] to get out or be put out of (office, politics, a campaign, etc).

**1901** *Democratic Standard* (Coshocton, Ohio) (Jan. 18) 8:
Now he returns to the senate as the champion of the same principles for the advocation of which he was rusticated by his constituents.

**1992** *Washington Post* (Feb. 18) D1:
Washington-based poll-taker Harrison Hickman...has been rusticated from the campaign since being caught dissembling to the press— about his dissemination of an attack fax assailing Clinton's draft record.

**1999** *Boston Globe* (Dec. 5) D4:
Maybe it's because Hussein is still in power, and Bush's father is rusticated, defeated the year after winning the Gulf War.

# S

**sachem** *n.* [< Narragansett *sachem,* 'chief or supreme head'] one of a body of high officials in the Tammany Society of New York; (*hence*) a leader.

**1622** *Relat. Plantation Plymouth, New Eng.* 49 in *OED*:
They brought vs to their Sachim or Gouernour.

**1842** *Brooklyn Eagle* (July 21) 2:
Sachems: A special meeting of the Grand Council of Tammany Society or Columbian Order, will be held.

**1850** J. Hammond *Hist. of Pol. Parties* 340:
The institution takes its name from the celebrated Indian Chief Tammany, whose attachment to liberty was greater than his love of life. It has a Grand Sachem and thirteen sachems, in imitation of the president and governors of the states, at the time it was founded.

**1894** W. Jones *Life of James Fisk, Jr.* (Nov. 4) 84:
Make impossible the substitution of Tweed for Stranaham, of Gilroy for Lincoln, or of any smirched sachem for Henry Ward Beecher in this beautiful city by the sea.

**1917** G. Myers *Hist. Tammany Hall* 77:
The Sachems were lobbying at Albany for charters of banks of which they became presidents or directors.

**1984** *Washington Post* (Aug. 2):
Business sachems had long resisted management-training courses lest they appear inadequate.

**2003** *New York Times Mag.* (Dec. 28) 38:
He ushered in a class of political experts who came not from the ranks of ward-heelers and party sachems but from advertising, public relations and television.

**Salt River** *n.* ¶In phrase:

¶**row** (someone) **up Salt River** [there are several claims about this term's origin; see H. Sperber and J. N. Tidwell in *AS* (1951) XXVI. 241-7] to defeat or to overcome. Now *hist.*

**1828** *Reg. Deb. Congress U.S.* (Feb. 2) 1341:
But, sir, I will venture to say this, that, in playing this game, if the Secretary of State is not influenced by the same courtesy which governed the courtiers of the great Frederick, never to beat the monarch at chess, that he could give the President twenty-nine, and as they say in Kentucky, "row him up salt river."

**1832** in *DAE*:
This was one of those threats which in Georgia dialect would subject a man to "rowing up salt river."

**1835** *New-England Magazine* (Apr.) 314:
I thought you would be into the administration-men like a streak of greased lightning, and row them a leetle farther up Salt river, than they have ever been before.

**1839** *Southern Literary Messenger* (Mar.) 206:
The next stage brought us to the bank of the Ohio at the mouth of the Salt river, which...is said to be...violent,...and consequently to require a navigator with strong arms and a stout heart to stem its current. This has furnished the Kentucky bruisers with a striking figure of speech: when they would terrify an adversary with a lively apprehension of rough usage, they threaten to "row him up Salt river."

**1908** *Washington Post* (May 31) 110:
The expression "Up Salt River," which was often used in former days to describe political defeat, owes its origin to a river of that name, a branch of the Ohio running through Kentucky. When Henry Clay was running against Jackson in 1832 he employed a boatman to row him up the Ohio...the boatman was an adherent of Jackson, and he missed his way accidentally on purpose, and rowed Clay up Salt River, and...Clay did not reach Louisville in time, and was defeated.

**scallywag** *n.* a white Southerner supporting Reconstruction. Also **scalawag, scallawag, scallowag.**

**1862** *Charleston Mercury* (S.C.) (Aug. 9) 1 in *OED*:
This invaluable class is composed...of ten parts of unadulterated Andy Johnson Union men, ten of good lord and good devil-ites, five of spuss and seventy-five of scallowags.

**1868** in L. Levy *Grace Notes* 36:
He calls me scallawag/While...I fills my carpet bag.

**1868** in McCorvey *Ala. Hist. Sks.* 174:
The scallawag is the foul leper of the community. Unlike the carpet-bagger he is native, which is so much worse.

**1878** in J. Haskins *Pinchback* 239:
The...Carpet baggers, and scalawags are determined to "make it worse" for me.

**1879** "Tourgée" *Fool's Errand* 125:
"Scalawags," the native whites who were willing to accept the reconstruction measures; and "Carpet-baggers," all men of Northern birth, resident in the South, who should elect to speak or act in favor of such reconstruction.

**1908** S.E. Griggs *Pointing* 90:
Wal, de bes' white people didun't think we wuz fittin' ter vote an' woulden't hab nothing' ter do wid us. Wal, we jes' had ter take de skallerwags.

**1994** *New York Times* (Nov. 13) 33:
Only carpetbaggers, scalawags (including Rhett and Scarlett) and Yankees have money.

**scratcher** *n.* a voter who declines to support his party's entire slate.

**1880** *Scribner's Monthly* (Feb.) 621 in *OED*:
Mr. Evarts will be obliged to look among the "scratchers,"..for the indorsement of...Civil Service Reform.

**1880** *Atlantic Monthly* (June) 764:
How are scratchers and bolters to be dealt with?

**1880** *Atlantic Monthly* (Nov.) 718:
We need more freedom; we must stiffen the knees of the judicious "bolter" and "scratcher" if we are to ever muster courage to insist upon a change.

**secesh** *n.* secession, a secessionist, or secessionists collectively. Now hist.

**1861** "Artemus Ward" in Vanity Fair (May 25) 251:
Secesh! I'm a Dissoluter. I'm in favor of Jeff Davis, Bouregard, Pickens, Capt. Kidd, Bloobeard, Munro Edards, the devil, Mrs. Cunningaham and all the rest of 'em.

**1862** in W. Cothren *Hist. of Ancient Woodbury, Conn.* (Mar. 7) 1152:
Now, embracing the first opportunity after arriving here, I appropriate some "secesh" pen, ink and paper, left in the hurried departure of the owners from this...recent home of the rebels.

**1880** *Elyria Republican* (Ohio) (Feb. 12) 4:
What illiterate ass represents the secesh Democracy of Medina in scribbling for their organ? Their pride must be divided between himself and his grammar. It is bad enough to murder the "bellowing leeches" without murdering the King's English.

**1900** *Anaconda Standard* (Montana) (Dec. 27) 6:
The Cape Colony secessionists hope to make more of a success of secesh than some other famous secessionists they have read about.

**security mom** *n.* a mother whose voting habits are said to be affected by her concern for her children's safety.

[**1993** *Dallas Morning News* (Oct. 23) 1J:
What began as a brainstorming session between coaches and parents resulted in adding a "security mom" to the team.]

**2003** *Time* (Feb. 17) 23:
When I was out campaigning last fall, this was all women wanted to talk about. Not schools, not prescription drugs. It was "What are you doing to protect my kids against terrorists?" Soccer moms are security moms now.

**2004** *News from CNN* (CNN-TV) (Jan. 26):
They're also looking for someone who can keep them safe—the famous security mom's vote.

**Sexgate** *n.* [*sex* + -GATE] a scandal involving sex; most famously any of several sex-related scandals involving Pres. Bill Clinton.

**1991** *St. Petersburg Times* (Apr. 5) 1B:
Some witnesses said House employees are staying late each night to watch the unfolding drama, which lobbyists have nicknamed "sexgate" or "As the World Turns."

**1998** *New York Post* (Sept. 10) 3:
One of two vans containing the 36 boxes of independent counsel Kenneth Starr's Sexgate report arrives at Capitol Hill amid tight security.

**2001** *New York Times* (Jan. 23) B1:
To Thomas Jefferson, [N.Y.C] was a "cloacina of all the depravities of human nature," but to one of his fellow Virginians it was a welcome refuge from scandal. It was where Nancy Randolph fled after being involved in the Sexgate of the colonial era.

**sexual McCarthyism** *n.* the condemnation of others for their sexual persepectives, behavior, or orientation.

**1981** *Washington Post* (May 7) D1:
Diamond said he is not worried that the women's tour will be consumed by a kind of sexual McCarthyism, damaged by unflattering rumor, suspicion and stigma by association.

**1985** *Chicago Tribune* (Dec. 4) C4:
Hugh Hefner decries the Reagan administration's commission on pornography as "sexual McCarthyism."

**2002** D. Brock *Blinded by the Right* 60:
Sexual McCarthyism had been introduced into modern right-wing politics.

**2003** *Arizona Republic* (June 25) B10:
We now have sexual McCarthyism in our state. It goes something like this: The next time you have a grudge against a young neighbor you can find out who he or she was dating at 14, find out if they had sex, and turn that person in for a crime against children. Case closed.

**sheeple** *n.pl.* submissive citizens.

**1984** *Wall Street Journal* (Feb. 27):
Mrs. Anderson begins every book sale with a lecture, and in this instance she derides taxpayers in general as submissive "sheep people"—or "sheeple" for short.

**1995** *Geraldo* (Jan. 30)(syndicated TV show):
Your real enemy is the white Anglo-Saxon, Protestant businessman in this country that's initiating this new world order where all of us are going to be herded up like sheeple.

**2003** *Iowa City Press-Citizen* (May 28) 11:
We've become a nation of compliant "sheeple," satisfied to give up our rights as human beings, just to feel "protected" by Big Brother.

**sherpa** *n.* an official or expert who makes preparations for a summit conference on behalf of a head of state.

**\*1980** *Times* (London) (June 23) 1 in *OED*:
The seven leaders inevitably based much of their comment on the draft communique drawn up for publication after the meeting by the seven government officials—known as the "sherpas"—who have been charged with preparing this summit.

**1981** *New York Times* (July 5) 4-4:
In preparation for the summit of Western leaders in Canada, experts known as "sherpas" have been preparing position papers for months.

**1989** *Federal News Service* (July 5):
This will be the 15th economic summit since it started in Rambouillet in 1975. They've become somewhat more institutionalized than they started out to be with sherpas and post-sherpas and so on.

**1991** *Wall Street Journal* (Apr. 15) 4:
Ms. Lauvergeon...will replace the mercurial Jacques Attali as the President's personal representative and "sherpa" for economic summit meetings, a key job that marks her as one of the president's closest and most trusted advisers.

**shift and shaft** *n.* having a tendency to increase taxes at a more local level by decreasing them at a regional, state, or federal level.—often *attrib.*

**1987** *San Francisco Chronicle* (Sept. 11) 1:
This is a tax shift and shaft bill.

**1992** *Portland Oregonian* (July 9) A13:
Essentially, what is happening is the federal government is shifting costs onto local government. It's what we call 'shift and shaft' federalism.

**2003** *Tulsa World* (Okla.) (Aug. 30) A9:
It's a shrink, shift and shaft policy. Services would shrink, state book

taxes would shift to local pocketbooks, and the shaft is a deteriorated quality of life.

**shirt-sleeve diplomacy** *n.* informal international relations.

> **1898** *Fort Wayne News* (Ind.) (July 29) 1:
> President McKinley is preparing to reply to Spain's peace overtures in a manner so direct and explicit that it will be regarded by Europe as another development of "shirt-sleeve diplomacy."

> **1919** *Star Journal* (Ohio) (Feb. 27) 13:
> This is Europe, not America. We know nothing about your Yankee methods; your shirt-sleeve diplomacy and dollar diplomacy.

> **1927** *Wall Street Journal* (July 19) 2:
> When John Hay, crusading for the Open Door in China, gave to the world both the spectacle and the label of Shirt Sleeves Diplomacy, his corruscating informalities shocked his friend Henry White.

> **1969** R. Kozicki in *Asian Survey* (May) IX 334:
> Israel's instruments for encouraging this process have been several varieties of effective shirt-sleeve diplomacy.

**shrieker** *n.* an anti-slavery advocate. Also **freedom shriekers**. Now *hist.*

> **1856** *Brooklyn Eagle* (Aug. 14) 2:
> The Freedom Shriekers begin to find that the dear people who flock in swarms to Kansas meetings, are more ready to pour out their sympathy than their cash, and that much as they may mourn over "bleeding Kansas," they are unwilling to "bleed" themselves.

> *ca*1859 *Scientific American* (Nov. 21) 337:
> An attempt was made to impress upon the mind of the Commissioner that Hyatt, the applicant, was what is known in modern polities as a "freedom-shrieker."

> *ca*1862 O. Victor *Incidents and Anecdotes* 265:
> They made that poor old man, who was a Methodist class-leader, sit by and see his son hang until he was dead, and then they called him a d——d Lincolnite Union shrieker, and said, "Come on, it is your turn next."

**shuttle diplomacy** *n.* negotiations involving a mediator travelling back and forth between disputing parties; in particular, the Kissinger peace attempts after the 1973 Arab-Israeli war.

> **1971** *New York Times* (Nov. 15) 1:
> A system of "shuttle diplomacy" for quiet contacts between visiting White House officials and Chinese diplomats at the United Nations on matters directly involving Washington and Peking has been set up here in recent days.

**1974** Q. Salim in *MERIP Reports* (May) 7:
By sending Kissinger to the Middle East to secure bilateral agreements (shuttle diplomacy), it aims at excluding the USSR and dividing the Arab states.

**1994** *Los Angeles Times* (June 18) A5:
The Jordan-Israeli track, which had been dormant in deference to [Warren] Christopher's shuttle diplomacy between Syria and Israel, is now going ahead in virtual defiance of Syria.

**2003** *USA Today* (Oct. 7) 11:
He said he would appoint a high-level negotiator to conduct shuttle diplomacy in the region.

**situation room** *n. Mil.* a planning center; (*hence*) a center for handling crises. Also **sit room**. Cf. WAR ROOM.

**1942** *New York Times* (June 3) 19:
Not only does his guiding information come from this small corps of women in the "situation room," but the messages are coded by another feminine platoon.

**1945** *Times Recorder* (Zanesville, Ohio) (Mar. 9) 8B:
An intelligence officer walked into the situation room and asked "what is the name of that new outfit that set up a command post in Brussels this morning?"

**1968** *New York Times* (Nov. 3) 278:
A messenger from the "Sit Room" takes the typed report upstairs to the President's living quarters at 6:30 A.M.

**1972** H.S. Thompson *Letter* (Dec. 19) in *Fear & Loathing in America* (2000) 503:
Even getting into a McGovern "situation room" on the night of a primary when the only other press person allowed through the door is John Chancellor.

**1985** *Record* (N.J.) (May 31) A27 [ref. to 1965]:
Located in the basement of the West Wing, the "Sit Room" was the crisis center of government.

**2001** *Time* (Nov. 26) 23:
Ridge and his staff at the Office of Homeland Security want to use the Sit Room, located in basement of the White House, for high-level meetings.

**slacktivism** *n.* [*slack*er + ac*tivism*] activism which requires little effort.

**1995** B. Palmer on Usenet: (rec.music.christian) (May 16):
Slacktivism 5 lectures.

**2001** *Newsday* (Feb. 27) A8:
They call it "slacker activism," or "slacktivism" (the term preferred by slacker typists). It's not that these e-mails don't intend to do good, the

experts say. It's that they go about it in a way that can too easily become utterly meaningless.

**2002** *New York Times* (May 29) B8:
It's all fed by slacktivism, the desire people have to do something good without getting out of their chair.

**2003** *Penscola News Journal* (Fla.) (July 1) 1C:
Another factor that contributes to e-mail clutter is "slacktivism," the practice of forwarding unconfirmed feel-good items.

**SLAPP** *n.* [strategic lawsuit against public participation] a lawsuit intended to intimidate opponents or activists.

**1989** *St. Louis Post-Dispatch* (Dec. 8) 3C:
In a recent article in Social Problems, Penelope Canan and George Pring of the University of Denver have given them a name: strategic lawsuits against public participation, or SLAPPs. "Every year," they wrote, "in the United States, hundreds, perhaps thousands, of civil lawsuits are filed that are aimed at preventing citizens from exercising their political rights or punishing those who have done so."

**1993** K. Sale *Green Revolution* (August) 89:
One favorite tactic from the mid-eighties on was called the SLAPP— ...filed in the hundreds by developers and polluters against environmentalists seeking to impede their businesses, embroiling individuals and community groups in costly...and lengthy...lawsuits regardless of outcome.

**2003** *Las Vegas Review-Journal* (May 21) 3D:
SLAPP statutes are generally intended to keep large companies or individuals from filing lawsuits with the intention of silencing critics or opponents who may not have the resources to effectively fight defamation suits.

**slash-and-burn** *adj.* aggressive and merciless, esp. when foregoing the possibility of reconciliation.

*****1979** *Gleaner* (Kingston, Jamaica) (Aug. 12) 12:
Mrs. Thatcher's policy of slash and burn among those items of the welfare state which the working class had come to take for granted, merely anticipates what will be forced on any government by 1985.

**1983** *Wall Street Journal* (Feb. 11) 23:
Litton also presented evidence to show that AT&T used "slash and burn" tactics calculated to make cutover from AT&T to Litton equipment as difficult as possible.

**1985** *Los Angeles Times* (Nov. 4) 1:
Argentine President Raul Alfonsin...decreed slash-and-burn assaults on runaway inflation and right-wing extremism.

*****1988** *Financial Times* (London, U.K.) (Sept. 14) 4:
By avoiding a detailed debate on the substantive problems facing

America and restoring to "slash and burn" campaigning, will the man who wins the White House find that when he takes up residence in January he will not have the stature to set a national agenda with any hope of seeing a significant part of it carried out?

**1989** *Wall Street Journal* (Jan. 20):
In picking his cabinet, he emphasized experience and team play, virtues by which he himself lives. This is no doubt prudent, given the prevalence of slash-and-burn politics in Washington.

**1991** *Washington Times* (Sept. 23) A4:
Republican promises like this are easy to discount, because slash-and-burn campaigning is the Democratic forte.

**1992** *U.S. News & World Report* (Sept. 14) 88:
It is cowardly for Bush to campaign around the country, looking like an unemployed airline pilot, alternately doling out goodies and practicing slash-and-burn politics.

**1998** (AP) (Dec. 19):
I stood on this floor yesterday and implored all of us to say that the politics of slash-and-burn must end.

**2003** *California Votes* (CNN-TV) (Oct. 7):
It's a night where the people of California have indicated we want accountability out of our government officials, and we don't want slash-and-burn politics.

**2004** *Centre Daily Times* (State College, Penn.) (Apr. 6) 6:
The president's unprecedented campaign war chest, almost as big as the federal deficits he has spawned, likely will mean an equally unprecedented eight-month air war of slash-and-burn ads against Kerry.

**sleeper** *n.* legislation, attached to an unrelated bill, which could have unexpected consequences.—often *attrib.*

**1927** *Gastonia Daily* (N.C.) (Mar. 31) 1:
As a result of the agitation aroused by the discovery of the "sleeper" clause in the automotive law...it has been found that the exact device specified in the law is manufactured by but one concern.

**1939** *Coshocton Tribune* (Ohio) (June 7) 8:
A "sleeper" clause was discovered today in an emergency bond authorization law enacted during the closing days of the 93rd general assembly which blocks extension of municipal ownership of public utilities.

**1949** *Holland Evening Sentinel* (Mich.) (June 4) 5:
A "sleeper" legislative amendment to an innocent-appearing state home rule act today stirred concern over its possible tax-upsetting effect in Michigan's 11 15-mill tax cities.

**1968** *Portsmouth Herald* (N.H.) (May 16) 5:
The law...could turn out to be a surprisingly important "sleeper" legislation.

**2004** *Sacramento Business Journal* (Feb. 20):
A sleeper clause in the new law—officially known as the Medicare Prescription Drug Improvement and Modernization Act—also alters the way HMOs are paid.

**snollygoster** *n.* a shrewd, unprincipled person, esp. a politician.

**1846** *Commonwealth* (Frankfort, Ky.) (Apr. 7) 2 in *OED*:
Now here I am a rale propelling, double revolving locomotive Snolly Goster, ready to attack anything.

**1895** *Columbus Dispatch* (Ohio) (Oct. 28) 4 in *OED*:
A Georgia editor kindly explains that "a snollygoster is a fellow who wants office, regardless of party, platform or principles, and who, whenever he wins, gets there by the sheer force of monumental talknophical assumnacy."

**1912** *Dialect Notes* III 590:
Snolly-goster, a shyster.

**2000** *San Francisco Chronicle* (Nov. 8) A26:
Advice to the new prez and all the other newly elected officials: Don't be a snollygoster.

**soccer mom** *n.* a mother who concerns herself with her children's after-school activities (such as soccer); (*hence*) a desirable bloc of voting women with busy families.

**1982** AP (July 3):
A judge has found a husband guilty of looting $3,150 from the treasury of the Soccer Moms booster club in Ludlow headed by his wife.

**1986** *Atlanta Journal-Constitution* (July 3) A18 (heading):
Former soccer mom Wagner learned game from sidelines.

**1997** *Vanity Fair* (Jan.) 48:
How foolish it was of Dole to pander to the so-called soccer mom, a phenomenon she depicted as the invention...of mewling feminists.

**2002** *Backwoods Home Mag.* (Nov.–Dec.) 78:
It is a volume every soccer mom, environmentalist, feel-good, knee-jerk do-gooder and politician should study because it will open their eyes to the reality of...fifty-plus years of social intervention.

**soft money** *n.* funds which can only be used for broad purposes, not for a specific candidate or campaign; (*hence*) donations which exploit loopholes in campaign finance laws. Cf. HARD MONEY.

[**1972** *New York Times* (Oct. 29) 47:
The unions are talking about what they call "soft money" from their general treasury that can be spent only to provide information for

members, and "hard money" voluntarily contributed by members to be used for political purposes generally.]

**1984** *Washington Post* (June 3):
In 1980, Republicans pioneered the channeling of corporate "soft money" into state parties to the tune of $12 million to $15 million.

**1990** *Manhattan Inc.* (June) 84:
The source of Coelho's largess was a seemingly endless supply of "soft money," the polite term for corporate and private contributions slipped through loopholes in federal laws limiting campaign gifts.

**1996** *PC World* (Aug.) 5:
Washington is now one of the world's grandest bazaars; the paybacks for last year's huge soft money contributions might be astonishing even by D.C. standards

**2003** *Philadelphia Inquirer* (May 15) A2:
The lower court said political parties could return to raising soft money. It also said they could spend it on a range of party-building activities, including get-out-the-vote drives, overhead, and...possibly ads on political issues, as long as they did not feature federal candidates.

**soft power** *n.* power derived from the influence of non-political and non-military factors, such as culture and media.

**1990** *Newsweek* (July 16) 31:
Nye offers an...analysis of "hard power" versus "soft power." The future, he suspects, lies with noncoercive forms of authority, and here he thinks the Americans have special advantages.

**1990** *Christian Science Monitor* (Aug. 14) 19:
This second aspect of power—getting others to want what you want—might be called co-optive or soft power, in contrast with the hard or command power of ordering others to do what you want.

**1998** *New York Rev. Bks.* (Nov. 19) 45:
They depended on the considerable influence of what Canadian Foreign Minister Lloyd Axworthy calls "soft power": a strong moral message, reinforced by their close partnership with nongovernmental organizations capable of mobilizing popular opinion.

**2004** *New York Times Mag.* (Jan. 4):
Hagel also observed that "the American image in the world is in need of immediate and long-term repair" and suggested such instruments of "soft power" as educational and professional exchange programs, as well as increased language training for American students.

**solid South** *n.* the South as a voting bloc, esp. historically as Democratic.

**1858** S. Colfax *Letter* in O.J. Hollister *Life Schuyler Colfax* (1887) 137 in *OED*:
We have fallen on strange times when the solid South in the House

and a score of Northern Democrats dare to vote "No" on a resolution approving existing laws against the African slave trade.

**1876** *Daily Republican* (Decatur, Ill.) (Nov. 2) 2:
Mr. Tilden is a crafty politician. While he was working up a solid south in his favor he carefully avoided anything that would interfere with rebel plans to plunder the United States treasury under the cover of the law.

**1925** *Century Mag.* (Jan.) 334:
How solid is the Solid South?

**1992** *Watertown Daily Times* (N.Y.) (Mar. 1) 2:
Mr. Bush has not lost California yet, but if the trend continues and the now-GOP solid South starts to break up, he will, in the terms of a part-time resident of Kennebunkport, Maine, be in "deep doo-doo."

**sorehead** *n.* a dissatisfied or disappointed politician.

**1862** *Rocky Mountain News* (Denver, Colo.) (Oct. 16) in *OED*:
What will the 'sore-heads' say now?

**1872** J. Parton in *Atlantic* XXX 273:
Thomas Jefferson as a Sore-Head.

**1884** C. Aldrich in *N. Amer. Rev.* CXXXVIII 93:
Every man of the party must vote the ticket or be set down as a bolter and a sorehead.

**Sore-Loserman** *n.* mocking allusion to the 2000 Gore-Lieberman presidential ticket.

**2000** *Washington Post* (Nov. 16) A28:
A picket-style sign stuck in an Austin Police Department traffic cone said "Clairvoyants Needed to Canvass Ballots." One, designed like the Gore-Lieberman logo, said, "Sore Loserman."

**2000** *New York Times* (Nov. 20) A15:
Each time a news camera ventures its way, the Bush group rushes forward to get their signs—"Sore Loserman 2000"—on television. This prompts the Gore group to rush in and thrust its signs—"George W. Bush is a moron"—in front of the Bush signs, which goads still more Bush partisans to rush in.

**2002** *South Florida Sun-Sentinel* (Sept. 19) 20A:
Florida voters and the entire nation have barely forgotten the Sore Loserman saga.

**2003** *Shreveport Times* (La.) (Nov. 26) 11:
You lost. That proves Louisiana voters prefer Democratic values over Republican values. So quit being a "sore loserman." Shut up, get over it and move on.

**sound bite** *n.* a brief excerpt of speech.

**1976** *New York Times* (Mar. 10) 20:
Faced with the need to limit the Reagan spot to just one minute and

five seconds, David Newman, the producer, had decided to cut the "sound bite"—that is, the portion of the spot that would be devoted to the candidate's actually speaking at his carefully staged news conferences.

**1980** *Washington Post* (June 22) L2:
Remember that any editor watching needs a concise, 30-second sound bite.

**1985** *San Francisco Chronicle* (Feb. 21) 56:
Blandness in public utterance is encouraged by television journalism which, because of the tyranny of the clock, specializes in what are known, in televisionspeak, as "sound bites."

**1999** *New York Times Mag.* (Oct. 24) 77:
But sound-bite politics is not a roaring success, considering that only 49 percent of the voting-age population bothered to cast a ballot in the last Presidential election and only 36 percent did in 1998.

**2003** *Oxford American* (Jan.–Feb.) 45:
My students are shocked to be expected to read or produce more than a sound bite. Hundreds of them have claimed to be unable to generate three pages on any subject, yet you could not convince them that there are deficiencies in their world of surfaces. They rely on pictographs, like cavemen, and the conversations I overhear in the hallway are ceremonies of largely nonverbal calls and responses.

**special interests** *n.pl.* a group, such as a corporation, industry alliance, or an advocacy organization, which seeks advantages for itself or its goals through lobbying or campaign funding. Also *sing.*

**1889** A. Shaw in *Pol. Sci. Quarterly* (June) IV 207:
As regards nominations by third parties or special interests, one might well expect to find them more numerous than they are.

**1894** J. Hill in *Quarterly Journal Econ.* (July) VIII 439:
If there had been a good deal of opposition to the income tax, it did not come from the people as a whole; for the great body of the people were not reached by it in any way. The clamor for the abolition of the tax was a "local and manufactured cry." It represented "a special interest."

**1910** G. Pinchot *Fight for Conservation* 134 in *OED*:
The people of the United States believe that...the Senate and the House no longer represent the voters by whom they were elected, but the special interests by whom they are controlled.

**1936** *Fortune* (Oct.) 115:
What was more serious perhaps was the unscrupulous character assassination to which executives who refused privileges to special interests were exposed.

**1991** *Nation* (Apr. 8) 446:
The war state is...much more *efficient* than the quasi-democratic

model practiced here, with its paralyzing quarrels, its contentious factions (also known during recent election campaigns as "special interests").

**spellbinder** *n.* an enthralling speaker.

1882 A. Alcott in R. W. Emerson 50:
But the free personal mind meets all, is apprehended by all; by the least cultivated, the most gifted; magnetizes all; is the spell-binder, the liberator of every one.

1888 *New York Tribune* (Nov. 15) 6 in *OED*:
The Republican Orators—"Spellbinders"—who worked during the recent campaign.

1925 *Amer. Mercury* (Feb.) 251:
He was already a favorite spellbinder, especially among the German voters.

1942 N. Balchin *Darkness Falls from Air* (1969) 68:
Everybody says Hitler's done a marvellous job in uniting Germany. Personally I think he's put up a mediocre show in losing so many of them. Any spellbinder worth his salt could collect that lot in ten minutes.

1998 *New York Times Mag.* (Jan. 12) 47:
This noisy super-salesman for God—the world's greatest shouter, a tent-revival spellbinder—is capable of modulating his voice to a whisper when he needs to get intimate with someone.

**spin** *n.* an interpretation of persons or events intended to influence others.

1977 *Washington Post* (Mar. 20):
What Pertschuk is accused of is being too ardent a consumer advocate, of "lobbying" members of the committee on behalf of things he thinks are good, of putting his own philosophical "spin" on options, of having excessive influence on Magnuson; in short of acting like the "101st senator."

1980 *New York Times* (Sept. 7) 35:
Charles L. Schultze, President Carter's chief economist, tried to put a positive spin on what has generally been perceived as a dismal economic picture.

1984 *Christian Science Monitor* (Oct. 15) 3:
There is what Robinson calls "media spin." If reporters constantly harp on how badly things are going, if TV news reports put a negative twist on the close of a story, that is "spin."

1988 *St. Petersburg Times* (Sept. 25) 1A:
Each campaign has prepared small battalions of spokesmen to provide favorable "spin" (campaign jargon for interpretation) in the makeshift press room at Wake Forest and on subsequent television programs.

**1990** *Business Week* (July 9) 26:
The spin campaign seemed to buck up some dispirited conservatives, but not much.

**spin** *v.* [perhaps related to the "spinning" of yarns or tales] to color or influence understanding of persons or events.

**1988** *San Francisco Chronicle* (Oct. 6) A1:
To "spin" is to try to ply reporters with self-serving post-event analysis in hopes of winning more favorable coverage.

**1989** *St. Petersburg Times* (Oct. 15) 4B:
I'm not going to spin it.

**1998** *USA Today* (June 29) 10A:
Regardless of how they try to spin it, losing the special congressional election in New Mexico's 1st District last week dealt Democrats a serious setback in their bid to regain control of the House of Representatives.

**2001** *Windspeaker* XIX (July) 21:
Luc Lavoie got paid $600,000 to spin that libel trial.

**spin alley** *n.* SPIN ROOM. Also **spin valley**.

**1988** *Baton Rouge State Times* (La.) (Oct. 5) A1:
The hall was ready for the debate after workers put the finishing touches on network anchor booths, patriotic bunting and even a red-carpeted "spin valley" where Democrats and Republicans will expound on their views of the debate for any reporter who wants to listen.

**1988** *Seattle Times* (Oct. 6) A3:
More than two dozen lawmakers from both parties were flown in for the showdown on "Spin Alley," the area of the press hall where campaign officials circulated to share with reporters their views of the debates in hopes of influencing what got said on the air or put in print.

**1992** *Houston Chronicle* (Oct. 20) A4:
Small armies of cameras and journalists quickly encircled these political propagandists in a wide, open area, affectionately known as "spin alley."

***2000** *Australian* (Jan. 8):
Unknown hundreds of others struggle for their souls while dealing with "the monarchs of spin valley," as Michael White terms the armies of propagandists employed to reshape truth.

**2004** *St. Louis Post-Dispatch* (Jan. 12) E1:
Celebrities in "spin alley" during the 2000 debate included Erin Brockovich, Joseph Lieberman, Richard Gephardt, Al Franken, Star Jones, Rob Reiner, Jack Danforth, Karl Rowe and Christine Todd Whitman.

**spin doctor** *n.* a person who SPINS, *v.*; (*hence*) a public relations person. Cf. SPINSTER, SPINMEISTER.

**1984** *New York Times* (Oct. 21) 4-22:
A dozen men in good suits and women in silk dresses will circulate smoothly among the reporters, spouting confident opinions. They won't be just press agents trying to impart a favorable spin to a routine release. They'll be the Spin Doctors, senior advisers to the candidates, and they'll be playing for very high stakes.

**1991** *Boston* (Apr.) 116:
He needed a top-notch spin doctor, someone who could turn a potentially negative story into something that would make the bank shine.

**1992** *Nation* (Mar. 16) 325:
His most pressing need is for a spin doctor, someone to proclaim victory and stoke the momentum.

**2004** *Calgary Herald* (Mar. 11) A3:
As hockey's body count rises, marketing Canada's national pastime as family friendly is becoming a spin doctor's nightmare.

**spinmeister** *n.* one who manipulates or frames the public debate. Cf. SPIN DOCTOR, SPINSTER.

**1988** *Chicago Tribune* (Nov. 7) 4:
Win or lose, he'll put on a hell of a show. He is a spinmeister extraordinaire.

**1992** *Dallas Morning News* (Jan. 26) 6J:
Mr. Lehrer, the newsman, gets to poke fun at every political spinmeister, portentous prognosticator, candidate handler and campaign consultant he's ever had to engage on the McNeil-Lehrer NewsHour.

**2003** *Wall Street Journal* (Jan. 26) 6J:
Clinton spinmeister Sidney Blumenthal inhabits a parallel universe, connected by various halls of mirrors to what most of us consider the real world.

**spinnable** *adj.* capable of being manipulated or influenced.

**1990** *Chicago Tribune* (Nov. 4) 2:
The supposedly unspinnable journalist becomes spinnable; the objective press is the phantom press.

**2001** *Washington Post* (Aug. 6) C1:
When Bush fell behind Vice President Gore in a crucial Labor Day survey, Stevens told campaign guru Karl Rove: "Spinnable."

**2002** *New York Times* (Oct. 2) B1:
A quick check reveals just one scrap with the law: a recent arrest for trying to sing at a rally protesting education cuts in New York. That's totally spinnable.

**2004** *New York Times* (Mar. 12) 21:
If they hadn't dropped out, the official unemployment rate would be an eye-popping 7.4 percent, not a politically spinnable 5.6 percent.

**spin patrol** *n.* campaign staff responsible for delivering a message to journalists.

**1985** *Houston Chronicle* (Nov. 24) A2:
The "spin patrol" said so. That's the group of White House and administration aides sent to mill among reporters to put the administration's desired gloss—or "spin"—on the meeting.

**1986** *Washington Post* (Oct. 20) A2:
Whatever the reason, history is likely to deliver a harsher verdict of the Reykjavik summit than did the White House spin patrol.

**1998** *Buffalo News* (May 14) C2:
The Julia Roberts spin patrol is in full deployment denying she wed distraction of five months Benjamin Bratt last weekend in London.

**2003** *Palm Beach Post* (Oct. 11) 10A:
Putting Dr. Rice on spin patrol reduces her focus and credibility, both of which she needs to succeed in her crucial new role.

**spin room** *n.* where publicity personnel, campaign staff, and journalists SPIN. Cf. SPIN ALLEY.

**1988** *Washington Post* (Sept. 26) C1:
Reporters tried to approach him, and were startled when a woman with the group screamed at the journalists, "Go down to the spin room!"

**1996** *Buffalo News* (Oct. 16) B3:
How would it be if we came into the spin room with six governors in sedan chairs on our shoulders?

**2004** *Milwaukee Journal Sentinel* (Feb. 16) 15A:
These voters saw the candidates in a way the large media contingent did not—without the filter of the post-debate spin room, or the "rapid response" updates churned out by the campaigns during the debate.

**spinster** *n.* SPIN DOCTOR, SPINMEISTER.

**1990** *St. Petersburg Times* (Oct. 5) 2:
If tax-weary voters overwhelmingly defeat the referendum as expected, political spinsters will suggest it was more a reflection of their views on the sheriff's managerial skills and his credibility.

**1994** *Toronto Star* (Apr. 20) A19:
What advice would Audrey have, as another Ottawa political spinster, for Campbell and her future of long, lonely nights in the nation's capital?

**2000** *Charleston Daily Mail* (S.C.) (Apr. 20) P1C:
Lees directed much of his ire this morning at Plante, calling him a "political spinster."

**2004** *PR Week* (Feb. 2) 24:
Taking a cue from the Pentagon's media policy for "Iraq War: The Sequel," I decided to embed myself with a candidate to study firsthand the tactics of the political spinsters.

**split ticket** *n.* a slate, ballot choice, or election result which includes candidates from more than one party, esp. in a pair such as president–vice president or governor–lt. governor; (*hence*) the simultaneous support by a voter of candidates from different parties as a way of hedging bets. Also as *v.*

**1836** J. Hoyt Let. (Nov. 21) in W.L. Mackenzie *Life M. Van Buren* (1846) 262 in *OED*:
I was reproached by you for having voted a "split ticket."

**1850** *Intl. Mag.* (Dec.) 140:
He was first chosen to the Legislature in 1814, and was reelected next year on a split ticket, which for a time clouded his prospects.

**1872** W. Garrett *Reminisc. of Ala. Public Men* 499:
He was a Democrat, and was elected on a split ticket, with...his Whig colleagues.

**2002** (AP) (Nov. 6):
Arkansans split ticket again: Democrat to U.S. Senate, GOP to mansion.

**standpatter** *n.* a person opposed to increases in taxes or tarriffs in the early part of the 20th century.

**1903** *New York Times* (Jan. 15) 8:
Senator Vest calls him and those who agree with him "stand patters."

**1910** *Current Literature* (Nov.):
It is among the old guard of "stand-patters" that the casualties have been so numerous.

**1916** Comm. on Taxation N.Y.C. *Final Report* 184:
It must be apparent to the densest standpatter that it is very expensive to business men of all sorts...to have to pay their share of the interest on the city debt incubus.

**starve the beast** See s.v. BEAST.

**stature gap** *n.* the perceived differences in electability, recognizability, or demeanor among candidates.

**1987** *Washington Post* (May 24) D1:
The good news for the Democrats is that their stature gap won't be permanent. Sometime between now and the party's convention in

Atlanta in July of 1988, a candidate of more or less presidential size is certain to materialize.

**1991** *U.S. News & World Report* (Oct. 14) 38:
While Democrats have long worried about Bush's "stature gap," the very fact that all their candidates lack much stature or experience could turn into an advantage at a time of such roiling animosity toward Washington insiders.

**1996** W. Strauss *Fourth Turning* 213:
Back in the 1980s, pundits coined the term "stature gap" to distinguish silent contenders from aging G.I. statesmen like Reagan and Tip O'Neill to whom the public still looked for a confident hand on the tiller.

**2001** B. Harpaz *Girls in the Van* 213:
Another big difference between the two...was what her advisors came to refer to the "stature gap," the notion that Hillary Rodham Clinton was simply more senatorial than Dick Lonzo.

**stealth campaign** *n.* low-profile politicking, lobbying, or electioneering, esp. that supported by groups with a non-public agenda, or by funds from non-traditional sources; *Joc.* a campaign which does not seem to have an effect.

**1980** *New York Times* (Sept. 28) 4-4:
To the entourages of the candidates for Vice President, theirs are the "stealth" campaigns. Vice President Mondale, George Bush and Patrick J. Lucey are traveling the country, shaking hands, attacking the opposition and shoring up their running mates' constituencies. But they move in a shroud of near invisibility.

**1980** *Newsweek* (Oct. 27) 38:
Vice Presidential campaigns this year are like black holes in space— swallowing vast quantities of time, energy and equipment so completely that you almost can't tell they are there. Reporters and television crews traveling on the Bush and Mondale campaign planes joke that their respective candidates are conducting "stealth" campaigns—a reference to the secret aircraft that is supposed to be invisible to enemy radar.

**\*1988** *Guardian* (Manchester, U.K.) (Aug. 22):
The Grand Old Party's pointed effort to contrast itself with the vagueness of the Atlanta Democrats (or the "stealth" campaign as Mr. Bush likes to call it).

**1988** *Reuters* (Aug. 23):
He accused the Democrats of running a stealth campaign to mask what he contends is their plan to raise taxes and weaken America militarily.

**1993** *Campaigns & Elections* (Oct.–Nov.):
So far, stealth campaigns have placed Christian Coalition candidates

on school boards, in state and local Republican Party office, and on the floor of the Republican Convention last summer in Houston.

**1997** S.B. Drury *Leo Strauss and the Amer. Right* (Aug. 23) 21:
Ralph Reed has defended the "stealth campaigns" of Christian Coalition candidates who have disguised their political agenda by campaigning on issues such as crime or taxes, but have revealed once in office that their real interests are in gay rights, abortion, and creationism.

**2003** E. Klein *Kennedy Curse* (Aug. 23) 110:
Joe hoped to use his ambassadorship as a stepping-stone to the White House and had directed a stealth campaign from abroad through "a prominent Washington correspondent."

**stealth candidate** *n.* a candidate receiving support outside the usual channels of power, usu. by means of a STEALTH CAMPAIGN; (*hence*) a candidate with unexpectedly strong support; *Joc.* one who runs for office to poor effect.

**1980** *Barron's* (Sept. 15) 1:
Then again, where would we be without her No. 1 son, the Stealth candidate in the Presidential debates, or even without that good old boy Billy to handle our relations with the Arabs?

**1980** *Newsweek* (Oct. 27) 38:
The Stealth Candidates.

**1987** *Los Angeles Times* (Nov. 25) 1:
They are unmeasurable in traditional political terms. They are a mystery. And that's why Robertson is starting to be known, among insiders, as the stealth candidate.

**1988** *Newsweek* (Aug. 22) 13:
He's the Stealth candidate...His campaign jets from place to place, but no issues show up on the radar screen.

**1990** *Business Week* (Sept. 17) 34:
By choosing a "stealth" candidate and by telling right-wingers that Bush's nominee next time around is likely to be more to their taste, the Administration is hoping to slip Souter through in time for the court's October term.

**1995** R. Timberg *Nightingale's Song* 300:
[John McCain] was, in effect, a stealth candidate, racing around auditioning for a job that didn't exist. To make matters worse, he couldn't tell anyone about it.

**1998** N.L. Rosenblum *Membership and Morals* 232:
Society for Good Government, for example. Even their ideological identity is obscure. They are the associational equivalent of "stealth candidates."

**2001** M. Ivins *Shrub* 126:
For some years now the board has been the target of "stealth candidates" from the Christian right.

**stemwinder** *n.* any event, person, or thing of exceptional character; (*hence*) an impassioned public speech or one who gives such speeches.

**1892** Gunter *Miss Divid.* (1893) 68 in *OED*:
"Ain't he a stem-winder, though?" goes on the boy. "He was the most popular man on the line when it was built."

**1896** H. Vachell in *Overland Monthly* XXVIII (Aug.) 170:
I'll give the readers of the *Enquirer* a stemwinder. I can make 'em wiggle.

**1940** *Stevens Point Daily Journal* (Wisc.) (Sept. 13) 16:
He told them that while the speech might look like "American history" to Mr. Roosevelt, it looked like a stemwinder to him.

**1945** *Gazette and Bulletin* (Williamsport, Pa.) (Nov. 16) 16:
The Yankees held a stemwinder of a press conference in their plush new offices yesterday.

**1960** *Great Bend Daily Tribune* (Ind.) (Apr. 13) 6:
A stemwinder is forecast as the athletes gun for first place ribbons.

**1987** *Mountain Democrat* (Placerville, Cal.) (May 22) A8:
It was a real Cuomo stemwinder of a speech, full of passion, humor, good sense and appeals to emotion and public service.

**2004** *St. Petersburg Times* (Fla.) (Feb. 28):
Kerry's early campaign speeches were more filibuster than stemwinder.

**still hunt** *n.* a surreptitious pursuit, campaign, or investigation.

**1828** M.S. Bidwell *Letter* in Toronto Publ. Libr. *MSS B104*. 69 in *OED*:
Under the guidance of Mackenzie, who did not conduct himself with the caution and reserve of a new member, the House went on a still hunt for grievances.

**1871** *Jeffersonian* (June 15) 2:
We have the assurance that this year there is to be no "still hunt"....All the best speaking talent of the Democratic party have volunteered their services, and wil make such a push for victory as has not been made for years.

**1876** M. Halstead *War Claims of the South* 6:
In the Southern Republican States the old Confederate army, reorganized in derringer clubs, is engaged in a deadly "still hunt" for the possession of power that "means business" in an eminent degree.

**1890** C.L. Norton *Polit. Americanisms* 109:
Still Hunt, originally a sporting term, but applied during the campaign

of 1876 to political methods conducted in secret, or underhanded methods.

**1899** L.G. McConachie *Amer. Journal Soc.* (July) V 70:
The still hunt that unduly lengthens the campaign backward from the election is no longer a factor.

**1919** *Sheboygan Press* (Wisc.) (Jan. 27) 5:
I was on a still hunt for the elusive "propriety line" observed by our best steppers—that dead-line of good behavior beyond which the dance referee cries "break."

**1928** *Nevada State Journal* (Reno) (Feb. 25) 8:
Prohibition Director Levi A. Moulton of Nevada yesterday morning went up in the air on a "still" hunt...seeking the telltale signs of steam that reveal the presence of illicit distilleries.

**1935** *Wall Street Journal* (June 22) 4:
A mortgage properly proportioned to *present* prices would be apt to prove a satisfactory investment. As a matter of fact something like a still hunt for this sort of thing has made its appearance already in many places.

**2001** H.J. McCammon et al. in *Amer. Soc. Rev.* LXVI (Feb.) 64 [ref *a*1915]:
Abigail Scott Duniway, an activist in the northwest, saw the merit of what she called the "still hunt"—quiet persuasion on many fronts so as not to arouse opposition.

**strike** *n.* legislation proposed with the intention of permitting it to be killed or vetoed in exchange for a favor or to make a point. Also **strike bill**.

**1885** *Century Mag.* (Apr.) 824 in *OED*:
When a member introduces a bill hostile to some moneyed interest, with the expectation of being paid to let the matter drop... [This proceeding is] technically called a "strike."

**1894** H. C. Merwin in *Atlantic Monthly* (Feb.) 247 in *OED*:
A 'strike' is a measure brought forward simply for purposes of blackmail.

**striped pants** *n.* an image referring to a diplomat or civil servant, or more broadly, artificial formality. Cf. COOKIE PUSHER.

**1941** *New York Times* (June 22) E5:
The United States finally came up this week with a modern definiton of the word "invasion." After three historic years we conceded official-ly what every good Austrian, Czech, Dane, Rumanian and Bulgarian discovered long ago—that a nation can be invaded not only by tanks, bombers and storm troopers, but also by sausage salesmen, mimeo-graphs, radios, ideas, economics and fake diplomats in striped pants.

\*__1955__ S.M. Lipset in *British Journal Soc.* (June) VI 209:
It is, of course, possible that Anglo-Saxon Protestant supporters of McCarthy react similarly to the members of minority ethnic groups to the mention of Groton, Harvard, striped-pants diplomats, and certified gentlemen.

__1955–56__ L. Bogart in *Public Opinion Quarterly* (Winter) XIX 375:
The people from whom we get the policy directives have one ambition—to wear striped pants and a morning coat.

__2000__ D.W. Drezner in *Amer. Journal Pol. Sci.* (Oct.) XLIV 741:
You put the Peace Corps into the Foreign Service and they'll put striped pants on your people.

**stump** *v.* to campaign and electioneer, usu. with a series of public speeches.

__1838__ R.M. Bird *Peter Pilgrim* (1839) 86 in *OED*:
I stumped through my district, and my fellow-citizens sent me to Congress!

__1858__ W.M. Thackeray *Harper's* (Dec.) 112:
In the contest between Judge White and Mr. Van Buren he took the field of White, and *stumped it* through the county.

__1874__ M. Field *Memories* 287:
He told me that during the Taylor campaign he stumped that state in favor of the hero of Buena Vista.

__1988__ R. Dole & E. Dole *Doles* 111:
For the next eleven months, I stumped Kansas in a '68 Oldsmobile.

__2004__ *Gleaner* (Henderson, Ky.) (Mar. 13):
Vice President Dick Cheney stumped for U.S. Sen. Jim Bunning as well as for himself and President Bush at a fund-raiser Friday night.

**stump speech** *n.* election-related oration given outside of a formal setting.

__1834__ *New-England* VII (Sept.) 178:
I once made a stump-speech nine hours long, and, probably, should not have stopped then, had not I been arrested and sent to bedlam for an insane man.

__1908__ *Journal of Accountancy* (Mar.) 409:
Mr. Bryan's address, both in substance and manner of delivery, had all the qualities of a successful stump speech—full of humor, half-truths, shrewd misrepresentation of opposing arguments

__1940__ L.B. Hill in *Journal Southern Hist.* (Feb.) VI 124:
Each, when he sat down to write a letter, was inclined to make a stump speech.

__1991__ *Columbia Journal Rev.* (Jan.–Feb.) 46:
From time to time Mondale's voice grew whiney as he fell back on his old stump speech.

**2003** *Washington Post* (Jan. 12) C1:
I have a mechanism for tuning out when politicians drone on with their stump speeches.

**summit-hop** *v.* to protest, as if on tour, at a series of economic and political summits, esp. as a form of entertainment or when one lacks serious commitment to a cause.

**2001** (AP) (June 10):
Most groups operate on shoestrings, so can't "summit-hop" outside their region.

**2001** *Ottawa Citizen* (July 21) B5:
The media treat professional agitators who "summit-hop" from city to city as conscientious objectors merely "doing their job."

*****2002** *Financial Times* (London, U.K.) (May 2) 8:
I never had the time or money to summit-hop, and I don't know many people who did.

**sunset law** *n.* **1.** a law closing polling stations at sundown. Now *hist.*

**1853** *Const. Conv. of Mass. Debates and Proceedings* (May 4) 592:
Section 9 repeals the Act of the 9th of March, 1839, the open ballot and sunset law.

**1889** *Trenton Times* (N.J.) (Mar. 7) 2:
The repeal of the Sunset law was a backward step. That this law was popular with the people there can be no question.

**1892** *Trenton Times* (Nov. 21) 4:
In view, however, of the haste with which a Democratic Legislature repealed the Republican attempt to introduce a sunset law in New Jersey, we have no hope of such legislation at present.

**1905** *Trenton Times* (Feb. 1) 4:
It is alleged that fraudulent voting is done after sunset. There is no good reason, though, why men not qualified to vote should select the hours after sunset for doing so in the preference to other times. The agitation for the enactment of a sunset law is utter foolishness.

**2.** an expiration date built into a law, after which the provisions it enacts will automatically cease unless the legislation is renewed. Also **sunset provision, sunset bill**.

**1976** *Edwardsville Intelligencer* (Ill.) (Mar. 25) 4:
Called the "sunset" bill, it has provisions to terminate any of Colorado's 44 departments, divisions, agencies, boards or commission that cannot justify continued existence.

**1997** *State Journal Register* (Springfield, Ill.) (Oct. 19) 11:
By creating this so-called sunset law, advocates believe lawmakers would be forced to make changes to the system that has grown increasingly complex and has created more and more problems for individuals and businesses.

**2003** *Wall Street Journal* (May 19) A1:
The bill says the dividend tax would return in full unless Congress acts to repeal it again. That's called "sunsetting" in Beltway patois. But neither friends nor foes of the dividend tax expect Congress to reinstate the tax in 2007. So why add the sunset provision?

**sunshine law** *n.* legislation opening government records to public scrutiny.

**1968** *Playground Daily News* (Fort Walton Beach, Fla.) (Aug. 19) 3:
This is a description of the Florida executive branch today, a government operating in a time when government in the sunshine law is in effect.

**1971** *New York Times* (June 5) 45:
Under the act, called the Sunshine Law because its aim is to bring all public matters out into the open, officials who conduct public business in private are guilty of a misdemeanor and can be punished by a fine...or by imprisonment for six months, or both.

**2004** *Webster County Citizen* (Mo.) (Mar. 12):
Contrary to what one elected official told us two weeks ago, the Missouri Sunshine Law wasn't "written by a bunch of journalists so they can snoop around and stir up controversy."

**Super Tuesday** *n.* a presidential primary held on a Tuesday in which many convention delegates are at stake. [Historically, the month and participating states have varied.]

**1976** *Holland Evening Sentinel* (Mich.) (May 27) 1:
The candidates are concentrating most of their efforts on the three contests on "super Tuesday" June 8.

**1980** *Washington Post* (May 28) A3:
Mostly this is a time to catch your breath and get ready for next week's Super Tuesday, the last big fling of this increasingly suspenseless primary season.

**2004** *Fort Worth Star-Telegram* (Feb. 1) 25:
Seven states hold presidential primaries or caucuses Tuesday in this year's first Super Tuesday. It could be do-or-die for some of the seven remaining candidates because pressure is building within the Democratic Party for anyone who hasn't won a state after Tuesday night to drop out.

**swartwout** *v.* [after Samuel Swartwout (1783–1856), customs collector of the Port of New York, 1829–1837. At the end of his service, he left for England on personal business, retaining more than $200,000 to settle outstanding claims. The true amount taken, whether legitimately or maliciously, was later claimed to be to more than a million dollars. The matter was eventually settled in *Murray's Lessee v. Hoboken Land & Improvement Co.*, of 1856, in which the Supreme

Court ruled unanimously that land sales made with the funds must be voided, and the funds recovered.] to embezzle public funds, then flee. [See 1839, 1848, 1934 quots. at LEG-TREASURER.] Now *hist.*

**1854** F. Fern *Fern Leaves* (Feb. 13) 141:
Not a blessed bit of gossip have I heard for a whole week! Nobody's run off with anybody's wife; not a *single* case of "Swartouting."

**1917** G. Myers *Hist. of Tammany Hall* 124:
The community was so impressed with the size of this defalcation that a verb "to Swartwout," was coined, remaining in general use for many years thereafter. A defaulter was generally spoken of as having "Swartwouted."

**swing voter** *n.* [fr. the phrase *to swing a voter* (from one party to another)] a voter not particularly loyal to any party; a voter who helps decide a close election.

**1958** *New York Times* (Oct. 11) 14:
The Republican problem in western Pennsylvania and West Virginia is to capture Democratic and swing voters to add to the usual Republican minorities.

**1965** *Holland Evening Sentinel* (Mich.) (Nov. 3) 22:
Miss Beck was followed by Philip VanAntwerp, considered a swing voter on the council.

**2003** *Time* (Nov. 17) 22:
The swing voter, so sought after during the 1990s, is getting his attention. The name of the game for both parties is getting their core voters to the polls.

**talk-show campaign** *n.* electioneering made (at least in part) of interviews or appearances on television and radio talk show, and in other forms of popular entertainment.

**1989** *Boston Globe* (Feb. 12) 73:
Ralph Nader requires a continuing reappraisal. The monkish activist ran a strong talk-show campaign against the pay raise, joining forces with a number of antigovernment lobbying organizations along the way.

**1992** *Newsweek* (June 29) 18:
Bill Clinton, Dan Quayle and even George Bush were mired in the muck of the talk-show campaign trail Perot had blazed.

**1999** *Record* (N.J.) (Feb. 3) Y3:
Not everyone is happy with the talk show campaign. In a letter to the candidates, Steve Scully, C-SPAN political editor, asked them to make their announcements "in a public setting" so the non-profit network could cover them.

**2004** *Washington Post* (Feb. 6) 18:
Clinton pioneered the talk show campaign in 1992, trading barbs with radio host Don Imus and playing the sax on Arsenio Hall's show.

**Tammany Tiger** *n.* symbol of the New York Tammany Society, the one-time core of the city's Democratic party, and associated with political corruption. [Created by cartoonist Thomas Nash.]

**1871** *Harper's Weekly* (Nov. 11) XV 1056 in *OED*:
The Tammany Tiger Loose. What are you going to do about it?

**1872** *Atlantic* XXIX (May) 642:
In one of his cartoons published during the war upon Tammany, called, if we remember right, "The Tammany Tiger loose," this is quite apparent.

**1896** *New York State Hearing Rel. to Greater New York* 83:
In his place and in theirs will be seen the typical representation of the Tammany Indian of whom the feet are fondly licked by the carnivorous chops of the typical Tammany Tiger.

**1896** *Scribner's* XIX (April) 488:
The metropolis inclined to scout the competency of "hayseed legislators" to deal with her problems, while the upcountry looked across the Harlem with more sorrow and jealousy than pride, longing to redeem the *imperium in imperio* from its wickedness and its Democracy—both, to the prevailing mind, embodied in the Tammany tiger.

**2001** *New York Daily News* (Aug. 18) 22:
In 1943, the Tammany tiger was toothless and forced to sell its headquarters to the International Ladies Garment Workers Union, which sold it in 1984 to the Union Square Theater.

**technocracy** *n.* rule by technical experts.

**1875** in S. Bauer *Economic Journal* V (Mar. 1895) 9:
Compare the ancient contest between "physiocracy," leading towards "nihilism," and "technocracy" in the history of medicine.

**1929** *Bookman* LXIX 12:
As an alternative to plutocracy, Mr. Evans suggest the establishment of a technocracy—a state in which government would be a business run by technicians created by selective breeding and trained for governmental duties.

**1978** D. Nelson in *Reviews in Amer. Hist.* (Mar.) VI 104:
Technocracy, that most eccentric of depression era radical causes.

**1999** R. Ireland in *Journal Interamer. Studies World Affairs* (Winter) XLI 131:
A third tendency is the march toward pure technocracy. As Latin American societies attempt to modernize and gain advantage in the global economy, considerations of economic efficiency and productivity tend to overtake those of equity and social welfare as technocratic elites prevail over popular associations and movements in governing society.

**technocrat** *n.* [assoc. in 1932–3 with Technocracy, Inc., established in New York by Howard Scott.] a technologically savvy leader or administrator.

**1932** *Sun* (Baltimore, Md.) (Dec. 12) 6 in *OED*:
The Technocrats, thanks...largely to a peculiarly fetching "trade label" which embodies in one word two of the most far-reaching of current concepts, technology and democracy, are succeeding in a remarkable degree in breaking down the apathy.

**1969** J. Kerouac *Visions of Cody* (1992) 264:
But at the same time he was a technocrat, you know this technocracy meetings and the, and the speaker would show how—like for example, victory gardens were foolish because if you put the man-hours and labor and, and the...bit of grass and all the seeds into...the manufacture of, ah—why you would build, a, you know, you know, understand, assembly line and all that.

**1987** *Atlantic* (Mar.) 32:
Rajiv Gandhi has replaced the Fabian socialists who had guided India since independence with a generation of young technocrats who are more interested in building industries that can compete with Hong Kong and Japan than they are in ideology.

**2000** T.L. Friedman *Lexus & Olive Tree* (June 15) 234:
They need a shrewd, honest, savvy pol who can attract the right technocrats around him and lead a democratic process to put in place the social policies and limited, but enforceable, regulations that are the necessary foundation for growth.

**techno-Democrat** *n.* Democratic technology wonk.

**1993** *Business Week* (Oct. 11) 115:
Techno-Democrats have taken over the White House and are going nuts over schemes for an information superhighway.

**1996** *Washington Monthly* (Dec. 1) 24:
There was Gore, the administration's chief Techno-Democrat and high priest of reinvention, extolling his vision of the future alongside Goldin, the superhero-cum-bureaucrat destined (in his own mind, at least) to reclaim the lost glory of the space program.

**\*1998** *Irish Times* (Sept. 12) 10:
Gore is an avid supporter of high technology. As long ago as the early 1980s, he was called a techno-Democrat.

**technopolitics** *n.* campaigning, voting, or participation in government by use of technology; the politics of technology. Hence **technopolitical**.

**1970** J. Goldbach in *Western Pol. Quarterly* (Mar.) XXIII 207:
Acceptance of the new "technopolitics" is not based on the economies of larger jurisdictions so much as the habituation of publics to comprehensive performance beyond scarcity.

**1986** *Los Angeles Times* (July 6) 2:
The manner of selection of the decision making body is very important in technopolitics.

**1991** *Washington Post* (Feb. 27) B6:
Washington-based Blackwell Corp. has another national series in the works....Its "TechnoPolitics" half-hour will debut on the Public Broadcasting Service.

**2001** *Electronic Engineering Times* (Apr. 16) 1:
Once deemed too exotic to ever be practical, extreme-ultraviolet lithography has proved itself in the laboratory but is now battling international technopolitics to show that it's commercially workable as well.

**teledemocracy** *n.* use of electronic media, esp. television, in the political process.

**1984** *PS* XVII (Spring) 361:
The Imminent Future of Tele-Democracy: Or It's Time We Talked Back to Big Brother.

**1994** *Chicago Tribune* (June 20) 1:
Even now the new technology poses the threat, or promise, of undermining representative democracy by rendering it unnecessary. Democracy is about to meet teledemocracy.

**1997** T. Luke in *Theory & Event* I:
Netcentric citizenship can follow virtual offices and factories out on to the Net. Might not digital beings of this sort be encouraged, for example, to press for teledemocracy in cybernetic referenda?

**2000** *Globe and Mail* (Toronto, Can.) (June 23) A5:
This weekend's vote will feature ballot-box voting in some ridings, and something called "teledemocracy" in others. Those living in ridings without large numbers of Alliance members will cast their votes by calling a 1-900 number.

**telephone banking** *n.* polls or telemarketing conducted via telephone.

**1988** *Chicago Tribune* (Jan. 12) 14:
Busloads of Dukakis volunteers—mostly students and, natch, Greeks—will head west for doorbell ringing and telephone-banking.

**1990** *Washington Post* (Aug. 29) A1:
The Post results are "totally at variance" with the results of her own telephone banking, an unscientific procedure that she said showed nearly 50 percent of the electorate undecided.

**1999** *Washington Post* (Mar. 8) B1:
Activists in both Republican and Democratic parties already have crossed the starting line for their marathon of organizing, polling, fundraising, telephone banking and mailing that culminates in the Nov. 2 general elections.

**theoconservative** *n.* a political conservative influenced by religious principles; a conservative who believes religion should play a role in politics and policy. Also **theocon, theo-con, TheoCon**.

**1989** *Newsweek* (Apr. 17) 25:
TheoCons. Hero: Pat Robertson. Enemy: TV sex and leering lyrics. Sacred Text: The New Testament (plain English version).

**1996** *New York Times* (Dec. 14) 1-9:
Challenging these "neocons" are what Mr. Heilbrunn labels

"theocons"—"mostly Catholic intellectuals who are attempting to construct a Christian theory of politics that directly threatens the entire neoconservative philosophy."

**1998** *Natl. Catholic Reporter* (Nov. 20):
Now another hyphenated word, theo-conservative, has appeared on the political scene.

**2003** *New York Observer* (Apr. 28):
"Journal of Religion and Public Life," home to Catholic neocon Father Richard John Neuhaus..., preeminent "theocon."

**think tank** *n.* an interdisciplinary institute or organization providing policy advice or research.

**1958** G. Shackle *Economic Journal* LXVIII (June) 362:
Professor Kenneth Boulding's conception in its universality of application and explanatory power seems entirely his own, and its creation will surely stand as one of the most striking products of the Center for Advanced Study in the Behavioral Sciences (known in some quarters as the Think Tank) and Palo Alto.

**1968** *Tri-City Herald* (Kennewick, Wash.) (Dec. 29) 51:
Those Super-Secret Think Tanks: Good or Evil?

**1999** *Columbus Dispatch* (Ohio) (Oct. 22) 20:
In the year after State Issue 2 went down in flames on May 5, 1998, money continued to go to campaign consultants and a think tank.

**third house** *n.* lobbyists. *Joc.*

**1841** *US Democratic Rev.* IX (Dec.) 583:
If the principle of general legislation should be adopted in this country, we should be struck with its purifying influences; the effect would be instantaneous in annihilating "the lobby," or "third house," that imbodiment of selfishness and gross corruption.

**1850** O. Turner *Pioneer History* 60:
In proportion as it was urgent, or interesting, would be the attendance of laymembers, or those who constitute "the third house," in modern legislation.

**2004** *San Francisco Chronicle* (Jan. 31):
Lobbyists—the so-called Third House—are waiting to see who will emerge as the new powers in Sacramento after the installation of a Republican governor who says he is hostile to special interest politics.

**third way** *n.* a strategy partially or wholly repudiating traditional policies of both the right and left.

**1988** *New York Times* (Sept. 11) 6-164:
We don't yet have a conceptual framework for these structures, or a vocabulary to describe them. This is not worker capitalism, and it's not state socialism. It's a third way, a new alternative that points toward the creation of democratic firms in a democratic economy.

**1992** *Boston Globe* (May 4):
"This is a third way," Clinton said in describing his idea of "empowering" community organization. He said it should replace traditional Democratic aid programs, as well as what he described as a decade of Republican neglect of urban problems.

**1993** P.L. Berger in L. Diamond *Capitalism, Socialism, and Democracy* (Aug.) 7:
All talk of a "third way" between capitalism and socialism stands revealed as nonsensical. There is no "third way."

**1998** *Omaha World Herald* (Jan. 28) 1:
We have moved past the sterile debate between those who say government is the enemy and those who say government is the answer. My fellow Americans, we have found a third way.

**2004** *Mercury News* (San Jose, Cal.) (Mar. 8):
Though the debate will now focus on where to cut programs or whether to raise taxes, there's an overlooked "third way" that can help close this gap: boosting government productivity, so that taxpayers get more for less.

**thought police** *n.* in a totalitarian state, a police force established to suppress freedom of thought.—usu. figuratively or accusatively today.

**1944** *Sunday Times-Signal* (Zanesville, Ohio) (Jan. 16) 2-7:
There was respect in his manner; but not the hushed, awful respect the Japanese show their emperor, whose name they never can mention. The cabbie worried that "thought police" might imprison him for something they imagined was on his mind.

**1949** "G. Orwell" *Nineteen Eighty-Four* 49:
He had denounced his uncle to the Thought Police after overhearing a conversation which appeared to him to have criminal tendencies.

**1979** *Washington Post* (May 29) B1:
One recent visitor from Southern California reported that 14-year-olds out there, which is to say the Thought Police of American popular culture, are approving things not as boss, hot, neat, bad, or tough but—are you ready?—"gnarly."

**1993** *St. Petersburg Times* (Dec. 15) 20A:
Do we really want a thought-police crackdown?

**2004** *Visalia Times-Delta* (Cal.) (Mar. 13):
While it may be offensive to people, we're not the obscenity police. We aren't the thought police.

**thugocracy** *n.* rule by thugs.

**1982** *New York Times* (June 20) 7-10:
The cruise ship is another Pequod, or ship of fools: one of those large symbols with strings attached, by means of which the writer snarls at

socialist thugocracy, the class warfare of crooks versus fools, third-world liberation movements, the United Nations and just about everything else.

**1988** *Washington Post* (Aug. 14) B7:
If Dukakis had been president in 1983, Grenada today would be a Cuban-run thugocracy.

**1993** R. Kaplan *Arabists* 279:
Some Arabists argue that the closed and totalitarian nature of the Saddam thugocracy made assessments of it problematic.

**2000** J. Dreyer in *Amer. Pol. Sci. Rev.* XCIV (Mar.) 207:
Perhaps An Chen could have addressed the question of whether the decline in party influence and unbridled corruption could have resulted in some other future for China than democracy, possibly the "thugocracy" experienced by parts of the former Soviet empire or a resurgence of regionalism and localism.

**timber** *n.* a character suitable to qualify one for office.

**1854** *Daily Telegraph* (Alton, Ill.) 4:
Rumors had reached us weeks ago that Col. Benton was undoubtedly prominent among the Presidential timber trees of 1856.

**1872** *Nevada State Journal* (Reno) (June 1) 2:
Messrs. Colfax and Blaine would unquestionably make excellent Presidential timber.

**1881** *Daily Republican* (Decatur, Ill.) (Dec. 19) 2:
It is generally understood among the politicians who are nearest the President that there will, when the cabinet is completed, be found no Presidential timber in its composition.

**1914** *Emporia Gaz.* (Jan.) 2:
He is everlastingly...N.G. as gubernatorial timber.

**1923** *Wisconsin Rapids Daily Tribune* (Dec. 19) 5:
The two names most frequently heard as vice-presidential timber on the democratic ticket, are E.T. Meredith and Gray Silver.

**1989** *Chicago Sun-Times* (Feb. 5) 14:
If Jews do not line up behind Sawyer, several community leaders said, it simply will be because they do not consider him to be good mayoral timber.

**2003** *San Antonio Express-News* (Texas) (Sept. 21) 4H:
Forgive me, but I don't think he is congressional timber, let alone qualified for president.

**tin pan** *n. Ohio.* a secret caucus of Democratic legislators working outside normal procedures and hierarchies to develop legislation to be forced by its majority power upon the state legislature. Hence tin-pan, v.—often *attrib.* Now *hist.*

**1840** *Huron Reflector* (Ohio) (Mar. 10) 2:
Another delegation bore aloft an old Tin-pan with the bottom knocked out, to show the condition of the TIn-pan party of Ohio...a very "dignified" body that has been cooking up a dish of unpalatable laws in Tin-pan this winter.

**1842** *Huron Reflector* (Ohio) (Aug. 16) 3:
You, the people of Ohio, have now an opportunity to crush this system of *Tin pan* legislation, whence has originated all the miserable laws, whereby your interests have been trodden down into the dust....We have appealed from the iron despotism of the *Tin Pan* directly to you, in whose hands rests all political power, and by whose breath alone, are we, as legislators, permitted to live.

**1842** *Huron Reflector* (Ohio) (Aug. 23) 2:
Night after night, they have "Tin Panned"—night after night, have they deliberated in darkness upon their various plans, and not until last night, after nearly three weeks of the session have elapsed, have they been able to agree *among themselves* upon any one scheme.

**1848** *Defiance Democrat* (Ohio) (Mar. 23) 1:
Finding themselves in a dilemma, brought upon them by an utter disregard of all political honesty, and all constitutional rights, invoked the aid of the tin pan; and as might be expected, and as was determined in this midnight caucus, they undertook by resolution to legislate upon the bill while it was in the possession of the Senate.

**1850** *Defiance Democrat* (Ohio) (Feb. 9) 2:
Most democratic members came here with honest hearts and independent minds, free from the shackles of tin pan, resolved to be upright and perform the duties of legislators in a manner which their better judgments may seem to dictate; but when they go in there, they have to ride the goat, their independence is frittered away, and they come out a machine, a prostitution of their liberties, and slaves to *tin pan*.

**tissue ballot** *n.* a ballot printed on onion skin or tissue paper, which, when stacked with others, has the appearance of a single standard-weight sheet, but when separated into individual pages, permits more than one vote to be cast.

**1878** *New York Times* (Nov. 7):
If the votes were counted as they were cast, Mackey would have 5,000 majority, but the boxes at nearly every poll in the district were stuffed with tissue ballots.

**1878** *Traveler-Herald* (St. Joseph, Mich.) (Nov. 23):
In all the counties where there was opposition, the Democrats voted a diminutive tissue ballot, inclosed generally in a larger one.

*Ibid.*:
The tissue-paper tickets are generally throughout Republican counties, showing that the scheme emanated from headquarters.

**1880** *Elyria Weekly Republican* (Ohio) (Sept. 23) 3:
In 1876, we had lost the South altogether, but there still lingered somewhat of the courage that fought for the right of the ballot against the fraud of the bull-dozer and the tissue ballot of the Ku-Klux.

**1880** in E. Pierrepont *Speeches* (Oct. 6) 17:
Is it a marvel that the Party which made the false count in 1868 and committed the tissue ballot crimes quite lately, should return a fraudulent Census?

**1883** G. Green in *North American Rev.* CXXXVII (Sept.) 263:
At the Eighteenth Ward caucus of that city, in 1881, more tissue ballots were found than there were voters in the whole ward.

**1891** *Bucks County Gazette* (Pa.) (Jan. 29) 2:
If they and some of their sister states should present themselves just as they are, with shot-gun, tissue-ballot, political terrorism, moral darkness and all, in the fore-ground, the angel of progress, instead of exulting, would be more likely to turn aside and weep.

**1920** *Indianapolis Star* (Mar. 27) 6:
From these states senators have been elected for the last half century by all manner of fraud upon the ballot from the time of the Klu Klux Klan and the tissue ballot regime to the date of disfranchising the negroes of the South by the grandfathers' clause and actual intimidation, coupled with fraud and murder.

**town hall** *n.* an informal gathering between a politician and voters.—often *attrib.*

**1977** *Washington Post* (Jan. 6) D1:
It's suggested that Carter have over some "just plain people" for lunch or dinner at the White House: that Carter and Mondale "meet periodically in public school auditoriums...in old-fashioned town hall meetings": that the Carters, Mondale, and Cabinet members "devote one Sunday afternoon to calling people all over the country for a three-minute conversation."

**1985** *Houston Chronicle* (Sept. 8) 34:
White, middle-income conservative types appeared to make up most of the audience of 200-plus at the town hall meeting last week

**1990** *Canada News Wire* (Aug. 17):
The political action campaign will include radio and newspaper advertising, distribution of a pamphlet explaining the funding situation in Metro, and a town hall election forum on September 28.

**2003** *New York Times* (Dec. 21):
Let's see now, Lieberman, Kerry's sister, Edwards twice, Dean twice, Sharpton did a town hall, Clark came by.

**tracker** *n.* a researcher who closely monitors opposing candidates.

**2000** *New Republic* (Sept. 8) 21:
The tracker...trained his digital camera on Lazio as the candidate worked the crowd....The man was...a "tracker"—a low-paid spy used to log hundreds of hours of video footage...that can be cut and spliced into an attack ad.

**\*2000** *Times* (London) (Oct. 11):
Mr Lazio said that Clinton "trackers" had begun appearing at his events as soon as he entered the Senate race in mid-May and since then had also turned their attention to his wife. Trackers have become a feature of US politics as campaigns try to keep tabs on opponents and ensure that they have videotapes of any gaffes they might make.

**2003** *New York Times* (Nov. 23) 22:
They include "trackers" who monitor and record rival candidates, researchers who delve into records and minions who spend their days sending these nuggets by e-mail to reporters in hopes of establishing negative story lines on the opposition.

**2004** *Boston Globe* (Jan. 2) A13:
But any sign of momentum, the Clark team knows, draws increasing scrutiny; at a town hall meeting in Newport on Sunday, at least three "trackers" from rival campaigns recorded Clark's every word on video cameras.

**transnational progressive** *n.* a person who espouses a multinational leftist political view opposed to hegemony and cultural domination, usu. accused by opponents of threatening national sovereignty or of having naiveté.

[**1982** C. Chase-Dunn in *Latin Amer. Res. Rev.* XVII 171:
A Gramsci of the world system would focus both on possible progressive coalitions within nations and an analysis of international and transnational progressive alliances for combating and resisting capitalism.]

**1994** S. Hartman in *Callaloo* XVII (Spring) 446:
At a panel I moderated on the practice of feminist theory, Jacqui Alexander raised the issue of coalition politics and the difficulty our proper name, "African American women," posed to developing a more encompassing transnational progressive agenda.

**2000** T. Haskell in *Rev. in Amer. Hist.* XXVIII (Mar.) 157:
Rodgers explicitly acknowledges that the exchange of information and opinions between Europe and America became more intense during and after the war than ever before... Yet he is quick to insist that during the 1940s the connection—in spite of having been the very wellspring of the transnational progressive impulse a few years earlier—ceased serving progressive ends.

**2003** *Toronto Sun* (July 20) C2:
I suppose the rationale is to include a range of opinion, but the anti-American, transnational progressive philosophy is all too well covered by other Canadian publications and media outlets.

**tranzi** *n.* TRANSNATIONAL PROGRESSIVE.— usu. considered derogatory, in part by comparison with spelling of "Nazi."

**2002** *Samizdata.net* (Aug. 18):
John Fonte has done us all a service by running his nails deliciously down that spot and we will hear more of him and, more importantly, much more of the "Transnational Progressives" ("Tranzis") he so graphically disects.

**2002** *NewsMax.com* (Aug. 30):
Tranzi stands for Transnational Progressive.

**2002** *Ottawa Citizen* (Nov. 5) A16:
Fonte defines this clash as one between liberal democrats and "transnational progressives" or "post-democrats"—the tranzis and the PDs, as they've been dubbed.

**trickle-down** *adj.* of a system or event in which a change at a macro level has repercussions at micro levels; (*specif.*) a system in which benefits or knowledge provided to an upper class, privileged group, or favored industry are said to pass indirectly to the less-advantaged. Also *v.* and *n.*

[**1924** *Gettysburg Times* (Pa.) (Aug. 19) 5 [advertisement]:
If a fountain pen or a furniture polish is worthy, sooner or later you are likely to hear of it. Even if you never read the advertisements, the good news may trickle down to you in time.]

[**1932** *Daily Times* (Burlington, N.C.) (Oct. 8) 4:
[Hoover] still wants to pour in relief from the top, expecting it all to trickle down to the bottom—from the banker down to the breadline.]

**1938** *Coshocton Tribune* (Ohio) (Apr. 20) 4:
The "trickle down" system was the idea of the late Andrew W. Mellon, who believed that if you fed business to the big firms at the top, without taxing them too much, the benefit eventually trickled down to the worker at the bottom. Only difficulty was that the system was too well named. The "trickle" which emerged at the bottom was, in fact, only a trickle.

**1954** A. Stevenson in *New York Times* (Oct. 3) 54:
The Republicans have stood together, consistent with their tradition of trickle down economics, favors for the few and prayers for the many.

**1968** P.L. Doerring & A.L. Rutledge in *Family Coordinator* (Oct.) XVII 258:
The "trickle-down" effect of the disturbance from the grandmother to the mother can be described as the mother's lack of having a model of

a woman whose personality was defined, feminine, consistent, and giving.

**1969** G.F. Rohrlich in *Journal Risk and Insurance* (Sept.) XXXVI 347:
This is not to deny that the "trickle-down" effect of economic growth without special ameliorative measures would improve matters, albeit gradually and slowly.

**1979** *Washington Post* (May 6) B1:
He wants development in rural areas but he does not want people separated from the land and packed into urban centers. He is skeptical of "trickle down" benefits from big industrial projects.

**1981** *Christian Science Monitor* (Dec. 7) B16:
The trickle-down knowledge from specialized marine-research schools needs to take into account the fact that this country was "discovered" by sea.

**1983** *Journal Intl. Bus. Studies* (Winter) 162:
Also lacking is any comment concerning "trickle down effect," and any mention of how an effective demand can be brought about by employment.

**1994** S. Eastaugh *Tough Choices* (Mar. 30) 58:
Some wags such as John Kenneth Galbraith suggested that the trickle-down was a yellow liquid filtered through the kidneys of the rich, or the solid droppings left by the rich for the poor birds.

**2002** *San Francisco Chronicle* (Jan. 11) D22:
The Bush administration also has a tax plan remarkably similar to the one implemented by Ronald Reagan, the old trickle-down, tax-cuts-for-rich-people, deficit-financing two-step. It didn't work then, and it won't work now.

**2004** *Saratogian* (N.Y.) (Mar. 15):
Gary Latti, owner of Marino's Pizza, has had to pay a surcharge of $5 or $10 on deliveries to his establishment because of surging gas prices. "It's just the trickle-down effect," he said.

**trickle-down government** *n.* a system of vesting power or funds in larger (national) government structures or programs, said to aid smaller (state or municipal) governments and programs.

**1988** *Washington Post* (Oct. 20) D4:
Keyes said Sarbanes wants a form of trickle down government, where power is vested in big government and the benefits filter down "through an intolerably complicated system" to reach those at the bottom.

**1992** *U.S. News & World Report* (Nov. 2) 36:
President Bush accused Bill Clinton of promoting "trickle-down government" during the third presidential debate...One of the things

Bush was alluding to is Clinton's plan to spend federal money on local infrastructure projects.

**1997** Federal Documents Clearing House (Aug. 6) transcript:
We've also learned that we cannot get there through trickle-down government, of government that, however well meaning, keeps all the power, all the authority, all the decision-making for itself. That approach does not empower anyone outside of the Federal Triangle.

**2000** *American Prospect* (May 22) 5:
Government benefits from universal programs do not simply "leak" to the rich; they pour out in a massive flood, leaving little to help the poor....Progressives have adopted a trickle-down philosophy about government programs. Big benefits for wealthy communities are deemed necessary because the poor will get a small piece of the pie. However, like trickle-down economics, trickle-down government is failing the poor.

**2001** AP (June 15):
Trickle down government has reached the local level.

**trickle-down liberalism** *n.* liberal policies which affect or penetrate areas of society and government other than those they are claimed to target; TRICKLE-DOWN GOVERNMENT. —usu. derogatory.

**1988** *Washington Post* (May 2) A21:
The theory seems to be that, when you give the middle class a big enough government subsidy, voters won't mind if a little bit ends up helping the poor. You might call this "trickle-down liberalism."

**1993** *Los Angeles Times* (July 6) 22:
All that liberals are likely to get under Clinton, in the view of many analysts, is leftover benefits from middle-class programs, or what amounts to "trickle-down" liberalism.

**1994** S. Eastaugh *Tough Choices* (Mar. 30) 58:
The real danger was trickle-down liberalism. Start a program in the name of helping the poor, but focus most of the dollars on the middle class and the rich.

**1999** *Capital Times* (June 14) 11A:
If you still don't like the reference to the book from which it came, "You will reap what you sow," to explain what has happened, then just call the phenomenon simply "Trickle-Down Liberalism."

**Triple-Headed Monster** *n.* an early name for the Constitution. [Usu. attributed to John Lansing (1754–1829) of New York.] See KITE.

**1887** *Atlantic* (Nov.) 687:
The Constitution was called the "triple-headed monster," and declared to be "as deep and wicked a conspiracy as ever was invented in the darkest ages against the liberties of free people."

**1988** in *WIlliam & Mary Quarterly* XLV (Jan.) 31 [ref. to 1787]:
The reason the results would not be quite that bad is that the new American state created by that "triple headed monster" of a Constitution was much closer to Madison's state than to Hamilton's— at least, that is for the rest of the eighteenth century and through most of the nineteenth.

**triumphalism** *n.* an (unwarranted) sense of invincibility which comes from previous success.

**1969** V. Lorwin in *Industrial & Labor Rel. Rev.* XXVIII (Jan. 1975) 252:
Its leaders have even shown a sensitivity to what its then president called a few years ago—in language drawn from the history of the church—"the danger in a successful movement of a certain 'triumphalism.'"

**1991** *U.S. News & World Report* (Mar. 11) 50:
To its credit, the Bush administration has avoided triumphalism or imperial designs, and has promised to bring U.S. forces home quickly.

**1999** *Journal Amer. Citizenship Policy* (Apr.–May) 8:
From the point of view of Gingrich-style Republicanism, the takeover of the House in 1994 was evidence that the American majority had recognized that Republicans, not Democrats with their false promises, had the people's true interest at heart. This view gave rise as well to another distinguishing characteristic of Gingrich's Republicanism: its triumphalism.

**2003** *Boston Globe* (Dec. 30) A15:
He was demonstrating that things could get better without the need for a complete victory by American unilateralists or anti-invasion multilateralists. He was demonstrating that progress in increments could lead to stability and lasting progress without chest-thumping triumphalism.

**trust-buster** *n.* a person who prevents or dismantles monopolies, or enforces laws against them.

**1897** *Marion Daily Star* (Ohio) (Mar. 3) 4:
As a trust-buster Mr. Lexow will not be pointed to with any great pride.

**1903** *Atlanta Constitution* (May 9) 7:
No permanent relief from the present railroad situation will ever come in Georgia until the state controls her railroads instead of the railroads running the state. And therefore we say, Georgia needs a trust-buster.

**1940** *Long Beach Independent* (Cal.) (Apr. 23) 17:
Trust Buster Would Ban Studio Ownership of Movie Theaters.

**2004** *Missoula Independent* (Mont.) (Mar. 11):
Is it conceivable that the Democrats would now put a Coal Trust buster a mere heartbeat away from the governor's office?

**truth deficit** *n.* a lack of honesty; (also) the withholding of information.

**1993** *Chicago Tribune* (Feb. 28) C3 [headline]:
Truth deficit is tough to rein in.

**1998** *New Orleans Times-Picayune* (La.) (Mar. 1) A8:
A president with a truth deficit cannot heal Washington's value deficits.

**2004** *New York Times* (Mar. 30):
What's really interesting is that with each attack, this administration is building up the truth deficit to go along with the jobs deficit, and the fiscal deficit, and their international intelligence-gathering credibility deficit.

**truth squad** *n.* a group formed to question statements made by an opposing party or campaign.

**1952** *New York Times* (Oct. 2) 25:
Republicans here, apparently nettled by President Truman's continuing attacks on Gen. Dwight D. Eisenhower, the party's Presidential nominee, during his whistle stop tour of the Far West, today dispatched a flying "truth squad" of Republican Senators that will play leap frog with the President for the remainder of his two-week schedule.

**1969** H.S. Thompson *Letter* in *Fear & Loathing in America* (Mar. 10):
I deliberately avoided using technical matter as far as possible, in order to avoid any chance of hassling with an Air Force "truth squad."

**1980** E. Marshall in *Science* XXIX (Aug. 1) 573:
It has helped placed industry technicians on television and radio talk shows, conducted an expanded pronuclear advertising campaign, and sent an "energy truth squad" to follow and correct Jane Fonda and Tom Hayden on their nationwide anti-nuclear campaign.

**2004** *Quad-Cities Times* (Mar. 10):
A similar conservative group...intends to conduct grass-roots organizing and air television ads, too, according to its Web site. It plans to act as an "issue truth squad."

**turkey farm** *n.* a department or agency staffed with political and patronage hirees; (*broadly*) an underperforming office.

**1977** *Wall Street Journal* (Sept. 26) 1:
Almost every department has a "turkey farm," a special division created to pool many of the department's incompetent workers where they can do minimum damage.

**1978** *Washington Post* (Oct. 19) C2:
"We don't plan to detail people to Alaska, or create 'turkey farms'" where government incompetents are often kept out of harm's way, but still on the payroll.

**1992** *Buffalo News* (Sept. 2) A5:
The Federal Emergency Management Agency, or FEMA, is widely viewed as a political "dumping ground," a turkey farm if you will, where large numbers of positions exist that can be conveniently and quietly filled by political appointment.

**1995** B. Eggers *Revolution at the Roots* (Sept. 20) 126:
When several nonperformers accumulate in the same department, it's called a "turkey farm."

**2002** S. Cohen *Effective Public Manager* (Sept. 6) 72:
If you have a large number of incompetent people working for you, it may be necessary to build a "turkey farm"—that is, detail people out of the organization, develop an unimportant special assignment, or use physical space to separate good staffers from bad.

**twinkie** *adj.* appealing but lacking substance.

**1991** (AP) (June 17):
Democratic presidential hopeful Paul Tsongas told the nation's mayors on Monday that leaders of his own party are advocating "Twinkie economics" by appealing to popular tastes without offering substance.

**1993** *Pantagraph* (Bloomington, Ill.) (April 18) E1:
The program is aimed at convincing companies of the economic benefits of voluntarily cutting pollution, although Greene dismisses it as "a bogus program" and "a Twinkie program" that doesn't provide enough technical and financial incentives.

**1994** *Orange County Register* (Cal.) (May17) B1:
John Raya, a Santa Ana mayoral candidate, called the new ordinance just more "Twinkie legislation."

**1997** *Roanoke Times* (Va.) (Oct. 30) A9:
Average voters are beginning to catch on to the developers' "Twinkie Economy."

# U

**ugly season** *n.* the early days in an election period; (*hence*) a
campaigning period when candidates of the same party seek
popularity at the expense of each other. See INVISIBLE PRIMARIES.

**2002** *Special Report* (FOX-TV) (Mar. 15):
We're on the threshold of the ugly season, is what's about to happen,
I think. And this is the first of what will be many, many really nasty
fights.

**2003** *New York Times* (Nov. 23) 22:
The campaign is now entering what Anita Dunn, a longtime Democratic
strategist, called "the ugly season," and she predicted that Dr. Dean's
rivals would collude with each other to try to bring him down.

**2004** *AlterNet* (Feb. 2):
We are in the ugly season for the Democratic Party. This is the part of
the presidential cycle where the challenging party's candidates rip
each other to shreds.

**2004** *Rocky Mountain News* (Feb. 18) 7A:
It's the ugly season, and, with many months before November, it will
stay ugly for a while.

**unconcede** *v.* to retract a concession (of election defeat).

**1996** *San Francisco Chronicle* (Nov. 6) A1:
In a final mishap of a campaign marred by strategic error, Dole
conceded the race more than an hour before the polls closed in the
West—only to turn around and "unconcede" later, after vice
presidential nominee Jack Kemp and other GOP leaders in California
protested the effect the early concession might have on highly
contested congressional races.

**2000** *Washington Post* (Dec. 11) C1:
But then "the roof fell in," Florida shifted, and Fox, like the other
networks, was left with two blown calls. Bush called back. "Gore
unconceded," he said. "You've got to be kidding me," Ellis said.

**2000** *American Prospect* (Dec. 18) 18:
The vice president, the networks report, has called the governor to concede (2:30 A.M.) and then unconcede (3:45 A.M.). The crowd on War Memorial Plaza—and the viewers at home—are dazed and stupefied.

**2001** *Masthead* (Can.) (Mar. 22) 6:
Gore had conceded, then unconceded.

**2001** *Crossfire* (CNN-TV) (May 28):
He calls George Bush before he makes a decision whether or not to call the election the first time around for Bush, which of course, Fox also got wrong, and then Bush calls him when Gore unconcedes.

**unconcession** *n.* a retraction of a concession.

**2000** *Austin American-Statesman* (Tex.) (Dec. 17) G3:
In the Governor's Mansion we would later learn, the elder George Bush and wife Barbara thought they were parents of a president-elect for about a half-hour—the interval between Al Gore's concession and unconcession.

**2003** *Tampa Tribune* (Jan. 19) 4:
He describes Gore's "unconcession" speech and Bush's reaction to it.

**unipolar** *adj.* having one superpower. Hence **unipolarity, unipolarists**.

**1961** F. Riggs in *World Politics* XIV (Oct.) 154:
If power in a macro-rule is highly segmented territorially, it contains many poles; if not only one pole. We may call the former case *poly-polar*, the latter *uni-polar*.

**1990** Inter Press Service (Aug. 21):
As Washington has taken the lead in the crisis, deploying unprecedented military force thousands of miles from its shores, the notion that the world has become "unipolar" rather than "multipolar" has begun to take hold.

**2003** J. Stromseth in *Amer. Journal of Intl. Law* XCVII (July) 634:
The post-September 11th conditions—which include a primary U.S. focus on counterterrorism, a unipolar world in which the United States enjoys predominant military power, and a desire among certain countries, most notably France, to counterbalance the United States—pose both doctrinal and structural challenges to the Charter system.

**un-policy** *n.* an absence of policy.

*1977 *Economist* (Aug. 20) 82:
Hurry to an election? Probably not yet, because of incomes unpolicy and unemployment.

**1985** *Washington Post* (Apr. 26) A22:
Thus did Congress kill the administration's policy and offer no substitute: our new Nicaragua unpolicy.

**1993** *New Republic* (July 12) 16 [heading]:
The foreign unpolicy.

**1995** *California Journal* (Sept. 1):
That was before affirmative action officially became what George Orwell might have called an "unpolicy."

**unterrified** *adj.* loyal.—usu. derisive. Also *n.* [Historically applied to Democrats or the Democratic party.]

**1832** in *DAE* VI:
Mr. Van Buren was taken up by the "unterrified Democracy" to run as Vice-President on the ticket of "old Hickory."

**1848** *Dialect Notes* VI (1938) 416:
The "unterrified democracy" are very hard [pushed] to understand the character of the Oregon Bill.

**1850** C. Lanman *Records of a Tourist* 31:
In politics they belong to the rank and file of the unterrified Democracy.

**1855** *Living Age* (Dec. 29) XLVII 780:
In the northwest of the state of Ohio, in the county of Auglaize, there is a township, the citizens of which are principally German, and notwithstanding their "sweet accent," they are all democrats of the regular "unterrified" stripe.

**1856** J.P. Hambleton *Sketch of Henry A. Wise* 354:
I retire from the "stump" the less reluctantly because I may now justly claim that I have faithfully tried to do my part, and I can confidently leave the rest to the unsubdued and unterrified Democracy and its loyal hosts.

**1876** W. Preston in *Proceedings of Natl. Democratic Convention* 173:
If you go in that spirit into the action, and, guided by the light of those principles, make no local modifications, but stand upon it, you will find the Democracy resuming a name long since abandoned—a name that, when I was a young Whig, struck terror to my heart—the name of the "unterrified."

# V

**vampire state** *n.* a nation or state seen as consuming excessive resources or taxes, esp. if it delivers services poorly or suffers from chronically weak economic conditions. [Often a play on "Empire State," a nickname for New York State.]

**1933** *Daily Northwestern* (Oshkosh, Wisc.) (Feb. 6) 6 [ref. to New York]:
The Vampire State.

**1990** *Newsday* (June 4) 20:
They used to call it the Empire State. Now it's known as the Vampire State. They're sucking the blood out of the working class with their taxes.

**1997** *Contemporary Sociology* (July) 502:
He offers the vivid metaphor in conventional discourse of the vampire state that is "compelled to suck the blood out of the economy" through unbridled increases in taxes to support wanton and wasteful spending that enhances neither economic growth nor development.

**1999** M.R. Somers in *Beyond the Cultural Turn* (June) 125:
Fred Block, for example, shows how our most accepted truths about the state and economy derive from enduring cultural images and metaphors (e.g., the image of a "vampire state" that sucks blood out of the economy), rather than from propositions that have been verified empirically.

**vast right-wing conspiracy** *n.* a coalition of political conservatives seeking to undermine the left, esp. those said to be responsible for instigating investigations during the two Clinton administrations. Also **vast right-wing plot**. Cf. VRWC [Popularized by Senator Hillary Clinton (D-NY).]

**1991** in *AS* (2000) LXXV 444:
All posited a vast right wing conspiracy propping up a reactionary government ruthlessly crushing all efforts at opposition under the guise of parliamentary democracy.

**1995** (AP) (Aug. 10):
Privately, a senior federal official said that the attack was probably not some kind of vast right-wing conspiracy but the work of maybe five malcontents, only two of whom did any "heavy lifting."

**1996** *Washington Post* (July 3) C1:
If anyone comes out with tough charges against the White House, they try to destroy him and call it a vast right-wing conspiracy.

**2004** *USA Today* (Feb. 9) A17:
The "vast right-wing conspiracy"—the John M. Olin Foundation, various Scaife family foundations and other endowments—fought back.

**veepstakes** *n.* [*veep* + sweep*stakes.*] the jockeying among politicians to be chosen as the vice presidential candidate on a party's ticket. *Joc.*

**1964** *News Journal* (Mansfield, Ohio) (Aug. 14) [headline]:
Veepstakes.

**1984** *Washington Post* (July 8):
Veepstakes: Who For Number 2?

**2004** *Boston Herald* (Apr. 4):
Speaking of the veep-stakes, one person Kerry apparently isn't going to consider is HBO comedian Larry David, co-creator of *Seinfeld.*

**Velcroid** *n.* a person who seeks the company of the powerful or famous in an attempt to borrow glory by proximity. Hence **velcrosis**.

**1991** *New York Times* (June 16) 1-1:
"Velcroids" are officials who form a Velcrolike attachment to President Bush at an event in Washington or on the road, sticking to him everywhere he goes in the hope of turning up next to him in newspapers or on television.

**1993** *New York Times* (Sept. 23) A1:
The acknowledged vizier of House velcroids is Sonny Montgomery, the Mississippi Democrat who has been a Congressman since Bill Clinton was a student at Georgetown.

*****1996** *Irish Times* (Jan. 5) 8:
The new Labour klingons...are not a great deal different from the Tory velcroids... what they both have in common is blind pursuit of power.

**Velcro president** *n.* a president caught in controversy and scandal. Also **President Velcro**.

[**1986** *Washington Post* (Apr. 20) C5:
Bush is Velcro to President Reagan's Teflon. To Bush, everything sticks.]

**1986** *Chicago Sun-Times* (Nov. 30) 1:
What began as a bizarre episode with an Alice in Wonderland quality grew last week into an ominous scandal that has stunned the most

self-assured administration in memory. Now, the Teflon president risks becoming the Velcro president. Things are beginning to stick.

**1995** *Wellsboro Gazette* (Pa.) (Feb. 8) 2:
Not smooth in the best sense but rather in the context of slick willie, the non-velcro president.

**2003** *Special Report* (FOX-TV) (Jan. 17):
Bill Clinton was a Velcro president, a man who attracted and could not shake off controversy.

**victim politics** *n.* the use of a group's (supposed) victimhood to gain advantage. Also **victimhood politics**.

**1991** *Chicago Tribune* (May 27) 9:
AIDS has gotten so entangled with civil-rights issues, victim politics and gay activism that public-health officials and politicians have not treated the disease like other infectious epidemics.

**1992** *Washington Post* (June 28) C1:
With pride politics challenging victim politics, there's terror among the career caretakers of our crippled nation, the ancien regime Camelot Democrats waiting for the restoration that will never come, the wet-look Republicans with their Northern Virginia mortgages, the journalists whom Perot has left riffling anxiously through their Rolodexes.

**1992** in J.H. Woodyatt (Oct. 20) on Usenet: talk.abortion [ref. to 1988]:
The psychology of victim politics.

**1994** *Chicago Sun-Times* (May 20) 41:
Thomas also is curiously selective in the way he talks about victimhood politics. Poor minorities aren't the only people who drape themselves in the mantle of victimhood.

**1996** H. Parker in *19th Cent. Lit.* LI (Sept.) 158:
Since he designed the collection as an "intervention" in the reputation of Whitman, for Martin to relocate the process of defensiveness and disguises was to participate, however unwittingly, in the appropriating of the poem by modish victim-politics.

**1998** *New York Times* (Oct. 7) E8:
The Robinson family story is told by several narrataors—the father, Susannah, Magdalena and Langley, as well as Pauline and Manuelito, all of them echoing the well-worn themes of Ms. Walker's victim politics.

***2003** *Courier Mail* (Australia) (Oct. 25) 32:
Mahathir's political style has remained that of the proud Asian leader standing up to the superpowers, and his speech to the recent Organisation of Islamic Conference exemplifies his victimhood politics in a strangely bipolar world inhabited by faith.

**2004** *Washington Dispatch* (Feb. 18) Internet:
Apart from being a victim of victim politics, *The Passion* arouses far

more difficult issues than the representation of certain sections of the Jewish people's leadership in Jerusalem in AD 33.

**Vietnamization** *n.* the process of reducing foreign influence in Vietnam, esp. after departure of American forces at the end of the Vietnam War.

**1957** *Holiday* (Aug.) 119 in *OED*:
When the new idea of "Vietnamization" is being fostered in the country...it is not surprising the Vietnamese prefer to approach...foreigners with care and reticence.

**1958** B. Fall in *Far Eastern Survey* XXVII (May) 71:
Vietnamization in the economy is carried out concurrently with a program of introducing Vietnamese language in Chinese schools, abolition of Chinese signs from shops, and the enforced Vietnamization of Chinese names.

**1969** A. Goodman in *Asian Survey* X 108:
Topics such as the progress and meaning of pacification and of the Vietnamization process have been extensively debated in Washington and Saigon

**2003** *Christian Science Monitor* (Nov. 13) 9:
Because it was rushed, politically driven, and pursued unilaterally by the US according to US timetables, Vietnamization was a dangerous fiasco for most of the people of Vietnam and helped usher in the period of abusive communist rule that followed.

**Vietnam syndrome** *n.* the reluctance after the Vietnam War to pursue foreign involvement, esp. as a result of distrust of government information or motives, or in fear of being defeated; (*hence*) the withholding of information from Congress or the public.

**1974** *New York Times* (Sept. 12) 5:
Mr. Church, a liberal who was one of the early critics of the Vietnam war, characterized the misleading testimony as "Part of the Vietnam syndrome." "There's become a pattern of deceiving Congress that I think began cropping up during the Vietnam war," he said.

**1975** *Coshocton Tribune* (Ohio) (Dec. 16) 1:
Sen. Frank Church, D-Idaho, called the administration program "the Vietnam syndrome all over again."

**1976** L. Carter in *Science* XCII 977:
Warren believes that in California there is now a widely prevalent attitude about nuclear power which can be likened to the "Vietnam syndrome," by which he means that people no longer accept at face value the reassurances given by utility executives and federal regulars that all is well.

**1982** L. Freedman in *Intl. Affairs* LVIII (Summer) 407:
Certainly, the "Vietnam syndrome" by which one legacy of the sorry

Indochina experience was believed to be an unnatural reticence in the conduct of American foreign policy, was always much more of an American than a European diagnosis.

**1983** M. Staniland in *Pol. Sci. Quart.* XCVIII (Winter) 601:
As used by the Left, the Vietnam syndrome operated to detect impending eruptions of American imperialism, to zero in on its puppets, and to spot forces of liberation to which solidarity might be addressed. In the hands of the Right, the syndrome worked to discover international communist inspiration in local uprisings and to alert a prennially complacent West to the need "to make a stand."

**2000** M. Pearlman in *J. of Mil. Hist.* (Apr.) LXIV 24:
The rebuilding of American high-tech military power permitted Ronald Reagan and George Bush to challenge those who accepted the Vietnam Syndrome, with its restraint on the use of American military power, by employing it in Grenada, Panama, and the Gulf.

**Visible Admixture Law** *n.* a post-bellum statute requiring voters who appeared to have African ancestry to answer certain questions. Now *hist.*

**1860** *Coshocton County Democrat* (Ohio) (Mar. 6) 1:
The Ohio Statesman, which lately attached so much sanctity to the decisions of courts, is prodigiously mortified at the late wiping out of the visible admixture law and talks about our Supreme Court being under the thumb of Giddings and in the grasp of Oberlin.

**1868** in *Dialect Notes* VI (1938) 419:
Viewing the whole question of the "visible admixture" law, the soliders' asylum law, etc., it is one of the most...characteristic chapters in modern Democratic history.

**1888** *Cambridge Jeffersonian* (Ohio) (Mar. 13) 2:
It repeals the "visible admixture law."

**Volvo Democrat** *n.* an upscale, educated, liberal white voter.

**1992** *Los Angeles Times* (Mar. 5) 5:
Tennessee and Oklahoma: Tsongas won't find many of his Volvo Democrats here: Relatively downscale, less well-educated states should reward Clinton with substantial margins.

**1999** *Los Angeles Times* (May 17) 5:
Bradley in early New Hampshire polls is running better among college graduates than those without advanced degrees. His appeal to those Volvo Democrats could allow him to threaten Gore in other states along the coasts.

**2000** *Beltway Boys* (Feb. 5)(Fox-TV):
Bradley has got college graduates and independents, you know, the Volvo Democrats.

**2004** *Capital Gang* (CNN-TV) (Jan. 17):
Bradley was a Volvo Democrat. He did very well with Democrats with college degrees, more upscale, socially liberal voters, he didn't connect as well with blue-collar folks, people who hadn't been to college.

**VPOTUS** *n.* [Vice President of the United States] (see quots.).

**1993** *Baton Rouge Sunday Advocate* (Sept. 26) 6:
The first lady is FLOTUS, and the vice president is VPOTUS.

**1996** 104th Congress *96-H-402-6 Corr. Between White House and Cong.* (May):
Agencies Providing Staff/Financial Support for POTUS/VPOTUS.

**2001** *Presidential Studies Quarterly* XXXI (June 1):
The manual even concludes with a directory of commonly used White House acronyms—POTUS, VPOTUS, and the rest.

**2002** *Larry King Weekend* (CNN-TV) (May 25):
[Lynne] Cheney: Dick is VPOTUS, vice president of the United States. So what does that make me? S-L-O-T-U-S, the SLOTUS, which is kind of a funny word. KING: Meaning, second lady of the United States.

**VRWC** *n.* VAST RIGHT-WING CONSPIRACY.

**1998** *Washington Times* (Feb. 5) A14:
As another charter member of the "vast right-wing conspiracy" (VRWC), I need to get a message to my fellow conspirators. Please publish the following, encrypted in VRWC code for security reasons.

**1998** *Pittsburgh Post-Gazette* (Apr. 1) A19:
The mood was downright sullen at last night's meeting of my local chapter of the VRWC (Vast Right-Wing Conspiracy).

**2002** *Chicago Tribune* (Mar. 20) 27:
Today the VRWC is variously a punch line, a Web site, a club, a T- shirt, a call-to-arms, a book title, a dogma, an annunciation and, in the case of one David Brock, a conscientious objection.

**2003** *Rocky Mountain News* (Denver, Colo.) (Nov. 14) 55A:
The party line, echoed by the chorus of paranoid liberal pundits in the media, is that CBS caved in to the VRWC (vast right-wing conspiracy) in its decision to remove from its schedule The Reagans docudrama scheduled for later in November.

**W**

**waitress mom** *n.* (see 1998 quots.).

**1996** *New York Times* (Oct. 20) 4-1:
Right now they are voting Democratic, but many of them are undecided....If you want to know the truth, it is now the Waitress Moms who are critical.

**1998** E. Burkett *Right Women* (Mar.) 81:
They are not, however, as important a force as the group Celinda Lake calls the "waitress moms"—blue-collar working mothers without college educations—who are twice as numerous as the soccer fanatics.

**1998** *Atlanta Journal-Constitution* (Oct. 25) A8:
Boggs is a "waitress mom," one of up to 25 million women voters in America who roughly fit Lake's profile: white, a high school graduate or less, under 55 years of age, married with a child at home, and living in the suburbs or a rural area. Many are working two low-wage jobs.

**2003** *Nation* (Oct. 13) 11:
When Time asked the accounting firm of Deloitte & Touche to analyze precisely how Bush's waitress-mom would be affected by his tax package, the firm reported that she would not see any benefit because she already had no income-tax liability.

**WAM** *n.* [*wa*lking *a*round *m*oney] discretionary funds.

**1987** *Patriot-News* (Harrisburg, Pa.) (Sept. 27) A11:
If leaders still are unable to rally enough votes to assure passage of a raise, they can turn to caucus initiatives, commonly referred to as "walking around money" or "WAM," to persuade fence-sitters.

**1995** *State Capitols Report* III (Nov. 24):
The court warned lawmakers to repair the budget-writing process that allowed $13.2 million in legislative initiative grants (a.k.a. WAMs or walking-around- money) to be passed contrary to budget rules.

**1996** *Crain's Detroit Business* (May 13) 1:
DCA has a proven track record with the Lottery, providing "The Big Pay Back," "Walking Around Money (WAM)," and "Play It Again WAM" promotional campaigns.

**2003** *Brandweek* (June 2):
For years, spirits companies have quietly given their sales staff WAM (walking around money), which was used to buy bar patrons drinks of their company's brands.

**war blog** *n.* a personal web site focusing on world affairs after September 11, 2001, esp. concerning terrorism and the wars in Afghanistan and Iraq. Also **warblog**. Hence **warblogger**.

*****2001** *Guardian* (Manchester, U.K.) (Sept. 20) 2:
A few, such as wtc-filter, Matt Welch's "warblog," and the Guardian's own crisis special, are instant publications set up to cover the story.

*****2001** "Born Again Manic" (Sept. 20) on Usenet (uk.local.london):
warblog.com is, amazingly, still available...I give it less than a week before it's gone.

**2002** *Star-Ledger* (N.J.) (Sept. 9) 53:
A new type of Weblog, sometimes called a "warblog," often focused on the war on terrorism and the aftermath of 9/11.

**2003** *New York Times* (Aug. 10) B9:
The number of blogs—liberally defined—has probably passed the half-million mark. That's up from just a few dozen five years ago, a spike that blog watchers say owes much to the events of Sept. 11, which spawned a whole new subgenre: the war blog.

*****2003** *Guardian* (Manchester, U.K.) (Mar. 24) 38:
It could be the nation's war blog—a forum for the hive in an environment that values truth over rumour, accuracy over speculation, reflection over anger.

**2003** Knight Ridder (Apr. 17):
It was a shock to the tight-knit blogging community when...when another hugely popular war blog was found to have lifted several postings from another source.

**war chest** *n.* campaign funds.

**1897** *Daily Northwestern* (Oshkosh, Wisc.) (Nov. 13) 1:
When the party needs a war chest there are various wealthy gentlemen always willing to subscribe

**1905** *Manitoba Free Press* (Can.) (Jan. 9) 4:
They begin to doubt whether two years hence they could hope for victory; they think that now, with a goodly-sized war chest and a taking fake election cry they would have a much better chance of winning.

**1911** H. Ames in *Proc. of Amer. Pol. Sci. Assoc.* VIII 186:
Such insertions can be arranged for, in nearly all the independent

journals, at advertising rates, and, though this procedure makes heavy inroads on the contents of the war chest, it is oftentimes an effective means of carrying the war into the enemy's country.

**1912** *Indianapolis Star* (Sept. 22) 7:
Dr. Harvey Wiley has contributed $300 in cash to the war chest of the Democratic national committee.

**1913** *Atlanta Constitution* (Nov. 2) 4:
How much money the war chest of Tammany holds this year is a problem.

**1915** *Manitoba Free Press* (Can.) (Feb. 15) 10:
When there's a war abroad, bring on the trouble at home, especially if you're well healed and your opponent has no war chest.

**1927** D. Lynch *"Boss" Tweed* 152:
The owners of grog shops contributed liberally to Wood's war chest, as did the keepers of gambling dens and bawdy houses.

**2002** R. Lau & G. Pomper in *Amer. Journal Pol. Sci.* XXXVI (Jan.) 49:
Any candidate, even one blessed with a large campaign war chest and other advantages, can campaign wisely or poorly.

**War Democrat** *n.* a Democrat who supported the Union during the Civil War. Cf. COPPERHEAD.

**1863** W. Cothren *Hist. of Ancient Woodbury, Conn.* (Jan. 12) (1854–1879) 1224:
Some of the Captains were war democrats, some republicans, and some of no politics.

**1869** in *Dialect Notes* VI (1938) 420:
I desire to say that I did not refer to War Democrats in using the term "Copperheads."

**1885** A.M. Loryea in *Overland Mo.* VI (Aug.) 198:
During the darkest hours of the great General's career, Senator Nesmith, one of the best known of war Democrats, was determined to sustain him, and Grant often made his headquarters while in Washington at the Senator's house.

**ward-heeler** *n.* HEELER. Now *S.E.*

**1887** E. Levey *Election in New York* 680:
I entered and saw a well-known ward "heeler"...pass a five dollar bill into each voter's hands with no effort at concealment.

**1897** J. Baxter *Old and New Municipality* 481:
The elevation of the character of legislative assemblies must necessarily follow its adoption, since it destroys completely the occupation of the ward heeler and makes the pathway of the politician who goes into ward politics for what he can make a difficult road to travel.

**1917** G. Myers *History of Tammany Hall* 153 [ref. to 1850–52]:
These sums were merely the beginning; committees would impress upon the candidate the fact that a campaign costs money; more of the "boys" would have to be "seen"; such and such a "ward heeler" needed "pacifying"; a band was a proper embellishment, with a parade to boot, and voters needed "persuading."

**2004** *Evansville Courier & Press* (Ill.) (Jan. 28):
When you meet a grizzled old ward heeler, it's a good bet that he is old indeed. There are many jerks, but few boors, in politics, and even the jerks smile these days

**war hawk** *n.* a supporter of military action. Cf. HAWK.

*__*1708__ [Philalethes] in *The Rehearsal* III 96:
This in his of the 24. last Month, N. 46, he Quotes out of the *Mirror* how the *Saxons* Conquer'd the *Britains* (War Hawk!) *there being no less then Forty of them who were Companions of the Soveraignty.*

**1798** T. Jefferson *Letter to J. Madison* (Apr. 26) in *Writ.* (1854) 238 in *OED*:
At present, the war hawks talk of septembrizing, [etc.].

**1852** *Amer. Whig Rev.* (Aug.) 127:
If they receive with equal enthusiasm the war *hawk* of Illinois or the handsaw of the Baltimore Cabinet makers, we may easily believe they are quite as philosophical in regard to opinions as in regard to men, and will receive the very antiquated politics of a Virginian delegation as readily as they accepted their very new and modern candidate.

**1999** *More* (Aug.) 87:
My goal was to understand the woman behind the down-to-earth heroine, the policy wonk who would become the administration's fierce war hawk.

**war horse** *n.* a veteran (of politics, the military, a sport, etc.).

**1835** *Republican Compiler* (Sept. 15) 1:
The White horse being fairly broken down and demolished, the old Tippecanoe war horse seems now to be the only one "available;" but he will not be able to stand under such a load a moment.

**1852** L. Woodbury *Writings* 199:
He was a lawyer as well as a doctor, a mechanic, a farmer, and, above all, a zealous politician—being called, during the last war with England, "the old war-horse of the mountain."

**1864** S. Carpenter *Logic of History* 105:
Wendell, the great war horse of the radical party in power, made a speech in Beecher's Political Synagogue, in 1862.

**1869** M. Smith *Sunshine & Shadow in New York* 645:
Mr. Leavitt, the old war-horse of anti-slavery, had many political enemies.

**1869** C. Halpine *Poetical Works* 343:
Elijah F. Purdy, city supervisor, was nicknamed the "War Horse."

**1954** *Gazette and Bulletin* (Williamsport, Pa.) (Mar. 2) 12:
Art Devlin, the "old" war horse of American ski jumping, is hot on the comeback trail.

**1967** *Post-Crescent* (Appleton, Wisc.) (Dec. 24) C11:
I'll admit I felt something like an old war horse let out to pasture.

**2004** *New York Times* (Feb. 2):
First it was Dean, then a bunch of people said Clark is the guy, now it's Kerry, the old war horse.

**war room** *n.* a (figurative or actual) room from where a (military or political) campaign is directed. Cf. SITUATION ROOM.

**1898** *Marion Daily Star* (Ohio) (Apr. 30) 2:
It will find its way quickly into "the war room," which has been fitted up in the White House for the especial use of the president.

**1900** *Mansfield News* (Ohio) (May 1) 3:
In the "war room" of the white house the pleasant face of President McKinley is not seen because he is absent from the capital, but he is nevertheless in closest touch with this famous nerve-center of the country—and the world, too, the United States and its possessions now being scattered over the earth.

**1964** H. Vinacke in *Journal Asian Studies* (Feb.) 293:
The author of this important study takes as its setting the war room, with the "arena of the Pacific...the council chamber rather than the coral atoll."

**1996** *USA Today* (Nov. 5) 12A:
But just as Clinton has become more reflective as he ends his last campaign, the aides who came of political age in 1992's "war room" will be comparing the two experiences in Little Rock tonight.

**2000** *Columbus Dispatch* (Sept. 10) F3:
Bush's tax cut is the elephant in his war room.

**Washington read** *n.* skimming a book index for one's own name in order to read about oneself, esp. when done with no intention of reading the entire book or of buying it.

**1985** *Washington Post* (June 12):
There was the usual jesting about the "Washington read," which consists of a flip through the index in search of one's name.

**1991** *Boston Globe* (June 24):
Former Kevin White deputy mayor Micho Spring pleaded not guilty the other day to doing a "Washington read" of the new book, *Boston Politics: The Creativity of Power,* that is making the rounds among political insiders. Spring swore she did not simply go to the index of

*Boston Politics* to find her own name, the way everyone does in Washington when a new political book comes out.

**2004** *Kitchener-Waterloo Record* (Ontario, Can.) (Mar. 31) D4:
I gave it the Washington read. You looked in the index to see if your name was in it.

**watchdog** *n.* a group or individual appointed to prevent abuses by, or to monitor activities of, government agencies.

**1826** *Adams Sentinel* (Pa.) (July 12) 4:
John Randolph—the Political watch Dog of the nation—may his growl ever ring in the ears of the existing Administration.

**1867** *Const. Convention Debates and Proceedings* (July 11) 41:
I do not know but my friend from Oakland...thinks that in that word the people will hear what they will conceive to be the growl of the watch-dog of the treasury. But to me it sounds, as I think it will sound to the people, more like the bray of some very different animal.

**1947** *Nashua Telegraph* (N.H.) (Oct. 9) 6:
The "watchdog" committee will avoid participation in any current labor-management dispute.

**2004** Knight Ridder (Feb. 8):
In December, he appointed a tough-minded watchdog to police unscrupulous accounting firms and tax preparers, and doubled that department's budget.

**Watergate** *n.* the Nixon-era scandals which lead to his resignation; (*hence*) any scandal, esp. one involving a cover-up. [See page 17.]

**1972** *Nation* (June 25) E2:
Watergate Caper: From the Folks Who Brought You the Bay of Pigs.

*Ibid.*:
The affair has become popularly known in the capital as the "Watergate Caper."

**1972** *Time* (Aug. 20) 28 in *OED*:
By coming down hard on Mitchell, the Democrats hope they can make Watergate a devasting—and durable—campaign issue.

**1981** *Oklahoman* (Oklahoma City) (Dec. 6):
His few defenders blame news media overkill, in which there is the tone and stridency of another Watergate.

**1996** *Christian Science Monitor* (June 25) 19 [ref. to 1974]:
What are you going to do to see to it that there are no more Watergates?

**2004** *Oakland Tribune* (Calif.) (Feb. 9):
This is a breakdown of trust that goes far beyond Watergate.

**watergate** *v.* to behave in a manner similar to those involved in the original Watergate scandals.

**1973** *New York Times* (May 17) 22:
Mr. Biaggis is being "Watergated" by the same people who wrecked our system of justice in Washington.

**1973** *Fond du Lac Reporter* (Wisc.) (Aug. 22) 4:
What sort of "Spanish Inquisition" is this? A mandatory snoop-sheet of one's personal affairs?...a "Self Watergating" on paper?

**1978** *Washington Post* (Sept. 7) 3:
Without a historical understanding of this process of human development, pro-growth elected officials are often Watergated, demoralized or bought off by anti-growth forces who basically see man as an impotent beast at the mercy of uncontrollable "natural phenomena."

**1981** W. Gibson *Johnny Mnemonic* in W. Gibson *Burning Chrome* 23:
Too much chance of interdepartmental funnies; they're too likely to watergate you.

**1994** *Gazette* (Montreal) (Apr. 23) K2:
The cybercops could have Watergated me while I slept—snuck in here and rewired the glove.

**2002** *Arkansas Democrat-Gazette* (Little Rock) (June 23) J4:
The ABA pointedly snubbed The Honorable Mr. Nixon back in his Watergated time (1973–74).

**water's edge** *n.* the boundary (geographical and figurative) between domestic policy (esp. elections) and foreign policy.

**1939** *Helena Independent* (Mont.) (Sept. 23) 4:
However, those sentiments demonstrate one thing—that politics stops at the water's edge when a menacing problem presents itself from outside.

**1946** *New York Times* (Oct. 7) 4:
President Truman's latest statement on Palestine illustrates the influence of domestic politics on United States foreign policy and demonstrates the limitations of the theory that politics stops at the water's edge.

**1950** *New York Times* (Apr. 9) E1:
Since the war a guiding prinicple in America's approach to foreign policy has been: "Politics stops at the water's edge."

**2003** *Wall Street Journal* (Aug. 20) A10:
Mr. Reagan's conservatism didn't end at the water's edge. Despite enormous opposition from congressional Democrats, he pushed back the Soviet Union on all fronts.

**2003** *New Pittsburgh Courier* (Sept. 24) A7:
As for that cliche "politics stops at the water's edge," an old Washington Post editor, Felix Morley, had the best answer: politics stops at the water's edge only when policy stops at the water's edge.

**weapons of mass distraction** *n.pl.* [fr. *weapons of mass destruction*] a tactic used to divert attention, esp. from scandal or unpopular policies. —usu. derisive.

**1996** *Boston Herald* (Nov. 17) 4:
Byrne...will star in the HBO movie "Weapons of Mass Distraction," a black comedy about two feuding media moguls who clash while vying to buy a Los Angeles sports franchise.

**1998** *San Francisco Chronicle* (Feb. 24) B8:
If the dispute between Iraq and the United Nations is settled without a fight, asks William Poole, will Bill Clinton be "deprived of a powerful weapon of mass distraction?"

**2003** M. Krantzler *Moving Beyond* 60:
"Deadbeat dad" is a fraudulent label that is a weapon of mass distraction.

**2004** *Counterpunch* (Feb. 6):
The American Republic is threatened...by the true WMD's (Weapons of Mass Distraction), more pervasive and more effective than Saddam's non-existent armory.

**wedfare** *n.* government incentives intended to promote marriage among welfare recipients. Cf. BRIDEFARE.

**1991** *Milwaukee Sentinel* (Feb. 23) 10:
Dubbed "wedfare" and "bridefare" by Democrats, the initiative is designed to encourage pregnant teens to marry by increasing their AFDC benefits if they do.

**1992** *Washington Post* (Feb. 4) A15:
Earlier this year, Wisconsin's governor proposed "wedfare," a plan to eliminate need-based increases to teen mothers with additional children while offering a "marriage bonus" of $73 a month to AFDC families headed by a married couple.

**2002** *Dollars & Sense* (Nov.–Dec.):
The Bush administration wants to divert an additional $300 million away from providing cash payments, health coverage, and child care assistance to poor families and into marriage promotion, or what critics call "wedfare," instead.

**wedge issue** *n.* a matter which could cause voters to deviate from their usual loyalties, esp. when splitting otherwise like-minded voters between two or more candidates and so strengthening any unified opposition.

**1986** *Washington Post* (Oct. 19) H7:
But more than that, education is the opposite of a wedge issue. It is a bridge issue for the diverse Democratic coalition.

**1989** *Boston Globe* (Sept. 17) 83:
To appeal to moderately conservative Democrats, the wedge issue

could be capital punishment; 12 years ago, it was the key to Koch's ability to break free of a large field in his first, improbable victory.

**1995** *Denver Post* (Aug. 212) A2:
It was heralded as the perfect "wedge issue," well-designed to split the Democrats.

**2003** *New York Times* (Mar. 5) 4-4:
People are more generous in their attitudes...Immigration is not a very good wedge issue in the current economic climate.

**wedge politics** *n.* electioneering or politicking which polarizes or divides voting blocs, usually by means of WEDGE ISSUES.

**1991** *New York Times* (July 21) E16:
The Democrats, intimidated by Mr. Bush's virtuosity in foreign affairs and harsh wedge politics back home.

**1991** *USA Today* (July 24) 4A:
The Republican Party has been a genius at playing wedge politics. We've got to be tough and responsive at answering these charges.

**1999** W.J. Clinton in *Public Papers of the Presidents* (Aug. 28):
We asked the Republicans to discard their hatred of government, and their blind faith that the only thing that would ever matter was having more tax cuts. And we asked them to abandon wedge politics.

**2003** *Pittsgurgh Post-Gazette* (Dec. 9) A21:
The fact that Democrats are arguing about the perils of wedge politics suggests an important turn in this presidential contest. Now that Dean is clearly established as the party's front-runner, the debate among rank-and-file Democrats as well as Democratic elites is over whether Dean himself will be a walking wedge issue for Bush.

**wheel-horse** *n.* an instrumental or hard-working party member.

[**1841** *Republican Compiler* (Gettysburg, Pa.) (Dec. 6) 1:
Jim Cash was Mo Mercer's right hand man—in the language of refined society, he was Mo's toady—in the language of Hardscrabble, he was Mo's wheel-horse.]

**1850** W. Gallagher *Progess in the North-West* 57:
The most stubborn moral or political wheelhorse to be found in any church or any party in the land, will not abuse the evidence of his senses so much, as to deny the material progress of the world.

**1860** D. Bartlett *Lincoln* 25:
For many years he was the "wheel-horse" of the Whig party of Illinois, and was on the electoral ticket in several Presidential campaigns.

**1892** *Fresno Weekly Republican* (Cal.) (May 2):
Sheriff Grant was a wheel horse, but he is a dead duck in the political puddle hereafter.

**1988** *Los Angeles Times* (Oct. 23) 5:
Bush, following an unsuccessful bid for the Senate, became his party's wheel horse.

**2001** *Denver Post* (Dec. 8) B7:
To the horror of Common Scold and the League, the first chief justice to exercise that decisive power was Paul Hodges—an old GOP wheel horse.

**whispering campaign** *n.* a systematic circulation of rumours, esp. in order to denigrate someone or something. Also **whisper campaign**.

**1909** *Mansfield News* (Ohio) (Nov. 19) 2:
Newspaper paragraphers and other wags characterize Mr. Moxley's fight as a "whispering campaign" because of his departure from the beaten paths of political methods.

**1925** *Bismarck Tribune* (N.D.) (Mar. 27) 4:
Voters should discount the whispering campaign which is the bane of politics. Bismark's city campaign has reached the "whispering" stage.

**1927** D. Lynch *"Boss" Tweed* 166:
The success of a whispering campaign—many campaigns have been won in this way—depends more on the secrecy with which it is waged than on any other element.

**1928** *San Mateo Times* (Cal.) (Mar. 28) 1:
A determined effort was made today to start a "whisper campaign" designed to harm the candidacy of Samuel D. Merk.

**1928** *Edwardsville Intelligencer* (Ill.) (Sept. 13) 1:
Charges of drunkenness are nothing new in the life of the Democratic presidential candidate. Probably because he favors modification of the prohibition laws he has had to deal with a "whispering campaign" about his personal habits in virtually every election campaign he has conducted.

**1929** T. Woofter in *Social Forces* (Mar.) 436:
One whose political reminiscences would have been of tremendous importance was Isaiah Montgomery of Mound Bayou, Mississippi, whos daughter Mrs. Booze, was the center of such acrimonious rumors in the whispering campaign of 1928.

**1940** *Nevada State Journal* (Reno) (Oct. 6) 1:
Whisper Campaign Draws Attack.

**1996** O. Frankel in *Amer. Hist.* (Dec.) 915:
In the year of Goldman's visit, she became the target of a vicious whispering campaign that accused her of disloyalty to the country and culminated in an attempt to impeach her in Congress.

**whistleblower** *n.* a person who publicly reveals inside information, esp. concerning wrongdoing. Hence **whistleblowing**.

**1958** *Mansfield News-Journal* (Ohio) (Oct. 10) 25:
The whistleblower on that $50,000 a month call-girl story was a witch, who tried to tap Bea Garfield, alleged madam, for $250.

**1960** *New York Times* (Apr. 15) 44:
In slamming the door on Mr. Hoffa's ambitions Mr. Hall, who also is president of the Seafarer's International Union, made a personal attack against the teamster president. He described Mr. Hoffa as a "notorious wink," a "whistle blower" and an "opportunist."

**1971** P. Boffey, in *Science* (Feb. 12) 550:
Some 200 or more persons attended the conference, and a number of the nation's more publicized whistle blowers described their personal experiences.

**1977** T. McAdams, in *Academy of Mgmt. Rev.* (Apr.) 203:
Protection for the whistle blower could only accelerate accomplishment of that task.

**1991** *Newsweek* (Nov. 11) 12:
Anita Hill is a whistleblower for human decency.

**whistle-stop** *adj.* to campaign quickly with stops in small communities. Also *n.* Cf. BARNSTORM.

**1948** *Wisconsin Rapids Daily Trib.* (Mar. 29) 2:
He will be following two Tafts, the senator and his wife, Martha, who have scheduled separate whistle-stop tours April 5, 6 and 7.

**1948** *Berkshire Evening Eagle* (Pittsfield, Mass.) (June 18) 14:
It was the whole performance at the "whistle-stops" that was the story, the talk by the President in his easy, informal, colloquial manner, the kindly interest of the people who had come from far and near to see their President, which was entirely different from that gained by reading some isolated sentence or two from what he said.

**1984** *Wall Street Journal* (Oct. 18) 1:
The late-afternoon sun, slanting through the trees, spotlighted the president of the U.S., standing on the observation platform of beautiful old U.S. No. 1, the Pullman car used in earlier whistle-stop campaigns by Franklin Roosevelt and Harry Truman.

**1993** Safire *Political Dictionary* 873 [refers to May 1948]:
My first formal experience at extemporaneous speaking had come just a few weeks before I opened the whistle-stop tour in June.

**wholesale campaign** *n.* electioneering which targets large voting blocs, as opposed to a RETAIL CAMPAIGN.

**1982** *New York Times* (Oct. 4) A1:
This retail rather than wholesale campaign, shown in reports from 63 battleground House races, does not reflect party fragmentation.

**1987** *Chicago Tribune* (Aug. 16) 27:
After we go through this retail period of Iowa, New Hampshire, South Dakota, etc., it's going to be a real wholesale campaign.

**2002** V. O'Regan & S. Stambough in *White House Studies* (Sum.):
This retail politics is nearly impossible in highly-populated states dominated by mass media markets and wholesale campaigning.

[**2004** *Mother Jones* (Jan. 29):
The contest is barely underway and already Sharpton, Kucinich and Lieberman are painfully short of the three things any candidate needs going into the big-state, "wholesale" phase of the primary season: money, media, and momentum.]

**2004** *Business Week* (Feb. 2):
Fact is, the campaign has moved from the retail to the wholesale phase, and Edwards can't meet enough voters for word-of-mouth to mean much.

**Wide-Awakes** *n.* [fr. a type of soft felt hat without a "nap" worn by the partisans] a young-men's club which supported Republican politics, from the middle of the 19th century.

**1854** *New York Daily Times* (Sept. 4) 8:
The difficulty is said to have had its origin in the "Wide-Awake" hats, which if accounts are to be believed, are held in great repugnance by the Irish...who commenced throwing bricks and paving stones at the "Wide-Awakes."

**1855** *National Era* (June 21) 100:
The Order of the American Star owes its origin to a young man named Patten, who started it in the spring of 1853, in the fourth ward...This organization was better known as the Wide-Awakes.

**1860** *New York Times* (June 2) 4:
At a large and enthusiastic meeting of the Hartford "Wide Awakes," held this evening, the Chicago nominations were heartily indorsed...The Hartford "Wide Awakes" are the originators of the movement, and all Republicans wishing information with regard to organizing can obtain such.

**wilderness years** *n.* an ineffectual or unnoteworthy period, esp. when out of power or office.

*1945 *Scotsman* (May 26) 6:
Europe's wilderness years were now at an end, and it had large visions of a promised land.

**1956** W. Brewer in *Journal of Negro Hist.* (Jan.) 7:
As financial watchman on the wall, President H. Council Trenholm deserves worthy mention in a triumvirate of leadership that has worked mightily during the wilderness years since April 3, 1950.

**1968** *New York Times* (Aug. 5) 20:
The difficulties are inherent in the Republican character as it was formed in the glory years between 1861 and 1912 and maimed in the wilderness years between 1932 and 1964.

**1990** B. Machado in *Journal of Mil. Hist* (Jan.) 109:
As was also true for Winston Churchill, Marshall's wilderness years finally ended in 1939.

**2004** *Los Angeles Times* (Jan. 4) A1:
Dean says he spent some of those wilderness years running from the man known as "Big Howard": his father.

**Willie Hortonize** *v.* [allusion to the Republican 1988 campaign issue of a convicted black murderer, Willie Horton, who while on a weekend pass from prison committed a rape] to invoke racial prejudice for political purposes. Hence **Hortonization**, **Hortonism**, **Hortonesque**.

**1989** *Washington Post* (Mar. 13) A15:
What came to be called "Hortonism" was not a single TV ad; it was a campaign.

**1989** *Newsday* (June 20) 5:
A supporter of the existing system...said that one reason there has not been a strong move toward the death penalty is, "We have not been Hortonized." He was referring to Willie Horton.

**1991** *Washington Post* (July 19) A8:
Asked whether Bush and the Republicans might be able to "Willie Hortonize" him, a reference to the advertising campaign against Michael Dukakis in 1998, he replied, "No."

**1992** *St. Louis Post-Dispatch* (June 21) 3B:
What we didn't anticipate was that the first attempt at the Willie Hortonization of the campaign would come not from conservative Republicans but from liberal Democrats.

**1994** *USA Today* (Oct. 10) 11A:
Singel warned his opponent not to "Willie Hortonize" the campaign, referring to the 1988 ads that George Bush ran about a convicted murderer who raped a woman while on a Massachusetts furlough program backed by then-Gov. Michael Dukakis.

**1996** *St. Louis Post-Dispatch* (June 5) 6A:
A federal appeals judge who was sharply criticized by Republican Sen. Bob Dole resigned Tuesday and warned that efforts to "Willie Hortonize the federal judiciary" would erode public confidence in the courts.

**2000** *National Review* (Apr. 3) 36:
Let's not attack Gore as soft on breast cancer. Willie Hortonize Al Sharpton. Shots of Gore and Sharpton with Freddy's Fashion Mart burning in the background.

**2002** *Rocky Mountain News* (Denver, Colo.) (Dec. 19) 7A:
It was a time when the dark stain of shameful collaboration with
racists was moving from the Democratic Party to the Willie-Hortonized-
Southern-strategy Republican Party.

**winner-take-all** *n.* a contest or election in which the most successful
competitor reaps all rewards.

**1943** *Marion Star* (Ohio) (Apr. 19) 5 [advertisement]:
Winner Take All!...There is no second place in a war. It's either win or
lose!

**1948** *New York Times* (May 16) E10:
In Oregon, it is winner take all. The entire delegation is bound by the
result of the popular statewide vote.

**1994** *Los Angeles Times* (July 17) 5:
The essential problem is that the very nature of our "winner take all"
electoral system discriminates against minorities, and no satisfactory
way has been found to fix it.

**1999** *American Pol. Sci. Rev.* (Mar.):
A sustained treatment of this subject is found in Brains (1978), who
argues that, under specified conditions, states with large, winner-take-
all blocs of electoral votes will attract substantially greater party
attention relative to those with smaller allocations, even out of
proportion to their size.

**wire-puller** *n.* [fr. the wires by which puppets are operated] a politician
or political agent who works secretly to further the interests of a
person or party. Cf. WIRE-WORKER.

**1833** J.R. Commons *Documentary Hist. Amer. Industr. Soc.* VIII 340
in *OED*:
Wire-pullers...for the furtherance of...party interest.

**1866** Barnum *Humbugs of the World* 59:
The party-leaders began to lay their plans early, and the wire-pullers on
both sides were unusually busy in their vocation.

**1913** *Gazette and Bulletin* (Williamsport, Pa.) (July 17) 7:
Champion Political Wire Puller Identifies Letters Disclosing Sensational
Plans.

**1997** R. Kluger *Ashes to Ashes* 229:
The firm's top strategist and behind-the-scenes wire-puller, Abe Fortas,
would shortly gain immortality in American jurisprudential annals with
his pro bono 1963 victory in Gideon v. Wainwright, expanding
indigents' right to counsel.

**wire-worker** *n.* a behind-the-scenes dealmaker or manipulator; WIRE-
PULLER

**1835** *Col. Crockett's Tour* (Phila.) 172 in *OED*:
He is the wire-worker, the very mover and organ of all those high-handed and lawless measures.

**1855** in P.J. Ethington *Public City* (1994) 119:
Of all the names that grace the roll of the political wire-workers in this city, the most conspicuous of all...as high over his compeers as was Satan over the fallen angels, and as unblushing and determined as the dark fiend, stands the name of David C. Broderick.

**1868** J. Brisbin *Lives of U.S. Grant* 364:
Despite the ability, tact, and shrewdness of the old political wire-worker, he only distanced his young competitor two hundred and thirty-eight votes, in a pull of over eighteen thousand.

**1887** "M. Twain" in C. Neider *Complete Essays of Mark Twain* (1985) 580:
The wire workers, the convention packers know they are not obliged to put up the fittest man for the office, for they know that the docile party will vote for any forked thing they put up, even though it do not even strictly resemble a man.

**1897** U.S. War Dept. *War of Rebellion* 976:
Having spent many years on the rude frontier, I freely admit that I know but little of the seductive arts of peace. I am no politician, no wire-worker, no representative man.

**1997** *American Hist. Rev.* (Dec.) 1572:
Wire workers tug behind the scenes, but [Sen. Lewis] Cass is all on the surface, his mind usually untroubled by doubts, theories, or abstruse thought.

**witch hunt** *n.* a relentless campaign against a group with unacceptable views or behaviour, specif. communists; such a campaign regarded as unfair or malicious persecution.

**1934** *New York Times* (Jan. 26) 9:
There are a thousand more pressing problems in the recovery program at the moment than a witch hunt.

**1973** E. Bentley *Thirty Years of Treason* 221:
At the universities, political witch hunts were staged, and campaigns were waged against motion pictures such as *All Quiet on the Western Front*.

**1977** *Washington Post* (Jan. 4) A4:
It took the 1952 general election, complete with pamphlets alleging "softness on communism " printed on pink paper, voting records used out of context and general appeals to a political witch-hunt mentality, however, to spur the suggested "eminent citizens" to action.

**WM²** *n.* [acronym for *w*hite, *m*arried, *w*orking *m*others (or *m*oms)]
White, married, working mothers, regarded as a desirable class of voter. Also **WMx2**, **WM squared**, **WMWM**.

**2000** *New York Post* (Aug. 20):
In fact, 2000's key voters appear to be white married working moms—in political junkie jargon, "WMWMs," "WM" squared or "WMx2"—because they back Bush by a giant margin that has Democrats wringing their hands.

**2000** *Orlando Sentinel* (Fla.) (Oct. 20) G3:
Women like me— the "WM2" target audience of white, working, married mothers—are, guess what, undecided.

**wolf-pack journalism** *n.* the obsessive coverage of the same stories by competing media.

**1979** in C.E. Kelley *Rhetoric of Hillary Clinton* (2001) 61:
The legacy of Watergate is wolfpack journalism.

**1983** *Christian Science Monitor* (June 28) 8:
She complained to a local journalist about "wolf-pack journalism" and found her supposedly private remarks picked up by newspapers, television, and radio stations around the world.

**1997** *Allentown Morning Call* (Pa.) (Jan. 12) F4:
Newspaper reporters don't like the wolf-pack journalism we often see on TV—a mob of reporters swarming people, poking microphones into their faces and screaming questions at them. It's rude, undignified and often counter-productive.

**2001** *Los Angeles Times* (Nov. 3) B23:
Wolfpack journalism has taken our attention away from serious issues happening in our own backyard, and we will seriously regret the consequences of our misdirected attention.

**2002** *Omaha World-Herald* (Dec. 22) 8AT:
There are so many 24-hour news outlets on television these days, we have what Allan calls "wolf-pack journalism."

**wonk** *n.* an expert on intricate policies; (*broadly*) a studious or hard-working person. Also **policy wonk**. Cf. POLICY WANK.

[**1962** *Sports Illustrated* (Dec. 21) 17 in *OED*:
A wonk, sometimes called a "turkey" or a "lunch," roughly corresponds to the "meatball" of a decade ago.]

**1985** *Washington Post* (Dec. 22) C7:
George Shultz has done the right thing. In an administration of policy wonks and junk bond junkies, he is a romantic.

**1994** *St. Louis Post-Dispatch* (Dec. 30) 7B:
Since Reagan was the very reverse of a "policy wonk," taking no deep interest in policy, he confined himself to initiatives—the "peace shield" in space being a great example—that even a child could understand.

**2002** *Akron Beacon Journal* (Ohio) (Nov. 26):
The two biggest newspapers in Northeast Ohio have, within the last 10 days, referred to departing U.S. Rep. Tom Sawyer as a "wonk."

**2003** *Broadcasting & Cable* (Dec. 1) 42:
He has largely given up the dream of running for office in Missouri but has found happiness as a policy wonk.

**2004** *New York Observer* (Feb. 16) 11:
If you're retail consultant Paco Underhill ("a tall, bald, stuttering research wonk on the cusp of his fifty-third year"), you would spend your time sniffing around 300 malls all across the country.

**wonkism** *n.* excessively deep knowledge of policies; the habits or character of a WONK.

**1993** S. Landsburg *Armchair Economist* 44:
Ross Perot was infected with an extreme form of wonkism during the 1992 presidential campaign when he called for Americans to produce computer chips rather than potato chips.

**1994** *St. Louis Post-Dispatch* (Dec. 30) 7B:
His recent recovery speech, while mercifully brief, was policy wonkism at its worst, echoing, on a modest scale, his Byzantine health-care reform package.

**2000** *Washington Post* (Jan. 5) A19:
Marshall Wittmann is the press corps's latest go-to guy on Congress....In his own words, Wittmann now exists "where pop culture and wonkism intersect."

**2001** *Orlando Sentinel* (Mar. 13) A8:
Wonkism consists of endlessly boring talk and written material, piles of useless statistics and graphs, and Utopian schemes that have as much chance of working as I do of climbing Mount Everest.

**work** *v.* ¶In phrase:

¶**work a room** to socialize aggressively at a gathering in order to win favor and attention; (*hence*) to circulate or mingle.

**1972** *New York Times* (Oct. 22) 84:
Once the introductions had been completed, many of the guests spent their time nibbling mushrooms stuffed with snail, Swedish meat balls and bacon-wrapped chicken livers, trying to find familiar faces and doing what is known in more plebian circles as "working the room."

**1977** *Washington Post* (Sept. 8) B3:
Once greeted by her host, she instantly began working the room much as she had during the months Jimmy Carter was trying to win the White House.

**1992** *Globe and Mail* (Toronto, Can.) (May 8) P31:
Talking about the hollywood side of L.A., [he] says, "It's a business of images," even as he works the room, keeping an eye on the passing diners, shaking the advantageous hands.

**2001** *San Antonio Express-News* (June 10):
A conjunto quartet worked the room, the bajo sexto and accordion lending a dreamy timelessness.

**2004** *Indianapolis News/Star* (Feb. 20) C1:
Say you have three viable candidates for a job, and you extend an offer for them to come into the network. They invite their friends and their peers, and for all intents and purposes you work the room.

**workfare** *n.* welfare benefits granted for government-arranged work.

**1968** *Gettysburg Times* (Pa.) (Feb. 23) 5:
He proposes what he calls a program of "workfare" featuring government-guaranteed jobs paying at least $50 a week.

**1977** *Washington Post* (May 6) A2:
Sen. Russell B. Long (D-La.), author of a welfare bill in 1972 which he called *workfare,* urged Califano to commit himself strongly to a federal takeover of local government welfare costs.

**2003** *Market Call* (CNNfn-TV) (Dec. 17) C4:
Students have been asked to leave college in order to do a work-fare assignment.

**working mom** *n.* a mother who works outside the home, regarded as a desirable voter. Also **working mother**.

**1988** *San Francisco Chronicle* (July 29) A1:
Dukakis, Bush Court Working Moms' Votes.

**1998** *Houston Chronicle* (Oct. 25) 9:
A Democratic hopeful who believes Texas teachers and working moms need help faces a Republican incumbent worried about suburban school district and subdivision problems in a contest to represent District 15 in the state Legislature.

**2000** *Ladies Home Journal* (June 1) 88:
This working mom is barely making ends meet. She may be divorced. She has no college education, so she holds down a blue-collar or service job and worries constantly about paying the bills. She's angry at all things political, describing herself as "disgusted with the whole process."

**2003** *Washington Post* (Dec. 16) A28:
The same degree of care and modulation that candidates in recent elections have put into displays of...solidarity with working moms...now goes into each utterance devoted to the events of a turbulent world.

# XYZ

**xerocracy** *n.* [*Xerox* + -*cracy,* 'rule by'] any underground populist movement which spreads its message by photocopies.

**1978** in E. Rogers *Communication Technology* 245 (1986):
We are struggling against autocracy, for democracy, by means of xerocracy.

**1980** A. Oettinger in *Science* (July 4) CCIX 194:
Khomeini's people struggled, as one wag put it, "against autocracy, for democracy, by means of xerocracy" using abundant and accessible modern and ancient consumer media

**1994** *San Francisco Chronicle* (June 16):
Numbers seemed to double monthly by Xerocracy, rule by Xerox.

**2000** *Sierra* (Sept.–Oct.):
Avoiding both confrontation and conventional PR, they publicize largely through "xerocracy," with individuals passing out their own flyers, applying whatever spin they want.

**yellow-dog Democrat** *n.* a steadfast Democrat party loyalist. See BLUE DOG DEMOCRAT.

[**1883** *New York Times* (Mar. 11) 1:
There is no eagerness shown, however, among Republicans to seek office at this time, when Democrats can see nothing but certain victory awaiting them. "Why, we could nominate yellow dogs this Spring and elect every one upon the ticket by a big majority," said one of the Democratic ward statesmen to-day.]

**1911** *Mansfield News* (Ohio) (Apr. 22) 14:
He favors a job for every "yellow dog Democrat" to keep him from want, exertion and worry.

**1972** *New York Times Mag.* (Mar. 5) 11:
The Republican party in Florida had been growing steadily in the postwar years; 2,400 new residents moved to the state every week, most coming from rockribbed Republican areas of the Midwest, and

even some Yellow Dog Democrats ("Hyad Druther Vote Fur A Yella Dawg Thenna 'Publican") were turning away from the New Frontier and The Great Society.

**2004** *City Paper* (Tenn.) *(Jan. 16):*
Not surprisingly, then, a yellow dog Democrat touring a home featuring autographed pictures of Ronald Reagan and George W. Bush might spend less time viewing the residence.

**young scratcher** *n.* a Republican in the 1880 presidential campaign opposed to old-guard "machine" politics.

**1880** E. Washburne in *Scribner's* XX (Sept.) 787:
In the Republican party, particularly, there were the "Young Scratchers," to whom the machine devoted a good deal of angry criticism, and who drew to their support, and won over to sympathy, some of the very best men in the party.

**1890** C. Deming *New Englander* LIII (July) 30:
It was in the autumn of 1878 that Mr. Henry Ward Beecher, addressing a Republican gathering of the faithful at Brooklyn, used, in substance, these words to satirize the "Young Scratchers."

**1928** *New York Times* (July15) N4:
Survivors of the Young Scratchers, Mugwumps and other Independent voters of the last fifty years must feel a certain pleasure in seeing how the "renegade" bolter, once about equally despised by both parties, has increased and multiplied.

**Young Turks** *n.* [from a name given in the 20th century to Ottomans who tried to rejuvenate and Europeanize the Turkish empire] young or new members (of an organization) impatient for radical or fast change. —also sing.

**1908** *Daily News* (Aug. 4) 7 in *OED*:
Will the glorification of the "Young Turk" kill this expression as one of reproach to be used in the nursery?

**1934** *Helena Daily Independent* (Mont.) (Feb. 6) 5:
The name Young Turks has now become almost synonymous with any youthful political group seeking to overthrow an established order and bring about a new deal.

**1975** *Business Week* (May 12) 42:
These no-so-Young Turks have been on the attack for years, without causing much of a stir.

**2004** *New York Daily News* (Mar. 13) 4:
Spanish reports detailed an internal split between ETA's old guard and a new generation of young turks pushing for more spectacular attacks.

**zoo plane** *n.* an airplane carrying journalists accompanying a traveling politician.

**1973** H.S. Thompson *Fear & Loathing Campaign Trail* (April) 425:
There were no McGovern staffers on the Zoo Plane? HST: A few tried
to get on it, but the press people had nailed down their own seats and
refused to leave them.

**1973** *New York Times Bk. Rev.* (July 15) 7:
The "Zoo plane" on which the journalists covering McGovern traveled
was evidently loaded with cocaine, marijuana and hashhish.

**1977** *Washington Post* (Apr. 1) B1:
He told me once he enjoyed riding on the zoo plane (the plane that
followed Carter) because everyone was more relaxed and less self-
important.

**1992** in *Guardian* (Manchester, U.K.) (Oct. 26) 21:
The zoo plane is a mobile party that never heard of seat belts, sitting
down for landings or any other of those tedious rules which take the
fun out of flying.

**2000** *Austin American-Statesman* (Sept. 3) J1:
The second, "zoo" plane, is packed with the leftovers, frustrated
journalists forced to wait until everyone lands before learning what
Bush had to say.

# Select Bibliography

Brown, Everit. *A Dictionary of American Politics*. New York: A. L. Burt Company, 1908.

Dickson, Paul. *The Congress Dictionary: The Ways and Meanings of Capitol Hill*. New York: John Wiley & Sons, 1993.

Lighter, Jonathan. *Historical Dictionary of American Slang: A–G*. New York: Random House, 1994.

———. *Historical Dictionary of American Slang: H–O*. New York: Random House, 1997.

Lindsay, Charles. "More Political Lingo." *American Speech* 2, no. 10 (July 1927): 443.

Norton, Charles Ledyard. *Political Americanisms; a Glossary of Terms and Phrases Current at Different Periods in American Politics*. New York: Longmans, Green & Co., 1890.

Philipson, Uno. *Political Slang, 1750–1850*. London: C. W. K. Gleerup Lund, 1941.

Safire, William. *Safire's New Political Dictionary*. New York: Random House, 1993.

Shafritz, Jay M. *The Dorsey Dictionary of American Government and Politics*. Chicago: The Dorsey Press, 1988.

Smith, Edward Conrad. *New Dictionary of American Politics*. New York: Barnes & Noble, 1949.

Sperber, Hans, and Travis Trittschuh. *American Political Terms: An Historical Dictionary*. Detroit: Wayne State University Press, 1962.

White, Wilbur Wallace. *White's Political Dictionary*. Cleveland: World Pub. Co., 1947.

Wimberly, Lowry Charles. "More Political Lingo." *American Speech* 2, no. 3 (Dec. 1926): 135–139.